DEAD SUBJECTS

DEAD SUBJECTS

Toward a Politics of Loss in Latino Studies

Antonio Viego

DUKE UNIVERSITY PRESS
Durham & London 2007

© 2007 Duke University Press
All rights reserved

Printed in the United States of America on acid-free paper ∞
Designed by Jennifer Hill. Typeset in Adobe Jenson Pro by Keystone Typesetting, Inc.

Library of Congress Cataloging-in-Publication Data appear on the last
printed page of this book.

Contents

VI

CONTENTS

Acknowledgments

A perspicacious reader of an early draft of this book commented to me that the book read like it was written under the sign of loss. She was terribly right. This project was conceptualized and carried through during the midst of some shattering personal losses. In the space of a very short time, I lost a father, a sister, a nephew, and my only mentor, Professor Lynda Hart, to sudden and tragic deaths. I watched an already brittle family of stubborn and rickety Cuban melancholics, who seemed willful in refusing to recover from the shock of exile experienced so many years ago, finally disintegrate. My mother refers to those still standing—herself, my sister Carmen, and me—as the three stray cats. The dogged, embarrassing force of Oedipus bearing down on my family with its sinewy "mommy, daddy, me" calculus seemed to draw me like a sleepwalker to psychoanalytic theory as an undergraduate. I've been sleepwalking toward and away from it ever since. Latino studies arrived later on the scene for me, as a first-year graduate student at the University of Pennsylvania. If this book has been written under the sign of loss in some way, my attempt to make sense of various kinds of losses—material, economic, psychic—relies on what I have learned from reading Lacanian psychoanalytic theory in concert and in tension with Latino studies and how the latter theorizes knowledge production in the context of university discourse. The reader may find in the pages that follow something particularly odd or simply wrong-headed in my claim that loss, a particular kind of loss that has to do with the human subject's inscription in language, is one of the important resources for subjective realization that continues to be unequally distributed to ethnic-racialized subjects. The book, in its shrillest moments, wants to reclaim that loss for disenfranchised subjects in order to offer the most complex and nuanced understanding of the historically situated human subject while banking on the faith that this reclamation of loss will have some impact on how we conceptualize and craft future forms of social and legal redress as ethnic-racialized subjects.

Several people have been instrumental in helping me think through this project. I thank Professor Laurie Langbauer, who introduced me to psychoanalytic theory while I was an undergraduate at Swarthmore College. During my PhD studies at the University of Pennsylvania, Professor Lynda Hart, Professor Rafael Pérez-Torres, and Professor Eric Cheyfitz were crucial influences in getting me to think about what it would mean to read Lacanian psychoanalytic theory with Chicano movement poetry and discourse. At Duke University, I have benefited from various streams and currents of intellectual inspiration stemming from many institutional sites and people— Kathy Rudy, Sibylle Fischer, Janice Radway, Robyn Wiegman, Karla Holloway, Anne Allison, Toril Moi, Cathy Davidson, Wahneema Lubiano, Walter Mignolo, Michael Hardt, Grant Farred, Jane Gaines, Alice Kaplan, Esther Gabara, Ken Surin, Fredric Jameson, Meg Greer, Ranjana Khanna, Claudia Milian. I thank all of those who have struggled valiantly and tirelessly along with me to establish a Latino studies program in the early and later years— Walter Mignolo, Orin Starn, Bill Mace, Jenny Snead Williams, Pedro Lasch, John French, Esther Gabara, Emilio Parrado, Victoria de Francesco, and Sally Deutsch. Outside of Duke University there have been some individuals who have, even though they may not know it, given me confidence to do this kind of work when I had little if any resources to draw on at the time—thank you, David Román, Miranda Joseph, and Sandra Soto. David's support over the years has been staggeringly generous. My dearest and oldest friend, José Esteban Muñoz, has been an unflappable source of intellectual stimulation over the years; he has challenged me to push at all disciplinary boundaries and has responded to my sometimes lame and timid fears with the Andy Warhol—inspired refrain, "So what?" My other dearest and oldest best friend, Ana-Margret Sanchez, has brought the wildest mix of joy, sadness, existential angst, and hope into my life, and many parts of this book were written with her *bruja*-spun notion of "care of the self" in mind. Students in two Duke University graduate seminars, "Race, Lacanian Psychoanalytic Theory, and Ego Psychology" and "Articulating Race and Psychoanalysis with Politics," challenged me to refine many of the questions that I ask in this book. Thank you: Neta Bar, Michelle Koerner, Jini Watson, Daniel Potuchek, Rizvana Braxton, Amalle Dublon, Selin Ever, Adair Hill, and Kevin James. I want to thank everyone in the Program in Literature at Duke University and Romance Studies, especially Pam Terterian, Karen Bell, Sandy Swanson, Tiwonda Johnson, Susie Waller, and Denise Wilborn. I would also like to thank my editor, Ken Wissoker, for his faith in this project, his wonderful guidance, and for helping me rework the very first sentence in the introduction. Anitra Grisales, Erika Stevens, Courtney Berger, and Justin Faerber at

Duke University Press have also been crucial contributors to the possibility of this book ever being completed.

This book is dedicated to those whom I have lost—Antonio Viego Sr., Mary Viego, Ian Beltran, and Lynda Hart—and to those who are still around trying to figure out what to do with the cranky remains—my extraordinary sister, Carmen Viego, and my mother, Margaret Zeliscovic-Viego. Finally, Mark Timothy Ziegler, who has put up with more secondary contact loss than anyone should ever have to endure, thank you for this, that, and the Other.

IX

All the Things You *Can't* Be by Now

S ix months deep into one of his most difficult seminars, *Seminar XX*, Jacques Lacan wondered aloud to those in attendance on May 8, 1973, "It is truly odd that the fact that the structure of thought is based on language is not thrown into question in psychology."[1] This is a simple formulation of a pointed but general critique of psychology that Lacan maintained throughout his teaching, beginning in the 1950s. From behind prison walls in the early 1960s, the famous Puerto Rican writer and activist Piri Thomas found himself wondering aloud in his classic autobiography after a somewhat different but, as we will see, related oddity attaching to psychology, "Maybe God is psychology, or psychology is God."[2] I want to begin by immediately placing Lacan and Thomas in dialogue on the question of the status of psychology, since a general exploration of the question Lacan thinks odd in its not being asked—that the structure of thought is based on language and that language as structure has certain privative and generative effects on the speaking human organism[3]—along with Thomas's spirited gambit—maybe God is psychology, or psychology, God—provides the general range of the desires detonating the problematics of this book.

I juxtapose Lacan and Thomas here in order to announce in the most general way my project's attempt to articulate psychoanalysis with a politics of race and with contemporary notions of Latino subjectivity and experience in particular. With Lacan I ask after the role of ego and social psychology in stirring, as I will explain, a kind of exacting trouble for ethnic-racialized subjects in clinical, extraclinical, legal, and extralegal contexts in the United States beginning in the mid-twentieth century. I would add a third related question to Lacan's and Thomas's queries above: Why do all manner of philosophical, legal, and popular cultural engagements with ethnic-racialized subjectivity and experience in the United States in the context of racism, discrimination, multiculturalism, and diversity appear to cede what will qualify as the dominant interpretation of ethnic-racialized trauma, loss, visibility, and the forms of social and legal redress we seek to the interpretative framework of ego and social psychology?

First, let's return to Thomas's cautious pronouncement. For readers not familiar with this classic autobiographical novel of Puerto Rican and Latino literature, I would like to recall some of the steps Piri, the narrator, has taken before landing in prison and articulating this strange missive. The events in the novel take place primarily in New York City in the 1940s, 1950s, and 1960s, precisely the time that Y. Kramer has described as the "golden age" of psycho-analytic ego psychology.[4] The struggle that ensues for the protagonist regards his ethnic-racialized identity in the most general way. He initially identifies as Puerto Rican but is in his immediate social environment racialized as an African American because of the color of his skin. For the better part of the text, these two ethnic-racialized identities sit in tremendous tension. Piri himself does not know what he "is," since he is constantly dispossessed of the agency that might allow him to name himself. Can he, the text repeatedly asks, reasonably claim an African American *and* a Puerto Rican identity in the United States of the 1950s? The novel illustrates how the racialization of Puerto Ricans was "entangled with the racialization of African-Americans" during this period, as Ramón Grosfoguel and Chloe S. Georas explain: "Given the large numbers of mulattos, blacks, and mestizos among the Puerto Rican migrants, many were initially 'confused' in the white social imaginary with African-Americans. The social construction of racial categories in the United States . . . was a fertile ground for the initial classification of Puerto Ricans as African-Americans despite their effort to maintain an autonomous identity."[5] Piri identifies as Puerto Rican, but as the darkest-skinned member of his embattled, working-class Puerto Rican family, he occupies there a marginalized position given the family's own disavowed politics of "pigmentocracy." His claims to the nominatory term *Puerto Rican* are constantly threatened within the familial space. The novel tracks the vagaries of his experience and underscores the absolute incoherence, ultimately, that attends any definition of Piri as either Puerto Rican or African American, an incoherence that we might understand in a more contemporary context as attending all of the contorted attempts to define *Latino*: is *Latino* an ethnic or a racialized designation? Who can count as a *Latino*? Are Latinos "white" or "not white?" We will deal with these questions at length in chapters 3 and 4.

By the time psychology makes its godly prison appearance in Piri's story, toward the close of the novel, the reader has traversed a blisteringly confused narrative rife with superegoic commands that direct Piri to assume an ethnic-racialized nominatory term *or else*. The novel never fully resolves Piri's identificatory dilemmas. The novel's reception at the time might be said to symptomatically act out this lack of resolution, given how critics have generally read the novel either along the lines I've pursued here or as a novel more centrally about rehabilitation—the transformation through the prison apparatus of an urban street-gang criminal into an enlightened, dutiful citizen-subject. Psychology does briefly appear to provide some promise for Piri by proffering an answer to his existential angst. What knowledge psychology might provide for him along these lines is, as Piri tells the reader, going to hurt: "It's not gonna be an easy thing to dig me, I thought. This psychology means that people's worst troubles are in their minds. That's cool."[6]

For Lacan, ego psychology also seemed to promise something painful—a dreadful distortion of Freudian psychoanalytic theory and technique that only deepened the alienation of the analysand at the same time that it inflated the power and prestige of the analyst. Using Piri's language in the preceding passage, Lacan might have remarked that the analysand's worst troubles are in the minds and therapeutic strategies of the Jewish-refugee ego-psychology analysts, who, forced to contend with coercive assimilatory mandates in mid-twentieth-century U.S. culture, responded in kind—"North American" style—with clinical strategies directed at strengthening the ego and adapting the analysand to the demands of some predetermined notion of "reality." In 1953, Lacan writes, "In any case, it seems indisputable that the conception of psychoanalysis in the United States has been inflected toward the adaptation of the individual to the social environment, the search for behavior patterns, and all the objectification implied in the notion of 'human relations.' And the indigenous term, 'human engineering,' strongly implies a privileged position of exclusion with respect to the human object."[7] Lacan's remarks are a commentary of sorts on Piri's own struggle, giving a bit of texture to the mysterious superegoic commandments forcing Piri to choose an ethnic-racialized nominatory term in order to be considered a socially and culturally intelligible citizen-subject and convincing him that failing to do so would condemn him to radical subjective illegibility.

I choose to read Piri's existential dilemma in this novel in relation to Lacan's critique of ego psychology because of how Piri's questions, although not directed at ego psychology, strictly speaking, appear to nonetheless enlist ego psychology's preferred strategies for adjusting and adapting the troubled and conflicted ego to the demands of "reality." Psychology appears to Piri in prison like a vision that half promises to serve as the balm that might narcotize Piri against the painful subjective division he feels as a result of not being able to lay claim to a nonconflictive ethnic-racialized nominatory term that could account for him in some exacting way and allow him to adjust to—and be rehabilitated for—the demands of "reality."

Piri's prescient remark—"Maybe God is psychology, or psychology is God" —accurately assesses the godliness of psychology at a particular time in U.S. history—a remark whose accuracy, we might add, still rings true today— especially with regard to the authority accruing to this field and its social scientists when remarking on ethnic-racialized psychological trauma. To wit, we saw the crucial role played by the social psychology experiments of Kenneth and Mamie Clark in the victorious 1954 *Brown v. Board of Education* decision, which I discuss in chapter 3. These experiments proved to the justices of the Supreme Court that African American children were psychologically traumatized by segregation in public schools. Kenneth Clark himself remarked, "The involvement of social scientists in the Brown decision set social science and the law on a common path. There can be no turning from it now."[8] At least ten years before the forging of a "common path" between psychology and the law, we know that Gunnar Myrdal's 1944 work *An American Dilemma* had already "served to push future work and policy on matters of race in decidedly psychological directions," in the words of Ellen Herman.[9] "Maybe God is psychology, or maybe psychology is God"—it would certainly seem this way. From within ethnic-racialized minoritarian discourses, we have found no way to dispense with certain assumptions in psychology—at the same time that we have steered steadfastly clear of psychoanalytic theory—any more than folks have found a way to exist without creating something in the image of "God."

This is the problem as the book sees it: critical race and ethnicity studies scholars have developed no language to talk about ethnic-racialized subjectivity and experience that is not entirely ego- and social psychological and that does not imagine a strong, whole, complete, and transparent ethnic-racialized subject and ego as the desired therapeutic, philosophical, and political outcome in a racist, white supremacist world. In the process we fail to see how the repeated themes of wholeness, completeness, and transparency with respect to ethnic-racialized subjectivity are what provide racist discourse with precisely the notion of subjectivity that it needs in order to function most effectively.

Although in recent years critics like Tim Dean and Lee Edelman have shown in very effective ways how Lacanian theory operates as a queer critique of the complementarity between the sexes—a queer theory *avant la lettre*, as Dean puts it—virtually no attention has been paid to how Lacanian theory also lends itself to an antiracist critique.[10] What may be compelling for some readers, as I explain in chapter 2, is the fact that the queer critique and the antiracist critique do not constitute two different critical operations but are rather mutually informing and revelatory. Readers who attend closely to the letter of Lacan's critique of ego psychology in many of the writings collected in *Écrits* will witness the antiracist charge of Lacan's position revealed in how he critiques North American coercive assimilatory imperatives working on ethnic-racialized subjects—in his example, Jewish immigrant psychoanalysts who fled Nazi Europe—that demand of them a certain mandatory adjustment and adaptation to North American "reality." In the midst of a very harsh critique of these Jewish psychoanalysts regarding the distortions they effected in Freudian psychoanalytic theory, he provides them with a guarded alibi of sorts: he locates the reasons for this distortion in the social and cultural forces acting on them as ethnic immigrants immersed in a culture of assimilation. In these moments, Lacan's position significantly overlaps with some of the basic positions in the best critical multiculturalist, antiassimilationist work and should, I think, for this reason, make his work of interest to critical race and ethnicity studies scholars. These are the topics of chapter 2.

The antiracist charge in Lacanian theory can also be located in the theory itself. Lacan's understanding of the subject in language, I would like to suggest, also provides an intervention into racist discourse. Lacan reworks the early-twentieth-century Swiss linguist Ferdinand de Saussure's notion of language as a system of signs into a system of signifiers and then argues that language, as paradigmatic structure, has certain privative and generative effects on the human speaking subject. The human organism must at some point choose language in order to express her or his needs, but language always has a somewhat distorting effect that never quite captures the need that is expressed in its medium. This is because the human subject is dependent upon a system of differentially constituted signifiers, a system in which signifiers signify only in virtue of their difference from other signifiers, and so any determination made about the human subject in language will be incomplete and insufficient to exhaustively defining who or what the subject is. In her cogent explication of the Lacanian subject as a subject "in language and yet more than language," Joan Copjec writes, "This subject, radically unknowable, radically incalculable, is the only guarantee we have against racism. This is a guarantee that slips from us whenever we disregard the nontransparency of subject to signifier, whenever we make the subject coincide with the signifier rather than its misfire."[11] Racism depends on a reading of ethnic-racialized subjects that insists on their transparency; racism also banks on the faith and conceit that these subjects can be exhaustively and fully elucidated through a certain masterful operation of language. Lacan's language-based psychoanalytic theory provides the tools to radically disrupt these colonizing, dominating, and ultimately racist interpretative practices.

Ego and social psychology generally ignore the linguistic dimension of human subjectivity and assume that the human subject can be adapted and assimilated to its environment and, related to that, can be made whole and complete. In contrast, because of the effects of language as structure on the human organism, Lacan concludes that the human subject is irredeemably divided in language—what he terms the "barred subject"—and can never simply make good on that division. I argue that the assumptions of ego and social psychology are still very much with us today in clinical and extraclinical contexts when we think about ethnic-racialized subjectivity and experience.

In his early work in the 1950s—the seminars and writings my book focuses on—Lacan argues that the themes of completion and wholeness that figure as theoretical touchstones in ego and social psychology are symptomatic of the dream of mastery and domination, the dream of absolute power over other human subjects as well as over the environment that is integral to the period we are defining as the "ego's era."[12] This book posits that the undisturbed dream of ego mastery, wholeness, and completeness not only threatens to inform how ethnic-racialized subjects craft a politics of recognition and re-distribution, to use Nancy Fraser's terms,[13] as well as threatening to inform the types of social and legal redress we seek, but is also, I argue, precisely what provides racist discourse with one of its most generative internal principles: the undivided, obscenely full and complete ethnic-racialized subject, transparent to itself and to others.

I hope that this book might inspire some critical race and ethnicity studies scholars to engage with some of Lacan's work. My analysis of ego psychology and social psychology in the United States may also encourage scholars in American studies to engage with Lacan's early work. His critique of the distortions of Freudian theory in ego psychology as attributable to North American assimilatory imperatives and high-speed capitalist practices registers a timely critique of U.S. exceptionalism and hegemony in the post–World

War II years. For critics interested in studying the flows of transnational capital and globalization practices and the role of the United States as author of these flows and practices, the role played by ego psychology in the United States and how it became a dominant global therapeutics of the self should play a part in the story told of U.S. hegemony. My book makes the argument that the new American studies' attempt to challenge the geographical, fiscal, and psychological boundaries that become naturalized in attempts to define what is American and what it means to study an area called America will find, curiously enough, that the mid-twentieth-century debates between ego psychology and Lacanian psychoanalytic theory provide crucial material for deepening their interventions.

Thus far, I have articulated the most significant distinction between Lacanian psychoanalytic theory and ego and social psychology as having to do with the attention Lacanian theory devotes to the effects of language as structure on the speaking organism. To be clear, this is certainly not the only difference between them, but it is, for me, the more remarkable given the concerns of this project and the interventions it hopes to effect. Before I provide a bit more texture to this claim, I would like to offer a brief and selective overview of the emergence of ego psychology, canvassing its major critical operations and assumptions with respect to a theory of the subject. I leave a more detailed description of social psychology for my discussion of the Clarks' social psychology experiments in chapter 3.

To begin with, although ego psychology cannot simply be reduced down to the work of the group Lacan famously refers to as the "troika"—Heinz Hartmann, Ernst Kris, and Rudolph Loewenstein[14]—Heinz Hartmann must be generally regarded as the leading figure of ego psychology. His *Ego Psychology and the Problem of Adaptation*, published in 1939, the year Freud died, has served as a major theoretical point of departure for ego psychology.[15] While it bears the word *psychology*, ego psychology does not emerge from within the general field of psychology but rather from a particular interpretation—Lacan uses the term *distortion*—of Freudian theory that fixes on Freud's construction of what is referred to as the "second topography" of id, ego, and superego that he introduces in his 1923 text *The Ego and the Id*. Hartmann saw himself as tracing out what he regarded as Freud's own wishes and aspirations for psychoanalysis, that it would eventually function as a general psychology "to refine, systemize, and increase our knowledge, thus advancing psychoanalysis as a general psychology."[16] In *Essays on Ego Psychology*, Hartmann wrote, "The consistent study of the ego and its function promises to bring analysis closer to the aim Freud has set for it long ago—to become a general psychology in the broadest sense of the word."[17] In the indispensable collection *The Hartmann Era*, Martin S. Bergmann rightly questions the veracity of this attribution to Freud of this particular aspiration.[18]

Generally, the ego psychologists concluded that the second topography served to replace Freud's previous topography of unconscious, preconscious, and conscious. By way of this conclusion, they definitively located the ego as the center of consciousness and lent it powers of mastery and adaptation that appeared to excise the role of the unconscious. In this regard, Hartmann saw himself as redressing the wrongs that had been supposedly brought to bear on psychoanalytic theory with Freud's introduction of the death instinct in his 1920 text *Beyond the Pleasure Principle*. Bergmann elaborates:

> By 1920 Freud is no longer a Darwinian, with the introduction of the concept of the repetition compulsion, which operates beyond the pleasure principle; the libido is in continuous struggle against its immortal adversary, the death instinct. The new theory fundamentally changed the model of the way the human mind functions. Hartmann's task, as Lichtenstein understands it, was to undo the damage that was done to psychoanalysis by the introduction of the death instinct. It was the ego system that, according to Hartmann, took over the adaptive regulation.[19]

Note the importance accorded the adaptive functions and the autonomous regality ascribed to the ego, as well as how adaptation and autonomy become the measure of mental health. In this context, adaptation itself served as the criterion for health. Yale Kramer explains, "Theoretically, the mentally healthiest individual is no longer the most sexually gratified one, but the one who is best adapted to the world in which he lives—the individual who, in theory, has reached an equilibrium between the gratification of his instinctual needs, his moral needs, and the demands of reality."[20] One of the fundamental points in Lacanian theory is that the relationship between the human subject and her environment cannot be thought of in terms of adaptation. Thinking this relation in terms of adaptation is a symptomatic and compensatory response to the fact of radical inadequation and lack of complementarity or natural correspondence between the human subject and the social.

David Beres wrote that the function of psychoanalytic treatment in ego psychology was mostly redefined "as the restoration of autonomy of ego functions" that had either been lost or compromised because of conflict or by repression.[21] Theorizing that there was an autonomous, conflict-free sphere in the ego, the ego psychologists argued that the ego should be strengthened so as to improve its chances of mastering conflict. In Lacan's first seminars and writings in the early 1950s, he clearly laid out his very different understanding of the ego and its function and why the strategy of strengthening the ego seemed, in theory, so misguided. In *Seminar II*, Lacan claimed that "the resistances always have their seat in the ego, so analysis teaches."[22] Two years earlier, he wrote, "This ego, whose strength our theorists now define by its capacity to bear frustration, is frustration in its very essence. Not frustration of one of the subject's desires, but frustration of an object in which his desire is alienated; and the more developed this object becomes, the more profoundly the subject becomes alienated from his jouissance."[23]

Returning for a moment to Piri's dilemma in *Down These Mean Streets*, it is precisely this alienation of desire that the novel cannot seem to remark upon. Given that the text speaks too fully and squarely within the vernacular of ego and social psychology, proffering as it does the strategy of strengthening Piri's ethnic-racialized ego as the only possible answer to his dilemma, it cannot even begin to address Piri's profound alienation as a human speaking subject. Psychology wins itself a godly, legally sanctioned victory and Lacanian theory gets the definitive boot.

We might take this moment to discuss some of the additional infelicitous effects that attend any interpretative or therapeutic strategy that seeks above all else to strengthen the ego, especially with regard to ethnic-racialized subjects in the context of racism, neocolonialism, and vacuous forms of multi-culturalism. As many who are familiar with Lacan's mirror-stage essay know, the ego is constituted through identification with a counterpart that, impor-tantly, appears as a point outside the ego. This captures the basic alienation and misrecognition that constitutes the ego and that corresponds to the Imaginary register. Since the relation between the ego and its counterpart constitutes an essentially narcissistic dynamic, aggressivity figures strongly. The Imaginary ego is caught in a false dialectic of either affirming or negating its sameness or difference from the other in a battle that presumably can only end in death, with the destruction of one or the other. The Imaginary register is organized around illusions of wholeness and synthesis, and to the extent

9

that ego psychology in theory imagines a way of making good on these illusory promises, it can be read as a psychology of the Imaginary, prompting the assessment by Paul Verhaeghe that ego psychology's insistence on the subject as a unity disqualifies it as a psychology and is more accurately named by the term "egology."[24]

The Imaginary fixity that characterizes the ego is opposed to subjective growth and change, and although psychoanalysis has very real effects on the ego it generally works on the subject, on stirring up desire in the subject, promoting a process of becoming. Homi Bhabha links the Imaginary fixity and rigidity that Lacan ascribes to the ego with the "fixity" that Bhabha identifies as a distinct feature of colonial discourse: "An important feature of colonial discourse is its dependence on the concept of 'fixity' in the ideological construction of otherness. Fixity, as the sign of cultural/historical/racial difference in the discourse of colonialism, is a paradoxical mode of representation: it connotes rigidity and an unchanging order as well as disorder, degeneracy, and daemonic repetition."[25] Ego psychology's ongoing hegemony in providing the basic outlines for how ethnic-racialized subjectivity and experience is interpreted and understood threatens to compel an Imaginary ego politics in ethnic-racialized minoritarian discourses that will not be able to offer a truly transformative vision of justice because instead of a subject, an ego is installed at the center of these politicized discourses.[26]

Freud theorized the ego as developing out of the id. Melanie Klein theorized the ego as present from the very beginnings of life, defining its primary function as a defense against an annihilating, disintegrating anxiety. Lacan theorized the emergence of the ego in the moments of the child's identification with and *captation* by a point outside its self. Hartmann and his group instead theorized the ego as emerging separately from the id. Moreover, they theorized the ego, as Judith Feher Gurewich explains, "as distinct from the defense mechanisms that prevent it from assuming its function as the agent of the reality principle. . . . The ego is therefore capable of regaining its discerning abilities and recognizing external reality for what it is."[27] Hartmann and David Rapaport theorized the ego as finding the best solutions for its adaptation to "reality."[28] The idea that reality is to be taken as something given in the outer world and that can be taught or learned is shared by both ego psychology and Kleinian theory, but is a notion radically alien to Lacan's teaching. The understanding of reality in ego psychology is what helps lend ego psychologists so much power in the analytical setting, since, in the end, they will serve as judge of what is real or not real; they function as masters of reality. In Lacan's scheme, reality is always seen through the window of fantasy, and so the analyst's reality is no better, no worse, no more real than the analysand's.

Understanding the nature and impact of ego psychology through Lacan's seminars and writings, one might get the erroneous impression that there were, apart from Lacan, no other critics of Hartmann's theories. Bergmann reminds us that this was not the case: "Criticism of Hartmann by his peers already appeared in 1961 in a paper by Glover. There were also those who believed that Hartmann and his followers had turned away from the unconscious, the most valuable part of psychoanalysis, as they preached conformity and adjustment."[29] A conceptual move that appears to attend this turning away from the unconscious is the new, intense focus on the analysis of children and infants during this time. I shall make more of this shift from the unconscious to "child analysis" when I discuss the Clarks' social psychology experiments in chapter 3. For now I want to conceptualize this shift as predicated on a certain pretension to mastery that lends psychoanalysis out to the strategies Michel Foucault calls "biopower"—the reproduction and control of biological life. The psychoanalyst André Green characterizes this shift in psychoanalysis as one that abandons the analysis of the "dream" for an analysis of the "child," and in this abandonment turns against the "true paradigm" of psychoanalysis: "The 'child' represents all this developmental point of view, the misunderstandings created by baby observation and what not. The 'dream' is the true paradigm of psychoanalysis."[30] Moreover, he makes clear how this shift to the "child" brings psychoanalysis into the purview of the disciplinary techniques of biopower: "There are two ways of considering the child. One way is to include the knowledge of the child into the knowledge of psychoanalysis. Psychoanalysis: you have different sorts—adults, children, psychotics, psychosomatics, delinquents, whatever. *But there is another way of including child psychoanalysis. It is to put it in a network of disciplines where you can find paediatrics, child psychiatry, pedagogy, child observation, and so on.* What happens then? It happens that the psychoanalytic point of view is drowned and we get child observation occupying the position of a fundamental 'science' in the general theory of the child and adult psychoanalysis."[31] When Lacan enumerates in 1953 what he thinks are the "current problems of psychoanalysis," his first entry is devoted to this shift toward the focus on the "child." He writes, "The impetus in this area has come from the analysis of children and from the favorable field offered to researchers' efforts and temptations by

11

the preverbal structurations approach."[32] Although it is not acknowledged in Lee Edelman's recent queer theoretical polemic *No Future*, on the status and image of the "child" as what "serves to regulate political discourse" in the United States, I think this shift from the "unconscious"/"dream" to the "child" effected so successfully by psychoanalytic ego psychology in the United States provides precisely the sort of historical texture and background informing the ascendancy of the "child." We might even read the following assessment by Edelman as providing the very alibi for this shift: "That figural Child alone embodies the citizen as ideal, entitled to claim full rights to its future share in the nation's good, though always at the cost of limiting the rights 'real' citizens are allowed. For the social exists to preserve for this universalized subject, this fantasmatic Child, a notional freedom more highly valued than the actuality of freedom itself."[33]

Not Romanticism

There is no doubt that ego psychology dominated North American psychoanalysis after World War II, even though virtually no analysts in Europe or South America drew inspiration from Hartmann's group's work. In a more contemporary context, the hegemony of ego psychology in the United States is so unquestioned that, as Jacques-Alain Miller reports, perhaps somewhat exaggeratedly, of a communication he received from a Chicago analyst in the mid-1980s, it has become like "wallpaper" for North American analysts.[34] Yale Kramer characterizes the "golden age" of ego psychology in particularly affecting terms: "The golden age of psychoanalysis, from 1945 to 1965, which many of us can still recall, raised Freud to the status of cultural hero in America. Every analyst had a full caseload, and those with middle-European accents had two-year waiting lists whether they were good or not."[35] Despite the prestige that attached to Hartmann and his work, interestingly, as Bergmann claims, Hartmann, unlike Lacan, Melanie Klein, and Heinz Kohut, did not have "disciples" but rather had "coworkers."

If there is one overarching point we might insist upon to characterize Hartmann's ego psychology, it regards a giddy optimism that is nowhere present in Freud's own work. There is a spirited trust in the human subject's capacity to develop, adjust, and grow, and where the occasion for a conflict between the ego and id or the subject and the environment might arise it can just as well be resolved into a conflict-free relation. At the other extreme, we might locate Lacan's vigorous, tireless pessimism—one that draws on Freud's own. Jacques-Alain Miller writes that after Lacan's troubles with the International Psychoanalytic Association in 1953, Lacan "adopts a more Freudian pessimism. To many, it was horrifying to see how sarcastic he was about the existence of human beings. If you are looking for a debasement of humanity, read Lacan."[36] I will come clean at this point: this book draws from that same sort of pessimism, insofar as I find very little reason, things being as they are in the United States, for contemporary ethnic-racialized subjects to invest in any political, theoretical, academic program that appears to draw its narcotizing charge from optimism, least of all the kind of optimism that imagines that a conflict-free relation might be effected with one's immediate social surround and environment in the absence of a radical transformation of the social structures in place. Working with the pessimism that Lacan might be said to generously lend my project, I want to characterize the pessimism that I think is needed along the lines of Foucault's "pessimistic activism." In an interview conducted shortly before his death, Foucault announced, "My point is not that everything is bad, but that everything is dangerous, which is not exactly the same as bad. If everything is dangerous, then we always have something to do. So my position leads not to apathy but to a hyper- and pessimistic activism."[37]

Although adjustment and conformity were interpreted by some as the central focus of ego psychology—that, in fact, the two went hand in hand—Hartmann himself did not equate them and did not necessarily see how adjustment necessarily gave way to conformity. Nonetheless, many analysts felt that Hartmann's work threatened to undo the basic tension Freud had elaborated between the individual and culture that he most famously articulated in his 1930 text *Civilization and Its Discontents*. Bergmann points out that although the specific era associated with the Hartmann group has passed, psychoanalytic ego psychology as a whole has not lost its significance. Indeed, I argue in this book that the more basic assumptions in ego psychology regarding its general optimism and its focus on adaptation and adjustment are alive and well in social psychology and in subfields like ethnic psychology and Hispanic psychology, as well as in Latino psychiatry, as I discuss in chapter 7, and in, more generally speaking, most psychoanalytic and psychological approaches and analyses of subjectivities marked out as ethnic-racialized, not to mention in much of the nonclinical work in critical race and ethnicity studies. In these approaches there is no understanding of the divided subject, the barred subject in language, or the subject of the signifier, no understanding of the effects of language as structure on the speaking human organism.

What does it mean to say that language as structure has both privative and

13

generative effects on the speaking human organism? What are the consequences in our work as critical race and ethnicity studies scholars if we fail to
consider the effects of language as structure on the human speaking organism
as we imagine ourselves committed, in theory, to knowledge projects that
intervene in systemic material and symbolic racist practices in the United
States?

For Lacan, language is the paradigmatic structure. One could say that
language is not *like* a structure but *is* rather "structure" itself and that language
transforms human organisms into subjects. We need to keep in mind that
Lacan does not understand language as simply reflecting reality. Reality is an
effect of the order of signifiers. Related to this point, Lacan understands
language as radically exterior to the body. For Lacan, language "is like an alien
body that grafts itself onto the order of the body and of nature."[38] Language is
composed of rules governing the formation of statements that precede every
human organism. Lacan writes, "The simple definition assumes that language
is not to be confused with the various psychical and somatic functions that
serve it in the speaking subject. The primary reason for this is that language,
with its structure, exists prior to each subject's entry into it at a certain
moment in his mental development."[39] What Lacan calls the Other as the
locus of language always precedes the subject and is in fact the first cause of
the subject. The Other, as the locus of language, is also referred to as the
Symbolic, the order of signifiers that determines for us all of the distinctions
that can be made and that organize reality for us. Although the subject is
founded in language and the signifier founds the Symbolic, this does not
mean, as Copjec explained above, that the subject is fully calculated in its
inscription in language.

Language is in and of itself meaningless; meaning emerges with speech, as
speech takes up with language and the rules governing the formation of
statements. Concepts do not precede their appearance in the material of
language and to understand this we must initially disabuse ourselves, as Lacan
writes, of "the illusion that the signifier serves the function of representing the
signified, or better, that the signifier has to justify its existence in terms of any
signification whatsoever."[40] Although most people tend to think of language as
particularly "human," in Lacan one is pushed to understand its *inhumanness* or
its *other-than-humanness*. Maire Jaanus rather pointedly explains that "the ana-
lytically defined 'human' is not the traditional knot of living flesh and eternal
spirit, but a subject constituted by the force and structure of speech and

14

language. And language as such has nothing human about it. Signifiers are dead. 'Humans' incorporate this deadness."[41] To be clear, the subject is an effect of the signifier, not a substance, not a preexisting essence that could precipitate itself outside the locus of the Other, the Symbolic, outside of language as structure.

As I briefly explained earlier, every human organism must at some point choose language in order to express his or her needs. Bruce Fink succinctly argues that the child *allows* "him or herself to be represented by words."[42] In *Seminar 1*, Lacan illustrates this point when he teaches, "All human beings share in the universe of symbols. They are included in it and submit to it, much more than they constitute it. They are much more its supports than its agents."[43] Since language is a system of signifiers in which each signifier means something only by virtue of its difference from another signifier, every demand we make in language will always have a distorting effect with respect to the need we try to express in its medium. There are, ultimately, no positive terms in language. When the human organism inscribes itself in language it becomes a subject of language, and as a result of this inscription every determination of the subject will be by necessity indeterminate. Lacan understands the inscription of the subject in language as constituting a loss, a loss of a hypothesized fullness prior to the impact of language that he will refer to as belonging to the order of the Real. This notion of fullness prior to language is also conceptually linked to Lacan's theory of jouissance. The privative effects of language as structure on the speaking organism, therefore, have to do with this primordial loss. Once we become subjects of the signifier we can never simply make good on this loss; it is irremediable.

And what of the generative effects of language as structure on the speaking human organism? These have to do with how language generates human desire. Dean describes how "the agent of the cut that produces both subject and object is, of course, language. According to Lacan, symbolic networks dissect the human body, producing leftovers that cause desire. The ill fit between language and the body introduces wrinkles and gaps that generate desire. We might say that the unconscious and desire exist only as a consequence of this disharmony between the structures of language and those of the body."[44]

The understanding of the subject as an effect of the signifier and the idea of this primordial loss that attends each human subject's inscription in language continue not to figure in theories of ethnic-racialized subjectivity and experience within critical race and ethnicity studies knowledge projects like Latino and Chicano studies, for example. Why, we might ask, should we even be concerned with these failures of engagement? What, if anything, do we stand to lose or gain by taking or not taking these issues into consideration? The result for our scholarship is an undertheorized explanation of loss and trauma at the psychic, political, juridical, and economic levels, as well as an overly simplistic and commonsensical conceptualization of human subjectivity in which we bracket the effects of language on the speaking organism in order to win back some empty promise of fullness and completeness. In this latter compensatory, falsely reparative critical move, we, against our best intentions, provide precisely the image of ethnic-racialized subjectivity as whole, complete, and transparent, an image upon which racist discourse thrives and against which we imagine we are doing battle.

With respect to the question of what the human subject loses or stands to lose in a world marked by radical disparities in social and material resources, we must stay attuned to what Dean describes as two different—but I think related—kinds of losses so that we might craft in critical race and ethnicity studies knowledge projects the most historically and psychoanalytically textured and nuanced explications possible. Dean writes,

> To recognize what Joan Copjec calls "the *unvermögender* Other," the Other who doesn't have what it takes, is to recognize that loss is constitutive of subjectivity rather than the consequence of an oppressive regulatory regime that has arranged the world to one's disadvantage. Recognizing this distinction should not delegitimate the impact of social inequities. Instead, articulating psychoanalysis with politics depends upon differentiating between losses and deficits that represent unequal distribution of social resources, including visibility and dignity, on the one hand, and losses and deficits that are constitutive, that indicate an ineliminable zone of subjective abjection (object *a*) on the other.[45]

As we have already explained, the losses constitutive of subjectivity have to do with the effects of language as structure on the human speaking organism.

An astute reader might ask about the universalizing tendencies buttressing such a claim.[46] Does language as structure have the same privative and generative effects on all speaking subjects, regardless of, for example, the position they occupy in a racialized social hierarchy? Speaking of the different kinds of languages humans engage in around the world, Lacanians would agree that different languages cut the body up in different ways. Bruce Fink explains,

"Each language cuts the body up or 'covers' it in slightly different ways, and the body becomes written with signifiers; language is 'encrusted upon the living,' to borrow Bergson's expression. The body is overwritten/overridden by language."[47] But with respect to understanding the primordial loss that a speaking human organism experiences as a result of being inscribed in language, is the nature of the loss the same across cultures, languages, racialized groups, and so on? Does it matter that a human organism before its immersion in language might already be marked as a disprized human body, seemingly already positioned in a racist culture to be the beneficiary of certain built-in losses and miseries reserved for certain bodies and not others? To flesh out a potential response that will shed light on how these losses in Dean's passage can be read in relation to each other in a way that attends to the particularity of the subject for whom the losses having to do with the unequal distribution of social and material resources are more likely to accrue, I'd like to turn to Lacan's "elementary cell" of the graph of desire and a passage from Hortense Spillers's 1996 essay "'All the Things You Could Be by Now If Sigmund Freud's Wife Was Your Mother.'"

In his 1960 essay "The Subversion of the Subject and the Dialectic of Desire,"[48] Lacan begins his elaboration of the graph of desire with the "elementary cell" (figure 1). The triangle figure in the lower right-hand corner represents the human organism before its inscription in language. Language in the diagram is represented by the vector running from left to right, S to S'. As Van Haute explains, the triangle in the lower right-hand corner refers to the "human being as simple being of needs, with vague, unstructured presentations (of hunger and thirst, light and dark, warm and cold, etc.) that are as such not yet taken up in the order of language and meaning."[49]

As we noted earlier, language grafts itself onto the human body, which is why we see in the figure of the elementary cell the two vectors prior to their intersecting moving in different directions, dramatizing, again, the exteriority of language to the human body. We can understand the effects of language as structure on the human organism as reflected in the elementary cell at the point where the vector representing language (S to S') intersects the other vector that begins with the triangle in the lower right-hand corner. The result of the effects of language as structure on the human organism is the "barred subject," the subject divided in language represented by the symbol in the lower left-hand corner.

Can we say so far that Lacan's idea of the effects of language as structure on

17

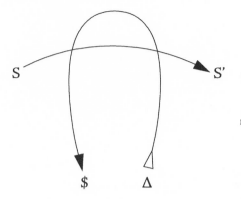

S   S'

$ Δ

1   Reproduced from Phillipe Van
    Haute, *Against Adaptation: Lacan's
    "Subversion" of the Subject: A Close
    Reading*. New York: Other Press,
    2002.

the human organism is universalizing in a problematic way, that it fails to consider the particularity of the human organism prior to language's impact on the organism's body? Does this model for understanding the effects of language as structure on the speaking organism describe any and all subjects, regardless of cultural, racialized, ethnicized, and other so-called differences? For critical race and ethnicity studies scholars interested in evaluating the feasibility of Lacanian theory for an understanding of the full range of objects a human subject stands to lose in the world, these questions are crucial.

In a passage I spend quite a bit of time attending to in chapters 3 and 7, Hortense Spillers writes, "The individual in the collective traversed by 'race'— and there are no known exceptions, as far as I can tell—is covered by it before language and its differential laws take hold."[50] I understand Spillers as arguing that there is a *signifierness* to race prior to the organism's subjection to language as structure. By "differential laws" of language, I take Spillers to be referring to the fundamental processes of metaphor and metonymy that constitute the two axes according to which all linguistic phenomena must be interpreted. I have worked up a slight variation (figure 2) of Lacan's elementary cell to graphically illustrate Spillers's point.

My version introduces a bar through the triangle originally meant to represent the organism of needs. This creates a formula that reads in the lower right-hand corner, "barred organism in relation to race." The organism is barred here to reflect Spillers's idea that race, its signifierness, somehow precedes language and its differential laws. The organism is already marked up by a kind of meaning, is already divided, as it were, by a signifierness

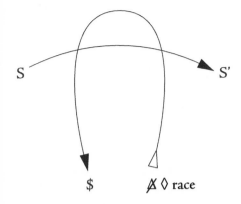

S S'

$ \$ $ $\cancel{A} \lozenge$ race   2   Graph of desire.

associated with race prior to the organism's encounter with language as structure. Spillers's point might be read as running contrary to Lacan's basic position because she seems to be granting race a Real status, lending it meaning prior to the organism's subjection to language as structure. How can race, one might ask, have meaning independent of its determination through language and language's differential laws?

I am not interested here in arguing, in the end, how Spillers's reading crosschecks or doesn't with Lacan's theory. I bring up Spillers's point in the context of the argument at this point in the introduction to entertain the possibility that language's intersection with the organism of needs might already find an organism marked by a kind of *metaphoricity* that yields from meanings associated with notions of racialized difference. Indeed, in Spillers's essay, as we will see later in my book, race is virtually equated with metaphoricity itself. I want to maintain an open-endedness to the question of whether or not Lacan's understanding of the privative and generative effects of language as structure is a problematic universalizing narrative. At the very least, it appears that taking into account Spillers's remarks means understanding that the metaphoricity of race in cultures suffused with racialized meanings is already stirring up a kind of signifying trouble prior to the moment of subjective constitution and that the metaphoricity of race here requires a more deeply textured narrative of this inaugural loss since it may be that it is not registered in the same way for all human organisms.

To attempt to provide a clearer picture here, we should recall that the human organism suffers a hypothesized inaugural loss as a result of having to

19

articulate its needs in the form of demands through the distorting medium of language. How, then, we might ask, does the metaphoricity of race and, more pointedly, the function of racialized difference in a racialized social hierarchy insinuate itself in the various moments of an organism's articulation of its needs in language? Does the fact that "the individual in the collective traversed by 'race' . . . is covered by it before language and its differential laws take hold" mean that race traverses and informs the scene of need prior to or at the very moment of the human organism's articulation of need in the form of a demand in language? I do not have the answers to these questions. It does seem to me that to articulate psychoanalysis with politics, as Dean suggests above, in the spirit of a discourse that wants to remain as alive as possible to the nature and impact of the different kinds of psychical and material losses experienced by the human subject means to dwell ferociously in the rich difficulties opened up by precisely these sorts of questions. Regardless of how one might field these questions, I think it is still imperative that we bring Lacan's theory of the divided subject in language to bear on how we conceptualize ethnic-racialized subjectivity and experience, if simply for the fact that it has so rarely if ever figured and because its not figuring reflects larger forces and practices of the domination of ethnic-racialized subjects.

20

I began this introduction with Jacques Lacan and Piri Thomas with very specific motivations in mind: to understand the relationship between their similarly mysterious and critical pronouncements on psychology and to signal the project's focus on certain aspects of Lacanian theory and Latino subjectivity and experience in the twenty-first century. Here, I would like to remark on a significant point of overlap between Lacanian theory's subject of the signifier, the barred subject, and Latino studies' conceptualization of the border subject that reveals, for me, the kinds of compelling links between Latino studies and Lacanian theory that ideally should encourage Latino studies scholars to engage Lacanian theory and Lacanian scholars to engage Latino studies. There is something, to put it simply, to the temporality of the signifying chain as Lacanian psychoanalytic theory understands it that is homologous to the temporality of *Latino* as this term currently circulates in academic and popular cultural narratives of the transformation of the United States that we are calling the Latinization of the United States. The indeterminacy of *Latino*, like the signifying chain, is predicated on equal parts anticipation and retroaction. I will discuss this in much greater detail in chapter 4, but for now I would like for us to imagine that in the following passage, the

Lacanian analyst Colette Soler, in explicating the temporality of the signifying chain, is also describing the temporality of *Latino* that precipitates in the twenty-first century version of the hailing "Hey, you, Latino" when she writes,

> What is the temporality of the signifying chain? It is a twofold temporality between anticipation and retroaction; it is what Lacan called reversible time. In other words, the temporality of speech is a time shared between anticipation, while you are speaking, of the moment of conclusion (the moment at which you grasped what you meant), and retroaction, for when you arrive at the anticipated end point, all previous speech takes on new meaning, that is to say, new meaning emerges retroactively. It is a time split between "*I don't know yet*" and "*Oh yes, I already knew that.*"[51]

Good.

The temporality of *Latino* unfolds according to first an anticipation of knowledge about the ethnic-racialized subject and then a retroactive determination, posthailing, which insists on already having known that knowledge about the subject. The temporality of *Latino* hinges on two different but ultimately related discussions. To begin with—and this is quite basic—the incoherent and inconclusive racialization of Latinos and Hispanics throughout the twentieth (and twenty-first) century in legal and extralegal contexts remarks quite directly on the nature of the meaning—"I don't know yet" and "I already knew that"—yielding from and accruing to this ethnic-racialized nominatory term, a term whose need it is ultimately to fully *know* ethnic-racialized subjects through the evidence collected for what will connote the signs of ethnicity and race. *Latino* operates a species of queer cut in the quasi-scientific discourses on race and ethnicity in the United States.

Throughout this project, I attempt to read for the overlaps whenever possible between the critical operations performed by *Latino* and *queer* with respect to ethnicity, race, sexuality, and sexual difference. Just as *queer* attempts to disturb binary categories like homosexuality/heterosexuality, female/male, masculinity/femininity, *Latino* similarly, due to its general inconclusivity with respect to remarking on categories of race and ethnicity, disturbs the logic by which ethnicity/race can be posed as a binary pair.[52] In short, *Latino* queers ethnicity and race. The hermeneutic similarity between *Latino* and *queer* also helps me make my second point. In contemporary Latino studies critique, *Latino* has been bonded to the future and to the past of the Americas, as I explain in chapter 4. Projects like the mammoth, multivolumed effort *Recovering the U.S. Hispanic Literary Tradition* read in concert with the ubiquitous

21

claims heard nowadays regarding "the inevitable Latinization of the United States" speak to a simultaneous backward- and forward-looking reading practice that drains the future into the past and burrows the past into the future. Insofar as *queer* too might be read as denoting temporality more so than ontology, *queer* then performs a similar homologous critical operation to *Latino*. The latter term—and the former term, too—is becoming increasingly responsible for compelling the new clock settings in the Americas.

This project's attempt to bring Latino studies and Lacanian theory into dialogue owes its inspiration to other, perhaps less theoretically sound and articulated reasons, given that it is based upon a general—and to this day still mostly unresolved—transference onto both Lacanian psychoanalytic theory and a certain history of politicized resistance in Chicano movement politics of the late 1960s and early 1970s. In 1935, Mrs. May Benzenberg Mayer was brought to a kind of justice in New York when she was fined for having promised and not delivered to a female patient a course of "dream therapy" that would have potentially provided for her patient some relief from paralysis in a limb.[53] During this time, what Freud called "wild analysis" was cause for some concern, especially in the bohemian East Village of New York City, where many artists and activists were generally quite enthused with the liberating promise they attached to Freud's psychoanalytic theory.[54] In this project I have often thought of Mrs. Mayer's fraudulent act as I have seemed to promise to bring to Latino studies not a course of "dream therapy" exactly, but a loosening of a very tightly bounded mode of partially paralyzed thinking on the constitution of subjectivity that we might characterize as predominantly "historicist," if we trust we can use Copjec's definition of *historicist* ("we are calling historicist the reduction of society to its indwelling network of relations of power and knowledge").[55] I am not suggesting that Latino studies' historicist traditions of scholarship represent "paralyzed thinking"—that would be preposterous. However, I am suggesting that the refusal to consider what might get remaindered in historicist analyses—that even the most rigorous historicist approach might leave important information about the human speaking subject in whatever historical period or epoch unremarked upon—is reflective of a refusal to engage psychoanalytic theory, and it is this refusal that strikes me as a species of paralyzed thinking. It paralyzes the field of Latino studies by effectively inoculating it against any new future critical strains. The Chicana lesbian feminist theorist, historian, and novelist Emma Pérez, whom

I discuss in chapter 6, attempts to craft a kind of rich and difficult balance between Chicano historicist practices and psychoanalytic approaches to analyzing and understanding history and individual and collective trauma.

On the issue of imposters, Lacan surmises in *Seminar XI*, "It would not be too much to say that, in the putting in question of analysis, in so far as it is always in suspense, not only in the popular mind, but still more in the private feelings of each psycho-analyst, imposture looms overhead—as a contained, excluded, ambiguous presence against which the psycho-analyst barricades himself with a number of ceremonies, forms and rituals."[56] Imposture looms over the head of my readers, I'm afraid to say: I am certainly not a trained psychoanalyst, but a reader trained in psychoanalytic theory and Latino studies who is operating under the same assumption that guides Spillers's project in " 'All the Things You Could Be by Now,' " that the outlines of an emancipatory strategy for ethnic-racialized subjects may be glimpsed in the self-regarding scrutinizing practices of a psychoanalytic hermeneutic that must mine Lacanian theory in particular. I see my engagement with Lacanian theory as part of what some may consider the problematic tradition of the reception of Lacan in North America, given, among other things, that I am working primarily only with those seminars and pieces of writing that have been translated into English.[57]

Some readers may, no doubt, find my focus on the Lacan of the 1950s somewhat restricted and limited, since I don't deal with the later Lacan and thus risk perpetuating, as Alenka Zupančič writes, the image of Lacan as the " 'philosopher of language' who insists on the price that the subject must pay in order to gain access to the symbolic order. Thus we get the primordial act of renunciation, enjoyment as impossible, and the end of analysis as the moment when the analysand must assume symbolic castration and accept a fundamental or constitutive lack (or loss)."[58] The difference between the early and late Lacan has been explained according to the distinction between Lacan's earlier focus on the subject of desire versus the later focus, already seen in *Seminar XI* in 1964, on the subject of the drive. Jacques-Alain Miller explains this shift as one in which desire is "devalued" by Lacan: "During a whole period of his theoretical elaboration, Lacan tries to prop up the life functions on desire. But once he distinguishes the drive from desire [in *Seminar XI*], a devaluation of desire occurs. . . . What then becomes essential, on the contrary, is the drive as an activity related to the lost object which produces jouissance, and secondly fantasy."[59] The reason I risk overemphasizing the Lacan of lack and loss is because of what I see as an underengagement with the universal condition of loss attributable to the effects of language as structure on the speaking organism within critical race and ethnicity studies, and this has consequences for how we think of the ethnic-racialized subject as a subject of desire, a topic I write about in chapter 2. Related to this reason, I focus on lack and loss because of how I understand racist discourse and racism, more generally, as reliant on generously extending a species of what Juliet Flower MacCannell characterizes as an "animal-like" jouissance to ethnic-racialized subjects, a kind of obscene fullness.[60] In other words, the fullness granted and the lack and loss that goes unconsidered work together to deny ethnic-racialized subjects their humanness and their status as subjects of desire.

I understand that Lacan comes to theorize desire as a defense against satisfaction and that the subject of desire in fact interferes with the subject of the drive's jouissance.[61] Again, ethnic-racialized subjects are often fantasized and hallucinated as possessed with a kind of jouissance—and are in fact symbolically and materially punished daily for this in myriad ways. We may then come to believe that we actually do, as ethnic-racialized subjects, possess this "animal-like" jouissance, that we have access to it in ways others do not, that we are tied to the order of the Real, prior to language, in ways others are not. Does this fact require us to think in more nuanced ways about how the end of an analysis—and what Lacan calls the "traversing of the fundamental fantasy" in order to gain a kind of second-order access to a jouissance after the letter—might play itself out differently in theory and practice for those subjects already thought to possess a kind of jouissance and where this possession is the condition upon which they are more likely to be *dispossessed* of certain social and material resources? Taking all of this into consideration, it is my hope that my focus on lack and loss with respect to a theory of the ethnic-racialized subject as a subject of the signifier might for the reader then call up generative metaphors of possibility, even excess and not metaphors of scarcity and lack and the placid gloom of renunciation.

After graduating from college, I worked from 1990 to 1992 in a variety of roles at a not-for-profit clinic, Camillus Health Concern, that provided free medical, social, and psychological services to homeless people in Miami—the first clinic of its kind in the United States. In one of my strangest roles, I worked as a translator in therapy sessions with Spanish-speaking patients and non–Spanish-speaking psychologists. I recall that I never seemed to translate word for word but rather attempted to insinuate myself, as imposter-qua-psycho-

24

therapist, in woefully problematic ways, no doubt, in order to forge what I thought would qualify as the best interpretive yield for the psychologist and the patient. "Wild analysis," indeed.[62] Am I practicing a species of wild (Lacanian) analysis in this book? Perhaps. Is the wild nature of this address compounded by the fact that over the years I have not only seemed to situate Lacanian psychoanalytic theory in the place of the critical methodology-supposed-to-know but have managed to engage a similar type of transference-like relationship with Chicano movement politics, attributing to its politicized resistance to assimilation an intoxicating power and knowledge? Probably. The following passage by Jane Gallop might be read as an accurate assessment of precisely the kind of interpretative transferential yield I continue to pursue through Lacanian theory and Chicano movement politics:

> From reading Freud and Lacan, I had developed, already, a transference onto psychoanalysis in general. I believed psychoanalysis knew, and that if I were analyzed, or better yet if I became an analyst (my analysis was started under the guise of a training analysis), then I would get "it." I thought that Lacan considers the goal of analysis to be the analysand's assumption of his castration. To assume mine, it seemed to me, would mean understanding that I would never get transparent knowledge of myself from psychoanalysis or elsewhere, and thus never achieve (phallic) self-mastery.[63]

It is no coincidence that I often identify Lacan as a quasi-Chicano activist given the overlap I discern between his critique of coercive assimilatory imperatives in 1950s U.S. culture and the similar critique of assimilation crafted by early Chicano movement activists. My transference onto the general ethos of Chicano movement politics is painfully obvious in my somewhat hagiographic salute to Mexican American *pachuco/a* and zoot-suit culture's quasi-Lacanian anti-identity politics of the 1940s and 1950s in chapter 5, and in my homage to the work of Emma Pérez in chapter 6.

In many places in this book I know I have run the risk of precipitating, along the lines of Gallop's assessment above, a new kind of mastery vis-à-vis symbolic castration. My insistence on the delusional nature of the Imaginary ego and my critique, more generally, of the ego's pretension to mastery only ends up repositioning the ego-as-the-center-that-is-not-the-center, without requiring the critic to disconnect from the need for mastery in order to uncover this lie and delusion. Although I have tried to remedy this problem, I know I have not always heeded the warning Lacan issues in *Seminar II*:

25

But do you think that we should be content with that, and say—the I of the unconscious subject is not me? That is not good enough, because nothing, for those of you who think spontaneously, if one can say that, implies the inverse. And normally you start thinking that this I is the real ego. You think that the ego is nothing but an incomplete, erroneous form of this I. In this way, you have accomplished the decentring essential to the Freudian discovery, but you have immediately reduced it. . . . you force the ego back into this I discovered by Freud—you restore the unity.[64]

In many ways, my loquacious, shrill insistence on subjective division and the irremediable loss reads to me during these very late stages of the project as oddly compensatory and restorative attempts on the part of the ego to master this very division and primordial loss. Somehow, garrulously confessing to the division and the loss can have the effect of embalming the ego, protecting it from any further change or movement.

As someone who has been closely involved with Latino students at my university as a past director of its Latino studies program and as a Latino activist in my community, I have also wondered, like the Latino literary critic and theorist Suzanne Oboler,[65] about what we both read as Latino students' confusion and ambivalence on college campuses today regarding what it means to be a Latino subject in the twenty-first-century United States and how an explication of this feeling and affect drawn solely from historicist analyses appears not to be enough. Rey Chow's theory of "coercive mimeticism"—a twenty-first-century mode of inhabiting ethnic-racialized identity where one's social and cultural intelligibility is predicated on one's coming to successfully resemble what is recognizably "ethnic-racialized"[66]—challenges us to come up with a more Lacanian psychoanalytic reading of how ethnic-racialized subjectivity is constituted in a social order suffused with racialized meanings so that we might stay alive to the full range of losses, those attributable to the unequal distribution of social and material resources as well as those attributable to the effects of language as structure on the speaking organism, and to how the meanings of those losses inflect and impinge upon each other. Chow's timely and gloomy diagnosis sheds considerable light on the confusion and ambivalence, not to mention the utter exhaustion, Oboler and I encounter among our Latino students.

In this book, I insist on a more Lacanian psychoanalytic approach to, in a quite general way, articulate psychoanalysis with politics for an ethnic-

Mimicry

racialized minoritarian discourse in the United States. An unambiguous hostility and dismissive attitude exists toward psychoanalytic theory and psychoanalysis, more generally, in North American society and universities. The hostility seems especially pronounced in critical race and ethnicity studies knowledge projects—and especially so, we might add, when it is that Lacanian psychoanalysis and theory is the object of discussion. Training in and exposure to psychoanalytic theory is becoming more and more a rarity in North American universities these days, reflecting the fact that, generally speaking, training in psychoanalytic theory has always taken place outside the university. As Douglas Kirsner explains, "Unlike psychology and psychiatry, psychoanalytic training does not take place in universities but in its own institutions which are supposed to serve not only training but also research functions. From the outset psychoanalysis has been organized around free-standing institutions, perhaps deriving from Freud's own unhappy experiences with the University of Vienna."[67]

I argue for a more Lacanian psychoanalytically literate approach, in particular, as opposed to a psychoanalytic object-relations approach, or an ego psychology approach, or a Kleinian approach, or a social psychological approach to theorizing ethnic-racialized subjectivity within Latino studies, and in critical race and ethnicity studies more generally, because of the significantly more complicated and less *psychologistic* picture it potentially promises. I use the term *psychologistic* to refer to what Karen Ro Malone and Stephen R. Friedlander call "psychologizing" modes of thinking, where consciousness is equated with subjectivity and where "the subject is usually conceptualized and researched in terms of material that consciousness provides: affect, awareness, will, perception, etc."[68] Lacan thought this type of psychologistic analysis completely misguided, as it ignores the unconscious and the symbolic order. Fink writes, "Lacan teaches us to seek explanations in the symbolic order itself: the unconscious, he says, is the discourse of the Other, i.e., the unconscious consists of linguistic elements, phrases, expressions, commands, social and religious laws and conventions that are part of the culture at large as well as being part and parcel of every household."[69] An antipsychologistic approach along these lines, attuned to how the unconscious is structured like a language, can therefore compel a culturally nuanced—not static and universalizing—analysis that should, in theory, remain alive to historical and epistemic shifts over time.

Fink has explained how in a 1966 text, "Science and Truth,"[70] Lacan coins the phrase "the psychologization of the subject" in his critique of the sociologist Lucien Lévy-Bruhl's analysis of the behavior of so-called primitive people and Piaget's analysis of children's mental development. The phrase captures the hegemonic interpretation of the human subject in critical race and ethnicity studies today. Fink writes, "Neither thinker ever seems to attempt to understand the particular workings of the primitive or child's system as it stands, to understand the complex series of synchronic relationships among terms, or the substitutions and displacements that take place in the diachronic unfolding of the system."[71] I am certainly not intending with this example to compare ethnic-racialized subjects with "primitives" and "children." I am, however, implying that in our failure as critical race and ethnicity studies scholars to understand the ethnic-racialized subject as a subject of the signifier and to understand, more broadly, the effects of language as structure on the human speaking subject, we inadvertently reproduce the kind of common-sensical and reductive approach that, in fact, ends up drawing an equivalence sign between the ethnic-racialized subject, Lévy-Bruhl's notion of the primitive, and Piaget's "children." Lacan's critique of the psychologization of the subject is closely tied to his more general critique of the "culturalist school" of psychology, which I liken in chapter 3 to the tradition of "social psychology" in the United States. In *Seminar II*, he asks after critical approaches that try to exhaust the meaning of the subject by solely or primarily attending to the social and cultural context in which the subject is immersed: "This so-called culturalism consists in emphasising in analysis those things which, in each case, depend on the cultural context in which the subject is immersed. . . . The question is to know whether this element should be given pre-eminent importance in the constitution of the subject."[72] The ethnic-racialized subject has been primarily theorized as the perfectly calculated sum of "the cultural context in which the subject is immersed." I read this psychologization of the ethnic-racialized subject as the refusal to interpret the subject as anything other than ego and according to no dimension other than the Imaginary register. My book maintains that there has been a thorough psychologization of the ethnic-racialized subject, a want-to-be-exhaustive explanation that ignores the indeterminacy of the subject that follows on the subject's vacillation in language and that these psychologization practices are political in nature, reflecting as they do on broader issues of power and knowledge in the context of systemic racism and discrimination.

For all of these reasons, in the final two chapters of my book I recommend we adopt Spillers's notion of "interior intersubjectivity,"[73] a species of practice that articulates psychoanalysis with politics and that refuses to cede the entire range of understandings that ethnic-racialized subjects might adopt with respect to what it means to be a subject marked out in culture as "ethnic-racialized" to the edifice of ego and social psychology and that might, in some way, interrupt the moribund lock-step movement between ethnic-racialized resemblance and ethnic-racialized social and cultural intelligibility. Her practice, which I interpret as a synthesis of the late Foucauldian notion "care of the self" and the late Lacanian ethical imperative that one at the end of analysis come to identify with one's symptom, takes the risk of ruining—in the form of "care"—the ethnic-racialized self-as-ego that has been installed, as I explain to the reader in chapters 1 and 3, in legal discourses as a result of psychology's insinuation and inscription in the legal apparatus since the end of the nineteenth century, and that circulates in extralegal, everyday contexts as common knowledge regarding what it means to be an ethnic-racialized subject in contemporary U.S. culture.

This book understands this caring ruination as imbued with the hope of precipitating new forms of ethnic-racialized subjectivities that, to borrow the words in the following passage from Foucault, are guided by the refusal of what we are currently made to be, of refusing the false amplitudes that yield from how our function in society has been reduced to our so-called difference: "Maybe the target nowadays is not to discover what we are, but to refuse what we are. . . . The conclusion would be that the political, ethical, social, philosophical problem of our days is not to try to liberate us from the state and the type of individualization which is linked to the state. We have to promote new forms of subjectivity through the refusal of this kind of individuality which has been imposed on us for several centuries."[74]

CHAPTER ONE

Hollowed Be Thy Name

Although provisions were not made to provide food, medical care, assist with resettlement and establish schools for recently freed African slaves until the Freedmen's Bureau was established by Congress in 1865, records do show that in 1862, fifty-eight African American subjects were treated for "insanity" at the Government Hospital for the Insane in Washington, D.C., for the very first time. In 1860 the federal census reported the existence of 766 "colored insane" out of a population of 4,441,830 African American subjects. By 1880, the number of "colored insane" had risen to 6,157 out of a total African American population of 6,580,793.

In 1890, American psychiatrist A. H. Witmer reported these facts in a paper he delivered before the Tenth International Congress at Berlin.[1] The numbers alarmed him, since in his conversations with former slave owners he had been told that although "colored idiots and epileptics" were not unheard of in the years before the Civil War, they had never heard of an "insane colored person."[2] In 1893, three years after Witmer's presentation in Berlin, another American psychiatrist, Dr. McGuire, also found a reason to panic over these numbers. He communicated his worries to the readers of the *Virginia Medical Monthly*: "During the days of slavery, insanity was very uncommon among the negro race. Now, our large asylums are not capacious enough to hold the insane negroes of both sexes."[3]

What is the definition of insanity in the "professional" community during this time in the United States? Researching one of the premier journals on the "science of the mind," the *Alienist and Neurologist*, between the years 1880 and 1920, I came across many attempts by researchers to hazard a definition for "insanity." In an 1888 editorial there is an entry, "The Nature and Definition of Insanity," where the author, imbued with a cautious certainty, offers, "But it is not impossible to define insanity or anything else if we fully understand the thing to be defined. The true basis of every rational definition of mental derangement must be delusive mental perversion *engendered by disease affecting the mind*, displayed in the conduct or speech of the individual, as compared with his natural self or what ought to have been (if perverted or arrested development had not prevented its display) the natural self-type of the individual."[4] The *Alienist and Neurologist* interests us because over an especially contentious twenty-year period from 1880 to 1900, in its pages one witnesses spirited, cantankerous debates over whose "scientific" discourse would reign supreme in the conceptualization of insanity precisely during the time—if we can be allowed here to add three new scenes of "ethnic-racialized trouble" to those already being spectacularly staged in the immediate post-Reconstruction years—of mass immigration and ethnic relocation to the United States, the beginnings of the institution of American immigration restriction policies, and the professionalization of the field of American psychology.

The simultaneity of these "scientific" conflicts, traumatic ethnic relocations, and the legal restrictions on immigration to the United States provides me with a craggy sort of scaffolding onto which I suspend hooks, around which I thread two ostensibly major lines of inquiry that support a great share of the weight in this project. Initially, I consider the dissimulating function of notions of ethnic-racialized difference in the field formations and theoretical assumptions of psychoanalysis, ego psychology, and social psychology in the United States. I then explore generally how the field of psychology—and its "experts"—would by the mid-twentieth century insinuate itself in the legal apparatus, crafting and codifying in the process enduring psychologistic and thus reductive legal and extralegal understandings of ethnic-racialized subjectivity, trauma, and loss that are still with us today.

In *A History of Affirmative Action: 1619–2000*, Philip Rubio argues that "whiteness as property," a term coined by legal scholar Cheryl Harris, emerges forcefully in the years following the Civil War and is intensely protected.[5] Although Rubio and Harris do not discuss this, we should add "insanity" to the list of holdings belonging to the property of whiteness. In the conversations and exchanges in the psychiatric and neurological community toward the last third of the nineteenth century, one sees in addition to the debates regarding what insanity is and what discourse most effectively conceptualizes its etiology another consideration: can African American subjects claim insanity? Returning to the 1888 definition for insanity, we might consider whether the African American subject is seen to qualify as an "individual" at this moment, possessed with a "natural self"—with a psychology, period. How might the scientific contributors to the journal have understood slavery as what could pervert or arrest the development of human subjectivity and effectively make one go insane and, to be generous, make the United States crazy?

They don't say. They don't want to know. Although these debates on the meaning of insanity and whose definition will rule the day, as well as the new question that emerges regarding whether or not African American subjects can make legitimate claims to insanity, are not explicitly linked in the literature, insofar as they are not seen to share space in the same argument put forth by any researcher, I would like to suggest that they are in fact related. This relation, moreover, reveals a larger issue my research has made obvious to me: that the history of psychology and psychoanalysis in the United States has always included as a crucial part of its history a witting and unwitting reflection on the meaning of ethnic-racialized difference in U.S. culture. When the fields of psychology and psychoanalysis in the United States have over the years asked themselves what they constitute as a practice, a science, a therapeutics, a curative, or a salve, they appear to have to call up the spectacle of ethnic-racialized difference in order to operate these moments of self-reflection. This complex and confusing problematic will become clearer to the reader in the pages to come.

The antagonism between alienists—the name used to refer to individuals who were basically superintendents of asylums—and neurologists was especially pronounced in the mid-nineteenth century. There was during this time a generally very negative view of North American psychiatry, with a more hostile attitude still waiting in the wings for psychoanalysis at the beginning of the twentieth century. As neurology began to claim possession of a more and more detailed and intimate knowledge of the nervous system and the human brain, their claims as to what they could treat became far ranging, covering everything from brain tumors to insanity to hysteria. The dream of neurology during this time, that it would be able to explain exhaustively all of the operations of the brain and nervous system and that all so-called mental diseases would be assigned specific physiological causes, is clearly still today on the minds of many in the medical profession. Neurologists' ability to persuade others, even in the absence of convincing, irrefutable evidence, of its explanatory power is partly responsible for the virtual eradication of psychoanalysis in the United States at the beginning of the twenty-first century.[6] Commenting on the current situation and the battle lines drawn between psychoanalysis and neuroscience, the psychoanalyst André Green remarks:

Co-evolution of Psychoanalytic & Racial Thought.

32

We have been attacked by the neuro-biologists and specialists of the brain, and this is the thing that we have to keep in mind. The closer people are to what we do, the brain and the mind or the body-mind problem, the more they fiercely attack us. This is not a problem of "objective knowledge"; this is a subjective problem of inner beliefs, of prejudice, of refusing to take into account some things that we think are very important things and cannot be ignored. Today, it is the progress of the neuro-scientist, the brain specialist, which is the most harmful to us.[7]

The conceit of American neurologists in the late nineteenth century was fueled by the first successful experiments using electrical stimulation to determine the localization of brain functions.[8]

Arnold Davidson has written that between the years 1870 and 1905 psychiatry was caught somewhere between neurology and pathological anatomy.[9] Can we mark a moment when psychiatry effectively distances itself from neurology and pathological anatomy in the manner in which it confronts and analyzes so-called mental disease? Davidson, following Michel Foucault's thesis in *Birth of the Clinic*, argues that psychiatry emerges as an autonomous medical discipline at the moment when pathological anatomy can no longer serve its purposes. Davidson uses the following passage, first cited in Foucault's text, to illustrate the nature of the pathological anatomist's gaze: "For twenty years, from morning to night, you have taken notes at patients' bedsides on affections of the heart, the lungs and the gastric viscera, and all is confusion for you in the symptoms which, refusing to yield up their meaning, offer you a succession of incoherent phenomena. *Open up a few corpses: you will dissipate at once the darkness that observation alone could not dissipate.*"[10]

In other words, the symptoms will offer up their real meaning once the seat of disease has been located—once the defective organ, upon the opening up of the corpse, is located. The diseased organ constitutes the disease. Returning to the 1888 definition of insanity, it is clear that insanity is being theorized as an organic problem and one whose seat of disease is the brain: "The true basis of every rational definition of mental derangement must be delusive mental perversion engendered by disease affecting the mind." If we are attempting to determine how these understandings play out when the subject in question is a subject like the recently, at the time, freed African American subject, what else informs the anatamo-clinical gaze? In her insightful study, Amina Mama writes,

33

It was to the new biological sciences that the establishment now turned. Insanity ceased to be associated with moral degeneracy and instead increasingly attributed to organic sources in the brain. Madness now became linked to 'evolutionary complexity' rather than degeneracy, and mental illness was re-theorized as an unavoidable result of the stresses of being civilized, as a by-product of the greater sensitivity and creativity of the white race. In a re-hash of noble savage ideas, black people's brains were now said to be too simple and retarded to be affected, and their apparent lack of insanity was taken as being further evidence of mental inferiority.[11]

Mama provides us with another layer for considering what changes may have been effected in the analysis of insanity in neurology, psychiatry, and pathological anatomy when one rotates the focus of the question slightly in order to train one's attention on the ethnic-racialized subject, and for assessing the impact notions of ethnic-racialized difference may have had on the reasoning strategies of pathological anatomy and psychiatry. Returning to Davidson's argument regarding when psychiatry emerges as an autonomous discipline separate from pathological anatomy, we know that, unlike pathological anatomy, psychiatry did not insist to the exclusion of everything else that disease was to be located in the brain, or sexual and reproductive organs. Mama's point above implies that when the bodies in question were African subjects, the pathological anatomist's focus on the organ-qua-brain still held sway in psychiatric reasoning on the nature of mental illness. In other words, the shift from pathological anatomical reasoning to psychiatric reasoning did not require a recalibration in logical reasoning when the subject in question was not a white European. There was no shift in reasoning.

Building on the kind of texture that Mama's point provides us, I would like here also to give the reader a sense for how so-called ethnic division and the "immigrant threat" in the United States between 1880 and 1920 (a period increasingly assuming a kind of magical aura) affected assumptions and reasoning in the field of psychology. Andrew Heinze argues that critical changes in American psychological thought coincided with attempts to come to grips with what personal and national identity meant in an era of mass immigration and ethnic relocation. He claims that before this historical moment, there was very little sense of identity as being subject to fragmentation along ethnic-racialized lines in the United States:

> The decade of the 1880s serves as a convenient point of demarcation, for those years witnessed both the emergence of professional psychology and the beginning

of American immigration restriction (i.e., the Chinese Exclusion Act of 1882). Until this time Americans were not conspicuously concerned about the ethnic divisions among them. . . . Between the 1880s and the 1920s, however, in synchrony with the Progressive drive for a unified and purified body politic, Americans problematized their "divided heritage" and "dualistic national identity." It was then that assimilation became a problem rather than a process that occurred in the case of some groups but perhaps not in others.[12]

Heinze presents a portrait wherein ethnic-racialized subjects are seen as stirring up all sorts of psychological trouble at the conceptual level in the field of psychology, and at the intersubjective level between American subjects differently positioned in a racialized social hierarchy. He links in not strictly causal ways the emergence of assimilation as a problem in American society to conceptual drifts in North American psychology where more value begins to attach to ideas of subjective wholeness, unity, and adaptation, thus anticipating, in part, some of the central tenets in ego psychology.

The concern with ethnic divisions that Heinze argues begins to rattle American society beginning in the 1880s is reproduced within the field of American psychology in the form of a virtual obsession with racialized divisions and the meaning of racialized difference that is revealed in their more general effort to understand human psychology. In 1902, Granville Stanley Hall, one of the pioneers of American psychology, who trained with William James and is considered to be the father of the American Psychological Association, remarked,

No two races in history, taken as a whole, differ so much in their traits, both physical and psychic, as the Caucasian and the African. The color of the skin and the crookedness of the hair are only the outward signs of the many far deeper differences, including cranial and thoracic capacity, proportions of body, nervous system, glands, and secretions, vita sexualis, food, temperament, disposition, character, longevity, instincts, customs, emotional traits, and diseases. All these differences as they are coming to be better understood, are seen to be so great as to qualify if not imperil every inference from one race to another, whether theoretical or practical, so that what is true and good for one is often false and bad for the other.[13]

Robert V. Guthrie has argued in his brilliantly titled *Even the Rat Was White* that psychology's obsession with the study of African subjects in the effort to understand human psychology was due to the initial union between psychology and anthropology in Germany, which took place when P. W. A. Bastain insisted in 1871 on the essential connection between psychology and ethnology.[14] An invaluable study published by George Oscar Ferguson Jr. in 1916, "The Psychology of the Negro: An Experimental Study," certainly confirms Guthrie's point. Ferguson's text is a study of all of the work conducted up to that point on the question of race and psychology, and he gives the famous anthropologist Franz Boas a certain pride of place in these discussions.

Ferguson explains that one of the more important questions Boas brings to the research has to do with what I will discuss below in my analysis of the American psychoanalyst Dr. John E. Lind's psychoanalytic study of African American subjects, the African subject's supposed inability to metaphorize. Ferguson glosses Boas's position: "Boas then takes up the arguments that primitive races cannot abstract, inhibit impulses or choose according to standards of value. . . . The specific differences which separate the primitive and inferior peoples from those which are higher are that the former races *have a relative incapacity to reason or associate, to compare and draw conclusions, to attend, observe and reflect, to exercise foresight, to persist in a given line of activity, to hold to a rather distant rather than a present end.*"[15] In a study whose twists and turns, lows and highs, require steady doses of Dramamine every twenty pages or so, the author's fickle investments—there *are* significant differences between the intelligence of blacks and whites; there *aren't* any remarkable differences between the intelligence of blacks and whites—finally appear to settle on the following claim: "It seems as though the white type has attained a level of higher development, based upon the common elementary capacities, which the negro has not reached to the same degree."[16] His argument eventually capitulates to what we earlier referred to as the mode of reasoning in pathological anatomy, one that insists on the seat of the disease to explain the nature of the disease, a mode of reasoning that does not give way to proper psychiatric reasoning when the subjects in question are African subjects. Ferguson's quasi-pathological anatomist's gaze wants to convince us that nonwhite subjects, in the end, simply have rickety and defective brains that are wrapped in misfiring neurons: "From the nature of the mental differences, one would infer that such neural differences as may be found will probably be mainly in the constitution of the cortical neurons, rather than elsewhere in the nervous system."[17]

Freudian psychoanalysis arrives fashionably late into these discussions in the United States. In "The Freudian Thing," Lacan writes that Freud is rumored to have turned to Carl Jung—Lacan claims the story came to him "from Jung's own mouth"—as they were rounding the Statue of Liberty at Ellis Island upon their historic first visit to the United States for Freud's delivery of his Clark University lectures in 1909 to say, "They do not realize we are bringing them the plague."[18] Almost ten years later, in the preface to the English-language edition of *Seminar XI*, Lacan revisits these remarks to say, "This conveys the idea he had of psycho-analysis—a plague—except that it proved to be anodyne in the land where he brought it; the public adopted/ adapted it quite painlessly."[19] Remarking on this mythic scene replete with mythic fathers, Jane Gallop draws the reader's attention to the plaque that appears beneath the Statue of Liberty with the inscription, "Give me your tired, give me your poor," which effectively "announces America's project to assimilate everything, including that rejected by the rest of the world."[20] This moment represents a compelling cluster of elements that establishes what seems like an odd link between the question of ethnic immigrant difference— the promise that they will be accepted, and then *melted*—and North America's attempt to grapple with Freudian psychoanalysis.

The treatment of the ethnic immigrant subject and the beginnings of psychoanalysis in the United States are condensed in the figure of James Jackson Putnam, whose importance in helping disseminate Freudian psycho-analysis in the United States cannot be underestimated.[21] At sixty-three, Putnam took a serious interest in Freudian psychoanalysis and was crucial in securing Freud and psychoanalysis a fair hearing in the United States. In the mid-1860s, Putnam was a neurologist very active in the debates between neurologists and alienists regarding the treatment of the insane in asylums. In 1872, he found himself holding the mysterious title of "electrician" at the Massachusetts General Hospital, in charge of its "magnetic and electric appa-ratus": "He worked in a small room on a small budget, treating patients, many of them immigrants, whose troubles ranged from paresis [partial to complete paralysis] to hysteria."[22]

Putnam, like many others—including Freud, of course, but also the much revered figurehead of American psychology William James who, incidentally, was never won over by psychoanalysis—began to question neurology's obses-sive focus on all things physical regarding the brain and nervous system to the absolute exclusion of psychological processes. Hale writes,

The brain was the "organ of mind," and every psychological state corresponded to a definite condition of the brain and nervous system. Complex functions of mind and brain could be analyzed into simple elements. Borrowing from faculty psychology, many neurologists assumed that mental states could be reduced to combinations of sensations and memory images. . . .

Nervous and mental illness, whenever possible, were ascribed to localized lesion, definite injuries to tissue. . . . Nervous and mental diseases occurred chiefly in those with defective heredity.[23]

One could characterize this moment as constituting the stage before what we might call, after Arnold Davidson, the constitution of an autonomous psychiatric mode of reasoning. Putnam, along with Morton Prince, another important figure in nineteenth-century American psychiatry and psychoanalysis, was very critical of the definitive exiling of the mind from the body—that the mind could have no influence on the body given the neurologists' insistence that the two constituted "closed-parallel systems."[24]

Granville Stanley Hall may have written the letter of invitation to Freud to present his ideas at Clark University in 1909, but it was Putnam who would be in charge of writing up the momentous events of this visit in a two-part publication in the *Journal of Abnormal Psychology* in 1909–10.[25] I'll cite a couple of passages from this publication to give the reader a sense for Putnam's vigorous support of Freud's theories at the time and his gentle chastising of the general psychological and psychiatric community in North America for being so reticent to engage Freud. I also want to point to the important differences between Putnam and Freud on some very key issues, namely, what we might call, with the title of Lacan's 1959–60 *Seminar VII* in mind, *The Ethics of Psychoanalysis*—specifically, what kind of ethics should drive psychoanalytic treatment and define the role of the analyst. The differences between Putnam and Freud on what I am referring to as "the ethics of psychoanalysis" anticipate the lines of division that would define the differences between Lacanian theory and ego psychology that I discuss in chapter 2.

Putnam characterizes the unfair prejudices against Freud up to that moment by subjecting those prejudices to a Freudian analysis of sorts:

The doctrines of Freud and his colleagues have been made known to us here more through the gossip of prejudice and misconception than by the testimony of those who have really tested them, and this, in itself, is an interesting fact. For these doctrines involve at every point the belief that the hidden motives which help to rule our lives, and which frequently show themselves as prejudices, are made up of "attraction," "desire," "acceptance," on the one hand, and, on the other hand, of "repulsion," "repression," "denial," mixed in equal parts. A strong prejudice often means a strong, instinctive attempt to set aside as false an influence which we feel that, if differently presented, we might be forced to accept, at least in part, as true, and the strength of the prejudice usually measures the importance of the half-felt but perhaps wholly suppressed truth. To say the least, our prejudices express feelings that at the moment we cannot or will not put to the test of reason.[26]

Earlier in the essay, Putnam questions the erudition of his North American colleagues, who, like him, have remained deaf to Freud's theories all of these years: "Though little known among us, Freud is no longer a young man, and indeed he outlined his life work and 'laid his course' so many years ago that it is a reflection on our energy and intelligence that we have not gained a closer knowledge of the claims and merits of his doctrine."[27]

In the following passage from part 1 of his report, train your eye on a question that appears—in the context of the entire report—as nothing short of a somewhat odd precipitation of concern: the question of self-knowledge in psychoanalytic treatment, that is, the question of why would one want to familiarize oneself with one's "crooked byways," as Putnam cutely puts it. I also want to draw the reader's attention to the end of the passage where Putnam already appears to anticipate the contentious issue that would define Lacan's trenchant critique of North American ego psychology in the 1950s— the role to be played by the analyst and the power she should be thought to possess and draw upon in the treatment. Putnam writes, "*It may not be necessary that every one should become intimately acquainted with all their crooked byways and obscure corners of himself,* or that each person should force himself to recognize his kinship with others whose qualities he deplores or whose acts he regards as criminal. But there are times when such knowledge becomes necessary for the preservation of the mental health, *and the physician should fit himself to be the guide to its attainment.*"[28]

What did Freud have to say about all of this? In a letter to Putnam dated January 28, 1910, barely two months after the appearance of Putnam's report, Freud writes,

You surely will understand when I tell you that it has been a long time since I have begun reading anything with such intense anticipation as I brought to your first article in the *Journal of Abnormal Psychology* in which my name has so honorable a place.

What I read did not surprise me in view of our correspondence. But it has given me pleasure and satisfaction. I hope your words will make a strong impression in America and will secure for psychoanalysis the lasting interest of your countrymen.[29]

He is particularly thankful for "the seriousness with which you came to my aid in the matter of sexuality,"[30] the focus of part 2 of Putnam's report. By 1914, Freud, according to Hale Jr., had started to take issue—gently—with Putnam's attempt to "place psychoanalysis 'in the service of a particular philosophical outlook on the world' and to 'urge this upon the patient for the purpose of ennobling his mind. In my opinion, this is after all only to use violence, even though it is overlaid with the most honorable motives.'"[31] In his "return to Freud," Lacan would echo precisely this same sentiment in reminding his listeners what psychoanalysis is and isn't. In the chapter "The Eye and the Gaze," from *Seminar XI*, Lacan maintains, "Psycho-analysis is neither a *Weltanschauung* [a world view], nor a philosophy that claims to provide the key to the universe. It is governed by a particular aim, which is historically defined by the elaboration of the notion of a subject. It poses this notion in a new way, by leading the subject back to his signifying dependence."[32]

What could have inspired this casually crafted but serious critique of Putnam by Freud? In the letters between Putnam and Freud, Putnam seemed especially fixated on the analyst's responsibility to the analysand and seemed obstinate in his claim that the analyst *needs* to provide guidance and direction for the analysand. In letter 14, dated February 13, 1910, Putnam writes to Freud,

> I feel that since you urge us to be completely truthful and completely thorough, you should urge us also to take in all the sources or knowledge and all motives and inducements for progress. *Our psychopathic patients need, I think, something more than simply to learn to know themselves.* If there are reasons why they should adopt higher views of their obligations [as based on the belief that this is a morally conceived universe, and that 'free-will' has a real meaning, *then these reasons ought to be made known to them.*[33]

Putnam is trying in his very early exposure to psychoanalysis to understand the ethics of psychoanalysis, the role and responsibility of the analyst and the nature of the value of truth and knowledge in the analytical setting. All of this business of psychoanalysis must be in the service of something, right? A kind of good old-fashioned American pragmatism informs Putnam's interpretation of the goals of analysis and his interpretation of the analyst as someone with whose "healthy ego" the analysand must come to identify and where this identification would constitute the end of a successful analysis. In the passage from Freud above, one sees that he characterizes this species of contract between analyst and analysand as suffused with a kind of violence and power that is run through with the conceit of mastery on the part of the analyst who buys into the fantasy that she really is the subject-supposed-to-know. In *Seminar VII*, Lacan reminds his readers and listeners of Freud's position on these matters and provocatively asks, "Are we analysts simply something that welcomes the suppliant then, something that gives him a place of refuge? Are we simply, but it is already a lot, something that must respond to a demand, to the demand not to suffer, at least without understanding why?—in the hope that through understanding the subject will be freed not only from his ignorance, but also from suffering itself."[34]

As I've remarked, Putnam's role in the reception of psychoanalysis in the United States at the beginning of the twentieth century provides the broad outlines for what would transpire in ego psychology with respect to the conceptualization of the role of the analyst, the goal of the treatment, and the status, more generally, of self-knowledge and subjective truth in psychoanalysis. Despite the differences between Putnam and Freud with respect to how one was to understand the role of the psychoanalyst and the nature of her clinical interventions, and despite the less than unanimous support garnered by Freud after his Clark lectures, this certainly did not affect how radically open the United States made itself to psychoanalytic discourse in both "high" and "popular" cultural arenas. Two years after Freud's lectures, in 1911, the American Psychoanalytic Association was established, along with the New York Psychoanalytic Society, the latter under the leadership of A. A. Brill, another crucial figure in the history of psychoanalysis in the United States. Putnam established the Boston Psychoanalytic Society in 1914. All of these groups belonged from their inception to the International Psychoanalytic Association that Freud founded in 1910. I would argue that the first notes struck in the conversation between Putnam and Freud about the nature of psychoanalytic discourse in the clinical setting and the specific role to be played by the analyst—her use of power, even violence, the word Freud uses in his letter to Putnam, in attempting to "ennoble" the mind of the suppliant— reappear in another later debate about psychoanalysis in the United States—

the question of lay analysis and whether analysts without medical degrees could practice psychoanalysis. In the excellent piece "Medicalized Psychoanalysis and Lay Analysts," Jeffrey Librett argues that "the theme of the relation between the psychoanalytic and medical discourses should therefore stand at the center of any examination of the institutional history of the reception of psychoanalysis in the United States."[35] He asks, as have others, why it is that despite the United States' relative, even spirited, openness to psychoanalytic discourse, "it was in the United States and not elsewhere, that the medical enframing of analysis became most radical."[36]

Common to both debates, as I read them—the role of the analyst and the power that should be allotted her and the question of lay analysis—is the refusal to dispense with a certain characterization of the analyst as the subject-supposed-to-know and medicine as the discourse-supposed-to-know. It is as though in his exchanges with Freud, Putnam could never stop speaking and understanding outside of his role as the medically trained neurologist. Putnam's exchanges with Freud not only foretell the future of what would become some of the central tenets and assumptions of ego psychology in the United States, they also embed, less explicitly, the debates about the role of medical training in psychoanalysis in the United States. Characterizing the argument put forth by Franz Alexander in a 1927 piece in the *International Journal of Psychoanalysis*, Librett writes, "Either one must subordinate psychoanalysis to medicine, or one must—even if this might seem absurd—subordinate medicine to psychoanalysis. That is, either one must submit the mastery of the soul to that of the body, or one must submit the mastery of the body to that of the soul. Freud, however, positions himself precisely between the two."[37]

The question of lay psychoanalysis and medical mastery—the soul as master to the body, the body as master to the soul—found another modality through which to articulate the terms of its debate as it was transferred to the scene of the ego-psychological clinical setting in the United States around the specific elaboration of the roles of the healing analyst and the suffering analysand. A passage from Lacan's "The Freudian Thing" serves as not only a commentary on the behavior of the ego psychologists but also an illustration of what was at stake in the much earlier debate over lay analysis in the United States. Lacan strikes quickly in this piece: "It is to return to the reactionary principle that covers over the duality of he who suffers and he who heals with the opposition between he who knows and he who does not."[38] The analyst here becomes, in theory, master of the analysand's soul and body, wherein the

42

analyst's healthy ego represents a certain mastery of some silently agreed upon reality; this healthy ego then serves as that which the analysand must emulate and with which it must come to identify in order to move toward the successful completion of an analysis.

How does the topic of race and racialized difference get articulated in early psychoanalytic work in the United States? The two earliest and most relevant pieces I came across were published in 1913 in the *Psychoanalytic Review*. Dr. John E. Lind's attempts to address from a so-called Freudian psychoanalytic theoretical perspective African American subjects as psychological subjects who may be initially thought to possess some psychical complexity presents a conflicted portrait, to say the least. If we noted above that the formative work in American psychology seemed incapable of defining its inquiries into the nature of human psychology without hallucinating the African subject as its necessary foil and producing patently racist ideas, we must add that early American psychoanalysis also finds itself similarly drawn to the strategy of exploring Freudian psychoanalysis on the backs of African American subjects and producing an equally problematic, if slightly more confusing and internally incoherent, racist discourse.

In "The Dream as a Simple Wish-Fulfillment," Dr. Lind, who collected his observations and data while working at the Government Hospital for the Insane in Washington, D.C., likens the African American subject to a child— an Anglo child, that is—and concludes that African Americans are not possessed of the ability to, basically, metaphorize: "In none of the eighty-four [dreams recorded] could distortion, condensation, latent content or secondary elaboration be determined. No associations could be obtained to the dream content, the dreamer simply recognizing the dream picture as a faithful visual representation of a wish which he had been obliged to suppress."[39] That certain subjects are thought incapable of metaphorizing has obvious implications for how we theorize their ability to sublimate, repress, and negate, to name just a few mental processes that would be affected. This understanding eviscerates any number of ways of how one makes sense of the world through the basic mechanisms of condensation/displacement and metaphor/metonymy, not to mention that it clearly theorizes a subject who appears immune to the effects of language as structure.

In "The Color Complex in the Negro," a second piece from the same year, Dr. Lind appears to reach a significantly different conclusion, although he seems oblivious to it.[40] In this analysis, he recounts different case studies of what he considers mostly psychotic African American men and women where the subjects in question express the belief that they are "white." Interestingly, it is only on the condition that the wish to be white can be detected in them that Dr. Lind then bestows African American subjects with the ability to metaphorize. In the absence of the African American subject's attempt to traverse a racialized divide by psychically crossing over to whiteness, Dr. Lind cannot imagine them as possessed of the ability to metaphorize and, more dramatically, as possessed of any ability to think creatively whatsoever. The effect of reading these pieces together is one of wild discordance: African American subjects become psychically complex subjects who might be possessed of the basic ability of creative thinking only on the condition that they make attempts, as psychotics, to hallucinate themselves as white.

Are the differences registered in Dr. Lind's analyses attributable to changing perceptions for what constitutes madness? Might light be shed on the discordant notes struck in Lind's analyses by attending to the history of madness more directly, as Foucault does in *Madness and Civilization*? Foucault's analysis, although possibly providing us with a general outline of the problematic, cannot explain the significantly more complicated situation in the United States around the period of the emergence and consolidation of psychiatry and psychology and the question of how to handle recently freed African American subjects and relocated ethnic-racialized immigrant subjects inserted into those discursive networks because of how race overdetermines the questions of madness, nonmadness, and general mental health from the get-go.

In one of his course summaries titled "Psychiatric Power," Foucault writes, "Power relations constituted the a priori of psychiatric practice. They conditioned the operation of the mental institution; they distributed relationships between individuals within it; they governed the forms of medical intervention. . . . *Now, what was essentially involved in these power relations was the absolute right of nonmadness over madness.*"[41] In Foucault's work, all of the physicians and their patients are assumed to be white and European. The power struggles around the mad and nonmad unfold within the racialized magnetic field of whiteness. White nonmadness has or does not have a right over white madness. Paul Gilroy reminds us that Foucault may indeed have underappreciated the central role made to be played by African subjects in "modern scientific thinking" and how, although Gilroy doesn't address this specifically, ideas about Africans as human subjects should have been seen as figuring crucially in the history that could be told about madness and nonmadness in the West:

"The extensive debate as to whether Negroes should be accorded membership in the family of mankind (a group whose particularity was inaugurated, proved, produced, and celebrated by the transformed relationship between words and things that crystallized at the end of the eighteenth century) might have been more central to the formation and reproduction of modern scientific thinking than Foucault appreciated."[42] The question of the mad versus the nonmad subject is a thoroughly racialized one in the United States in the nineteenth century (and in the United States of the twenty-first century as well, I might add).

Critics like Ann Laura Stoler have discussed how the specific charge that ignites race in a North American context is simply not present in Foucault's work because it didn't circulate in intellectual discussions to any significant extent during his time in France.[43] Of course, this does not mean that Foucault does not allow one to see the specific operations attributable to race in his histories of human subjectivity. Both Stoler and more recently Rey Chow have argued for the determining presence of race and ethnicity in his work. Chow, for example, insists that Foucault's theory of "biopower" and his notion of "deployment of sexuality" in volume 1 of the *History of Sexuality* can be read as remarking on the "ascendancy of whiteness" in the Western world: "I would like to propose that Foucault's discussion of biopower can be seen as his approach, albeit oblique, to the question of the ascendancy of whiteness in the modern world."[44] Building on Chow's claim, I want to add that this ascendancy is underwritten by the assumption of a remarkable and riotous psychical complexity that does not get extended to ethnically and racially marked subjects.

In his 1976 lectures at the Collège de France, Foucault seems especially wary of being construed as providing a history of racism, or whiteness, even though the lectures themselves sometimes appear to compel these very characterizations of his historical inquiries. He is quite explicit regarding one particular shift in understanding racism: "I think that racism is born at the point when the theme of racial purity replaces that of racial struggle, and when counter-history begins to be converted into a biological racism."[45] Throughout this book, I argue that the exhaustive interpretative reduction of ethnic-racialized subjectivity and experience to the "indwelling network of relations of power and knowledge"[46] constitutes a new form of biologism, evolutionism that is also a species of ethological analysis since the specifically human dimension—the effects of language as structure on the human or-

45

ganism—are not taken into consideration when we conceptualize ethnic-racialized subjectivity and experience. Moreover, I claim that this is occurring both within and outside academic and popular cultural discourses that can be described as racist, as well as in those critical interventions that attempt to challenge these racist discourses. If Lacanian psychoanalysis's sole "moral maxim" is, as Slavoj Žižek maintains, that you "not surrender your internal conflict, your division,"[47] then this need not apply to the ethnic-racialized subject, who, as I argue throughout, is not divided or conflicted in the psychoanalytic sense because the effects of language as structure are never thought to bear on his or her body. Mama has argued that "ideas about the minds of Africans, and about the sanity and insanity of both Africans and Europeans, have been integral to the subordination of the enslaved and the colonized."[48] I maintain that the failure to conceptualize the ethnic-racialized subject as a subject of the signifier, as subject to the privative and generative effects of language as structure, represents another species of racist elaboration on "ideas about the minds of African" and other ethnic-racialized subjects that is integral to the ongoing subordination of ethnic-racialized subjects today.

Agreeing with Chow that Foucault can be read as remarking on the ways in which categories of ethnicity and race are internal to the management and reproduction of biological life, I would like to add that crucial to this early form of diversity management is the necessity of rendering these same marked bodies as psychologically unremarkable, or, as I prefer to say, hollow.[49] We might locate this idea in Foucault's explication of "deployment of sexuality," developed toward the end of *History of Sexuality*:

> If it is true that sexuality is the set of effects produced in bodies, behaviors, and social relations by a certain deployment deriving from a complex political technology, one has to admit that this deployment does not operate in symmetrical fashion with respect to the social classes, and consequently, that it does not produce the same effects in them. We must return, therefore, to formulations that have long been disparaged; we must say that there is a bourgeois sexuality, and that there are class sexualities. Or rather, that sexuality is originally, historically bourgeois, and that, in its successive shifts and transpositions, it induces specific class effects.[50]

I am for the moment aligning "class sexualities" with ethnic-racialized subjectivities wherein the joint that serves as the hinge is "psychical inte-

46

riority." Before this discussion in the passage above, Foucault attempts to explain why the "working classes" were extended a remarkable sexuality that had previously been bestowed only to the bourgeoisie: "There is little question that one of the primordial forms of class consciousness is the affirmation of the body; at least this was the case for the bourgeoisie during the eighteenth century."[51] What I would like to concentrate on here, and Foucault certainly compels it in his discussion, is the assumption and hallucination of a vast, complex, and remarkable interior domain—in short, the psychic domain, that served as the very foundation to a claim of class hegemony. The affirmation of body is also the affirmation of a psychical interiority that is remarkable (Foucault is quite clear on this); the affirmation of body depends absolutely on a prior presumption of psychical interiority.

This is hardly a new claim. Many critics have remarked upon how the notion of psychical interiority and psychological complexity had in late-nineteenth-century and early-twentieth-century North America been tied to a particular class and ethnic-racialized positioning.[52] For example, Joel Kovel writes: "within our (North American) culture, introspection signifies participation in a particular class and social relation. . . . I am not saying that working-class people do not develop insight, but for them to do so in analysis means pursuing an activity foreign to their experience of the world."[53] Kovel's point is right as far as it goes, but it cannot speak to the historical instantiation of these kinds of understandings. Here's a question that begs to be asked: why is introspection "foreign to their experience of the world?" I think Joel Pfister, Nancy Schnog, Kovel, and many other theorists working on the question of the invention of the psychological miss the fact that the power exercised over, say, the working classes and ethnic-racialized subjects in a racialized, class-stratified social hierarchy is expressed in the very act of attempting to convince "them" that "introspection" is foreign to their experience of the world.

47

CHAPTER TWO

Subjects-Desire, Not Egos-Pleasures

To look at race and racism, then, is to encounter fantasies of castration and escape from it, fantasies of "Who has the jouissance?" The "possession" of jouissance is still an irrational element in all thinking about race, and it taints even antiracism today.

JULIET FLOWER MACCANNELL,
The Hysteric's Guide to the Future Female Subject

On the one hand, we need to preserve the jouissance of the Other in order to be able to define our own: but on the other hand, we seek to destroy the Other enjoyment because we suspect it may be more superabundant than our own.

DYLAN EVANS, "From Kantian Ethics to Mystical Experience: An Exploration of Jouissance"

The rallying point for the counterattack against the deployment of sexuality ought not be sex-desire, but bodies and pleasures.

MICHEL FOUCAULT, *History of Sexuality, Volume 1*

In recent years, as I noted in my introduction, critics such as Tim Dean and Lee Edelman have argued that Lacanian theory is a species of queer theory. I argue that Lacanian theory is also a radical antiracist theory, and its antiracism functions as a deepening and extension of its antiheteronormative charge. Lacan's theory of the incalculable subject in language can be seen to operate in both the scene of the queer Lacanian critique of the complementarity between the sexes and the antiracist Lacanian critique that challenges any explication of the ethnic-racialized subject as wholly reducible in and exhausted by language.

Given what I have been arguing thus far regarding how racism depends on a certain representational capture of the ethnic-racialized subject—rendered as transparent to the signifier, potentially whole and unified—in order to manage this subject more masterfully in discourse, then this insistence on the incalculable and indeterminate should be very welcome in our antiracist analyses. Since the human subject is, as I explained earlier, dependent upon a system of differentially constituted signifiers in which signifiers signify only in virtue of their difference from other signifiers, any determination made about the subject in language will by necessity be incomplete and insufficient to defining who or what the subject is. Joan Copjec has argued that these built-in failures in language are what provide us with one of the best tools to contest racism.[1]

Many antiracist positions in critical race and ethnicity knowledge projects do not endorse Lacanian theory because understanding the precipitation of subjectivity as an effect of language seems, among other things, ahistorical, apolitical, universalizing, and antihumanist—the kind of antihumanism that few can stomach, because it allows for none of the residual comforts that attend forms of antihumanist thinking where an ego will still be seen to have survived the wreckage of antihumanism and where, from the scene of its survival, it can then manage to raise the human from the dead.

If some of the most crucial work done in fields like Chicano studies and African American studies has involved, as a kind of basic first step, narrativizing previously invisible subjectivities and erased histories, then one can imagine that defining the human subject in our research as, for example, "nothing other than what slides in a chain of signifiers, whether he knows which signifier he is the effect of or not," or as "the intermediary effect between what characterizes a signifier and another signifier"[2] can be interpreted as simply reproducing the themes of invisibility and erasure on another, more fundamental level. The Lacanian subject here is defined as a kind of absence, and absence—the conspicuous absence of this tradition or that experience in the routine accounts of the histories that get transmitted from one generation to the next—broadly conceived and related to "invisibility" and "erasure" is precisely what our antiracist scholarly and activist work has courageously and tirelessly fought against.

But to follow Lacan's theory of the subject in language does not mean that ethnic-racialized subjectivities and our histories, routinely threatened with erasure, must go unremarked upon once again according to new terms and conditions. Ranjana Khanna sharply captures the gist of a certain criticism of Lacanian theory along these lines when she writes,

> In Lacan, it is not so clear how to conceive of historical occurrences that appear to cause and be caused by particular psychical traumas and identifications, in spite of the fact that Lacanians insist on singularity and contingency. While the structural split or antagonism seems to be intrinsic to the subject in Lacan's corpus, and

49

therefore attains the status of universal condition, it is not clear where there is very much room for understanding how the particular, with all its historical permutations, exists alongside this universal. *Although the universal does not necessarily trivialize the particular*, it certainly seems to in much Lacanian thought.[3]

I agree with Khanna that this trivialization of the particular, as she calls it, is something we do find in some Lacanian commentary. I'm less certain that this is a necessary outcome of Lacanian theory than it is the result of a limited and somewhat cowardly deployment of Lacanian theory that backs away from some of the more radical commentary that can be made about the universal and the particular, especially when the spectacle of ethnic-racialized difference, to return to the spirit of Paul Gilroy's comments about Foucault in chapter 1, is already seen to be scrambling the distinction between word and thing. Gilroy's comments share a certain affinity with Spillers's quandary, which we addressed in the introduction. As Lacanians attuned to questions of race, not backing away means taking seriously her quandary: "The individual in the collective traversed by 'race'—and there are no known exceptions, as far as I can tell—is covered by it before language and its differential laws take hold."[4]

My project fixates on the hope that Khanna leaves intact when she writes that the universal condition of loss that yields from the effects of language as structure on the speaking organism "does not necessarily trivialize the particular." The challenge for us would be to craft analyses that can read for the historical specificity and texture of the loss that is constitutive of subjectivity in relation to those losses that can be attributed to the unequal distribution of social and material resources, losses that continually appear to accrue more on the side of some people than others. We should understand the relationship between these different kinds of loss as a dynamic one where we see the losses inter-informing each other, lending "signifierness" to each other's explanation for what gets lost. The unequal distribution here should also be understood as the unequally distributed function of loss within narratives that attempt to explain the vicissitudes of ethnic-racialized subjectivity and experience but neglect to comment on the losses attributable to the effects of language as structure on the speaking organism. This means including as part of the more gradated and textured history we recollect, narrativize, and transmit of ethnic-racialized subjectivity and experience the fact that we are, to begin with, subjects in language—that this is our history too, to have been subject to the effects of language as structure, that our network of signifiers can be mapped. We are not pure, statuary, brute densities existing either outside language or produced through its medium but exempted from having to suffer any of its effects.

To refuse in our antiracist critical practices to engage with the universal condition of loss attributable to the effects of language as structure is in fact to leave untouched one of the most powerful ways in which racism creates among humans an internal division that bestows some humans with human status and others with an animal-like status. Juliet Flower MacCannell helps me make this point clearer in the following acute formulation, where the reader might understand her use of "castration" as indexing the cut introduced by language on the human organism. She writes,

> The human being is "castrated" by the signifier, or put another way, it gives up a large portion of jouissance to become a member of the human community, whose only universal characteristic is speech. Hence castration is linked to language, that blade that carves out a body out of an animal substance. In racism's focus on the phenomenology of color, however, there is no true line dividing animal from human, and castration cannot have the meaning it has when it is linked to speech. Instead, a secondary, imaginary idea of castration compounds the original difficulties of "castration by the signifier" (the common work of civilization) and is used to divide human beings another way, shading some more toward the animal of full jouissance, shading others more toward the human free of this animal "stain." Politically it is used against certain peoples both to deny them their humanity and to limit their access to cultural goods, including (or perhaps especially) their own.[5]

If we accept that what is distinctly "human" about the speaking organism's experience is her use of language and its effects on her and her precipitation as subject through its medium, then we might have to agree that the charge that Lacanian theory is antihumanist is somewhat misguided and imprecise. The charge of being antihumanist might more accurately be directed at those forms of psychoanalysis and psychology that do not consider what is distinctly human about an experience, that "the structure of thought is based on language."[6]

Just because Lacan has famously insisted that "the unconscious is structured as a language," that "the unconscious is neither the primordial nor the instinctual," and that "what it knows of the elemental is no more than the elements of the signifier" does not mean that the historical specificity and texture of an individual's life goes missing somehow.[7] It means approaching the unconscious as a history; it means attending to the history of "the other scene," as Freud coined the term, and to this end Lacan writes, "What we teach the subject to recognize as his unconscious is his history—in other words, we help him complete the current historicization of the facts that have already determined a certain number of the historical 'turning points' in his existence. But if they have played this role, it is already as historical facts, that is, as recognized in a certain sense or censored in a certain order."[8]

By the end of this chapter, I hope to have made the case that given the contemporary situation in the United States regarding the diversity management of ethnic-racialized life as a strategic form of "biopower," especially in some university settings where students and faculty are slotted to play the roles of what John Champagne terms "privileged marginals," and given the morbid, paltry terms and conditions granting some modicum of social and cultural intelligibility to ethnic-racialized subjects that Rey Chow names "coercive mimeticism," that Lacanian theory opens up the possibility of developing strong critiques of and engaged responses to racism and white supremacy. Crucial to what yields as a response to racism in Lacan (although he certainly does not discuss "race" or ethnic-racialized subjectivity in his seminars and writings in any clearly recognizable way), is the utter refusal to promote the idea of a stronger ego—and thus a more alienated subject—as the natural, desired outcome for negotiating the traumas attending the experience of systemic institutional racist practices.

The introduction provides the reader with a thumbnail sketch of ego psychology, and although it is clear in that brief presentation that Lacan in his "return to Freud" sets himself up against the ego psychologists—that, in fact, the Lacanian explanation of the "return to Freud" can seemingly take its shape only in the vigorous battle that he wages against ego psychology—I would like in this chapter to give the reader a somewhat more detailed picture of Lacan's critique of ego psychology. At the same time that we must understand that Lacan's critique cannot, as Philippe Van Haute reminds us,[9] be taken seriously as a critique of all contemporary forms of North American psychoanalysis, I would suggest that many of the basic assumptions in ego psychology, especially with respect to the focus on adaptation, the definition of "reality," and the concept of the "autonomous ego," still resonate in subfields of psychology, such as ethnic psychology and Hispanic psychology, points we will address in chapter 7.

What does Lacan think is so egregious about ego psychology, and why should this be interesting as part of a discussion on, in the broadest possible formulation, race, psychoanalysis, and contemporary ethnic-racialized subjectivity and experience in the United States? Some may think my engagement with Lacan's critique of ego psychology not worth the time spent on it, given how much ink has been spilled and how many toner cartridges emptied on the topic. Michael Zeitlin outlines the routine account of this debate quite succinctly:

> The main outlines of Lacan's narrative are well-known: in the course of Ego Psychology's passage to success and institutional power in America, the essential meaning of the Freudian project was betrayed in the service of an American culture based on profit. Thus, for Lacan, this transplanted "American psychoanalysis" was nothing but a facile medical program, based on "the reactionary principle operant in the duality of the sick and the healer, the opposition between someone who knows and someone who does not" (Lacan, 1977, 115), aimed at adapting human subjects to the values of an American ideology, practice, and "style."[10]

Lacan's critique of ego psychology can be read as both a critique of the colonizing tendencies increasingly taken on by the ego as a kind of agency, especially if it is strengthened—which is precisely the strategy he sees proffered in ego psychology as an actual therapeutic goal—and, more broadly, as a critique of the increasing colonization of the analytical field by ego psychology, to the point of becoming the dominant theoretical and therapeutic treatment paradigm in the Western world. However, I would maintain that no one has really bothered to consider how this critique might resonate for an antiracist position where the significant point of overlap regards the critique of assimilationist imperatives in both Lacanian theory and in critical race and ethnicity studies knowledge projects like Chicano and Latino studies.

I'm attempting to flesh out what I think are homologous critical pursuits and mutually supportive interests shared by Lacan's critique of the masterful ego who makes everything over into her own likeness and by critical race and ethnicity studies' critique of systemic racist practices in the United States in legal and extralegal contexts that reveal similar investments in seeking out Imaginary likenesses and similarities. Basic to both of these positions is a rejection of the notion of a stronger ego, whose strengthening then bodes only for the further alienation of the subject—this is explicit in Lacan, less explicit in critical race and ethnicity studies. Related to this point, they also both reject the conflation of the ego with the subject, explicit in Lacan, less so in critical race and ethnicity studies, a conflation that functions as a fundamental support for the internal logic of racism we see operative in contemporary discourses of multiculturalism inside and outside North American universities.

The specific aspects of Lacan's critique that I feel help illustrate these links best have to do, first, with Lacan's rejection of the ego psychologists' reliance on the themes of adaptation, synthesis, integration, and assimilation in their attempt to make sense of the ego's relationship to the environment. Second, I think one might insinuate common critical links between Lacanian theory and critical race and ethnicity studies on the basis of how Lacan's critique of the role played by the analyst in the ego psychological setting reveals a more capacious, less clinically centered critique of the power and domination accruing to the United States in a particular historical period and milieu in which ego psychology thrives, a critique of power, domination and U.S. world hegemony that is shared by many critical race and ethnicity studies scholars. There is established for him a foreboding, discordant harmony—and for Lacan, harmonies can only ever be discordant—achieved between the political and economic global aspirations of the United States after World War II and the theory of the ego and treatment strategies espoused by ego psychology as it consolidated itself in the United States during this same time.

As good a place as any to begin would be to turn to the central role played by "America" and "the American way of life" in Lacan's critique of the "troika," the word Lacan uses to refer to the three central figures in ego psychology, Heinz Hartmann, Rudolph Loewenstein, and Ernst Kris. Some critics have remarked that Lacan's tireless critique of America runs the risk of setting America up as a "moralizing fiction" in which America becomes a stand-in for the alienating register of the Imaginary itself. Alexandre Leupin writes, "His America is a moralizing fiction, an imaginary construct, which in the end produces a blindness to the success of American happiness. Insistence on pure theory, on the Symbolic order and the Real at the expense of the Imaginary (but successful) fictions satisfies here a certain Old World haughtiness, justified by a theory but leading to impotence on a pragmatic level."[11] Lacan's early critiques of ego psychology seem to need to reject America, aligned as it is for him with the Imaginary, in order to argue for the supremacy of the Symbolic, but Elisabeth Roudinesco maintains that this should not be read as a form of cultural chauvinism on Lacan's part. "When Lacan would lash out against what has been incorrectly called 'American psychoanalysis,' it would be to criticize the aims of a practice cut off, he felt, from Freud's true message. He would never be 'anti-American,' since at no point in his life did he adhere to the chauvinistic ideals of the psychology of nations. Had he done so, he would not have been an authentic theoretician."[12]

As it turns out, Lacan's strong critique of American culture and the "American way of life" seems most likely to have been shared by those ego psychologists—arguably, the main targets of his attack—who fled Nazi Europe for the United States during World War II. Douglas Kirsner's invaluable history of psychoanalytic institutes in the United States, *Unfree Associations*, details how European analysts pushed American analysts aside in their attempt to rule the New York Institute because they saw themselves as preserving "true psychoanalysis," "excluding those whom they saw as not directly linked with the Europeans who possessed psychoanalytic truth."[13] As "keepers of the flame," they thought that psychoanalysis "required protection from alloy or contamination through vulgarization—and from Americanization, which in their eyes amounted to the same thing. This schism between American and European analysts was so great that they often barely knew one another. . . . From the 1940s until the mid-1980s the European analysts kept their distance from most American analysts whom they regarded as uncultured."[14]

"America," therefore, serves similar functions for both Lacan and the ego psychologists who each see themselves as the true heirs of Freudian theory and see "Americanization" as a veritable threat to the elaboration of the truth of Freudian psychoanalysis. I am going to take a slightly different tack in this debate and suggest that Lacan's admittedly complicated and at times moralizing attack of America is in places oddly sympathetic to the plight of the Jewish ego psychologists. I don't read him as attacking America, per se, but rather the assimilationist imperatives guiding American culture and reflecting the ideology of whiteness. The troika, it would appear, never had a chance in hell. They were defenseless. It is in the guarded alibi he extends to the ego psychologists for why they couldn't help but distort and betray the Freudian cause that we see Lacan's incisive critique of not only North American exceptionalism and its dreams of global mastery but also the critique of the force of assimilation as it bears down on ethnic-racialized subjects—here, Jewish immigrant psychoanalysts.

To be clear, my point in this discussion is not in the service of proving who the real heirs of Freudian theory are, whether they be Lacanians, object relations theorists, Kleinian theorists, or ego psychologists. Because of this, I do not concentrate on the various different ways in which Freud might be read as theorizing the ego throughout his work, and especially, in *The Ego and the Id* (1923). Bruce Fink, for example, numbers at least four different readings of the ego in this text by Freud, the text that introduced the second topography.[15] Nonetheless, I shall attempt to provide the reader in what immediately follows with some idea as to how Lacan understood the function of Freud's introduction of the second topography as well as how he responded to the errant interpretation of it on the part of the troika.

A good part of Lacan's critique of ego psychology in his first seminars and writings in the 1950s is concerned with proving how Freud's second topography—the id, ego, and superego, which ego psychologists read as replacing in total the previous topography, preconscious, conscious, unconscious—had been woefully and passionately misinterpreted, "Where have we got to today? To a theoretical cacophony, to a conspicuous revolution in positions. And why? In the first place, because the metapsychological work of Freud after 1920 has been misread, interpreted in a crazy way by the first and second generations following Freud—those inept people."[16] Lacan explains that Freud thought it necessary to introduce the structural model of ego, id, and superego because of perceived setbacks in clinical results after a kind of flourishing that was experienced initially with the first wave of psychoanalysts: "What Freud introduced from 1920 on, are additional notions which were at that time necessary to maintain the principle of the decentring of the subject. But far from being understood as it should have been, there was a great rush, exactly like the kids getting out of school—Ah! Our nice little ego is back again! It all makes sense now! We're now back on the well-beaten paths of general psychology."[17] Lacan refuses to read Freud's second topography as replacing the first one. He insists that they are to be read as "subsisting side by side."[18] According to Jacques-Alain Miller, by the time Lacan delivers *Seminar XI, The Four Fundamental Concepts of Psycho-Analysis*, in 1964 his analysis of the drive allows for a unification of Freud's first and second topographies, moving from the unconscious—of the first topography, unconscious, preconscious, conscious—to the id—from the second topography, ego, id, superego—by relating the drives to the id.[19] Regarding this "theoretical cacophony," Freud isn't simply let off the hook by Lacan: "In the article on *The Ego and the Id* which is read so sloppily, because attention is paid solely to the famous, idiotic schema, with the stages, the little bob, the irrelevancies, the gadget he brings in which he calls the super-ego, *what got into him, to come up with that, when he must have had other schemata.*"[20] Lacan relates the ego psychologists' sloppy mistake of collapsing the ego with the subject directly to their misreading of the second topography: "It is therefore always in the relation between the subject's ego and his discourse's I that you must understand the meaning of the discourse if you are to unalienate the subject. But you cannot possibly achieve this if you cleave to the idea that the subject's ego is identical to the presence that is speaking to you."[21]

There is a general ambiguity in Freud's theory of the genesis of the ego. What appears to be particularly compelling for Lacan's theory of the genesis of the ego regards what Jean Laplanche and Jean-Bertrand Pontalis have argued is a shift in Freud's own thinking about the ego during the period 1914–15.[22] I want to point to two closely linked ideas that were worked out at this point by Freud: narcissism and identification as constitutive of the ego. Lacan's theory of ego formation in the mirror stage is predicated on how he understands narcissism as the erotic attraction to the specular image. I will speak more centrally to Lacan's mirror stage theory and the function of ethnic-racialized difference in relation to it in chapter 3. For now, we should keep in mind that Freud quite clearly argues that the ego is not a unity that is already there, that the point of the ego is not to arrive at some fully formed state, that a new psychical action requires its formation, and that the dialectic between fragmentation and unity has something to do with the disarticulating force of sexuality.

Lacan picks up on all of these points along the way to teaching that the ego is formed by identification with a point *outside* itself, with an *image* of itself, which is why Lacan refers to the ego as an imaginary structure. This is crucial for understanding why Lacan argues that the strengthening of the ego as proposed by ego psychologists will result in a thoroughly alienating effect that will in turn only increase the resistances: "The resistances always have their seat in the ego, so analysis teaches us. What corresponds to the ego, is what I sometimes call the sum of the prejudices which any knowledge comprises and which each of us has as individual baggage. It is something which includes what we know or think we know—for knowing is always in some way believing one knows."[23] In 1953 Lacan writes—and we should understand the object in this passage as the ego—"This ego, whose strength our theorists now define by its capacity to bear frustration, is frustration in its very essence. . . . the more developed this object becomes, the more profoundly the subject becomes alienated from his jouissance."[24] The notion, for example, attributed to prominent ego psychologist David Rapaport that "the healthy ego is slave neither to the drives nor the environment," that it "solves problems, makes choices, and permits pleasure,"[25] ignores what is central to Lacan's teaching: that the subject emerges in language, in relation to the Other, that the subject is an effect of the gap between one signifier and another signifier, "The Other is the locus in which is situated the chain of the signifier that governs whatever may be made present in the subject—it is the field of that living being in which the subject has to appear."[26]

Lacan's theory of the ego, in contradistinction to ego psychology's, stresses what must be considered one of the fundamental insights of Lacanian theory: the radical maladaptation between the human subject and its environment. Lacanian theory is rigorously opposed to the idea that psychic life must be generally understood as a problematic of adaptation. Van Haute explains, "The psyche must assist the organism in its attempt to adapt itself to reality. Just like psychoanalytic orthodoxy, academic psychology believes that psychic life must be understood primarily and fundamentally as 'adaptation,' or in terms of an 'adaptive' problematic. Lacan radically rejects this assumption."[27] Basically, the ego is thought to possess functions that work as internal principles in its development toward harmony with its environment and, of course, these functions are to be strengthened. Regarding this picture of the ego, Lacan can barely contain his laughter in the following, exceedingly arch remarks: "The ego is a function, the ego is a synthesis, a synthesis of functions, a function of synthesis. It is autonomous! That's a good one! It's the latest fetish introduced into the holy of holies of a practice that is legitimated by the superiority of the superiors. It does the job as well as any other."[28] Note that this theory of the ego as well suited for adaptation to reality—a notion of reality again drawn from the material provided by the consciousness of those in power—is in synchronicity with the concerted focus on assimilation and adaptation in the mainstream racialized politics of U.S. culture in the 1950s.

Lacan links the focus on adaptation in ego psychology to the experiences of adjustment undergone by the troika upon coming to the United States as immigrants and having to contend with a general ethos of coercive immigrant assimilation. How does the insistence that the ego be fitted to its environment resonate for ethnic-racialized subjects who experience, seemingly from the get-go, hostile social surroundings? I would argue that Lacan's critique of the ego-psychological interpretation of human subjectivity, which sees it in terms of the problematic of adaptation, allows for an additional way of critiquing coercive assimilatory imperatives by unveiling the orthodoxy of adaptation and adjustment for what it really is: a political and economic tool for the psychological domination of ethnic-racialized subjects who will be burdened and deadened by the pressure to assimilate and yet who will always be seen as coming up short of whatever normative ideal. It is for these reasons that we must seek out the resonances of these ego psychological notions in contemporary clinical and extraclinical, legal and extralegal accounts of ethnic-racialized subjectivity and experience to expose them and to imagine, again, a different, less dominating, nonpsychologistic account of ethnic-racialized subjectivity, one alive to the effects of language as structure on the human organism.

Other tropes come in the muddy tow of adaptation, principally those of harmony and reciprocity, which, we will see shortly, Lacan argues reflect a prior default setting—adult, mature genital harmony and the presumed reciprocity between the sexes. I will add to this that the ego-psychological position also barely veils the presumption of whiteness. There is a kind of privilege that is thoroughly racialized—and not remarked upon—as white that attaches to the conceit in the imperatives of adaptation and adjustment to and harmony with "North American reality." Lacan's critique of what ensues in the ego-psychology clinical setting interprets what goes on there as a distorted, compensatory attempt to cover over the lack of relation, reciprocity between the sexes, lending Lacan's critique of the power wielded by the analyst in the ego-psychology clinical setting the charge of a queer theoretical critique of the assumed complementarity between the sexes.

Recall that Lacan theorizes a radical lack of adequation between "man" and the sexual function: "In man, as we know, an eminent disorder characterizes the manifestations of the sexual function. Nothing in it adapts. This image, around which we, we psychoanalysts, revolve, presents, whether in the neuroses or in the perversions, a sort of fragmentation, of rupture, of breaking up, of lack of adaptation, or inadequation."[29] Shortly thereafter, in the same seminar, Lacan links up the nature of the function assumed by the analyst in the ego-clinical setting with the analyst's attempt to make good on this inadequation: "Well, what is the end of the treatment? Is it analogous to the end of a natural process? Genital love—this Eldorado promised to analysts, which we quite imprudently promise to our patients—is it a natural process? Isn't it, on the contrary, simply a series of cultural approximations which are only capable of being realized in certain cases."[30] Five years later, in *Seminar VII*, Lacan makes explicit in the two passages I quote here the link between this way of theorizing "adjustment" and the impossible promise of genital harmony between the sexes as the ultimate "analytical ambition":

> Goodness only knows how obscure such a pretension as the achievement of genital objecthood remains, along with what is so imprudently linked to it, namely, adjustment to reality.

> That is the ideal of genital love—a love that is supposed to be itself alone the model of a satisfying object relation: doctor-love, I would say if I wanted to emphasize in a comical way the tone of this ideology; love as hygiene, I would say, to suggest what analytical ambition seems to be limited to here.[31]

So insistent, according to Lacan, is this focus on the "ideal of genital love" that he fears future civilizations might think of the purported goals of psychoanalysis that they were committed to nothing else than helping analysands achieve the "perfect orgasm": "Yet, in reading our work, should any of it survive into a time when people will no longer know what these effervescent words corresponded to in practice, people might imagine that our art was designed to revive sexual hunger in those afflicted with retardation of the sexual gland."[32]

The ego psychologists, as well as the object relations theorists that Lacan accuses as being equally guilty of promising to deliver on the dream of genital harmony, can believe in this dream because the dimension of the signifier, its effects on the subject, does not figure in their theory of human subjectivity; there is no built-in failure in their theory because language is seen by them, although they aren't explicit about this, as able to provide determinate meaning about the subject. This same view allows them to give the impression that language can be operated in a masterful way because the clinician or researcher working the scene of interpretation is not her- or himself a subject divided in language. Lacan's theory of radical inadequation—between the sexes, between the subject and the environment, between, to some extent, the subject and the signifier, insofar as the subject will never fully coincide with the signifier—emerges from having to consider this linguistic dimension and its real effects: "That is to say that, with regard to the agency of sexuality, all subjects are equal, from the child to the adult—that they deal only with the part of sexuality that passes into the networks of the constitution of the subject, into the networks of the signifier—that sexuality is realized only through the operation of the drives in so far as they are partial drives, partial with regard to the biological finality of sexuality."[33]

I am posing, perhaps too starkly, Lacan against the ego psychologists, but I do so because the historical moment of this confrontation in the 1950s is significant for this project's study of coercive assimilation and the critique of it by ethnic-racialized subjects during the time of the civil rights movement. Lacan's critique of the ego psychologist's privileging of her own position, her "healthy ego," and her own take on reality as a dominating tendency calls up the relationship between ethnic-racialized subjects and ideological state apparatuses who appear guided during this time by white, Anglo, assimilatory imperatives.

How does Lacan imagine, and I shall present this as I have above, in a general and schematic manner, the clinical setting, especially with respect to what the analyst should and shouldn't do? To begin with, before Lacan, the analysand's speech was regarded simply as a form of "talk" whose value was determined solely in its ability to refer to some "reality." Theorizing the psychoanalytic experience as an experience of discourse, Lacan located the subject "within the very act of talking."[34] Let's return to a passage I quoted in chapter 1 regarding Freud's criticism of James Jackson Putnam's understanding of what psychoanalysis should be and, importantly, how the role of the analyst should be defined. Recall, Freud was opposed to the idea that the patient in psychoanalysis should be encouraged to ennoble her mind through the guidance of the analyst, since this was "after all only to use violence, even though it is overlaid with the most honorable motives."[35] This species of ennobling violence is practiced by the analyst when she, with the best of intentions, uses her power to correct, educate, and strengthen the ego, a practice Lacan considers anathema to a true psychoanalytic praxis. Sadly, Lacan recounts, one finds this educative violence in the work of even some of the finest clinicians, like that of object-relations theorist Michael Balint: "That is how someone like Balint and one whole trend of analysis have come to think that, either the ego is strong, or else it is weak. And if it is weak, they are obliged, by the internal logic of their position, to think it has to be strengthened. As soon as one holds the ego to be the straightforward exercising of self-mastery by the subject, the high point of the hierarchy of the nervous functions, one is completely committed to the task of teaching it to be strong."[36]

The fact that Lacanian psychoanalysis, unlike most forms of psycho-

61

analysis and psychotherapy, doesn't answer to the need—in fact, it opposes it—to be "happy" may strike some readers as somewhat intolerable, cruel, elitist, perhaps, just plain crazy, or all of the above. Bruce Fink writes, "Analysis is not pragmatic in its aims, if pragmatism means compliance with social, economic, and political norms and realities. It is a praxis of jouissance, and jouissance is anything but practical. It ignores the needs of capital, health insurance companies, socialized health care, public order, and mature adult relationships."[37]

Consider these three passages from Lacan's *Seminars I, VII,* and *XI,* representing admittedly different contexts and different moments in his teaching. Read together, they show how Lacan theorizes the clinical setting, and the consistency with which he theorizes this idea over time, with the specific function and role of the analyst in mind.

> That means essentially that, for him, the interest, the essence, the basis, the dimension proper to analysis is the reintegration by the subject of his history right up to the furthermost perceptible limits, that is to say into a dimension that goes well beyond the limits of the individual.[38]

> When in conformity with Freudian experience one has articulated the dialectic of demand, need and desire, is it fitting to reduce the success of an analysis to a situation of individual comfort linked to that well-founded and legitimate function we might call the service of goods? Private goods, family goods, domestic goods, other goods that solicit us, the goods of our trade or our profession, the goods of the city, etc.
>
> . . . To make oneself the guarantor of the possibility that a subject will in some way be able to find happiness even in analysis is a form of fraud.[39]

> Analysis is not a matter of discovering in a particular case the differential feature of the theory, and in doing so believe that one is explaining why your daughter is silent—for the point at issue is to *get her to speak,* and this effect proceeds from a type of intervention that has nothing to do with a differential feature.[40]

By "differential," Lacan can be read here to mean "distinctive" or "distinguishing." In analysis, one does not go about trying to highlight the distinctive and distinguishing features of the theory, one goes about trying to get something done, "to *get her to speak.*" Lacan, following Freud, is adamant that psychoanalysis is not a *Weltanschauung,* a worldview or philosophy. "The point to which analysis leads, the end point of the dialectic of existential recognition, is—*You are this.*[41] To be clear, it is not that Freud and Lacan were unconcerned with alleviating what seemed intolerable to an analysand regarding her or his symptoms. The point is that this was not their principal aim. The Lacanian psychoanalyst Marie-Hélène Brousse explains, "Their aim does not concern the symptoms as developed in ego behaviors or attitudes. What they strive to change is the subject's position, not his or her identifications."[42]

Lacan's critique of power in the ego-psychological setting overlaps with the critique of power crafted by ethnic-racialized minorities on the question of what will qualify as "reality" and "health" as defined in a prior moment by a well-adjusted person in power—a "reality" and model of "health" one has to answer to, adapt to, and assimilate to in order to be read by others as a socially intelligible human subject. Regarding the definition of a healthy ego, Lacan writes that it is virtually impossible to determine what is healthy unless the analyst resorts to using her own ego as the measure:

> Isn't it clear that there is no way to discern which is the healthy part of the subject's ego except by its agreement with your point of view? And, since the latter is assumed to be healthy, it becomes the measure of things. Isn't it similarly clear that there is no other criterion of cure than the complete adoption by the subject of your measure? This is confirmed by the common admission by certain serious authors that the end of analysis is achieved when the subject identifies with the analyst's ego.[43]

63

Lacanian psychoanalysis cannot, strictly speaking, be characterized as a discourse of power and domination, although the question of variable-length sessions in Lacanian analysis historically has made believable to some the accusation that Lacanian analysts abuse their power when they decide to punctuate an analysand's articulation by drawing the session to a close.[44] Less time in the office, more money. Yes, some do and some don't use this opportunity to abuse their power as subjects-supposed-to-know. Who can know? However, the power that Lacanian psychoanalytic theory attempts to abuse is the Imaginary power that the analysand's ego fights for and hordes in its attempt to squash the appearance of the subject. As Fink explains, the Lacanian analyst draws on a kind of power, but it uses this power to challenge the want-to-be-masterful-ego's attempt to block the precipitation of the subject and thus the path to the unconscious: "It deploys a certain kind of power in the analytic situation, a power that is unjustifiable according to many American schools of psychology wherein the 'client's' autonomy (read: ego) is sacrosanct and must remain untrammeled and unchallenged. Psychoanalysis deploys the power of the cause of desire in order to bring about a reconfiguration of the analysand's desire."[45]

Insofar as ego psychology addresses itself primarily to the ego, to strengthening and empowering it, and to holding up the ego of the analyst as the healthy ego with which the analysand should identify, we would be right to characterize it as a discourse of power. That these therapeutic conceptions continue to figure in fields like Hispanic psychology and ethnic psychology and how we generally go about crafting strategies in clinical, extraclinical, legal, and extralegal contexts in response to the psychological traumas of racism and the ongoing systemic social disenfranchisement of ethnic-racialized subjects should give us pause and should certainly compel us to think differently about how we understand and respond to loss. We are failing to develop a language to talk about ethnic-racialized subjectivity and experience that is not entirely ego psychological and that does not imagine a strong ego as the desired therapeutic and politicized outcome in a racist, white supremacist world. This strategy comes to us, as Lacan makes clear, from a psychologistic therapeutics predicated on power and domination at the individual and global level: the ego's dream of power over the environment as this dream collects its bits and shreds of daily residues from the social surround of the United States in the mid-twentieth century—a United States that, in turn, is also caught dreaming of power over the world's environment.

The pronouncement "You are this," announced by Lacan as the ideal (although often never reached) "end point of the dialectic of existential recognition"[46] to which psychoanalysis leads, has a particularly significant relevance for questions on ethnic-racialized subjectivity and experience in contemporary U.S. culture, specifically regarding multiculturalism and the forms of recognition that currently undergird diversity rationales in most North American universities. Where a Lacanian analysis approaches this end point through the "dialectization" of the analysand's desire, ultimately compelling the analysand's separation from the demand of the Other by, as Lacan explains in *Seminar XI*, "leading the subject back to his signifying dependence,"[47] the existential recognition "You are this," which confronts ethnic-racialized subjects in contemporary clinical and extraclinical contexts, works to obscure if not raze entirely the path leading to her signifying dependence. This species of recognition is antidialectical by nature and achieves its predetermined synthesis on the basis not of argumentation, and thus speech and language, but of the unpaid labors of ethnic resemblance that Chow terms "coercive mimeticism": "the level at which the ethnic person is expected to come to resemble what is recognizably ethnic . . . to resemble and replicate the very banal preconceptions that have been appended to them, a process in which they are expected to objectify themselves in accordance with the already seen and thus to authenticate the familiar imaginings of them as ethnics."[48]

The searing commentary by Chow is a deepening of the questions she brings up in an earlier text, questions that might be read as serving as the background to the diagnosis she offers in her theory of "coercive mimeticism." In a passage in *Ethics after Idealism*, she comments in a more pointed way on the anemic, emaciated critical engagements with the cultural productions of ethnic-racialized "groups." These comments sadly still ring true in academia in the twenty-first century. She writes,

> I feel strongly that, until and unless we grant non-Western authors and texts—be these texts fiction, theory, film, popular music, or criticism—the same kind of verbal, psychical, theoretical density and complexity that we have copiously endowed upon Western authors and texts, we will never be able to extricate our readings from the kind of idealism in which the East-West divide . . . is currently mired. Granting such density and complexity would mean refusing to idealize the non-West . . . and reading the non-West in such a manner as to draw out its unconscious, irrational, and violent nuances, so that, as an "other," it can no longer simply be left in a blank, frozen, and mythologized condition known perfunctorily as an "alternative" to the West.[49]

How does one intervene here? The lack of attribution of density and complexity is related to the manner in which ethnic-racialized subjectivity and experience, in a preliminary conceptual move, continues to be theorized according to whatever interpretations can be gleaned from an analysis of the social and cultural network of power relations that inform said experiences, interpretations that continue to believe on some level in the transparency of the subject to the signifier, a belief—a certainty—that Lacanian theory might ascribe to the psychotic subject.

The ethnic studies scholar and theorist George Lipsitz continues to mine the concerns raised by Chow above and challenges us to ask after the reading practices we deploy when we interpret the knowledges generated in minoritarian discourses: "The knowledges generated from within aggrieved ethnic groups can serve as a rich repository for understanding national, international,

65

and transnational cultures, if we learn to read them in the most fully theorized and knowing way."[50] I want to consider precisely what it would take, using Lipsitz's words, "to learn to read" these knowledges "in the most fully theorized and knowing way," and I want to make clearer what is perhaps only implicit in Lipsitz's passage—that the readers interpreting these knowledges include those who are ostensibly not members of these aggrieved ethnic groups, as well as those who are. That is, the project of developing more subtle reading practices in order to remain as alive as possible to the complex forms of knowledge generated by "aggrieved ethnic groups" is one that has to be cultivated in every reader, regardless of the reader's perceived ethnic-racialized affiliation.

In response to Lipsitz's passage, I would answer that we need to begin by theorizing these "aggrieved ethnic" subjects in a more Lacanian psychoanalytic register, as subjects in language. This means deepening our understanding of what constitutes human grief and the full range of objects we stand to lose, so that we can interpret the losses that attend the speaking subject's inscription in language and the losses attributed to the "unequal distribution of social resources, including visibility and dignity,"[51]—and, I would add, so that we can interpret how those losses may relate to each other, how they may be read as interpenetrating each other's seemingly discrete and separated scenes of human loss.

The contemporary "aggrieved" ethnic-racialized subject is instantiated, according to Chow, as the always already protesting, contesting, quasi-proletarian subject *only* in relation to social and economic structures and political forces.[52] Language as a structure with very real effects on the human organism never figures in this interpretative scenario, dismissed, perhaps, as too "psycholinguistic," to use the American studies scholar John Carlos Rowe's term: "Scholars of ethnicity and minority cultures considered poststructuralist treatments of repression largely esoteric, often excessively psycholinguistic, issues rather than concepts designed to address explicitly the continuing effects of racism and internal and external conditions."[53] We might insist on a more Lacanian language-based approach to interpret ethnic-racialized subjectivity and experience not only because the refusal to read ethnic-racialized subjects as subjects of the signifier who experience the loss that presages human subjectivity and desire constitutes one of the "continuing effects of racism," but also because, returning to the specificity of Chow's remarks in *Ethics after Idealism*, it will affect how we conceptualize the initial approach to the interpretation of minoritarian, as she puts it, "fiction, theory, film, popular music, or criticism."

One could draw a somewhat shaky but no less reasonable and convincing line connecting three different scenes: the underlying assumptions revealed in the nineteenth-century North American psychoanalyst Dr. Lind's claims, cited in chapter 1, that the dream work of African American subjects showed no evidence of any ability on their part to metaphorize (unless they were psychotic African American subjects who believed they were white), to the contemporary assumptions undergirding the refusal, as Chow explains, to grant "verbal, psychical, theoretical density and complexity" to non-Western "authors and texts," to our—and this includes minoritarian and majoritarian subjects—ongoing inability to, as Lipsitz describes, "learn to read" "the knowledges generated from within aggrieved ethnic groups" "in the most fully theorized and knowing way." In short, Lind's refusal to recognize the processes of metaphorization—more basically, human creativity and signification—in the dream work of African American subjects is a species of the same kind of refusal that blocks complex theoretical engagement with, according to Chow, the cultural productions of ethnic-racialized subjects and with the forms, according to Lipsitz, of learned grief they generate in response to racism and systemic social disenfranchisement.

To continue arguing that certain theories are, to use Rowe's words, overly "esoteric" in their "psycholinguistic" excess is to occlude a very significant mechanism in the production of racist thinking that renders some subjects potentially fully calculable through the medium of language. There must be much less pretension to understanding in this regard, since ethnic-racialized subjectivity has suffered from too much understanding. This is not to say that ethnic-racialized subjectivity and experience has been understood, but rather to say that the project of understanding it is imagined as completely within reach. Language, in this instance, is imbued with the remarkable ability of telling it all, with nothing remaindered, because the ethnic-racialized subject in question—the consummate captive of representation—seems somehow immune to the effects of language as structure, seems, in fact, to be the kind of sum that can be perfectly, because exhaustively, calculated in language. Lacanian theory opposes the masterful tendencies embedded in acts of understanding, however well intentioned, since, as Jacques-Alain Miller puts it, "One only understands what one thinks one already knows. More precisely,

67

one never understands anything but a meaning whose satisfaction or comfort one has already felt."[54] Lacan himself warned his analysts against understanding too much:

> How many times have I said to those under my supervision, when they say to me—*I had the impression he meant this or that*—that one of the things we must guard against is to understand too much, to understand more than what is in the discourse of the subject. To interpret and to imagine one understands are not at all the same things. It is precisely the opposite, I would go as far as to say that it is on the basis of a kind of refusal of understanding that we push open the door to analytic understanding.[55]

The "idealization" that Chow comments on above regards, in my take, the idealization of the subject who got away, the subject never subjected to the effects of language. It is an idealization that proceeds apace with the fantasy of pure, undivided, prediscursive, obscene Being and jouissance, and the ethnic-racialized subject has been made to inhabit this fantasy for others and, on some level, for herself too. Juliet Flower MacCannell reminds us of the links between racism and the belief that some humans continue to have access to a prelinguistic jouissance and animal-like substance when she writes, "To look at race and racism, then, is to encounter fantasies of castration and escape from it, fantasies of 'Who has the jouissance?' The 'possession' of jouissance is still an irrational element in all thinking about race, and it taints even anti-racism today."[56]

Earlier I referred to the alibi (of sorts) that Lacan provides the ego psychologists in an otherwise ruthless critique. This alibi drains some of the blame for the so-called inexcusable distortions they effected in Freudian psychoanalysis in the direction of North American culture, specifically with regard to the assimilatory imperatives operating in the culture. The piece of writing that I think most frontally addresses these issues is Lacan's "The Freudian Thing" (1955).

A passage from the essay brings together several topics that I have been tracking throughout this chapter, but I am mostly interested in the idea that Lacan develops regarding the ego psychologists' reduction of their difference—which I read here as their Jewish ethnic and cultural difference—to their function—as "managers of the soul"—and in how we might read this idea in concert with Chow's theory of "coercive mimeticism." This may resonate in

68

our current situation concerning the ethnic-racialized pedagogue's role in teaching "difference," managing souls, in contemporary multicultural and diversity-driven U.S. university settings. Lacan writes:

> The shock waves were to reverberate to the very confines of our world, echoing on a continent where it would be untrue to say that history loses its meaning, since it is where history finds its limit. It would even be a mistake to think that history is absent there, since, already several centuries in duration, it weighs all the more heavily there due to the gulf traced out by its all-too-limited horizon. Rather it is where history is denied with a categorical will that gives enterprises their style, that of cultural ahistoricism characteristic of the United States of North America.
>
> *This ahistoricism defines the assimilation required for one to be recognized there, in the society constituted by this culture. It was to its summons that a group of emigrants had to respond; in order to gain recognition, they could only stress their difference, but their function presupposed history at its very core,* their discipline being the one that had reconstructed the bridge between modern man and ancient myths. *The combination of circumstances was too strong and the opportunity too attractive for them not to give in to the temptation to abandon the core in order to base function on difference.* Let us be clear about the nature of this temptation. It was neither that of ease nor that of profit. It is certainly easier to efface the principles of a doctrine than the stigmata of one's origins, and more profitable to subordinate one's function to demand. *But to reduce one's function to one's difference in this case is to give in to a mirage that is internal to the function itself, a mirage that grounds the function in this difference.* It is to return to the reactionary principle that covers over the duality of he who suffers and he who heals with the opposition between he who knows and he who does not. How could they avoid regarding this opposition as true when it is real and, on that basis, avoid slipping into becoming managers of souls in a social context that demands such offices? The most corrupting of comforts is intellectual comfort, just as the worst corruption is corruption of the best.[57]

The "troika" sold out, Lacan maintains, for recognition, for money; they confused recognition with the receipt of money. Still, I find Lacan here uncharacteristically generous when he remarks that certain cultural factors were *working on* the ego psychologists—"This ahistoricism (characteristic of the United States) defines the assimilation required for one to be recognized there, in the society constituted by this culture"; "in order to gain recognition, they could only stress their difference"; "The combination of circumstances was too strong and the opportunity too attractive"; "How could they avoid . . . slipping into becoming managers of souls in a social context that demands such offices?"

When Chow writes, "the level at which the ethnic person is expected to come to resemble what is recognizably ethnic . . . to resemble and replicate the very banal preconceptions that have been appended to them, a process in which they are expected to objectify themselves in accordance with the already seen and thus to authenticate the familiar imaginings of them as ethnics" to diagnose a contemporary dilemma for ethnic-racialized subjects in the United States, how can we not hear in it the same charge and diagnosis in Lacan's critique above: "But to reduce one's function to one's difference is to give in to a mirage that is internal to the function itself, a mirage that grounds the function in this difference"? If the culture of assimilation in North America has changed somewhat in the time between Lacan's remarks and Chow's, it is with respect to what is to be assimilated. Instead of the 1950s edict "turn white or disappear," it's more like "turn mottled or disappear" at the beginning of the twenty-first century in the United States.

According to both Lacan's and Chow's diagnoses, these coercive assimilatory imperatives operate on the condition that the subject be confused with the ego and that whatever conflicts present themselves are to be remedied with the strengthening of the ego. If Lacan can be said to link the confusion of the subject with the ego in ego-psychological theory—the sine qua non, according to him, of the distortion of Freudian theory—to certain North American assimilatory imperatives with which the ego psychologists had to contend, then we can say that Chow illustrates the outcome of this confusion—of the subject with the ego—in a contemporary situation as the price to be paid for ethnic-racialized subjects to be legible subjects in the United States.

In the passage from "The Freudian Thing," we also have what qualifies as a commentary on the "privileged marginal," to use John Champagne's resonant term: "privileged members of cultural minorities whose disciplinary role is to contain the threat of a much more radical deployment of difference that might destabilize homogeneous intellectual culture."[58] The "privileged marginal" I have in mind, depending on the particular vicissitudes of his experience in an institution where he has been entrusted with the task of disseminating the knowledge of cultural differences—for example, as a representative of Latino studies—will have, no doubt, been coerced or compelled to reduce his function to his difference. He sells out. He needs the job. He is a diversity manager of souls? A manager of diversified souls? A diversifier of managed souls? Prior to his involvement in the university's elaboration of the discourses on multiculturalism and diversity, what will be defined as "diversity" will have already been subjected to a kind of management, so that diversity, now inoculated, can be dispersed and dispensed safely. The concern with safety comes from the desire to safeguard the university from any real transformation in the politics of knowledge production that a more infectious, more generatively noxious, unsafe notion of diversity might compel. How might the "privileged marginal" subject craft more transgressive uses of her difference, to which her function has been reduced, given that the dictates of "coercive mimeticism" have already worked her over in lending her pedagogical authority to begin with?

Lacan might be said to have at least once referred to something like multiculturalism: "With our jouissance going off the track, only the Other is able to mark its position, but only insofar as we are separated from this Other. Whence certain fantasies—unheard of before the melting pot. Leaving the Other to his own mode of jouissance, that would only be possible by not imposing our own on him, by not thinking of him as underdeveloped."[59] Dylan Evans's gloss on this passage is revealing: "But as soon as we are forced to have recourse to the Other in order to mark the position of our own jouissance . . . a curious paradox results. On the one hand, we need to preserve the jouissance of the Other in order to be able to define our own; but on the other hand, we seek to destroy that Other enjoyment because we suspect it may be more superabundant than our own."[60] We are left with a vicious Imaginary a-dynamic: on the one hand, a ruthless refusal to grant psychical complexity to ethnic-racialized subjects, which is to say, the refusal of the lack that generates desire and the subject's incalculability that springs from the human subject's inscription in language, coupled with the weird generosity— the compensatory psychical act of those in power—that offers a pure, riotous Beingness followed by a kind of disgust and shame for the ethnic-racialized subject's perceived unbounded pleasure, which, in turn, necessitates strategies to circumscribe and destroy those very lives.

In the final pages of *The History of Sexuality, Volume 1*, Foucault crafts one of his more infamous formulations: "The rallying point for the counterattack against the deployment of sexuality ought not to be sex-desire, but bodies and pleasures."[61] The title of this chapter, "Subjects-Desire, Not Egos-Pleasures" is playing off of Foucault's mysterious pronouncement in a very contradictory manner, although less so than one might think if the point here is to achieve

71

maximum volume in a counterattack. The value that I am attaching to desire, Lacanian psychoanalysis's theory of desire and its relation to the law of the signifier, is precisely what Foucault is critiquing as the generative principle of disciplinarity in psychoanalysis's theory of sexuality.

Foucault's phrase "deployment of sexuality" should generally be taken to refer to a historical moment when sexuality was constituted as an area of investigation. It could be constituted as such because "power had established it as a possible object," and if power could take it as a target, it "was because techniques of knowledge and procedures of discourse were capable of investing it."[62] The term "deployment of sexuality" refers to the various strategic modes of investing, naming, and disciplining the body as a result of sex having become, at a particular time, a "crucial target of a power organized around the management of life rather than the menace of death."[63] It is clear that Foucault in this text understands Freudian psychoanalysis as internal to this deployment: "In its historical emergence, psychoanalysis cannot be dissociated from the generalization of the deployment of sexuality and the secondary mechanisms of differentiation that resulted from it."[64] As I maintain in chapter 1, Foucault's history of madness assumes that every human subject has been carved up the same way by the various sciences of the mind. I argued that Foucault's assumption of a white, Western European context in order to make his claims cannot explain the very different manner of approach effected by psychiatry's and psychology's take-up with ethnic-racialized subjects in a U.S. context, given that the distinction between the mad and nonmad in the latter part of the nineteenth century becomes a thoroughly racialized one.

I follow the Lacanian reading of the unconscious, a reading that insists on the instantiating (but not exhaustive) importance of language as structure. I also follow that desire is born in this process as well. Yet it makes little difference where my own investments lie, since the point that should be remarkable is that the effects of language on the subject as—let's play devil's advocate for a moment—constituting no more than simply an account of, among others, a technology of disciplinarity predicated on capitalism's metaphorics of scarcity and lack are not thought to affect all subjects. Why? Does the fact that the effects of language as structure are seen not to bear down on some subjects make them different kinds of human subjects, who, by virtue of this freedom from the impact of the cut introduced by language, can't really be said to desire after all, since it is language that opens up the dimension of desire in the first place?

Arnold Davidson provides a useful gloss on Foucault's distinction between desire and pleasure and the theoretical appeal of pleasure over desire: "Desire has psychological depth; desire can be latent or manifest, apparent or hidden; desire can be repressed or sublimated; it calls for decipherment. . . . Pleasure is, as it were, exhausted by its surface; it can be intensified, increased, its qualities modified, but it does not have the psychological depth of desire."[65] Although I understand the compelling nature of Foucault's antipsychologistic use of "pleasures" in his formulation, where "pleasures" cannot be said to speak to the particularity of the subject, to the psychology of the subject experiencing (and experienced by) the pleasures, I also hear in the use of the word the pleasures that attend ego mastery. That is why, ultimately, in the context of my argument here, I line pleasure up on the side of what we might do battle against. I'm not, to be sure, against pleasure, just this kind of pleasure. I think Foucault's critique of psychoanalysis misses an opportunity to clarify that in fact it's more pointedly and accurately directed at ego psychology and not Freudian or Lacanian psychoanalysis.

Consider these three passages from Lacan's *Seminar XI*. The third passage should be read as a hinge that joins the first two.

> Where it was, the Ich—the subject, not psychology—the subject, must come into existence. And there is only one method of knowing that one is there, namely, to map the network.[66]

> In analytic practice, mapping the subject in relation to reality, such as it is supposed to constitute us, and not in relation to the signifier, amounts to falling already into the degradation of the psychological constitution of the subject.[67]

> The unconscious is constituted by the effects of speech on the subject, it is the dimension in which the subject is determined in the development of the effects of speech, consequently the unconscious is structured like a language.[68]

In her brilliant Lacanian reading of "hysteria" in a Puerto Rican barrio of north Philadelphia, Patricia Gherovici writes, "Ultimately, the consequence of a position that excludes the access to psychoanalysis for poor Hispanics would be that a poor Hispanic's unconscious is out of reach."[69] One might go a little further and suggest that the ethnic-racialized subject's unconscious is not so much out of reach as it is nowhere to be found, because language as structure is thought to never have effects on this subject in the first place, compelling the question of whether we can even use the term *subject* to describe them, as well as suspending the attribution of desire to these "subjects." The rallying point for the counterattack against the conceptualization of psychical complexity internal to the deployment of sexuality that carves up the body of the ethnic-racialized subject ought not to be egos-pleasure, but rather subjects and desire.

CHAPTER THREE

Browned, Skinned, Educated, and Protected

The involvement of social scientists in the Brown decision set social science and the law on a common path. There can be no turning from it now.

KENNETH CLARK, "The Social Scientists, the Brown Decision, and Contemporary Confusion"

I don't think law is capable of resolving or banishing this contradiction. In that sense law is incapable of guaranteeing social justice. Social justice for people of color and for other stigmatized minorities will require a revolutionary cultural transformation, one more sweeping and more penetrating perhaps than any we've seen. Perhaps one more profound than any society can achieve while remaining the same society.

RICHARD T. FORD, "Beyond 'Difference': A Reluctant Critique of Legal Identity Politics"

Need and reason are harmonized only in law, but everyone is left a victim of the egoism of his private needs, of anarchy and of materialism. Marx aspires to the creation of a State where, as he puts it, human emancipation will be not only political but real, a State where man will find himself in a non-alienated relation to his own organization. . . . the two terms of reason and of need are insufficient to permit an understanding of the domain involved when it is a question of human self-realization. It is in the structure itself that we come up against a certain difficulty, which is nothing less than the function of desire.

JACQUES LACAN, Seminar VII

In 1951, social psychologist Kenneth Clark almost forgot his dolls on a train en route to South Carolina to perform experiments that would come to figure crucially in perhaps the most important legal decision in U.S. history—the 1954 Brown v. Board of Education decision ending segregation in public schools. Kenneth and Mamie Clark's 1947 doll experiments, whose purported focus was to study the development of "racial identification as a function of ego development . . . in Negro children" and the children's racial preferences,[1] eventually came to solidify in quite dramatic fashion the place of the psychologist and psychology in the U.S. legal machinery. "Give me the doll that looks bad. Give me the doll that is a nice color. Give me the doll that looks like a white child. Give me the doll that looks like a colored child," the Clarks asked 253 black children enrolled in segregated and racially-mixed nursery schools in Arkansas and Massachusetts.[2] They concluded that both the northern and southern black children's overall preference for the white doll over the brown doll was evidence that "the children suffered from self-rejection, with its truncating effect on their personalities, and the earliness of the corrosive awareness of color. I don't think we had quite realized the extent of the cruelty of racism and how hard it hit."[3] Shortly after prosecuting attorney Thurgood Marshall enlisted Kenneth Clark as one of his experts in the Brown case, Clark set out to perform his experiments at the Scott Branch School in South Carolina. Clark, terrified of flying, took the train, where he almost left his suitcase full of brown and white dolls.

Might Lacan, upon invitation, have joined Kenneth Clark on Thurgood Marshall's list of expert witnesses in the Brown case? Would he have defended the Clarks' findings and the service into which Marshall was pressing these findings—that segregation psychologically traumatized black children?

Picture it: "Dr. Lacan, do you swear to tell the whole truth and nothing but the truth, so help you God?" Lacan might have responded with what he told a French television audience in an interview aired in 1973, "I always speak the truth. Not the whole truth, because there's no way, to say it all. Saying it all is literally impossible: words fail. Yet it's through this very impossibility that the truth holds onto the real."[4]

During the time frame of these trials, initially argued in December 1952, reargued in December 1953, and finally decided on May 17, 1954, Lacan was busy preparing and delivering his first two public seminars, *Freud's Papers on Technique* (1953–54) and *The Ego in Freud's Theory and in the Technique of Psychoanalysis* (1954–55). Two days after the Brown decision ending segregation was issued in the United States, Lacan, in a session titled "The Nucleus of Repression," insisted that a clear distinction be made between the ego and the subject:

> The fundamental fact which analysis reveals to us and which I am in the process of teaching you, is that the ego is an imaginary function. . . . If the ego is an imaginary function, it is not to be confused with the subject. What do we call a subject? Quite precisely, what, in the development of objectivation, is outside the object. . . . The ego is deprived of its absolute position in the subject. The ego acquires the

status of a mirage, as the residue, it is only one element in the objectal relations of the subject. Are you with me?[5]

Would the Clarks' 1947 experiment of the development of "racial identification" as a function of ego development have sounded a new kind of direction for Lacan on how one might theorize the construction of the ego as formed by identification with the specular image in the mirror stage?

This chapter is divided into three sections. In the first, I explore, on the prompting of Hortense Spillers's landmark 1996 essay "'All the Things You Could Be by Now, If Sigmund Freud's Wife Was Your Mother': Psychoanalysis and Race," the many historical and theoretical questions that elect themselves when one juxtaposes race and psychoanalysis in the specific context of rights discourse. I also consider the question of what emancipatory potential for ethnic-racialized subjects may be mined in psychoanalytic theory, keeping in mind Spillers's sobering claim "that the psychoanalytic object, subject, subjectivity now constitute the missing layer of hermeneutic/interpretive projects of an entire generation of black intellectuals now at work."[6] I think we could easily extend the reach of Spillers's claim to note that it represents the missing hermeneutic, as well, among a generation of scholars working in Chicano and Latino studies, and other critical race and ethnicity studies knowledge projects. After considering the question of the emancipatory in psychoanalysis, I consider the same question in relation to social psychology, where I unpack the theoretical assumptions that can be said to be shared by ego psychology and social psychology on the topic of strengthening the ethnic-racialized ego, the theme of adjustment to reality, and the importance allotted to social and cultural influences in determining psychological trauma for ethnic-racialized subjects.

In the second section, "Haunted by *Brown*," I provide the reader with a brief history of the Brown case and an analysis of the Clarks' experiments to understand not only the moment when, as Kenneth Clark remarks, "The involvement of social scientists in the Brown decision set social science and the law on a common path,"[7] but to also understand the specific nature of ethnic-racialized psychological trauma that was, in effect, being codified in law. Building on this, the concluding section reads Lacan together with Kenneth and Mamie Clark and Hortense Spillers on the topic of ego development and the place that should be allotted to the meaning and function of racialized difference in a theory of ego development in a Symbolic order like that of the United States, in which racialized meanings suffuse virtually all aspects of life—cultural traditions, rituals, customs, modes of thinking, structures of feeling, and so on. Is there a conceptual meeting place, conflictive, even, but not for that reason necessarily cross-canceling, between Lacan's work on the ego in his mirror stage article, the Clarks' experiments on ego development and black children's consciousness of "self" as racialized, and Spillers's claim that the signifierness of race covers the individual before language and its differential laws take hold of the speaking human organism? I conclude this section by speculating on how we might theorize rights discourse for ethnic-racialized subjects with a more psychoanalytic notion of the subject in mind, which, again, tries to engage a more varied and textured understanding of the losses experienced by ethnic-racialized subjects in a white supremacist society. By the end of this chapter, I hope to have forged a space of overlap between Lacanian psychoanalytic theory, social psychology, rights discourse, and critical race and ethnicity studies theory.

I am not sure how successful or promising the reader will find this admittedly forced dialogue, but I insist upon it in order to imagine how we might bridge analytic approaches to conceptualizing and theorizing ethnic-racialized subjectivity in the humanities, law, and the social sciences in an effort to craft the most complex characterization of ethnic-racialized subjectivity and experience that we can. By the mid-twentieth century in the United States, the social sciences—psychology, specifically—along with law and rights discourse had together participated in hallucinating, scaffolding, and inscribing in the popular cultural, political, and intellectual imagination enduring accounts of ethnic-racialized subjectivity and experience that are still with us today. We might say that the way had been prepared for the insinuation of the "sciences of the mind"—psychiatry and psychology, for example—into the legal apparatus since the mid-nineteenth century, as Michel Foucault remarks: "I simply want to underline this strange fact, that psychiatrists have tried very stubbornly to take their place in the legal machinery."[8] Kenneth Clark reminds us that by the middle of the twentieth century in the United States, social scientists had with respect to "this strange fact" taken the lead over psychiatrists. "The involvement of social scientists in the Brown decision set social science and the law on a common path," Clark writes.[9]

In an essay known for a rhetorical opacity and density that rivals and mimics Lacan's own writings in its desired analytical training effects, Spillers locates, in one of the essay's most straightforward and unambiguous formulations, the emancipatory potential of psychoanalytic theory for black cultural and political critique in psychoanalysis' scrutinous self-regarding practices:

> At the very least, I am suggesting that an aspect of the emancipatory hinges on what would appear to be simple self-attention, except that reaching the articulation requires a process, that of making one's subjectness the object of a disciplined and potentially displaceable attentiveness. To the extent that the psychoanalytic provides, at least in theory, a protocol for the "care of the self" on several planes of intersecting concern, it seems vital to the political interests of the black community, even as we argue (endlessly) about its generative schools of thought.[10]

Spillers's essay has been hugely influential for scholars working at the intersection of race and psychoanalysis, although it has been woefully underengaged with over the years. The difficulty of this essay, somewhere between speech and writing like Lacan's "The Instance of the Letter in the Unconscious, or Reason Since Freud" can be read as a strategic attempt on Spillers's part to effect in her readers something along the lines of the analytical training effect Lacan has on his readers and listeners through his writings and seminars. The specific training effect achieved by Spillers has to do not with teaching readers and listeners how to be better clinicians, strictly speaking, as in Lacan's case— although her essay might have that effect as well, especially for those analysts compelled to read for and listen to the text and noise of race in the Symbolic, as Franz Fanon did. Rather, Spillers's essay compels us to understand how we might be better culture and political theorists as a result of engaging psychoanalytic theory—which is not at all to say, by the way, that our engagement must remain faithful to whatever Freudian or Lacanian psychoanalytic doxa.

Spillers circles the insinuation of an intersection between race and psychoanalysis in the same manner in which a drive deliriously circles a partial object, leaving always open and thus suffused with desire what, in other theorists' hands, might compel an entirely closed circuit of argumentation wrestled down into a well-worn proof. Who's circling whom? Does race circle psychoanalysis? Does psychoanalysis circle race? Finally, why ask this question, and what is the function of the conjunction *and*, which appears to set

79

them up as related before the question of that possibility is even broached? I have intentionally left some questions regarding the role of ethnic-racialized difference in the field formations of psychoanalysis and psychology unaddressed in chapters 1 and 2 so that I might take them up here, with Spillers's study serving as a catalyst and guide. I would like to begin by pushing at either end of the potential theoretical relationship between psychoanalysis and race and attempting to answer some of the questions with which Spillers begins. She asks, "By juxtaposing psychoanalysis and 'race,' is one bringing them into alignment in the hope that these structures of attention will be mutually illuminating and interpenetrative? By contrast, does one mean to suggest the impossibility of the latter, which reinforces the impression that these punctualities are so insistently disparate in the cultural and historical claims that they each invoke that the ground of their speaking together would dissolve in conceptual chaos?"[11] Keeping this question in mind, let's attempt to deploy the next quotation as a kind of partial answer to Spillers's question. In *Freud, Race and Gender*, Sander Gilman argues, "For Sigmund Freud, an acculturated Jewish medical scientist of late-nineteenth-century Vienna, one of the definitions of the Jew that he would have internalized was a racial one, and it was a definition that, whether he consciously sought it or not, shaped the argument of psychoanalysis. Being a male scientist-physician and being a Jew were linked at the turn of the century in many complex ways."[12] After Gilman, then, we might note that Freudian psychoanalysis emerges from a quasi-intentional ("whether he consciously sought it or not") juxtaposition of it and "race"—in that Freud's and many of his Jewish disciples' and followers' experiences of being racialized as Jewish inform the theorizations themselves.

However present in these initial formulations "race" may be—something that no psychoanalytic school of thought appears to entertain, including Lacanian theory—Freud's accomplishments, again following the logic of Gilman's argument, strike one as effectively removing race from psychoanalysis' moment of instantiation, if we trust Gilman's point: "As virtually all of Freud's early disciples were Jews, the lure of psychoanalysis for them may well have been its claims for a universalization of human experience and an active exclusion of the importance of race from its theoretical framework."[13] What is never quite clear in Gilman's text is how the experience of being racialized as nonwhite did in fact inform or shape certain psychoanalytic notions and tenets. Ranjana Khanna attempts to give specific shape to how Freud's experience of anti-Semitism might have translated into certain changes in his theories when she writes, "Freud recognized the problem of European genealogy as the death of the synthetic European neurotic ego. He found in its place a destructive splitting. Freud recognized this as his own relationship to his nation changed because of anti-Semitism. It is through the notions of disavowal and melancholy that Freud begins to develop a different notion of self, one that embodies a critical nationalism."[14]

With Gilman's observations regarding race's place at the inception of Freud's invention of psychoanalytic theory in mind, let's return to Spillers: "Perhaps we could argue that the 'race' matrix was the fundamental interdiction within the enabling discourse of founding psychoanalytic theory and practice itself. But it is the missing element here that helps to define Freud's significance as one of the preeminent punctualities of Western time in modernity."[15] Believing Gilman's claims means shifting the stress Spillers places on the nonplace occupied by race in psychoanalysis. It's not that it's not there; it's not that race was the "fundamental interdiction." Rather, it constitutes a peculiar presence—a silent letter that goes unpronounced in a word, perhaps, but is still materially present in the writing and visualization of the word and in the effects the word achieves. "The 'race' matrix" might be read as helping ignite aspects of psychoanalytic theory but then appears to go missing as the dissimulating agent or force of whatever aspect in question. I think one addresses the intersection between race and psychoanalysis not in an effort to think something new but rather because they require each other. Not talking about this relationship is precisely to disappear race in the manner in which psychoanalysis has so often been accused of doing in its so-called universalizing applications. Having said this, I do not want to come to any conclusion here regarding precisely how race and ethnic-racialized difference figure in the psychoanalytic invention. We have to keep in mind what Nicolas Rand and Maria Torok argue in their critique of those readings that remark on the vicissitudes of psychoanalytic theory by weighing the importance of Freud's ethnic-racialized difference:

81

> We fall short in the search for the origin of Freudian theories if we confine our study to the history of ideas in medicine, biology, psychiatry, psychology, literature, philosophy, or sociology, if we limit our inquiry to nineteenth-century habits of mind and social attitudes. The paradoxes of Freudian psychoanalysis as a theory of psychotherapy cannot be sufficiently elucidated through Freud's intellectual biography and the degree of conservatism or enlightenment in his scientific convictions

and social beliefs or practices. The contradictory development of Freudian theory does not derive its essence from historically or ethnically motivated factors—such as Freud's secular Judaism, the insidious effects of widespread anti-Semitism in Central Europe during his time, or his acquaintance with Talmudic forms of exegesis.[16]

The relationship Sander Gilman establishes between the racialization of Jews as other than white and the invention of Freudian psychoanalytic theory is generally revisited when Lacan takes up with the Jewish ego psychologists and how their experience as Jewish immigrants contending with coercive assimilatory imperatives in the mid-twentieth-century United States would, in Lacan's view, ultimately inform the distortion of Freudian theory, as we discussed at length in chapter 2. In following this link established by others between Jewish difference, anti-Semitism, and psychoanalysis, we need to be careful that we not then turn psychoanalytic theory's past, present, and future into a fun-house mirror of Jewish experience. It may appear that I want it both ways—to claim that Freud's experience of being racialized as other than white both does and doesn't inform the theory of psychoanalysis from its inception—and that would not be an erroneous reading.[17] In the end, we may find that the history of psychoanalytic theory always appears to include the spectacle of ethnic-racialized difference, articulated in slightly different ways depending on the historical period in question. This is, after all, what I imply in chapter 1.

Since the beginnings of psychoanalysis, theorists have been considering what, if any, emancipatory potential it might have, especially in the context of capitalism and whether psychoanalysis serves or doesn't serve its needs. Some have pointed to the conservative, human engineering function of psycho-analysis, seeing it as a corrective, disciplinary therapeutics committed to ad-justing troubled subjectivities for proper and productive citizen-subject-worker status. One might seek confirmation of this point in Freud's own work. Take, for example, how Freud at the Budapest Congress in 1918 envi-sioned the response of psychoanalysis to the demands of the masses: "When this happens, institutions or out-patient clinics will be appointed, so that men who would otherwise give way to drink, women who have nearly succumbed under their burden of privations, children for whom there is no choice be-tween running wild or neurosis, *may be made capable, by analysis, of resistance and efficient work.* Such treatments will be free. It may be a long time before the

82

States come to see these things as urgent."[18] No doubt, from even a loose Marxist perspective, the proffering of "free treatments" might be said to sit in some tension with the attending desire to cultivate "efficient work."[19] The equivalence sign that some have tried to draw between psychoanalysis and capitalism has been forged through the condemnation of psychoanalysis' so-called slavish adherence to a theory of lack, one that is, in turn, to be attributed to capitalism's need to circulate a structure of feeling organized around scarcity and loss.

Others have argued for psychoanalysis' more radical, intrinsically anti-capitalist function, one that might be seen to issue from analytic discourse itself that, at least in Lacan's presentation of the ethics of psychoanalysis in *Seminar VII*, defines analysis in opposition to the imperative that subjects should or can be adjusted to the demands of reality, or his theory of the end of analysis in *Seminar XI*, the seminar, incidentally, that Spillers mines most directly in her essay, in which the analysand traverses the fantasy and reaches the strange dignity of "subjective destitution" by realizing that the Other does not exist— nor does the subject, for that matter. Along these lines, Patricia Gherovici writes, "Since it cannot avoid being caught up in the capitalist mode of production, psychoanalysis is, in Lacan's view, the very 'symptom of capitalism,' insofar as it encourages the symptom to produce meaning rather than commodities."[20] What is often not taken into consideration when assessing the conservative or radical function of psychoanalytic theory has to do with the fact that there are, simply put, different kinds of psychoanalysis, and that very different assumptions and strategies attend these different forms of analysis and theory. For example, Lacanian analysis could not be more different than object relations theory or ego psychology on the question of the role and function of the analyst, as I explained in chapter 2, and these differences have consequences for how we imagine the supportive or adversarial roles played by psychoanalysis and the psychoanalyst in the context of capitalism.

The question of synthesizing Freudian psychoanalysis and Marxist theory and more generally of inquiring into psychoanalytic theory's relevance for emancipatory projects is still being asked, although, as I argue throughout this book, it is mostly absent in knowledge projects emerging from critical race and ethnicity studies. Where psychoanalysis has been deemed not especially promising for the development of a politicized discourse in critical race and ethnicity studies, social psychology, on the other hand, has historically been presumed to possess some potential for a politicized antiracist discourse.

Social psychology has a long history in the United States. Even though we can maintain with confidence that ego psychology is hegemonic in the United States between the years 1945 and 1965, precisely during the time that includes the peak of the civil rights movement, we would be simplifying the picture considerably if we did not add that before the consolidation of ego psychology in the United States, it had to contend with the strong presence of "social psychology" and "behaviorist psychology." Despite ego psychology's concerted focus on adaptation, Heinz Hartmann and his group "showed little interest in the outside world."[21] The social, cultural, and historical textures and resonances of what will pass as the agreed-upon "reality" go mostly unremarked upon in ego psychology. Things could not be more different in the case of social psychology. In the early 1950s, Lacan argued that social psychologists like Erik Erikson risked overemphasizing the social and cultural in their reading of human psychology:

> A man called Erikson, who describes himself as an advocate of the culturalist school—for the good it will do him! This so-called culturalism consists in emphasising in analysis those things which, in each case, depend on the cultural context in which the subject is immersed. . . . The question is to know whether this element should be given pre-eminent importance in the constitution of the subject.
>
> . . . You will be surprised to see that this culturalism converges quite singularly with a psychologism which consists in understanding the entire analytic text as a function of the various stages in the development of the ego.[22]

Lacan reveals how the preeminence given in social psychology to the cultural context of the analysand—a fact that was read as a good sign by analysts and therapists battling against the ethnocentrism of psychoanalysis and psychology in the United States—proceeds apace with an understanding of the human psyche in terms of stages of ego development. This latter point sheds some light on why ego and social psychology could, in theory, see themselves as sharing some of the same basic assumptions about the ego, its stages, its development, and how the question of adaptation figures in these stages and development, even though they appeared to part ways when it came to understanding the importance of the role played by an analysand's specific social and cultural context.

Eric Fromm, a theorist associated with the Frankfurt School, early on attempted to craft a kind of synthesis between Marxism, psychoanalytic theory, and social psychology: "Man to Marx has certain basic drives (hunger, love, and so forth), which seek gratification; acquisitiveness (the desire to attain, possess, etc.) was merely a product of specific social conditions. Marxism was, however, in need of additional psychological insights. . . . Psychoanalysis could provide the missing link between ideological superstructure and socio-economic base. . . . The task of social psychology was to understand unconsciously motivated behavior in terms of the effect of the socio-economic substructure on basic psychic drives."[23] More recently Neil Altman has tried to integrate social psychology with psychoanalytic theory in his work as an analyst in urban inner city settings. In the preface to *The Analyst in the Inner City*, he writes, "My project in this book is part of a large contemporary project of integrating the social with the psychological within psychoanalytic theory and practice."[24] In *Cultural Diversity: Its Social Psychology*, Xenia Chryssochoou provides a more contemporary definition of the scope and task of social psychology when she writes,

> What makes social psychology distinct as a discipline is not only its object, but also its way of looking at it. Moscovici suggests that what differentiates social psychology from the related disciplines of psychology and sociology has been its efforts to understand the conflict between the individual and the social, along with its particular way of looking at this relationship. Within a social psychological framework, the relationship between the individual (as ego/organism) and the social object needs to be studied through the relationship between this individual and a social subject (an Alter that can be real, symbolic, represented, an individual, or a group).[25]

In juxtaposing Fromm's, Altman's, Chryssochoou's, and Lacan's earlier characterizations of social psychology, I want to draw attention to precisely the kind of Lacanian psychoanalytic concern that seems to fall out in social psychology—the effects of language as structure on the speaking organism. Some readers might think that what falls out of the Lacanian paradigm because of the attention trained on language as structure is precisely the engagement with the deep social and cultural texture of an individual's life, but that is hardly the case. In fact, the focus on the signifiers that collect and pool in the narrative of an individual's life requires that the analyst be rigorously attentive to the analysand's specific cultural background, as Bruce Fink reminds us: "Lacan suggests that analysts have to be consummately familiar with the elements of the signifier that constitute the analysand's particular, perhaps quite idiosyncratic or foreign cultural background."[26] Moreover, as

Patricia Gherovici makes explicit, Lacan's notion of the Other as the locus in which speech is constituted is suffused with social and cultural texture, "For Lacan, the Other is the signifying treasure, the reservoir of language, human laws, and culture, which is, obviously, social. . . . Lacan's conceptualization of an unconscious 'structured like a language' does not mean that the common elements of language are arranged in the same way for everyone. Each subject will have a particular history that has been written on the body as the first signifiers."[27]

My argument for a more Lacanian reading of the ethnic-racialized subject in rights discourse understands, as the Latino studies scholars Antonia Darder and Rodolfo Torres put it, that "the terrain of social change is shifting as the role of litigation for social change seems to be declining and the role of public policy, increasing. . . . Thus, 50 years after the monumental victory in Brown vs. The Board of Education, it is strikingly evident that the traditional approach to framing public policy is insufficient to address effectively racialized, gendered, and class inequalities."[28] I don't necessarily think that social justice, given these shifts, will be won for minoritized subjects as a result of bringing to bear on the understanding of ethnic-racialized subjectivity that gets scripted in rights discourse a more Lacanian-inflected reading. That said, even if the role of litigation in achieving social justice for minoritized subjects is declining, this does not change the fact that work on matters of race in public policy is still conceptualized through a psychological apparatus and that psychologists participate heavily in policy making.

My intervention attempts to answer to the kind of work Darder and Torres suggest we undertake when they write, "There is a dire need then to engage not only with the technical dimensions of public policy (i.e., initiatives, referendums, and the ballot box), but also with its conceptual ideological apparatus. This requires us to question more deeply the philosophical dimensions and political interests that undergird public policy discourse."[29] Gunnar Myrdal's conviction, detailed in his 1944 publication *An American Dilemma*, that psychology held the key to eradicating racism not only "served to push future work and policy on matters of race in decidedly psychological directions"[30] but also revealed psychologists' desire to have *direct* impact on social and public policy, as Ellen Herman explains: "This was perfectly consistent with the desire (so evident in Myrdal and in many other contemporary experts) to make behavioral expertise inform government policy and inspire social action."[31] Public policy on matters of race in the United States is run through

86

with an ideology we might describe as "psychologistic," recalling my explication of this term in the introduction, and that has the potential to convince everyone that the assumptions and tenets of ego and social psychology provide the only tools available for understanding, interpreting, and resolving the psychological impact of systemic racist practices as experienced daily by ethnic-racialized subjects in legal and extralegal contexts. In this book Lacanian theory's position on the subject in language serves to, returning to Darder's and Torres's words, "question more deeply the philosophical and political interests that undergird public policy discourse" on matters of race.

HAUNTED BY *BROWN*

Brown v. Board of Education, perhaps one of the most significant decisions in U.S. legal history, is a palimpsest of ethnic-racialized psychological traumas. The case's background immerses its researcher in the force field of Mexican American, Japanese American, and African American psychological and historical trauma. To begin to tease out these layers of trauma, we need to turn our attention first to *Mendez v. Westminster*, a case many believe was instrumental to the later victory in the Brown decision.[32] In 1946, Gonzalo Mendez, along with four other parents, filed a lawsuit claiming that his children were discriminated against when they were not allowed to enroll in an Orange County school in Los Angeles. Edward Escobar explains how "Los Angeles city school officials placed many Mexican American children in special segregated 'Mexican schools.' The curriculum in these schools emphasized vocational instruction and Americanization at the expense of academic course work. While not segregated by law, housing segregation and the gerrymandering of districts forced many children into these separate schools. School officials also used Mexican Americans' alleged lack of English proficiency as an excuse to segregate them."[33]

Thurgood Marshall had actually filed briefs in the Mendez case. Now that many have forgotten the Mexican American struggle for recognition and rights underpinning the Brown case, it constitutes a ghost case. The challenge to segregated schools for Mexican American children in the Mendez case was initially framed as a violation of the Fourteenth Amendment.[34] Although this first challenge wanted to take up with the unconstitutionality of the separate-but-equal clause, a challenge held by the district court initially in the case, the

Court of Appeals for the Ninth Circuit did not rule in this way. It supported the claims for Mexican American children, not because it considered the Plessy decision invalid but rather because there was no California statute that authorized segregated schools.[35]

The Mendez decision is already suffused with ethnic-racialized trauma. Two years before filing the complaint, Gonzalo Mendez, his wife, Felicitas, and their children moved to a farm in 1944 that Gonzalo agreed to manage while its Japanese American owners were interned. It's never clear if the Japanese American family in question returned to their farm, if they were ever allowed to return to their farm as its original, rightful owners. Here we have a strangely infelicitous moment of payback where what could have been imagined as originally Mexican land before the land theft / agreement we call the Treaty of Guadalupe Hidalgo of 1848 is returned to a Mexican family, but the land must first be stolen from a Japanese American family. This is not what Reies Lopez Tijerina and his Alianza de las Mercedes movement had in mind, I imagine, when at the beginning of the Chicano movement in 1966 they fought for the reappropriation of lands stolen from Mexicans and small farming communities after the Mexican-American War.[36] Where the Mendez case functions as a kind of ghost in the Brown decision, the Japanese American family whose farm the Mendezes came to possess functions as a ghost in the Mendez decision. To this day I have been unable to track down the name of the Japanese American family or find out what happened to them.

The specter of the ghost that hovers in and around the Brown case might be said to have made its first appearance in the weird, haunting, inanimate line drawings of "white boys," "colored boys," "lions," "dogs," "clowns," and "hens" that the Clarks had 150 black children in a segregated Washington, D.C., nursery school choose from. In their first important study, "The Development of Consciousness of Self and the Emergence of Racial Identification in Negro Preschool Children," published in 1939 they pursue a question that they attribute to having first been explored by Ruth Horowitz, from whose work the Clarks draw much sustenance: "Her study dealt with race-consciousness conceived as a function of ego development."[37] William E. Cross Jr. strongly and persuasively critiques, and rightly so, the overestimation of the Clarks' contribution to the discourse on black identity, since the Clarks appear to be mostly extending when they don't simply, to use Cross's word, "replay" Ruth Horowitz's position.[38]

The Clarks specify their study as "an attempt to investigate early levels in the development of consciousness of self in Negro preschool children with special reference to emergent race consciousness."[39] Their focus is not unlike the question Spillers formulates: "How might psychoanalytic theories speak about 'race' as a self consciously assertive reflexivity, and how might 'race' expose the gaps that psychoanalytic theories awaken?"[40] The reader should keep in mind that this early study is in the service of understanding at what age and with what frequency young black children express "appropriate racial identification" by choosing line drawings of "colored boys" and not "hens" or "white boys." They conclude this early study by noting that with the increase of age, there is a consistent increase in the appropriate choice of "colored boy" by black children. What is never entirely clear in this early study on "appropriate racial identification" is whether or not the Clarks ultimately think children racialized as black undergo the same or a completely different developmental schema with regard to ego formation than do nonblack children. The question that lurks in the background to their study appears to want to ask whether race consciousness comes to figure only after the child has already ostensibly developed an ego, or do black children's egos develop through the calculus of race consciousness from the get-go. It is a question that bears some affinity to the remarks made by Spillers regarding how she understands race as traversing the individual in the collective before language and its differential laws take hold of the speaking subject, if we understand that the organism of needs prior to being inscribed in language has yet to develop an ego.

Although the 1939 study has been influential in social psychology, a 1947 study by the Clarks, "Racial Identification and Preference in Negro Children," came to play the more crucial role in the Brown decision. In this experiment, the Clarks bring more loaded questions and change from line drawings to dolls. The crucial word added to the description of this experiment is "preferences": "Because the problem of racial identification is so definitely related to the problem of the genesis of racial attitudes in children, it was thought practicable to attempt to determine the racial attitudes or preferences of these Negro children—and to define more precisely, as far as possible, the developmental pattern of this relationship."[41]

The 253 black children from segregated nursery and public schools in three different towns in Arkansas and from racially mixed nursery and public schools in Springfield, Massachusetts, were given four dolls from which to choose: "Two of these dolls were brown with black hair and two were white with yellow hair. In the experimental situation these dolls were unclothed except for white diapers. The position of the head, hands, and legs on all the dolls was the same."[42]

These dolls were selected in response to eight different questions:

1. Give me the doll that you like to play with—(a) like best. 2. Give me the doll that is a nice doll. 3. Give me the doll that looks bad. 4. Give me the doll that is a nice color. 5. Give me the doll that looks like a white child. 6. Give me the doll that looks like a colored child. 7. Give me the doll that looks like a Negro child. 8. Give me the doll that looks like you. Requests 1 through 4 were designed to reveal preferences; requests 5 through 7 to indicate a knowledge of "racial differences"; and request 8 to show self-identification.[43]

The Clarks note that they had to begin with the preference questions, because when they began with the identification questions and then moved to the preference questions, the children generally chose the doll that they had initially identified with, suggesting, as the Clarks put it, that there was a "reflection of ego involvement."[44]

The authors conclude,

Analyzing the results of requests 1 and 2 together, it is seen that there is a marked increase in preference for the white doll from the three- to four-year level; a more gradual decrease in this preference from the four- to the five-year level; a further decrease from the five- to the six-year level; and a continued decrease from the six- to the seven-year level. These results suggest that although the majority of Negro children at each age prefer the white doll to the brown doll, this preference decreases gradually from four through seven years.[45]

What should strike us about this conclusion is that it does not in fact entirely support the idea of "black self-hatred," an idea the Clarks' doll studies have sometimes been used in the service of proving, since, as we see, the children approaching the age of seven show a reversal in the trend toward choosing the white doll over the brown doll. At the same time, we cannot fail to register that throughout all ages, from three to seven, the black children preferred the white doll to the brown doll despite the gradual decrease in this trend as the children got older. Black self-hatred, no. A preference for "whiteness," yes.

Additionally significant about this conclusion in the context of our discussion on psychoanalysis, ego psychology, and social psychology is how it bears on a general theory of ego development—whether Lacanian, ego psychologi-

90

cal, or even Kleinian. If we keep in mind that the ego is developed and consolidated at an earlier age, just before the age during which the Clarks note that black children are more likely to prefer the white doll to the brown dolls, then we might read their—to use the language from the Clarks' earlier study—"inappropriate" racial identification as pointing to a kind of splitting experienced at the moment of the black child's formation of an ego. Unfortunately, a conversation was never really struck up between the Clarks, Horowitz, and ego psychologists in the United States on how race consciousness might or might not bear on ego development and, more broadly, on a theory of ego development in psychoanalysis. The reader should keep in mind that in ego psychology's magisterial 1945 address to the study of children in *The Psychoanalytic Study of the Child*, a three-volume series edited by Anna Freud, Heinz Hartmann, and Ernst Kris that collected work that was contemporaneous with Horowitz's and the Clarks' studies, there is no mention of how race or "racial consciousness" might figure in ego development, how race, to return to Spillers's remarks, might be seen as traversing the human organism before the organism is inscribed in language.

One is left to wonder how Mexican American children would have responded in these experiments. How would they have chosen? Brown dolls? White dolls? From what I have gathered, experiments performed on Mexican American children were mostly in the service of testing for intelligence.[46] There is very little evidence that Mexican American children were approached as psychological subjects who could experience psychical distress as a result of segregation. I would argue that one of the reasons why the Mendez case so often fails to get invoked is because the decision reached doesn't provide an opportunity for the meeting up of social science and the law, and where, revealingly, we might or might not find an engagement with Mexican American children as, say, psychological subjects damaged by segregation. Most of the studies performed on Mexican American children that I have read are ultimately in the service of proving that they are constitutionally feeble-minded. In one study from 1943 by D. K. Garretson, despite the fact that the researcher takes into account the transient patterns of Mexican children who are often frequently moving about as their families look for agricultural work, which affects their schooling and education, he will still insist that this doesn't help explain the so-called low intelligence possessed by these children.[47] The spectacle of damaged Mexican American children does not resemble here in even the remotest manner the way in which the possibility of black children's damaged psyches informed—because it could be thought, conceptualized—the Clarks' experiments and how they were used in the Brown decision.

But how would the doll studies be used to secure a victorious decision in the Brown case? Throughout there was a problem of specificity with regard to proving exactly what psychological damage is done to children as a result of the specific fact of segregation. Prosecuting attorneys Carter and Marshall had to "isolate the psychological damage caused specifically by segregation in schools as singled out from other manifestations of prejudice in society as a whole."[48] A prominent psychologist at New York University, Elsa E. Robinson, looked at Kenneth Clark's studies and concluded, after consulting with a number of her colleagues, that "there is as yet no scientifically verified material of an empirical nature which bears directly on the issue."[49] While offering testimony in the South Carolina case, *Briggs v. Elliott*, Clark testified, "'The essence of this detrimental effect is a confusion in the child's concept of his own self-esteem—basic feelings of inferiority, conflict, confusion in his self-image, resentment, hostility towards himself, hostility towards whites, intensification of . . . a desire to resolve his basic conflict by sometimes escaping or withdrawing.'"[50] The defense teams in the trials in Virginia were able to call a couple of psychologists and psychiatrists who referred openly to the doll tests as "blunderbuss" and who insisted that segregation was natural, warranted and beneficial for all and that "Negro inferiority" was a natural fact of life. Even Dr. Henry Garrett, professor to both Kenneth and Mamie Clark at Columbia University, took the stand for the defense, taking more than a couple of jabs at Kenneth, telling the court that Kenneth was an exceedingly average and unremarkable student. What never quite emerges in any explicit way in the vast amounts of material—clinical, legal, and otherwise—produced on the Brown case is how racialization practices themselves are what are primarily detrimental. Before one might even consider the cultivation of a positive ethnic-racialized identity in children, one needs to ask after the damage that comes with understanding that one is the result of an approximation of an extracategory of humanness found nowhere in nature. We will consider this very question in more depth in chapter 7 when we look at a more contemporary experiment conducted in the field of political psychology.

Returning to Clark's passage, I want to concentrate for a moment on how the "essence of this detrimental effect" is being characterized. All of the emotions and modes of self-regard described by Clark are very loaded psychical experiences. Is Clark attempting to be too exhaustive in his explication of the children's experience of psychical distress as attributable to segregation? To be clear, I am not questioning the obvious detrimental psychological (and otherwise) effects of segregation on the young black children Kenneth and Mamie Clark have studied. Rather, I am wary of the explication's pretension to exhaustiveness because, approaching it from a more Lacanian perspective as I do, I think it woefully undertheorizes loss and I am equally wary of how—although perhaps beneficial to the case—it helps codify black identity, as many scholars have noted, as always already damaged. This accomplishes the deadening task of radically reducing and simplifying an understanding of black children's psychical complexity—understandings, I might add, that I think are still with us today when we think generally about the psychology of ethnic-racialized subjects in the United States and how we conceptualize their/our experiences of loss and trauma.

This has more to do than with arguing that, in fact, the Clarks' experiments do not prove black self-hatred or that they generalized unfairly about the black experience in the United States, or that they used experiments performed on very young children in order to draw conclusions about black adult subjectivity. Amina Mama has strongly argued that "the subject at the heart of black psychology, like that of mainstream psychology, was still assumed to be a unitary, static and rational subject, and the emphasis here too was on what was measurable, quantifiable and observable," and where "white racism" was to be read as "the sole factor in black identity formation" that "ignored the existence of diverse cultural referents available to many black people."[51] Mama's well-intentioned recommendation that we begin multiplying in our research these "diverse cultural referents" in order to reach a more complex picture of black identity does not, however, prevent the possibility of reinscribing a "unitary, static and rational," even moribund black subject, because we will have ignored how, despite the impact of all of these "diverse cultural referents," the black subject is first and foremost a subject in language, a subject divided in language who experiences, like all other speaking subjects, the privative and generative effects of language as structure on the speaking organism. If, in our critiques of the Clarks' experiments and the uses to which they were put, as well as in our critiques of how black subjectivity is theorized in black and mainstream psychology, we continue to remain situated within the field of ego and/or social psychology and thus wedded to an understanding of loss and trauma that refuses to consider the effects of language as structure on the speaking human organism, we miss the opportunity to craft a deeper, paradigm shifting critique.

We lose the opportunity to ask why we have seemingly ceded the entire discussion of what ethnic-racialized subjectivity and experience can mean with respect to loss and trauma in the context of systemic racism and discrimination to the general explanatory framework of psychology.

LAW, PSYCHOANALYSIS, AND ORDER

I began this chapter by asking in a rather forced way if we could have imagined Lacan accepting Thurgood Marshall's invitation to appear as an expert witness in the Brown case. Would Lacan have agreed with the Clarks' theory of racial consciousness and ego development? Regarding the Clarks' assumption of the basic ego-psychological confusion of the subject with the ego, one can imagine Lacan would have been quite critical. But how would he have responded to the specific analytical charge attaching to the focus on race—"racial identification," to use the Clarks' words—as a "function of ego development" in black children?

I would like to turn to Lacan's most focused and well-known piece on the question of ego formation, "The Mirror Stage as Formative of the I Function." The work by Ruth Horowitz, Kenneth and Mamie Clark, and the Lacan of the mirror stage article are mostly contemporaneous. I want to carry into my reading of Lacan's article the questions that the Clarks' work compels regarding the force of racialized difference in the constitution and formation of the human organism's ego. Specifically, I want to provide a bit more analytical texture to the central problem they address in their studies—the relationship between race consciousness and ego development—by looking to Lacan's article. The question that the Clarks appear to be asking but never formulate as such is: How does one account for the function of racialized difference in a theory of the construction of the ego? Are we to understand race as "behind" or "in front" of the ego, as it were, in how we theorize the construction of the ego? This is not in an attempt to critique the Clarks' ego- and social psychological assumptions through Lacan's concerted focus on the distinction that must be made between "ego" and "subject," since I will claim that perhaps Lacan's theory of ego construction does risk bleeding out the social too much—or the "socionom" as Spillers might characterize it[52]—and too early, to the point where it's difficult to theorize the "I" function when racialization practices already appear to be doing their dissimulating work on the infant prior to the construction of the ego.

In Lacan's theory of the mirror stage, the ego is formed through an identification with an image as counterpart in a reflective surface. He writes, "It suffices to understand the mirror stage in this context *as an identification*, in the full sense analysis gives to the term: namely, the transformation that takes place in the subject when he assumes [*assume*] an image—an image that is seemingly predestined to have an effect at this phase, as witnessed by the use in analytic theory of antiquity's term, 'imago.'"[53] Lacan will date this stage in human development, locating it somewhere between six and eighteen months of age. We should keep in mind, however, that as Lacan builds his theory over the years that the mirror stage is meant less to reference a particular historical moment that can be isolated and is meant more as a commentary on the structure of subjectivity itself, which is to say a structure of subjectivity where the subject is precipitated according to a fundamental misrecognition in which she identifies with a point outside herself—with an image of herself.

An important tension that Lacan attributes to the infant's response here arises from a general motor uncoordination that it feels and what it spies as a unified image of itself outside, precipitating a tension between fragmentation and unity:

95

> This development is experienced as a temporal dialectic that decisively projects the individual's formation into history: the mirror stage is a drama whose internal pressure pushes precipitously from insufficiency to anticipation—and, for the subject caught up in the lure of spatial identification, turns out fantasies that proceed from a fragmented image of the body to what I will call an "orthopedic" form of its totality—and to the finally donned armor of an alienating identity that will mark his entire mental development with its rigid structure.[54]

The infant is compelled to identify with the counterpart because this appears to resolve the tension and this compromise of sorts is what forms the ego.

Where might we locate the function of "racialized difference" in this scenario? In a passage that I addressed in my introduction in conjunction with Lacan's "elementary cell" of the graph of desire, Hortense Spillers writes, "The individual in the collective traversed by 'race'—and there are no known exceptions, as far as I can tell—is covered by it before language and its differential laws take hold."[55] This would seem to be a point that could not be supported in Lacan since, as I have explained, it implies that there is a signifierness to race before language, that race means something before the acquisition of language—before, that is, language lends it meaning. If this were possible, how might it work? Where is race before language? And the other question: where is race when we theorize the assumption of the ego in Lacanian psychoanalytic theory? Can we say, along with Spillers, that race is *already there* before the human organism emerges as a speaking subject in language? If the human organism is in some essential way always born prematurely, according to Lacan, because of its radical helplessness when compared to other species, then how does race's presence work on that prematurity—if it does—before the assumption of the specular image, before the infant stuffs herself with the contents in the mirror reflection, before the consolidation of the ego?

The mirror scene is very often imagined as one organized around two terms, the child and the counterpart image. Tension between fragmentation and unity characterizes the relationship between those two terms. However, in the 1949 version of the mirror stage—the article was first presented in 1936 and published in 1939—things are presented in a more complicated manner. The difference in the later version has to do with the involvement of the Symbolic, which in effect introduces a third term into the child/counterpart image scenario.[56] Dominiek Hoens and Ed Pluth explain, "The idea of a Symbolic point from which the child identifies can be found for the first time in the 1949 version of the mirror stage, where the child is said to receive the guarantee of its image from the parent who says: 'Thou art that.' . . . in other words, this point is thought of as some sort of *signifier*, and no longer as an *image*. The 'two' in the Imaginary thus actually includes a third."[57] Another way to articulate this new difference is to say that the Symbolic now operates the Imaginary, or that the Imaginary is regulated by the Symbolic, as Lacan explains in *Seminar I*:

> Now let us postulate that the inclination of the plane mirror is governed by the voice of the other. This doesn't happen at the level of the mirror-stage, but it happens subsequently through our overall relation with others—the symbolic relation. From that point on, you can grasp the extent to which the regulation of the imaginary depends on something which is located in a transcendent fashion, as M. Hyppolite would put it—the transcendent on this occasion being nothing other than the symbolic connection between human beings.[58]

What Lacan accomplishes in the later version is a virtual purification of the mirror stage by, as Dany Nobus writes, reducing "its basis in the physiology of perception":

The symbolic control of the imaginary implies that the assumption of a "self-image" may be distorted despite the presence of mirrors, but also that it can still be formed in the absence of mirror images. Furthermore, the symbolic control of the imaginary implies that the assumption of "self-image" can occur outside the field of vision. . . . Insofar as the symbolic governs the imaginary, a blind child can still assume a self-image, *as long as the symbolic is there to replace and control its eyes, for it will then see itself through the words of the Other.*[59]

In the later version the mirror function is, in a sense, taken over by the Symbolic, which now assumes the labors of reflection where words and signifiers can serve as reflecting surfaces for the child. The new emphasis on the Symbolic also requires Lacan to rethink how he had characterized the infant's experience of deficient motor coordination. Although he still sees the human infant as essentially born too soon, when compared with other species, he now understands the infant's attempt to remedy its feelings of fragmentation in the mirror stage as not in response to a Real biological lack, but rather a Symbolic lack, a lack that is introduced by the Symbolic. What does this mean? Instead of understanding the infant's identification with or assumption of an image that promises unity as a response determined by the Real biological lack of motor uncoordination, one is to understand the infant's identification with or assumption of an image as its attempt to reaccess the hypothesized fullness of unity and being that it experienced prior to becoming inscribed in language. Understanding this in terms of Symbolic and not Real lack lends an elegiac quality to the ego, insofar as the ego that is consolidated in these moments of identification can be seen as a memorial to the primordial loss suffered by the human organism as a result of the effects of language.

A question the Clarks, Horowitz, and Spillers all seem to be pursuing regards the relationship between the function of "racialized difference" and the formation of the ego. Specifically, how does one understand the figuring, disfiguring presence of racialized difference in ego formation? Again, Spillers writes that the signifierness of race carves up the human organism's body prior to the subject's inscription in language, prior to the formation of the ego. The Clarks say something a bit different, insofar as the question they pose regarding the impact of race on ego development seems to assume that something like "racial consciousness," or consciousness of self as racialized, comes after the ego has been formed. In other words, it is a mostly formed ego that encounters the function of racialized difference. Does the later version of the

97

mirror stage theory, in emphasizing the role of the Symbolic in ego formation, allow us to read the possibility of race's impact in a new way because the signifierness of "racialized difference," being of the Symbolic order, operates this moment of ego formation in a way the earlier version wouldn't have allowed to be theorized? Does this later version then lend credence to Spillers's point regarding the individual's having been "traversed" by "race" before language and its "differential laws" of metaphor and metonymy?

To continue with this line of thinking, let's imagine where we might locate the *signifierness* of race and the force of racialized difference in the following passage, in which Bruce Fink explains the relationship between the unconscious and the symbolic order:

> Lacan teaches us to seek explanations in the symbolic order itself: the unconscious, he says, is the discourse of the Other, i.e., the unconscious consists of linguistic elements, phrases, expressions, commands, social and religious laws and conventions that are part of the culture at large as well as being part and parcel of every household. The unconscious is composed of the speech of the child's parents and family members, itself largely determined by the social/linguistic world around them. Explanations are thus, to Lacan's mind, to be sought in the symbolic order insofar as it has become the basis for an individual's unconscious.[60]

We may regard the signifierness of race and the force of racialized difference as embedded, for example, in those unconscious elements such as "social and religious laws and conventions that are part of the culture at large." If the signifierness of race and the force of racialized difference are of the symbolic order, and if the symbolic order precedes the human organism's entry into it, as Lacan writes, "This is the point of insemination for a symbolic order that preexists the infantile subject and in accordance with which he has to structure himself,"[61] then Spillers's remark that race traverses the individual before language and its differential laws take hold of the organism is right on point. This in turn must affect how we read the construction of the ego, since it shows that race is behind the ego and not in front with regard to a theory of how the ego is consolidated in the identification with a specular image.

I would like to conclude this chapter by completing the space of overlap I have been crafting between Lacanian psychoanalytic theory, social psychology, critical race and ethnicity studies theory, and rights discourse. I begin by turning to an intervention and series of questions asked by Judith Butler in her exchange with Slavoj Žižek and Ernesto Laclau in *Contingency, Hegemony,*

Universality in order to understand psychology's role in forging a particular understanding of the ethnic-racialized subject as a rights-bearing subject who is, as I have been arguing up to now in this book, entirely reducible to analyses of the relations of power and knowledge in a society. How might we intervene to posit a different kind of rights-bearing ethnic-racialized subject—one alive to the human dimension of language and its effects on the ethnic-racialized subject—and by way of that, fathom what a more psychoanalytically inflected rights discourse for minoritarian subjects might look like?

In a discussion of Hegel's *Philosophy of Right*, Butler writes,

> Although it does turn out in the *Philosophy of Right*, for instance, that the national state conditions every other sector of society, . . . it is equally the case that the legal apparatus of the state gains its efficacy and legitimacy only through being grounded in an extra-legal network of cultural values and norms. The dependency works both ways, and the question that I would like to pursue in closing my contribution is: how can the dependency of the legal dimension of the state on cultural forms be mobilized to counter the hegemony of the state itself?[62]

Butler here echoes the critical interventions staged by critical legal studies, whose theorists and scholars, in debunking the deterministic notion of the law as simply reflecting society, focused on legal discourse as "a crucial site for the production of ideology and the perpetuation of social power."[63] This chapter has attempted to explore how legal discourse becomes a site for the production of a certain ideology and perpetuation of power that is predicated on a particular understanding of the ethnic-racialized subject as a psychological subject who is only ego, who can be exhausted by explanations of its experience that draw solely from what can be gleaned from the social and cultural script. To this end, it asks a very similar question to the one Butler asks above, only we would need to understand the specific role of social psychology in this scenario, keeping in mind Kenneth Clark's somewhat foreboding remark, "The involvement of social scientists in the Brown decision set social science and the law on a common path. There can be no turning from it now."[64]

Butler asks, "How can the dependency of the legal dimension of the state on cultural forms be mobilized to counter the hegemony of the state itself?" Building on this question, how might we short-circuit the legal dimension's dependency on ego and social psychology in constructing the ethnic-racialized subject as a rights-bearing subject who experiences loss and trauma *and* the ethnic-racialized subject's dependency on the legal dimension to understand how it should live in this world and how it should articulate the meaning of its experiences of loss and trauma? Although I am somewhat tentatively attempting to bring some Lacanian ideas to bear on legal theory as it takes up with ethnic-racialized subjects, I do not see my project here as a concerted attempt at *applying* Lacanian theory to legal theory.[65]

Having said this, I do think that Lacan's theory of the subject in language and in particular how a certain loss of being is constitutive of subjectivity should perhaps figure in how critical race theory conceptualizes ethnic-racialized subjectivity in relation to rights discourse. In our assessment and study of legal measures that have attempted to secure fuller rights for ethnic-racialized subjects beginning around the time of the civil rights movement, we have to attend closely to how we have been instantiated in the law as particular types of psychological subjects since the extension of rights required that a psychological portraiture be created of ethnic-racialized subjects as psychological subjects experiencing social injury. That these legal measures are for the most part in response to, not always explicitly, the psychic pain that yields from being marked as a disprized subject whose human rights are always potentially under the threat of erasure means to me that we must bring to the discussion some engagement with psychoanalysis, but more specifically a Lacanian psychoanalytically-inflected theory of the ethnic-racialized rights-bearing subject as a subject in language, so that the losses that are constitutive of subjectivity can be read in concert with the losses that are attributable to real social and material inequities.

The problem is that we have entirely ceded all attempts at understanding the ethnic-racialized subject, its relationship to rights discourse, and its demands and needs for protective rights, more generally, to the interpretative framework of psychology. Because of the theory of the ego we find there, a theory that does not attend to the specifically human dimension which has precisely to do with the effects of language on the speaking human organism, we risk reproducing in the law an undersubjected notion of the ethnic-racialized subject and where the nature of this undersubjection is precisely what secures a racist discourse, insofar as it helps render the ethnic-racialized subject as a thoroughly calculable and exhaustible—that is, dead—subject.

If it is the case, as Pierre Schalg argues,[66] that for the most part contemporary legal theory inscribes and is subsequently plagued by the assumption of a legal subject who is rational, autonomous, potentially whole, and most definitely not split (again, ego psychology's subject), this is doubly problematic and troublesome for those subjects who are inscribed in the law as minoritized, for example, ethnic-racialized subjects for the reasons having to do with the double remove, or what Rey Chow calls the work of "extra categories" (such as Asian American, Latino, etc.). I might call it a double alienation. The ethnic-racialized subject should ideally be given the opportunity to make her peace with language as structure, to bear a certain loss of being, but she must also make her peace with an extracategory of humanness that attempts to seduce with its mirage of real and complete identity, a seduction whose wicked lure makes any attempt to address and bear the first difficult peace with language as structure seem irrelevant.

If indeed it has been the case that there has been no turning from the common path forged by social science and the law, and if, as I have been arguing, ego and social psychology are deeply responsible for the kind of ethnic-racialized subject inscribed in the law and recognized by the state, we might understand the supremely radical revolution that would be required to approximate what Foucault suggests:

> Maybe the target nowadays is not to discover what we are, but to refuse what we are. We have to imagine and build up what we could be to get rid of this kind of political "double bind," which is the simultaneous individualization and totalization of modern power structures. . . . The conclusion would be that the political, ethical, social, philosophical problem of our days is not to try to liberate us from the state and the type of individualization which is linked to the state. We have to promote new forms of subjectivity through the refusal of this kind of individuality which has been imposed on us for several centuries.[67]

In this well-worn passage that has served as a general inspiration for our inquiries, I am translating what Foucault calls the liberation "from the state" into my own project's terms, to mean liberation from the kinds of psychological subjectivities codified by the state and its legal apparatus.

Some contemporary positions address the efficacy of rights discourse and identity-based advocacy models where the rights dispensed and the identity in question concern ethnic-racialized subjects. I would like to begin with a brief characterization of the role played by "race" in debates between critical legal theory and critical race theory by turning to the introduction to *Critical Race Theory: The Key Writings That Formed the Movement*, by Kimberlé Crenshaw, Neil Gotanda, Gary Peller, and Kendall Thomas. The authors write, rights discourse held a social and transformative value in the context of racial subordination that transcended the narrower question of whether reliance on rights alone could bring about any determinate results. Race crits realized that the very notion of a subordinate people exercising rights was an important dimension of Black empowerment during the civil rights movement, significant not simply because of the occasional legal victories that were garnered, but because of the transformative dimension of African-Americans re-imagining themselves as full, rights-bearing citizens within the American political imagination.[68]

Consider the scope and domain of this transformation. Although intensely felt, this transformation is experienced at the level of the ego and, crucially, locates all problems and solutions from an ego- and social psychological perspective because an ego- and social psychological understanding for subjectivity is what informs the understanding in law and in the "political imagination" of a rights-bearing citizen. Legal scholar Patricia Williams also values the kind of transformation effected in black subjects as a result of the acquisition of rights: "For the historically disempowered, the conferring of rights is symbolic of all the denied aspects of their humanity: rights imply a respect that places one in the referential range of self and others, that elevates one's status from human body to social being. For blacks, then, the attainment of rights signifies the respectful behavior, the collective responsibility, properly owned by a society to one of its own."[69] She argues against those who would rather see the oppressed emphasize needs rather than rights—that this shift in focus amounts to nothing more than a word game. She writes, "The argument that rights are disutile, even harmful, trivializes this aspect of black experience specifically, as well as that of any person or group whose vulnerability has been truly protected by rights."[70]

The concept of "rights" condenses needs, demand, and desire in extremely complex ways, and I do not have the space to unpack that complexity here. I am not, to be clear, critiquing the concept of "rights" in such a way that leads to the dismissal of the history of legal victories that have secured basic human rights for ethnic-racialized subjects under the law. That would be preposterous. I'm asking after the possibility for a kind of ethnic-racialized subject construction alternative to the one that currently sits at the center of these debates. I am also wondering whether the rights secured, codified in law, do not then repeat a certain dynamic in the historical rendering of ethnic-racialized subjects that reduces them—the entire range for what can be attributed to the cause of their experience of loss in the social—to whatever can be gleaned from an analysis of the social and cultural forces that affect these subjects. Such an analysis imagines the best strategy as one that strengthens the ethnic-racialized ego—and thus, from a Lacanian perspective, alienates the subject—and that aspires to a full, complete, and transparent elucidation of the ethnic-racialized subject, the very same account that nurtures racist discourse. The hopelessly utopic charge here announces itself as an inquiry into how we might craft a discourse of rights that understands the ethnic-racialized subject as a subject in language who suffers the losses that are attributable to social and material inequities and the losses that are constitutive of subjectivity as such.

The concept of needs in a capitalist society is almost entirely subsumed under "consumer needs." Thus "needs" in the legal sense, as it relates to rights, contains within it capitalism's past, since, as Wendy Brown argues through Karl Marx, the emergence of rights discourse coincided with the "triumph of the bourgeoisie in post-feudal Europe, with capital's pressing need for the free circulation of land and labor."[71] I do not think it possible any longer to use the concept of needs as though it could be separated off from consumer needs at the beginning of the twenty-first century. What, in fact, could "needs" have meant before capitalism?

In *Seminar VII*, Lacan maintains that we are still immersed in "the foundation of the State, of the bourgeois State, which lays down the rules of a human organization founded on need and reason." However, "the two terms of reason and of need are insufficient to permit an understanding of the domain involved when it is a question of human self-realization. It is in the structure itself that we come up against a certain difficulty, which is nothing less than the function of desire."[72] As Tim Dean has argued, we live in a society that effectively confuses—advertising companies do this best—among its variously positioned consumers the concepts of desire and need, in effect, fooling us into thinking that desires can be fully exhausted and that we would actually want them completely satisfied.[73] With respect to the real effects laws that protect ethnic-racialized subjects through rights discourse have on these subjects, one might remark that a similar confusion occurs between needs and desire, but I would add that the notion of the ethnic-racialized subject's desire is withering away to such an extent that we won't know that there were two terms that became confused but will rather think that there was always just *needs*. In "The Direction of the Treatment and the Principles of Its Power,"

Lacan writes, "Desire is produced in the beyond of demand, because in linking the subject's life to its conditions, demand prunes it of need."[74] What indisputable right the oppressed should have is to desire beyond need and demand.

The editors of *Critical Race Theory* write, "We began to think of our project as uncovering how law was a constitutive element of race itself; in other words, how law constructed race."[75] My project agrees with this assessment, but I would extend the law's reach a bit more to suggest that it also constructs ethnic-racialized subjects and in this sense plays in concert with what Chow names "coercive mimeticism" by helping circulate scripts for what it means to be a proper, that is, *identifiable* ethnic-racialized subject worthy of protection. My position is like and unlike the critical legal theory position that, in the editors' words, is skeptical, even disdainful, of any political project organized around race. One could say that any concerted effort to focus on race risks reifying it. That's old news. I'm more concerned with addressing how any engagement with race by the legal apparatus produces a hollowed-out subject, an ego- and social psychological subject, how the legal apparatus encourages the sad imbecility of feeling compelled to resemble that which is ethnic-racialized and how it disseminates impoverished readings of ethnic-racialized subjectivity over scores of generations—its bullying effects—and how this affects social and political movements staged by ethnic-racialized subjects. It may be that justice for ethnic-racialized subjects in a white supremacist society can be achieved only on the condition of the exhaustive reduction of these subjects to social and cultural explications, to the utter exclusion of understanding them as subjects in language, subjects of the signifier, subjects with an unconscious.

The following quotation by the legal theorist and scholar Richard T. Ford echoes my own sentiment with respect to whether the law, dependent as it is upon an ego- and social psychological framework for theorizing the ethnic-racialized subject that partly reproduces the reductive and calculating logic of racism in the very act of protecting disprized subjects from discrimination, can ever guarantee social justice. Ford writes, "I don't think law is capable of resolving or banishing this contradiction. In that sense law is incapable of guaranteeing social justice. Social justice for people of color and for other stigmatized minorities will require a revolutionary cultural transformation, one more sweeping and more penetrating perhaps than any we've seen. Perhaps one more profound than any society can achieve while remaining the same society."[76] Allow me to speculate on what I think might set the ground work for a "cultural transformation." To begin with, we might react to Ford's claims by noting—with a rather broad stroke—that the revolutionary transformation that will have to be effected will necessitate a radically different theorization of ethnic-racialized subjectivity—one that willfully refuses to allow these questions to be ceded entirely to the social sciences, especially psychology.

In the essay, Ford develops a notion, "compelled performance" that sheds important light on how Chow's theory of "coercive mimeticism" plays out in the legal apparatus. He writes, "Contemporary multiculturalism worries a lot about 'silence,' 'absence,' and 'exclusion' but very little about 'speaking for others,' 'conscription,' and 'compelled performances.' If misrecognition is a serious harm, then we must be concerned that legal recognition may go wrong, misrecognizing already subordinated groups and codifying that misrecognition with the force of law and the intractability of stare decisis. We'd better be pretty sure that the traits the law recognizes are the right ones."[77] To translate this into the terms of my argument, I would say that since the law can recognize and codify only traits based on ego- and social psychological notions, a profound misrecognition is built into the law's ability to see and comprehend the human subject as a rights-bearing subject. I'm not suggesting that there is a pure line of vision that would perfectly capture the traits of the subject in some brilliant and exasperating explanation, as though that were even a desirable goal. To the contrary, I am suggesting that the law won't own up, can't own up to the fact of misrecognition, denying the Lacanian lesson taught in the mirror stage article, that "misrecognition" constitutes the very structure of subjectivity. But "misrecognition" may simply be the price to pay for "protective custody," as Ford explains: "Cultural or identity rights are a form of protective custody: the witness gets protection, sure. The violent accused is thwarted in his plot to silence the witness or exact revenge. But the price of protection is incarceration."[78]

Shifting gears somewhat abruptly in an effort to link Lacan's theory of the subject who precipitates in the Symbolic versus legal recognition's attempt to safeguard against the very appearance of the subject in deference to the masterful ego ensconced in the Imaginary, I want to transfer Ford's notion of "incarceration" into the context of the clinical setting, one gone awry, where the analyst erroneously engages the analysand only along the imaginary axis in Lacan's Schema L (figure 3), from one ego (a) to the other, counterpart ego (a'), in effect incarcerating the analysand in the Imaginary.

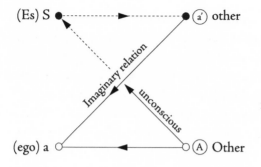

3 Dylan Evans, *Introductory Dictionary of Lacanian Psychoanalysis*. New York: Routledge, 1996.

The analyst failing to be fully imbued with the understanding of the difference between the Symbolic and Imaginary effectively prevents the appearance of the Subject (and the unconscious), represented by the S in the upper left-hand corner. What emerges from this in the legal context is an ego politics of the Imaginary. As I explained earlier in the book, the Imaginary in Lacan is dominated by rivalry and hostility. Moreover, to be trapped in the Imaginary, in addition to compelling a kind of social psychosis, as Teresa Brennan argues in *History after Lacan*, radically undermines the human subject's ability to make linkages and connections between historical events—undermines, in fact, the ability to historicize, period. Brennan writes,

> And as we shall see, when Lacan refers to making connections he says that the process is also one of "rewriting history." To avoid confusion, it should be emphasized at the outset that rewriting history, in the sense of making connections, is for Lacan an attribute of the symbolic. His theory of history is an account of how that symbolic activity, and a great deal else besides, is curtailed by the imaginary ego's era. In other words, Lacan is describing a specific era in history—that of the ego. But the era he is describing is one that curtails historical thinking.[79]

Making connections and links between historical events is threatened by the interference generated by the Imaginary in symbolic relations. In the 1950s, Lacan saw the reduction of this interference as the primary analytical goal. We might return now to ego psychology and its role in helping inscribe an image of ethnic-racialized subjectivity in the letter of the law. Again, Martin Bergmann reminds us that the ego psychologists who came to the United States seemed to forget history: "In spite of the emphasis on adaptation, the Hartmann group showed surprisingly little interest in the outside world. Hitler, World War II, and the Holocaust left no discernible impression on their thinking. . . . Denying what happened in Europe appears to have been a necessary defense for their adaptation to America."[80] The field of ego psychology established in the United States is not only a symptom of the ego's era, in whose language it speaks, it is also run through by a kind of turning away from making historical links and connections. The codification of an ego psychological understanding of ethnic-racialized subjectivity in the service, ostensibly, of crafting legal forms of social redress that correct upon a history of legal and extralegal systemic racist practices, oddly enough, in that very move, accomplishes a kind of refusal to engage this same history because of how it theorizes these subjects only along the Imaginary, thus rendering the project of making historical links and connections virtually impossible.

My argument in this chapter has insisted on the intimate historical links between ego psychology, social psychology, rights discourse, and the power of the state to weigh in on what ethnic-racialized difference and psychological trauma means, as predicated upon ego- and social psychological assumptions and tenets, and why I think we're tragically stuck since we are fueled by the false amplitudes that yield from being addressed as ego and only as ego. If it appears to be the case that legal and political recognition for disprized ethnic-racialized subjects in U.S. culture in the twenty-first century can be secured only to the extent that we be hallucinated as psychological subjects at risk according to the Imaginary politics of ego and social psychology, then employing a more Lacanian psychoanalytic reading of ethnic-racialized subjects as rights-bearing subjects in language would precipitate subjectivities that we probably wouldn't even recognize. Returning to some of Judith Butler's language in a passage quoted above, we might ask what price would have to be paid in order to bring to a definitive close the U.S. legal dimension's long-standing dependency on ego and social psychology in crafting visions of ethnic-racialized subjectivity and experience in a white supremacist society. Ford has a provisional answer to this question: "It may be that the price of providing our descendants with a world free of social stigma and oppression of identities such as race, a world we could be proud to call more just, is that they would not share our identities, that they would be our heirs but *not* our descendants."[81]

Latino Studies' *Barred Subject* and Lacan's *Border Subject*, or Why the Hysteric Speaks in *Spanglish*

I will be dead by 2050—I'm sure of it—which is a shame, since the ethnic-racialized nominatory term I currently come to rest under, *Latino*, promises to have finally scaled its way up the demographic ladder of the Americas, making U.S. Latinos, upward of 96 million and some say as high as 100 million by that time, constitute the third largest Latin American nation, behind Brazil and Mexico.[1] I've always wanted to be a part of a winning team, but *people like us,* my mother reminds me, *aren't winners, don't you forget it.* Even if I were still alive in 2050, I probably wouldn't figure in this new scenario anyway since the giddy triumphalism that mines the impending fact of these demographic swellings in order to proclaim that the future of the Americas will be Latino and that it will be broadcast in Spanglish strikes me as already leaving out its queer Latino contingency. The interpretative contortions necessary to think that Latinos in the United States can constitute a nation in the first place are not only a testament to the ways in which the idea of "nation" is significantly up for grabs these days. They are also a sign of the more general interpretative contortions that mark the contemporary discourse on *Latinidad.* Theorists of all stripes discuss Latinidad in relation to the future, the tense that appears to naturally elect itself for these discussions. But, as the reader will see in this chapter, this future-regarding tense is Janus-faced, because the broadcasting of the Latino future is intimately dependent upon what will have already been claimed back as evidence of a Hispanic past.

By 2050, I will have left behind a pile of bills, no children, a mangy, nasty cat, and a mangy, nasty dog. My mother made of equal parts iron and stone, will have outlived me and, saddled with the irritating responsibility of having to handle my funeral arrangements, will read my shabby last will and testament against the grain—I mean *really* against the grain. She will have had my head shrunken and placed in one of her home *altares,* somewhere between the sliver of Tía Cuca's femur bone—long story—and a one-legged ballerina figurine from the dollar store—I'm just guessing here with respect to the exact arrangement of the ephemera that crowd her two altares. I will have no descendants and no heirs, which is fine by me. I will take this to be a reflection of an ethical decision on my part to have refrained from burrowing my generative, tireless symptoms—the transgenerational queer Cuban exile melancholic phantoms that were so generously passed on and drilled into me, no questions asked—into the next generation. But I do teach. I'm a professor— that's what they tell me. This is where things get tricky. Even though I have not been at this very long, I see how my symptoms have managed to live on in some of my students, and not only my graduate students who are just looking to be haunted any chance they get.

I can't seem to stop thinking about Richard T. Ford's startling, deliciously macabre statement with which we concluded chapter 3—"It may be that the price of providing our descendants with a world free of social stigma and oppression of identities such as race, a world we could be proud to call more just, is that they would not share our identities, that they would be our heirs but *not* our descendants"[2]—and how it might be read as necessarily bearing on our responsibilities as educators in critical race and ethnicity studies knowledge projects like Latino studies, the critical knowledge project that will be the focus of this chapter. I take Ford's affecting remarks quite seriously and think that what he suggests as the price that might have to be paid for "providing our descendants with a world free of social stigma and oppression of identities such as race"—"that they would not share our identities" and that they would "be our heirs but *not* our descendants"—is one whose sum *we must begin calculating now* in the critical race and ethnicity studies knowledge projects in which we engage in the university structure.

Why do I hear in Ford's provocation a certain Lacanian resonance? Why does Ford's drama of transmission—that they "would not share our identities" —strike me as reflecting on the goal Lacan too had in mind with respect to what should, among other things, not be transmitted in psychoanalytic theory —the ongoing confusion of the ego and the subject, for one, that attended the misreading of Freud's second topography? We know that Lacan's introduction of two of his more referenced "mathemes," $\$ \lozenge D$, the formula for the drive, and $\$ \lozenge a$, the formula for fantasy that he worked out in his "graph of desire" in 1957, were attempts on his part to prevent his readers from grasping psychoanalytic concepts in an intuitive or Imaginary way as well as an attempt at securing a mode of scientific transmissibility of psychoanalytic concepts from one generation to the next.[3]

Lacan's interest in mathemes and formulas in the service of preventing intuitive and Imaginary and thus reductive understandings that might attend the transmission of psychoanalytic concepts can also be read as his attempt to prevent from happening with his work what happened with the reception of Freud's work in *The Ego and the Id*. Psychoanalysts grasped Freud's schemata of the ego, id, and superego in precisely the Imaginary and intuitive ways that resulted in a woeful misreading, according to Lacan, of what Freud was really up to in his introduction of the second topography. Lacan himself noted, "In the article on *The Ego and the Id* which is read so sloppily, *because attention is paid solely to the famous, idiotic schema, with the stages, the little bob, the irrelevancies, the gadget he brings in which he calls the super-ego,* what got into him, to come up with that, when he must have had other schemata."[4] One need only compare Freud's spongy-looking, cerebellum-inspired diagram for the ego and id (figure 4), whose general shape we see nowadays reproduced in ads depicting depression and the latest new magical pharmaceutical drug that will cure it, with Lacan's frightening insectlike carapace figure—the belly of a cockroach or the more appetizing, to some, belly of a soft-shell crab?—of the completed graph of desire (figure 5), to see the lengths Lacan went to prevent any intuitive or Imaginary grasp of his theory of the subject. Lacan's graph of desire makes you work, makes you calculate, makes you do the math, as it were. It absolutely prevents any intuitive or Imaginary grasp of the subject in language.

Lacan intended for his "algorithms" and "analogs" in the graph to "allow for a hundred and one different readings, a multiplicity that is acceptable as long as what is said about it remains grounded in its algebra. . . . They are not transcendent signifiers."[5] Lacan's graph of desire and the mathemes and formulas, more generally, not to mention Lacan's later interest in knot theory, string theory, and topological theory and his introduction of surfaces like the Möbius band, the torus, and the impossible-to-render surface of the cross-cap[6] are—if I can be allowed to continue reading Ford's provocation as homologous to Lacan's refusal to allow for an Imaginary and intuitive capture of psychoanalytic concepts—in the service of securing the transmission of knowledge to future generations. These generations "would not share our identities"—how we currently define, understand, and inhabit identity. They might claim us as critical heirs of some sort, but *not* as descendants.

For these reasons, Lacan's theory of subjectivity should serve us as a fruitful model for crafting a theory of the ethnic-racialized subject as a subject of the signifier. This theory might compel the transmission of knowledge in our work that gestures to the broad outlines of the shape of "a world free of social

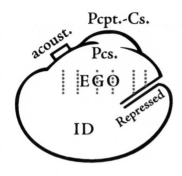

4 Reproduced from Sigmund Freud, *The Ego and the Id*. New York: W. W. Norton & Company, 1960.

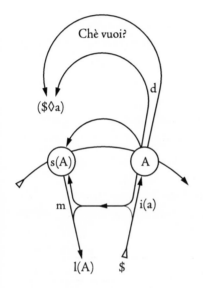

5 Reproduced from Jacques Lacan, "The Subversion of the Subject and the Dialectic of Desire." In *Écrits: A Selection* trans. Bruce Fink, New York: W. W. Norton & Company, 2002.

stigma and oppression of identities such as race." The price we'll have to pay, the very least we'll have to pay, is what some might feel is an untenable loss—the loss of a kind of *substance* with respect to an understanding of human subjectivity that we are challenged to risk losing if we embrace Lacan's definition of the human subject as "what slides in a chain of signifiers, whether he knows which signifier he is the effect of or not."[7] He also teaches, "What I call men, women, and children—means nothing qua prediscursive reality. Men, women, and children are signifiers."[8]

What Lacan allows us to transmit in a theory of ethnic-racialized subjectivity attuned to the effects of the signifier on the speaking human organism is not a kind of substance—the substance that Ford describes as clotted with the stigma and oppression associated with race—but a set of formulas that will "allow for a hundred and one different readings."[9] These formulas may allow us in any particular historical formation or epoch in human history to, if not recognize what passes as life according to the Imaginary ego's needs to discover, first and foremost, gestaltlike similarities or differences in an endless battle onto death, then determine the general speed and always just vacated location that defines the subject's fleeting movement in the chain of the signifier.

Years ago, I might have said that queer subjects are probably best outfitted for calculating the sum required to be paid in the critical project we might cobble together out of Ford's remarks where something is being transmitted, but with a difference because of queer subjects' fundamentally different relationship to questions of lineage, offspring, successors, scions, brood, the whole bit, but our increasingly mad, earnest dash to courthouses and legal offices around the United States to marry and fill out queer adoption papers has altered my assessment. That's another story for another place. But perhaps I'm exaggerating the radical nature of Ford's recommendation, since the difference between "heirs" and "descendants" might not be so great after all. Both still allow for the transmission of symptoms. Neither challenges the desire to pass on a symptom, only its pedigree. It's that desire to reproduce ourselves in our children, in our students, even in our pets, that cannot help but strike one as reminiscent of the ego's desire for an Imaginary reflection of sameness while caught in the very dialectic onto death between sameness and difference, unity and fragmentation. That Lacan might be seen to help us out here confirms what Tim Dean has argued, that Lacan can be read as a queer theorist avant la lettre[10] and, on my reading, as an antiracist theorist, as well.

It seems to me, returning for a moment to the argument at the end of chapter 2, that one of the most crucial aspects to our critical multiculturalist pedagogy must involve teaching our students the terms and conditions under which "faculty of color," entrusted to disseminate the knowledge of difference for the delectation of the masses in the context of contemporary university multiculturalism discourses, are, as Lacan accused the Jewish ego psychologists of doing, forced to reduce our function to our difference. We should be wary, at the same time, of passing on to them as a set of symptoms the kind of politics of resentment that yields from being reduced in this way, so that we might secure the possibility, returning to Ford's passage, that they "would not share our identities."

This should be read not as an attempt to do away with symptoms entirely and thus with hysterics—because we will never be without symptoms, which is to say without narrative, without history—but rather as an attempt to cultivate new symptoms, new hysterics, new hysterias, and thus new forms of knowledge and new ways of *getting off* on knowledge, if we understand, as I will explain below, that the hysteric undermines the master's discourse by producing new symptoms and by requiring the production of new knowledge, more knowledge, because the hysteric, as Bruce Fink reminds us, *gets off* on knowledge.[11] Insofar as Latino studies critique stands to bring some noise regarding how the production of knowledge is conceptualized in the university—the role of knowledge, its purpose, whom does it serve—I liken Latino studies critique to Lacan's "hysteric's discourse." Latino studies gets off on knowledge and gets off on undermining the master just as much as the hysteric does.

I want to hold on to what I still read as the queer theoretical charge animating Ford's articulation and attempt to think it through in the specific context of Latino studies critique in U.S. universities and how its theory of the border subject[12] calls up Lacan's theory of the barred subject. Latino studies' reliance upon a psychologistic approach to defining Latino subjectivity has obscured the ways in which the indeterminate and incalculable nature of *Latino* as an ethnic-racialized nominatory term overlaps with Lacanian theory's notion of the incalculable, indeterminate subject in language and has thus made us overlook the fact that we are not best served in Latino studies, not at all, by precipitating a subject as determined by ego and social psychology, since these forms of psychology are simply inadequate to the complex task at hand. Latino studies still entertains the mirage of a subject as potentially fully transparent to itself—especially, for example, in narratives about Latinos as a class formation. Do the assumptions of "resistance" and "contestation" that have historically attached to Latino studies knowledge projects require an ego- and social psychological subject? If so, why? Where precisely does the Latino subject resist? Why, one might ask, does the ego- and social psychological subject work against or behind the back, as it were, of Latino studies?

I intend for this chapter to serve readers as a general, if necessarily incomplete, account of some contemporary theoretical and critical drifts in Latino studies that is heavily informed by my idiosyncratic approach to these theoretical and critical drifts and that reflects the vexed conditions of my own training in Latino studies during a particular time at a major university when Chicano and Latino studies were being pressed into the unity of one. In what follows, I hope to show how the promise that many scholars and activists attach to Latino studies critique may be even deepened by highlighting what I think are some implicit spaces of critical overlap between it and Lacanian theory on topics such as the barred subject and the border subject, the question of how the temporality that is currently theorized as reflecting the radical processes of transformation we are referring to as the Latinization of the United States is virtually identical to the temporality of the signifying chain as Lacan theorizes it, and how Latino studies critique as it is thought to bear on business as usual in U.S. universities bears a striking resemblance to Lacan's explanation of the "hysteric's discourse."

RESETTING THE CLOCKS IN THE AMERICAS: LATINO FUTURITY,
RECOVERING THE HISPANIC PAST, AND REVERSIBLE TIME

In a recent commentary by Latino studies scholars Antonia Darder and Rodolfo Torres, we're reminded that Latinos now constitute the largest minority group in the United States and that the inevitable Latinization of the United States is something we can no longer deny:

> In January 2003, the U.S. Census Bureau estimated the Latino population to be 37 million, constituting 13% of the population. With these new numbers, Latinos have the dubious distinction of being the nation's largest minority group, surpassing African Americans with an estimated population of 36.2 million. In order to make sense of the current condition, we must remain attentive to the impact of such changes in the regions where large Latino populations reside. Along the same lines, we must also consider carefully what these changes mean to the local, national, and international political economy. *It is impossible to ignore what many are calling the "browning" or "Latinazation" of vast metropolitan areas in the U.S.*[13]

Does it matter that we don't precisely know what we mean or whom we mean to include or exclude when we invoke Latinidad or the process of Latinization? Mike Davis's response is, "Yet, if there is no reducible essence to latinidad—even in language or religion—it does not necessarily follow that there is no substance. . . . To be Latino in the United States is rather to participate in a unique process of cultural syncretism that may become a transformative template for the whole society."[14] Given the capaciousness of the term *Latino* right now, can we expect it to continue to swell and lengthen its sticky tendrils' reach, or will it shrink and become miserly in its old age, holding stubbornly to a ruthless, discerning door policy?

Not everyone is pleased as punch about the Latinization of the United States. It has driven the political scientist Samuel P. Huntington to profound, paranoid distraction. I might compare his grand paranoid delusions of an irredeemably split nation to Daniel Paul Schreber's poetic construction of a version of the end of the world, replete with capricious gods, in his *Memoirs of My Nervous Illness*, but that would be an insult to Dr. Schreber, even if we might still catch glimpses of Dr. Schreber's "rays of God," if not exactly penetrating Huntington's body as they did Dr. Schreber's, then penetrating his discourse, serving as the legitimating ground for lamentations on behalf of what is good and right and godly and truly American. In "The Hispanic Challenge," Huntington writes, "In this new era, the single most immediate and most serious challenge to America's traditional identity comes from the immense and continuing immigration from Latin America, especially from Mexico, and the fertility rates of these immigrants compared to black and white American natives."[15] Here, a supremely devious Latina woman emerges as the most dangerous, toxic figure. Huntington, in language reminiscent of the eugenics movement's characterization of Mexican American women and children in the 1920s, imbues her with awesome reproductive capacities that she mindlessly uses to litter the American landscapes with her brood and—more devastating still—through her brood then disseminate the Spanish tongue.

The essay cringes at this simultaneous bastard of a link forged between the seemingly random and riotous, trigger-happy reproduction of Latino children and the Spanish language that bleeds out in their tow, inspiring the sobering question, "Will the United States remain a country with a single national language and a core Anglo-Protestant culture? By ignoring this question, Americans acquiesce to their eventual transformation into two peoples with two cultures (Anglo and Hispanic) and two languages (English and Spanish.)"[16] Of course, the whole point about the Latinization of the United States is that we no longer need think in terms of two separate cultures; the "Spanglish ethos" that grounds the concept of what I call Latino futurity works to

115

erase that specious border.[17] To give credit where credit is due, at least Huntington has noticed the sea change, unlike many commentators, whether they be political theorists, economists, cultural theorists, or university administrators and presidents, either on the perennial left or on the right, who refuse to take note of this radical transformation. If Huntington's discourse can be described as paranoid, then the positions I reference in the preceding sentence can be characterized as structured by the disavowal of the fetishist: "I know very well that transformations are taking place, nonetheless I will act as though this is not happening."

The claims that make up the discourse of Latino futurity in Latino studies today do not only draw their dramatic charge from commentaries about the present and inevitable future demographic changes that we are already witnessing, but also draw their charge from a simultaneous empowering cultural claim that is being made on the past of the Americas. A mammoth project like *Recovering the U.S. Hispanic Literary Tradition*, now fifteen years old, has brilliantly remapped the American historical literary terrain. In the introduction to volume 1 (1993), Ramón A. Gutiérrez and Genaro M. Padilla remind the reader that the Hispanic presence in the United States can be traced back to at least 1513, the year in which Spanish explorers had already made their way to Florida; by 1540 they were in the Grand Canyon; by 1548, the San Diego Bay, and by 1598 they had already established outposts in New Mexico. All of this occurred a very good, long time before Jamestown was founded in 1607 and before the arrival of the Pilgrims at Plymouth in 1620.[18] This claim assumes immediate temporal interest for us when read in concert with the claims made regarding the Latino future. The historical narrative of Latino experience is simultaneously working its Janus-faced way backward and forward. Gutiérrez and Padilla write, "Our mission and goal is nothing less than to recover the Hispanic literary heritage of the United States, to document its regional and national diversity, to view from various perspectives and angles the matrix of power in which it was created, and to celebrate its hybridity, its intertextuality and its polyvocality."[19] By the time of volume 3's publication, the materials that will qualify as evidence of a Hispanic past have become incredibly diverse: "chronicles, travel narratives, diaries and testimonials; administrative, civil, military and ecclesiastical records; musical and theatrical compositions; prose, poetry and other rich primary sources constitute the earliest extant Spanish American literature in what is today the United States."[20] The editors of volume 3 make explicit how the *Recovery Project* links up with the contemporary claim on the future to which *Latino* is being pressed: "What then, does it mean to be Hispanic or Latino (a) in American society at the crossroads of the millennium? How have we persevered and created community in two world contexts? How indeed have we shaped the Americas? Like bridges to the past, the recovered heritage prepares the groundwork for understanding the complexity and totality of the U.S. Hispanic heritage."[21]

Moving to the scene of contemporary Latino theater, I want to read two mostly recent and successful pieces as providing the kind of past and future bookends that I think define the current discourse on Latino futurity. Nilo Cruz's *Anna in the Tropics*, which critics have made entirely too much racket about, gushing to the point of inanity, is set in the early-twentieth-century town of Ybor City, close to Tampa, Florida, and features a family of old-school Cuban cigar makers. This play constitutes one of the few literary attempts over the years to represent the Cuban *tampeño* community, who owned and worked in cigar factories and who also established a successful Spanish-language theater tradition, *teatro bufo*, between 1878 and 1895.[22] Cruz's play explores this community's links to the Cuban past through the figure of the *lector*—the person entrusted to read to the cigar workers as they rolled cigars in the factory. The *Anna* in the title of the play refers to *Anna Karenina*, the novel the lector reads to the workers. With the exception of one character, all of the Cuban workers in the play as well as the Cuban owners of the factory cannot bear to see the past—represented here as the nostalgia for the pre-modern mode of producing cigars, the tradition of the lector, and a pre-modern nineteenth-century "Spanish" colonial version of Cuba—give way to the future. The other bookend, this one future-oriented, is Puerto Rican playwright José Rivera's surreal, apocalyptic play *Marisol*. The end of the world is finally upon us, and our guide into the future world order is Marisol, a semi-*arrepentida*[23] young Puerto Rican advertising company employee from the Bronx.

On one end, there's Tolstoy's Anna wafted into a smoky Cuban cigar factory in early-twentieth-century Ybor City, Florida, through the tradition of the lector, and on the other end, there's Puerto Rican Marisol in twenty-first-century Manhattan. Where Marisol gets shot into the future like a cannonball and mostly loves it, the Cuban cigar factory owners and its Cuban workers are dragged into it, one might say, kicking and screaming.

In Cruz's play, the factory owner's wife, Ofelia, remarks of the push by another employee to modernize by using machines instead of humans to roll

117

cigars, "If working with machines means being modern then we're not interested in the modern world."[24] Juan Julian has to be literally murdered at the
end of the play to suggest even the hint of the possibility that the factory and
its employees might embrace the future and "go modern." At the end of
Rivera's play, a future-looking Marisol stands knee-deep in the rubble of a
bombed-out Manhattan and closes the play with the lines, "New ideas rip the
Heavens. New powers are created. New miracles are signed into law. It's the
first day of the new history . . . Oh God. What light. What possibilities. What
hope."[25] We will put to the side the significance we might make of the fact that
with little effort we could craft a somewhat reductive reading that explores
how these two plays reveal that the Cuban American's truck is with the past
tense forced into the future, and the Puerto Rican's with the future tense
bored and drilled from a bombed-out past.

Related to the question of the Latino claim on the future and the past of
the Americas, I want to consider more closely the pronouncement often
repeated these days, that the United States is being Latinized or Hispanicized. We are challenged to understand this idea of Hispanicization or
Latinization, as Darder and Torres remind us above, not only in terms of
cultural transformation, that the United States is increasingly becoming
marked by a kind of Latino savoir-faire but that this process of Latinization is
also affecting our landscapes and economies.

Davis, for example, echoing the views of many others, eloquently argues for
how Latino immigrants are breathing new life into dilapidated American
ghost towns, performing a virtual cardiopulmonary resuscitation on towns
that have been ignored.[26] To suggest this is, again, to comment on myriad
effects, effects registered on everything from the political economy to the daily,
often unremarked upon, mostly silent intake and consumption of cultural
resonances and influences. Where I live, in Durham, North Carolina, this has
certainly been the case, although I want to be fair to Durham here and say
that it's hardly a ghost town, even if it does sport its fair share of phantom
spaces bearing the traces of the racialized politics of city planning from the
not-too-distant segregated past of the South. Along a stretch of road called
Roxboro Avenue, one sees in 2007 a flurry of Latino commercial and cultural
activity where only five years earlier one saw barely any signs of life, outside of
the lazy-eyed, erratic blinking of traffic lights at the quiet, almost pointless
intersections.

One could say that verbs pass time into lives, that they pass time through speaking human subjects. If one were to understand the increasingly used *Hispanicization* and *Latinization* as verbs, this opens up some interesting areas of inquiry that sit somewhere between the study of grammar and psychoanalysis.[27] In a classic book of English grammar, Ralph Long writes, "Then tenses are the recognition that verbs give to the passage of time. The common mode makes more distinctions than any other. In the common mode four tenses have the time of speaking or writing as their center: the present, the present perfect, the present future, and the present future perfect, the last with some future time as a more immediate center. These are the tenses of proximity, or the present tenses."[28] To say that contemporary U.S. culture is being Hispanicized or Latinized is to suggest that these ethnic-racialized nominatory terms, used as verbs, are passing through us a particular kind of time, the present future tense, I would say, where some future time functions as its more immediate center. But what does this mean?

The obsessive take-up with the past in, for example, the project *Recovering the U.S. Hispanic Literary Heritage* is the obverse of the other ubiquitous discursive-qua-temporal tic in Latino cultural criticism—a claim on the future—and to say that the United States is being Latinized or Hispanicized is to effect the passing of a future tense through the lens of a recollected and archived past, approximating in the process the temporality of the signifying chain. I'd like to return to Colette Soler's characterization of Lacan's notion of "reversible time," a passage I called upon in my introduction. She writes,

> It is a twofold temporality between anticipation and retroaction; it is what Lacan called reversible time. In other words, the temporality of speech is a time shared between anticipation, while you are speaking, of the moment of conclusion (the moment at which you grasped what you meant), and retroaction, for when you arrive at the anticipated end point, all previous speech takes on new meaning, that is to say, new meaning emerges retroactively. It is a time split between *"I don't know yet"* and *"Oh yes, I already knew that."*[29]

Perhaps embedded in the claim that the United States is being Hispanicized and Latinized is another claim, that the United States is being Lacanized, since the temporality that charges the claims regarding what I call Latino futurity is the temporality of the signifying chain and, as I argued in the introduction, is also the temporality that figures in the inconclusive hailing of the Latino subject, a hailing whose certainty of belief is split between "I don't know yet" and "I already knew that."

Regarding the inconclusive and incoherent hailing of the Latino subject, we need here to engage a problematic that up to now I have left untouched regarding how we are to read the term *Latino* in relation to Rey Chow's notion of "coercive mimeticism,"

> the level at which the ethnic person is expected to come to resemble what is recognizably ethnic. . . . What makes this third kind of mimeticism intriguing is that the original that is supposed to be replicated is no longer the white man or his culture but rather an image, a stereotyped view of the ethnic: I am referring to the "Asianness," "Africanness," "Arabness," and other similar kinds of nativenesses with which ethnics in North American society, for instance, are often expected to conform.[30]

If we are arguing that there is a general terminological inconclusivity and incoherence that attends the ethnic-racialized nominatory term *Latino*, an inconclusivity that I have already likened to Lacan's incalculable subject in language, then this must certainly impact the extent to which *Latino* can be captured in the net of Chow's theory of "coercive mimeticism." If one listens to the stream of speech coursing through contemporary Latino studies scholarship regarding Latino hybridity, *mestizaje*, border subjectivity, and so on, it may appear that the Latino subject is offered an exemption of sorts, a get-out-of-jail-free card with respect to the prison houses of race and ethnicity, since it may be that she cannot be entirely captured by Chow's notion of the "ethnic" above. At the very least this is to say that the coercion might not work quite as seamlessly or effectively, because it's not clear what or whom is being hailed when the call issues, "Hey, you, Latino." The passage from Chow may already leave open a space or suggest a doubt given, the reader will note, that "Latino-ness" does not number among the other "kinds of nativenesses"—"Asianness," "Africanness," "Arabness"—in the list she provides.

Some Latino critics have worked in the space of this incoherence and inconclusivity in an effort to argue that the Latino subject represents the postraciological subject of the future. The Latino as postraciological subject is, I would argue, a key feature of the discourse I'm referring to as Latino futurity, insofar as "Latino" is seen to signify beyond ontologies of race and ethnicity. This, in turn, is seen to bode well for analyses of the social, cultural, and economic that do not corral, partition, and quarter-draw human subjects and groups according to the calculus of race and ethnicity.

In *Living in Spanglish*, an informative if at times glib commentary on contemporary Latinidad, Ed Morales writes, "Living in Spanglish is an informal invitation to those who seek to end the tyranny of black and white. . . . But Latino culture, particularly our Spanglish variation, has never been about choosing affiliation with a particular race—it is a space where multiple levels of identification are possible. It may be what Michel Foucault calls a hetero-topic space."[31] In a polemic addressing the political strategies that might be enacted by Latinos in Los Angeles, Victor Valle and Rudolfo Torres argue, "Counterdiscourse based upon inclusion, that renders hybridity, ambiguity, and border experience meaningful and empowering, and that makes racial-ized categories uninhabitable will provide a nation as heterodox as the United States the acid with which to deconstruct its prisons of race and gender. To the degree a discourse of cultural mestizaje is not touted as a new orthodoxy, we believe it represents the greatest contribution Latinos will yet make to the United States."[32] Morales, Valle, and Torres conceptualize the cultural and racial mestizaje of Latinos as forging an example of an existence beyond race as a category, a queering of race, if you will, from the site of Latino.

Might we not more productively read the term *Latino* as a term outside and beyond ontologies of race and ethnicity, not because it appears to point to the postraciological but rather because in fact it is a term that is first and foremost remarking on questions of temporality? *Latino* as a term is resignifying tem-porality, not just race and ethnicity; it should affect how we will tell the time and the history of the Americas in the future.[33] Might we think of these current forecasts and backward historical Janus-faced glances that mark the discourse of Latino futurity as I've described it as dabbling with the future anterior of a Lacanian analysis?

In "The Function and Field of Speech and Language in Psychoanalysis," Lacan writes, "In order to be recognized by the other, I proffer what was only in view of what will be. In order to find him, I call him by a name that he must assume or refuse in order to answer me. I identify myself in language, but only by losing myself in it as an object. What is realized in my history is neither the past definite as what was, since it is no more, nor even the perfect as what has been in what I am, but the future anterior as what I will have been, given what I am in a process of becoming."[34] I want us to hear in this last sentence the voice that animates accounts of Latino history today, the voice that animates the pronouncement in Latino studies that the United States is being Latin-ized. Aren't we hearing in the quality of the voice that animates the charge of Latino futurity today the same accent, timbre, and tonality we hear in the first-person voice that speaks in Lacan's passage above? What is being realized in Latino history and the Latinization of the United States is the future anterior of what the United States will have been, given what it is in the process of becoming. If it has been said of Lacan that in his writings and seminars he at times adopts the analysand's discourse,[35] choosing more often than not to impersonate the hysteric in order to achieve certain training effects in his listeners and readers, we might add that he manages in a curious way in the passage above to also impersonate Latinidad. Reading this passage from the vantage point of the beginning of the twenty-first century in the United States, knee-deep in the cultural, economic, and political transformations we are calling the Latinization of the United States, I would like to add "Latino" to those subject positions Lacan might be said to adopt in his writings.

LATINO SUBJECTS, INSIDE AND OUTSIDE OF LATINO STUDIES; LATINO STUDIES, INSIDE AND OUTSIDE OF LATINO SUBJECTS

Let's clarify a bit more what we mean by the Latino subject, since so far I appear to be using the term to designate real Latino constituencies living and luchando[36] in the world as well as a theoretically construed Latino subject, the subject imagined to sit at the center of academic oriented discourses, whose bordered, transnational experiences compel in it a kind of interpretative strategy, a "methodology of the oppressed"[37] that allows for the opening up of new vistas on cultural and political issues. In what follows here I would like to provide a kind of theoretical pedigree and palimpsest for how the Latino subject has been thought in relation to the tropes of resistance and contestation both as a real political constituency and as a theorized subjectivity in critical race and ethnicity studies and cultural studies, more generally. This is a selective list, obviously, that attempts in broad strokes to give readers not entirely familiar with these debates a sense of the theoretical, cultural, and political assumptions and operations underwriting the construction of a Latino subject installed in and around the center of the critical enterprise we are calling Latino studies.

In order to flesh this out, I will have to unpack *Latino's* and *Latino studies'* relation to *Chicano* and *Chicano studies*. This is a very difficult—on some levels impossible—task to fulfill. Generally, I think that we have not come close to resolving the unwieldy issues that come up in both conflictive and generative ways when we think Chicano studies and Latino studies together and apart. Chicano studies and Latino studies are not identical knowledge projects, and yet I find that increasingly theorists are forgetting this fact. But by pointing to something here that gets forgotten, what is one saying? What is it that one has in mind as having been forgotten?

Importantly, it seems as though we're not historicizing the blurring between them carefully enough, which means we don't know precisely (or approximately) from where—not to mention why—the pressure to combine them, to blur them originates. I have not given myself the time or space in this project to do justice to all of the specific historical questions that I need to consider regarding the emergence of each, their geographical specificity, and how this kind of specificity informs the vicissitudes of their critical trajectories, and of course how contemporary forms of diversity management and soft multiculturalism in U.S. universities often require that *Chicano* and *Latino* be combined in the service of a general bottom-line imperative. The pressure that pushes them toward a quantity of one is attributable to a myriad number of cultural and political and fiscal reasons inside and outside—to lean lazily on this fake distinction—the universities. In the useful collection *Critical Latin American and Latino Studies*, Chicano studies is rarely invoked in the discussions of contemporary Latino studies knowledge projects, and yet it's there all the same, unspoken, but present. It's not named because it—and this is my impression—is assumed to persist, like a silent letter, in the pronunciation of the newer formulation *Latino studies*.

123

In a recent interview, the Latino studies scholar Frances Aparicio notes that "the appearance of the 'border subject,' its theorizations by feminists such as Gloria Anzaldúa (1987), as well as by immigration historians, literary and cultural critics, and social scientists, has been the most important concept that Latino studies has contributed to cultural studies in the United States, Europe, and Latin America."[38] I quote this passage not to debate the general veracity of its claim—she's right, of course—but rather to think about what it means that she's attributed the theorization of the border subject to the field of Latino studies. Not too long ago—and perhaps still today—one might have said that the border subject as a concept hails from Chicano studies, not Latino studies. One might even have maintained this in a contestatory manner.

As some may know, Anzaldúa's work, especially, has served as the battleground for many debates regarding unacceptable appropriations of her theory of the border subject to describe experiences entirely alien to the specific geographical and cultural context that compelled the crafting of the concept in the first place. Generally either the critic is taken to task, or the field into which Anzaldúa's concept is being smuggled is taken to task, and the entire nefarious process is shown up for reflecting larger strategies of power and domination in the academy that reward some forms of mining and poaching while maintaining the raw generative material at the margins of acceptable academic discourse.[39] Should we now be engaging a new dialogue regarding how the border subject has been appropriated by Latino studies from Chicano studies? Who is responsible for nurturing this somewhat silent, unremarked-upon appropriation? I point to Aparicio's comment in order to gesture to some questions that I won't be able to resolve fully here. However, the reader should know that they hover in the background to a chapter that announced itself as addressing the border subject and as ostensibly focused on Latino studies.

The Latino subject, as a subject construction for a theoretical strategy of resistance, has been precipitated in Latino studies critique. Let's begin by texturing the notion of resistance as it has been deployed vis-à-vis Chicano and Latino subjectivity and Chicano and Latino cultural production. In a now classic text, *Chicano Narrative: The Dialectics of Difference*, Ramón Saldívar has famously written, "As resistant ideological forces in their own right, their function is to shape modes of perception in order to effect new ways of interpreting social reality and to produce in turn a general social, spiritual, and literary revaluation of values."[40] I quote this passage because I think it captures a familiar characterization of the Chicano subject and Chicano cultural production as resistant. I don't want to contest whether or not this is true, but I do want to consider how Chow's argument now compels us to approach our valuations of resistance, protest, and contestation in Chicano studies and Latino studies in the twenty-first century differently. We need to know how much Chicano and Latino resistance really *resists* these days.

Chow understands two basic options yielding from the modern construction and assignation of "ethnicity": in the first one, "the essence of humanity is always already there," inscribed in customs and literary and cultural representations, and in the second one, ethnicity is defined in terms of "opposition and resistance." What she calls "the essence of humanity," I understand as her manner of referencing that reading of the ethnic-racialized subject as fully transparent to itself and to others, as entirely exhausted in language. The second option announced by Chow should serve the function of a red flag of sorts for those working in Latino studies and Chicano studies, since opposition and resistance have been the fields' preferred modus operandi. Chow goes on to ask how the ethnic subject might go beyond the constricting and instantiating terms of this definition of subjectivity: "What ideological forces are there, if any, that would enable the individual representative of an ethnic minority to move beyond, or believe she could ever move beyond, the macro sociological structures that have already mapped out her existence—such as, for instance, forces that allow her to think of herself as a 'subject' with a voice, as a human person? What makes it possible for her to imagine that her resistance-performance is her ultimate salvation, her key to universal humanity, in the first place?"[41] So far in my project I have tried to offer what I think might serve as provisional answers to Chow's questions. My answers require that we lace our critical race and ethnicity studies inquiries with a Lacanian theoretical understanding of the Latino subject as a subject of the signifier to understand where the Latino subject resists and where it doesn't, to understand that language as structure determines the subject but does not exhaust it, which can be read as meaning that the subject resists at the very level of language. Joan Copjec explains, "In language and yet more than language, the subject is a cause for which no signifier can account. Not because she transcends the signifier but because she inhabits it as limit."[42]

125

What kind of cognitive, intellectual acuity is Latino studies' "border subject" thought to possess that she then deploys as a critical and interpretative practice in making sense of the world? I will use as a frame for the three theorists I engage below the resonant concept of "border gnosis" developed by Walter Mignolo: "Border gnosis/gnoseology and border thinking will be used interchangeably to characterize a powerful and emergent gnoseology, absorbing and displacing hegemonic forms of knowledge into the perspective of the subaltern. This is not a new form of syncretism or hybridity, but an intense battlefield in the long history of colonial subalternization of knowledge and legitimation of the colonial difference."[43] Again, I am being selective here as I isolate three broadly conceived practices and strategies that are roughly cognitive in nature and boldly transformative in their design and desire and that dwell ferociously in the trenches of the battlefield Mignolo describes above: Tomás Ybarra-Frausto's "rascuache aesthetic"; Chela Sandoval's "oppositional consciousness"; and José Estéban Muñoz's "disidentificatory practices." I choose these three particular theorists because of how they appear caught in a species of politicized call and response with each other and how when considered together from a distance—like the necessary distance a viewer needs to effect in order to take in the complete image of a painting in the pointillist tradition—appear to precipitate what I consider to be the contemporary figure of the politicized Latino subject installed at the center of the discourse of *Latino futurity*. These three strategies, along with Anzaldúa's "border subject," constitute a palimpsest of sorts of the contemporary notion of the resistant, oppositional Latino subject in Latino studies critique that is queer, third world feminist and, for the most part, working class.

Ybarra-Frausto's famous "Rasquachismo: A Chicano Sensibility" argues for a unique sensibility guided by the improvisational that emerges from the demands of survival. In describing a home altare as the object that perfectly captures the sensibility he is theorizing, he writes, "The rasquache inclination piles pattern on pattern, filling all available space with bold display. . . . The composite organization has a sort of wild abandon yet is subtly controlled with precise repetitions, replications, and oppositional orders of colors, patterns and designs."[44] The strategies used to craft the altares are simply illustrative of the more general strategies used to craft a life-world in the barrio: "The visual distinctiveness of the barrio unites the improvisational attitude of making do with what's at hand to a traditional and highly evolved decorative sense. . . . In yards and porches, for example, traditional items like religious shrines (capillas) and pottery mingle with objects from mass culture, such as pink flamingos of plaster animal statuary. Throughout, there is a profusion of textures and colors and a jumble of things."[45]

As I move on to the Chicana feminist theorist Chela Sandoval's equally famous and groundbreaking essay, also published in 1991, "U.S. Third World Feminism: The Theory and Method of Oppositional Consciousness in the Postmodern World," keep in mind the focus in the passages above on "improvisation" and the species of reading practice that must entertain multiple levels and profusions of phenomena as the backdrop to the "consciousness" that Sandoval describes. I also want to read Sandoval's theory of "consciousness" as illustrating the very cognitive aesthetic practices outlined by Ybarra-Frausto. In the first paragraph of her essay, Sandoval links the "differential consciousness" that will be the rich outcome of her theory to a historical consciousness that emerges from the practices of U.S. third world feminism. She defines her idea of "differential consciousness" as representing the strategy of another form of oppositional ideology that functions on an altogether different register. Its power can be thought of as mobile—not nomadic but rather cinematographic: a kinetic motion that maneuvers, poetically transfigures, and orchestrates while demanding alienation, perversion, and reformation in both spectators and practitioners. Differential consciousness is the expression of the new subject position called for by Althusser—it permits functioning within yet beyond the demands of dominant ideology. This differential form of oppositional consciousness has been enacted in the practice of U.S. third world feminism since the 1960s.[46]

As though taking its direct cue from Sandoval's gesture to the cinematographic, the Latino studies queer theorist José Estéban Muñoz theorizes "disidentification" in relation to the visual register of filmic and performance texts. Centrally concerned with the politics of U.S. queers of color, Muñoz echoes Ybarra-Frausto's and Sandoval's focus on mobility and deft maneuvering as he crafts a critical practice that labors within and along the meandering currents of power: "Rather, disidentification is a strategy that works on and against dominant ideology. Instead of buckling under the pressures of dominant ideology (identification, assimilation) or attempting to break free of its inescapable sphere (counteridentification, utopianism), this 'working on and against' is a strategy that tries to transform a cultural logic from within."[47] Read together, these three strategies emerge from working class Chicano aesthetic sensibilities, U.S. third world feminist politics, and the politics of U.S. queers of color.

Powerful and hugely influential as these theories have been and continue to be for scholars working inside and outside Latino studies and Chicano studies, a somewhat negligible but not unremarkable problematic persists in all three of them. This has to do with the failure to theorize opposition to—the working on and against—the cultural logic of ego and social psychology that serves as the discursive psychologistic background for how the subject operating in these passages is being theorized. I don't think the lack of engagement with a more psychoanalytic reading of the subject necessarily challenges in any significant way the nature of the powerful claims being made in the passages above. However, deploying a more Lacanian psychoanalytic reading of the subject in language would give us an additional way of understanding what is lost and gained in working within and against a cultural logic. In our example, we attempt to isolate a cultural logic whose racism is internally guided by a

127

psychologistic principle that attempts to instantiate the ethnic-racialized subject as potentially socially and culturally intelligible on the condition that the subject is conflated with the ego so that she might be fully calculated, controlled, and managed in the distorting medium of language.

I would like to extend my guarded and respectful critique of these three theorists' reliance on ego- and social psychological notions of the subject to make a similar point regarding how Latino studies' "border subject" and the experience of Nepantla have been traditionally conceptualized. Speaking to the experience of Nepantla as Latino studies scholars have mined this concept, Aparicio writes,

> Latino scholars have emphasized what is called Nepantla in Nahuatl: that experience of living between two cultures, not always as victims but never completely free as cultural agents or historical subjects. . . . Latino academic production has tried to offer an alternative perspective in which Latinos, as border subjects, are not a homogeneous group, but rather a multiple entity whose ideologies are being constantly negotiated, tolerating hegemonic forces and dominant structures as well as resisting and opposing them, while introducing social changes at different levels and producing new and complex positionalities for the cultural subject.[48]

We need to mine the metaphorical potentialities in the concept of Nepantla more deeply. It suggests that prior to living between two cultures, the transmovement of the human subject is reflected in its fleeting and vanishing movement between two or more signifiers. Lacan could be said to have Nepantla in mind when he remarks that "the subject is nothing other than what slides in a chain of signifiers, whether he knows which signifier he is the effect of or not. That effect—the subject—is the intermediary effect between what characterizes a signifier and another signifier, namely, the fact that each of them, each of them is an element."[49]

With respect to Anzaldúa's theory of the border subject, we should recall that whatever split, whatever breach or division implied by the term *border* is ultimately explained according to social, cultural, and historical determinants. Even when Anzaldúa writes in the preface of the "psychological borderlands" and remarks later that she "knows things older than Freud,"[50] she is still operating a theory of the border subject that replicates an ego- and social psychological conception of human subjectivity. The privative and generative effects of language do not figure here. Even in the service of complicating the notion of duality that theoretically attaches to ideas of wholeness and unity by adding a third element, she still shows herself as committed, in the end, to synthesis: "In attempting to work out a synthesis, the self has added a third element which is greater than the sum of its severed parts."[51] Although she eloquently discusses how the Chicana/o subject is traversed and bordered by different languages,[52] this subject is never bordered or divided as a result of the effects of language as structure on the speaking human organism. We need to be able to reference the effects of language that cross and split the Latino speaking subject before we can articulate in language the general coordinates of the geographical border space in which she dwells.

What we need to bring to the Latino studies concept of the border subject is a more Lacanian, psychoanalytic-language-based account, one that is in some ways already implicit in the concept of the border subject. This will allow us to understand the bordering and splitting of the subject as not only predominantly social, cultural, and historical in its origins and effects but as additionally linguistic and psychical. In short, by insisting that the border subject is a subject in language, we would deepen further the overall complexity and profundity of our explanations for what is suffered as lost, since we would be challenged to read for both the losses that constitute subjectivity as such as well as those losses attributable to the unequal distribution of social and material resources.

129

Before drawing out the homologous critical operations between contemporary Latino studies critique as theorists conceptualize it and Lacan's ideas on the "hysteric's discourse," I want to give readers a sense for how Latino studies is imagined as constituting an important locus of critique in contemporary U.S. universities that is fast disappearing. Mignolo identifies the critical potential of Latino studies by drawing out the important epistemological differences between it and Latin American studies knowledge projects with respect to how each does or does not reproduce the oppressive, colonial dynamics of knower and known: "While Latin American (and area) studies are part of the larger paradigm of the modern/colonial world, together with Occidentalism and Orientalism, Latino studies are part of the paradigm shift today identified as ethnic studies, which is precisely not the location of the knower but the location of the known. Latino studies, in other words, is accomplishing the formidable task of turning the place of the known into the location of the knower."[53] We'll note later that the hysteric's attempts to undermine the master as Lacan explains it can also be understood as an attempt at reversing the places of knower and known by, if not exactly usurping the place of the knower, making the knower's claim to knowledge so precarious that the knower herself can't even buy into her own claims as master of knowledge.

One can't help but love the kind of charge in Mignolo's passage, but I fear Mignolo's claim has not quite realized itself, which is certainly not to say that it can't. At the same time, I maintain that Latino studies will not realize its full potential unless it learns to strip itself of all psychologistic thinking on human subjectivity. Juan Poblete echoes Mignolo's claims and dramatizes Latino studies' potential critical impact, but, in contrast to Mignolo, points to how the field exceeds ethnic studies as it is traditionally configured:

> Latino studies seems to provide the institutional basis for in-depth understanding of the processes that have normally been resisted or have escaped the radar of nation-centered paradigms, be those ethnic or area studies–based. As a field in the borders of ethnic and area studies, Latino studies mines the analytical space where borders themselves can be investigated and with them all kinds of transnational, translingual, and transcultural phenomena. Thus Latino studies can, in this view, perform the very healthy job of criticizing the nation-centered limitations of area and ethnic paradigms.[54]

These are, to say the least, some very heady and radical goals that have been identified as integral to Latino studies critique.

I would like to add my own voice to Mignolo's and Poblete's regarding how to assess the potential of Latino studies critique to intervene in how business as usual is conducted in the university. However, in my effort to continue mining the spaces of productive overlap between Latino studies and Lacanian theory or, stated somewhat differently, of articulating Lacanian psychoanalysis with Latino politics, I would like to draw out the similarities between Latino studies' critique of power in the university and the hysteric's critique of the master's power as Lacan describes it in his formulation of the hysteric's discourse.[55]

We can characterize the different kinds of institutional relationships Latino studies may have with the university in terms of what Lacan understands as the four possible types of social bond among human speaking subjects that he first begins to develop as the "four discourses" in *Seminar XVII* in 1969–70.[56] Lacan develops these discourses during a time of cultural and political unrest and contestation in France and the United States; the events surrounding May 1968 in France, generally, and the student strikes are certainly on Lacan's mind during this time, and they no doubt serve as the background for the invention and further elaboration of these four formulas in his later seminars.[57]

Commenting on Lacan's 1969 lecture to students at the university at Vincennes, Copjec writes, "he comes fresh from his 1969 seminar *L'envers de la psychanalyse*, on the four discursive relations to knowledge. . . . To counter the romantic assumption that all institutions are necessarily confining and the voluntarist notion that the imagination would be free outside them, Lacan warns that the structures are not merely imposed on otherwise freely existing practices. All practices are always part of some institutional structure beyond which no practice, no critique, no speech is possible."[58] The students were hardly receptive to Lacan's position. A couple of student interventions seemed to really crystallize the students' general dismissal of Lacan and his message: "Up there to the right of God, that's Lacan" and "What is a Master? It's Lacan."[59] These years happen to also mark the height of the Chicano student movement in the United States, a movement that led to the establishment of the first Chicano studies programs and without which we would probably have no Latino studies programs today. As we move through this discussion, we would do well to try to understand how Latino studies programs respond—given the university politics of soft multiculturalism and diversity management within which they must operate—to thorny institutional issues underlined in Copjec's passage above. How do Latino studies programs critique and/or endorse the "romantic assumption that all institutions are necessarily confining"? Does Latino studies obscure or make explicit the fact that "practices are always part of some institutional structure beyond which no practice, no critique, no speech is possible"?

The four discourses developed by Lacan include the master's discourse, the university's discourse, the hysteric's discourse, and the analyst's discourse.[60] For clarification, given the names of these discourses and what we generally think these names signify, this does not mean that a psychoanalyst functions or will automatically adopt the analyst's discourse, or the hysteric subject the hysteric's discourse, or the university the university's discourse, and so on. The analyst may operate within the hysteric's discourse, the university within the master's discourse, the hysteric within the analyst's discourse, and so forth. As Fink explains, "A particular discourse facilitates certain things and hinders others, allows one to see certain things while blinding one to others."[61] In my examples, given the nature of the critique Latino studies can unleash in the university, it should ideally come to be represented by the "hysteric's discourse," as I will explain shortly. Given the ways in which the university these days puts Latino studies (and other ethnicity and race-based studies programs) to work on its behalf, in such a way as to neutralize if not cancel the force of its critique, I think the university currently functions within the master's discourse.

Earlier I argued that Lacan's impersonation of the hysteric in his adoption of the analysand's discourse can also be read, with a slight rotation, as Lacan's impersonation of the twenty-first-century Latino subject, through what I interpret as his curious adoption of the contemporary discourse of Latino futurity in the description of temporality and history he offers in "The Function and Field of Speech and Language in Psychoanalysis." A more explicit connection between Lacanian theory and Latino studies might be forged, as I've already suggested, as a result of how Lacan's barred or split subject calls up Latino studies' border subject and vice versa, and where the hysteric's discourse functions as the critical hinge that attaches one to the other. If it is true that Lacan is most often heard as speaking with a hysteric's accent in his writings and seminars, then it must be that the analysand's discourse we claim to hear in his voice today when we read him in the context of the Latinization of the United States betrays a kind of English in translation that's been broken by Spanish because the twenty-first-century hysteric, whose accent he liberally borrows, will most likely claim Spanglish as her first language.

Distributed throughout Lacan's four discourses are four mathemes, S_1, S_2, a, and $\$$, and four positions that can be filled by each of the mathemes. S_1 refers to the master signifier; S_2 represents knowledge; a, or object a, can stand for what persists as a remainder after the symbolization process, representing the loss in the register of the Real attributed to the effects of language as structure on the human organism; $\$$ represents the barred subject, the speaking subject inscribed in language. The four positions available to be filled can be represented as in figure 6. The role that a particular matheme—S_1, S_2, a, and $\$$—will come to play will be determined by the position—agent, other, product/loss, and truth—it is made to occupy in the formula.

Looking at the formula for the master's discourse in figure 7, we note that the master is situated in the upper left-hand corner, S_1 representing the signifier that needs no alibi or justification for its manipulation of power; it just is because it says it is. Again, for the purposes of reflecting early-twenty-

$$\frac{\text{agent}}{\text{truth}} \xrightarrow{} \frac{\text{other}}{\text{product/loss}}$$

6   Reproduced from Bruce Fink, *The Lacanian Subject: Between Language and Jouissance.* Princeton, N.J.: Princeton University Press, 1995.

first-century articulations and elaborations of multiculturalism in North American universities and illustrating the university's role in helping perpetuate and deepen the alienated labors of ethnic resemblance that Chow names "coercive mimeticism," I identify the university as speaking the master's discourse in relation to Latino studies as a field, which is why I choose to represent the university with the matheme S_1.

Directly across its way is S_2, representing the body of knowledge that S_1, the university, puts to work. In my example, I have two laboring bodies in mind: the body of knowledge called Latino studies and the instrumentalized body of the Latino studies professor. The Latino studies laborer produces something in the way of knowledge, but the master is unconcerned with the nature of this knowledge. The production of this knowledge doesn't affect how business as usual is conducted. It is not allowed to have transformative potential. The only requirement is that the work keeps getting done and that the worker keep doing it. Let's think of the requirement as that of the ongoing circulation of difference just for difference's sake or, more specifically, as the packaging of Latino cultural difference in the service of teaching about and codifying so-called Latino cultural difference for the delectation of the masses. That "difference" is represented by the *a* in the lower right-hand corner; this is the surplus produced by the Latino studies professor's labor in the context of contemporary university multiculturalism and diversity rationales.[62] The university-qua-master appropriates this surplus.

Generally speaking, the master's discourse is primarily concerned with giving the appearance of having not been submitted to symbolic castration— not having been subjected to language as structure like the other human subjects laboring in language. Translated into the terms of my example, the university must ensure that it is not transformed or challenged in any substantive way by a broadly conceived and far-ranging Latino studies critique of knowledge production. The split or crack in the master's discourse—the

133

Discourse of the master

$$\frac{S_1}{\$} \longrightarrow \frac{S_2}{a}$$

7   Reproduced from Bruce Fink, *The Lacanian Subject: Between Language and Jouissance.*
Princeton, N.J.: Princeton University Press, 1995.

revelation through Latino studies critique of the motives for the university's production and appropriation of difference as knowledge for prestige (the ego's prestige) and financial profit—is represented by $, which occupies the place of truth in the lower left-hand corner.

In the hysteric's discourse (figure 8), the upper left-hand corner is occupied by $, the split or barred subject who interrogates and puts S_1, the master signifier, to the test, calling it into question, making it prove that it has what it takes.

Where both the master's and university's discourses try to cover over a basic lack that blisters any attempt at complete knowledge that is fully transparent to itself, the hysteric's discourse keeps pointing to the breach, to the hole in the discourse that wants to be free of lack and division. "The hysteric maintains the primacy of subjective division, the contradiction between conscious and un-conscious, and thus the conflictual, or self-contradictory, nature of desire itself."[63] The cultural and political critique deployed in Latino studies possesses the ability to hystericize university discourse. This hystericization of university discourse would ideally necessitate an intensive study—and reorganization—of the politics of knowledge production in the university and the uses to which we think we are to put those knowledges. Darder and Torres write, "Latino Studies is forthrightly directed toward promoting critical scholarship—schol-arly work carried out with the expressed intent of challenging the current nature of economic inequality and social oppression."[64]

In my example of the hysteric's discourse, I situate Latino studies in the position of agent, represented by $, referring to both the barred subject and the border subject. Latino studies interrogates the university represented by S_1, the master signifier, putting it to the test and calling it into question, working to, as Mignolo writes above, turn "the place of the known into the location of the knower." The hysteric "gets off on knowledge" because "knowl-

Discourse of the hysteric

$$\frac{\$}{a} \longrightarrow \frac{S_1}{S_2}$$

8   Reproduced from Bruce Fink, *The Lacanian Subject: Between Language and Jouissance.*
    Princeton, N.J.: Princeton University Press, 1995.

edge is perhaps eroticized to a greater extent in the 'hysteric's discourse' than elsewhere."[65] The product that yields from Latino studies' interrogation of the university-qua-master, is a form of knowledge, S_2—a critical literacy and reading practice drawing on Ybarra-Frausto's "rasquache aesthetic," Sandoval's "oppositional consciousness," and Muñoz's "disidentification"—that sheds light on the politics of knowledge production and, more broadly, the uses we think are to be made of the knowledge produced in the university. The barred and border subject of Latino studies also reminds the university that ethnic-racialized subjectivity cannot be wrestled down into a set of calculable proofs   135 and memorizable experiences to be bought and sold in the market of difference under the veil of diversity and multiculturalism.

This is to say, once again and with a bit more force and conviction, that Chow's disciplinary notion of "coercive mimeticism" does not necessarily capture *Latino* and *Latinidad* in its net given the generative and ongoing confusion that undermines all attempts to exhaustively understand who or what *Latino* and *Latinidad* really are. Enrolling *Latino* and *Latinidad* in the service of teaching difference in the university will always invite a bit of "ethnic-racialized trouble"—or at least it should—because the questions the terms pose are not ontological ones but performative and temporal ones. It is not about what *Latino* and *Latinidad* are but about what Latino and Latinidad *do* and the time that it takes to do it, where time is measured according to the pulse and beat of the future perfect tense that defines the unfolding of historical time we are calling the Latinization of the United States.

Still, the pedagogical task of providing proper, specific versions of the various histories that get crowded under the umbrella *Latino* is an important and widely promoted strategy in contemporary Latino studies. But what should the Latino student actually know about what makes up a "Latino" in this moment of "coercive mimeticism" and "compelled performance," and how might our teaching reflect Ford's idea that "the price of providing our descendants with a world free of social stigma and oppression of identities such as race, a world we could be proud to call more just, is that they would not share our identities, that they would be our heirs but *not* our descendants?"[66] Suzanne Oboler argues that the affirmation of Latinidad among students on college campuses today appears to proceed apace with an ahistorical, even dehistoricizing analytics and is having a negative impact on Latino students:

> Instead of historical knowledge which could ground the meaning of the umbrella term under which the students "are supposed to" rally, the affirmation of Latinismo ultimately ends up becoming the cause for dissent. For it is based on abstract, stereotyped, and certainly ahistorical and homogenizing definitions of what "a Hispanic" actually is (or is supposed to be) culturally and politically, as well as in looks, social class, status, behavior and beliefs. The absence of information about their respective groups' histories, which could help students to better appreciate the historical, socio-cultural and national specificities involved, has lead to a search for symbols of unity grounded in a stereotyped version of the ideal Latino or Latina, against which the new generation seems to be both defining and measuring itself.[67]

What compels the angst made of ambivalence and confusion that Oboler comments upon later in her essay among Latinos is the effect registered by a label that over the last thirty years or so has effectively erased the historically varied texture of Latino communities and groups in academic and popular narratives about Latinos. It has literally cultivated ignorance among the students at the same time that it has served to swell the ranks for who can be counted as Latino. Oboler continues, "In this context, we have to ask: to what extent are we seeing on campuses today, not the affirmation of identity, the strengthening of the self, but rather its opposite?"[68]

I propose that we think a bit more critically regarding the investment in the "strengthening of the self" that figures in the passage above. Again, this seems to reflect the fact that we have developed no language to talk about ethnic-racialized identity that is not entirely ego- and social psychological and that does not imagine a strong ego, a strengthened "self," and thus a more alienated subject as the desired outcome in a racist, white supremacist world. This invites precisely what Ford warns against: passing on social identities clotted with the stigma that will have been determined through the calculus of race.

Why is it that what we need to be doing, and are not, regards this general therapeutic and conceptual capitulation to the ego? I have listened carefully to my students' speech but have arrived at slightly different conclusions than Oboler as to what it may be that is being communicated by them. I would claim that the students' responses are telling us that they are partly choking on this edict of affirming an identity because they understand the grim reality that Chow names "coercive mimeticism" and Ford names "compelled performance." Are these Latino students speaking the hysteric's discourse? And are we speaking only the university's discourse? Are these students symptomatically acting out the effects of a certain kind of psychologistic state language on the body of the ethnic-racialized subject? By ignoring a more psychoanalytic approach, are we condemned to continue not hearing the full range of losses (and the new strategies that are trying to emerge in response to those losses) as they are articulated in our Latino students' speech? Are we refusing them the right to choose *not* to be our descendants?

Although we can say that Latino studies may be operated in such a way as to force a hystericization of the university discourse, we should be clear that this attempt at hystericization will work effectively only to the extent that Latino studies also learns to challenge the master in her attempts to come off as a subject not divided in language and not just in her attempts to qualify as master by virtue of her having hoarded all of the economic and political goods for herself. To this end, Latino studies must borrow more literally and liberally from the hysteric's arsenal and Lacan's more language-based analyses to confront the master with her basic and constitutive division in language, a division she tries to cover over by mastering the social field through oppressive practices that help perpetuate and maintain economic inequalities.

To the degree that Latino studies can learn to draw on the critical labors performed by both the barred and the border subject, it will be poised to craft a psychoanalytic-historical-materialist reading practice capable of commenting, in the richest ways possible, on the nature of those losses that are attributable to the unequal distribution of social and material resources and those losses, constitutive of subjectivity, that are attributable to the effects of language as structure on the speaking human organism. Latino studies must teach the university not Latino cultural difference, per se, but rather how to speak, read, and write in Spanglish, the hysteric's mother tongue.

CHAPTER FIVE

Hysterical Ties, Latino Amnesia, and the *Sinthomestiza* Subject

Recently at a dinner table in a Mexican home in Los Angeles, an eleven-year-old boy turned angrily to his parents, "Well, who says I'm a Mexican? The doctor or the police?"

BEATRICE GRIFFITH, *American Me*

Puppet. They killed Puppet.

MARGARITA COTA-CÁRDENAS, *Puppet*

Sinthomosexuality, on the other hand—denying the appeal of fantasy, refusing the promise of futurity that mends each tear, however mean, in reality's dress with threads of meaning . . . —offers us fantasy turned inside out, the seams of its costume exposing reality's seamlessness as mere seeming, the fraying knots that hold each sequin in place now usurping that place.

LEE EDELMAN, *No Future*

This is a suicidal gesture, because the pachuco does not affirm or defend anything except his exasperated will-not-to-be. He is not divulging his most intimate feelings: he is revealing an ulcer, exhibiting a wound. A wound that is also grotesque, capricious barbaric adornment. A wound that laughs at itself and decks itself out for the hunt.

OCTAVIO PAZ, *Labyrinth of Solitude*

The precocious Mexican American boy's Foucauldian query in the opening epigraph to this chapter is taken from Beatrice Griffith's 1948 corny and compelling *American Me*. The eleven-year-old boy asks after the terms and conditions granting him social and cultural intelligibility through the stamp of the name *Mexican* in 1948 Los Angeles, knowing this is dependent upon who issues the call. He appears to already understand that those terms and conditions will draw their disciplinary exactitude from either medical and/or criminalizing discourses that are themselves more than a little beholden to psychiatric discourse since the end of the nineteenth century in the United States. The understanding for what constituted the etiology of criminality in the criminal subject as introduced in a new way by Cesare Lombroso's 1876 *The Criminal Man*—that criminal behavior, reasoned through a species of biological determinism, was to be chalked up to the inherently defective quality of the individual or group and not to weak and dodgy morals[1]—was precisely the understanding underpinning early- to mid-twentieth-century popular cultural and social scientific research's hallucination of the Chicano subject as inherently criminal, which is not to say that we are no longer under the spell of this pernicious mode of reasoning today.

The passage that follows Griffith's in the epigraph, on my reading, attempts to dramatize how both medical and criminalizing discourses kill and mortify him, the eleven-year-old in 1948, and the young Chicano male named Puppet in Margarita Cota-Cárdenas's classic Chicana novella, *Puppet*. This mortification concerns the mad swarming of the Chicano body with a ready-made discourse built from narratives forming "the perceptual grid that precedes them" devoted to instantiating them as types. As David Palumbo-Liu understands the problematic for ethnic-racialized subjects, more generally, "The real difficulty in making this move [from ethnic-racialized typecasting to recognizing individual identity] is that 'identity' is predicated upon a set of behaviors that, for racial and other minorities and women, is geared to a set of historical narratives about 'them' precisely as groups, rather than as individuals, and these narratives form the perceptual grid that precedes them in the social discourse of identity."[2] In an important 1974 essay, "La Evolución del 'Bandido' al 'Pachuco': A Critical Examination of Criminological Literature on Chicanos," Larry Trujillo points to the interpretive labors shared by eugenics movement discourse and culturally-biased psychologistic social science research in lending content to the historical narrative about Chicanos as an inherently criminal group: "Once they were satisfied that Chicano children were intellectually inferior, mentally retarded or feeble-minded, they went on to 'scientifically prove' other personality traits that supposedly resulted from this low mentality. One of their most popular conclusions was a propensity for criminal behavior."[3] Carl Gutiérrez-Jones explains that how Chicanos have over the course of a century become "institutionally and popularly associated with criminality has a long and complex history that is intimately related to their very construction as a social group in the United States."[4]

This constitutes a very different conceptualization and instantiation of ethnic-racialized subjectivity from that which one witnesses in the social science research on African American subjects, for example. The psychological portrait offered by Kenneth and Mamie Clark of African American children in the late 1930s and 1940s would have been virtually impossible to offer

139

of Mexican American children also suffering the effects of segregation due to the very different way in which the latter subjects were conceptualized as psychological subjects. Mexican American children first emerge as psychological subjects in eugenics movement discourse only insofar as they could be tested for intelligence. Questions having to do with psychological trauma and loss are pushed to the side in order to deal chiefly with that aspect of psychology thought to pertain to intelligence. The research reveals that the Chicano male subject, in particular, is not so much damaged—in the absence of any quota of psychological complexity the idea of trauma simply goes missing—as he is profoundly criminal and damaging to society.[5]

Before the police gun down Puppet in Cota-Cárdenas's novella—before the police and popular cultural discourses today literally and metaphorically speaking continue to gun down Chicanos—I would argue that the criminalizing discourses have already turned him into living, breathing stone. Before this petrification through a ready-made criminalizing discourse he will have, in an even more fundamental initiatory moment, found himself condemned to a kind of solitary confinement outside the chain of the signifier, excluded from the drift and movement of meaning that attends the distinctly human experience of being a subject in language.

There are two aspects to the discursive process I refer to as the fossilization of Chicano subjectivity. One aspect regards the deleterious, rigid, and fixed narrative content of the criminalizing discourse itself that precedes the Chicano subject's entry into a linguistic universe, a Symbolic order into which the Chicano subject is born and through which she or he will become a socially legible subject in U.S. culture. The second, less remarked upon part of this process, which, in fact, helps secure the immobilization of the ethnic-racialized subject required in the first part, regards how the Chicano subject has been petrified as a result of being exempted—gunned down—from the chain of the signifier because the ethnic-racialized subject is here granted a kind of immunity from the privative and generative effects of language as structure. This generously bestowed immunity doesn't protect, it kills through inoculation, allowing the discursive networks of power and domination in a racialized social order to silently wrestle the Chicano subject down into a set of well-worn proofs, precipitating, in the process, the seductive mirage to others and to ourselves of a potentially whole, full, and unified subjectivity. When rendered as such, and when we help render our selves as such, we provide the enabling conditions for a managed and disciplined existence.

140

That, as Latino and Chicano studies scholars, we have also bought into this reductive and ego amplifying narrative of Latino and Chicano subjectivity shows us to be problematically in thrall with the unspoken conditions of our subjugation and shows us to have become overinvested in and insufficiently critical of ego- and social psychological explanations of human subjectivity that continue to obsess over notions of subjective unity, wholeness, adaptation, adjustment to reality, "mental health," and that definitively place in parenthesis all of the poststructuralist lessons we have learned about language and the effects of language as structure on the speaking subject. Recall how Lacan observed, "It is truly odd that the fact that the structure of thought is based on language is not thrown into question in psychology."[6] We need to *start* wondering aloud ourselves more about this oddity or, at the very least, wonder why we're not wondering about this oddity in our scholarship. We need to *stop* wondering, like Piri Thomas, "Maybe God is psychology, or psychology is God."[7]

I think a Lacanian psychoanalytic approach to thinking through Latino subjectivity in the twentieth and twenty-first centuries announces itself, although we have remained somewhat deaf to its call, in one of the more yielding objects-qua-subjects of study over the years within Chicano cultural studies: the *pachuco/a* and zoot suit figures and cultural formations of the 1940s and 1950s. Chon Noriega, a theorist of Chicano film and culture, may already put us on the path to understanding the pachucos'/as' and zoot suiters' politics of resistance in a more psychoanalytic register, given the interesting gloss he provides of the Chicano playwright, film director, and activist Luis Valdez's presentation of the zoot suiter over the years: "Valdez suffuses the volitional and politically symbolic act of assuming an identity with the secret fantasy of dressing up. In so doing, he opens the door to such unruly things as desire and the unconscious."[8] Something about zoot suiters and pachucos/as "just doesn't make any sense," as one of the classic studies of zoot suit culture by Mauricio Mazón explains, "The zoot-suiters projected a deceptively anarchistic image. Especially nonsensical to adults were aspects of their garb, gait and argot. . . . Zoot-suiters were nonsensical because among other things they took pride in their ambiguity."[9] Edward Escobar reminds us that the "nonsensical" was only deepened by the fact that "Mexican American youths who adopted the zoot suit left no record regarding their motives."[10] Not only did they appear to leave no record, but, as Sanchez-Tranquilino and Tagg explain, they never "read the manuals": "Pachuco culture was an assemblage, built from machines for which they never read the manuals. It was a cultural affirmation not by nostalgic return to an imaginary original wholeness and past, but by appropriation, transgression, reassemblage, breaking and restructuring the laws of language."[11] If Noriega, after Valdez, seems to encourage a psychoanalytic reading, Sanchez-Tranquilino and Tagg encourage a specifically Lacanian psychoanalytic reading, given the undeniably Lacanian resonances they draw out regarding pachuco/a culture's refusal to buy into ego- and social psychologistic notions of wholeness and unity and their attention to the laws of language that transform us into subjects of the signifier.

In the previous chapter, I argued that what Latino studies scholar Suzanne Oboler identifies as Latino student confusion and ambivalence on college campuses today might be attributable to their reaction to the edict that they affirm an identity according to the reductive tenets of ego and social psychology that confuse the ego with the subject and that serve to underwrite soft forms of multiculturalism and diversity rationales in universities. From the vantage point of the twenty-first century, we will see that the pachuco's/a's and zoot suiter's response to the hailing "Hey you, Mexican American" is to offer up an incalculable, unreadable, and unrecognizable text, revealing a prescient understanding of the sad labors of ethnic-racialized resemblance that would come to inform late-twentieth- and early-twenty-first-century terms and conditions for Latino social and cultural intelligibility. They dramatize the signifying meanderings of the fleeting, vanishing subject in language who cannot be wrestled down into some determinate meaning, because language, no matter how masterfully one tries to operate it, can never provide a determinate meaning about the subject. Where I suggested in the previous chapter that Latino studies critique hysterizes the university discourse that poses as master, here I will show how the zoot suiter and pachuco/a figures hystericize all discourses, whether social scientific or Chicano activist, that pose as masterful in their attempts to explain and make sense of these figures.

The zoot suiter and the pachuco/a emerged from a rebellious Mexican American youth culture of the 1940s, predominantly on the West Coast. To say the least, they occupied a certain pride of place in the criminalizing and pathologizing discourses that surrounded them. Escobar has argued that nothing moved the Mexican American community more "to large-scale activism like the twin issues of the zoot-suit hysteria and the police misconduct of the 1940s. While other issues may have forced people to think of themselves as Mexican Americans, no other issue made people act politically as Mexican Americans. For them, identity politics began in 1943."[12] One could make this claim, of course, but it seems to me that what the pachuco/a and zoot-suit youth cultures introduce is a species of anti-identity politics that, although clearly linked to Mexican American culture, also runs beyond identity and culture as defined according to categories of race and ethnicity. Their ability to trouble identity categories is nowhere more present than in the social scientific literature where, again and again, the research, whether pathologizing or sympathetic, points to the nonsensical and inexplicable nature of pachucos/as and zoot-suit cultures, revealing how these cultural formations remain for the most part unreadable, and at a certain level incalculable.

I'm certainly not saying anything new here. I am in fact following closely on the heels of Sanchez-Tranquilino and Tagg, who note, "The pachuco was an indecipherable mythology. (The Pachuca—the Black Widow—could not even be thought.) And so it goes on. Tragic, heroic, delinquent, or grotesque, without a clear identity and location, the pachuco is a scandal of civilized meaning."[13] What I hope to add that is new regards how, what I'm calling their quasi-Lacanian anti-identity politics might be mined as a rich resource for contemporary Chicano and Latino identity politics that refuses the falsely amplifying terms and conditions for social and cultural intelligibility extended to ethnic-racialized subjects based on forms of self-mimicry and that begins the process of severing its ongoing commitment to ego- and social psychological models for understanding human subjectivity.

This chapter is divided into two sections. In the first, I schematically and selectively track the pachuco's/a's and zoot-suit figure's appearance in material ranging from Anglo social science research to Chicano historical analysis to African American poetry to give the reader a sense for the cacophonous responses they have elicited—from awe and disgust to adoration, hatred, and jealousy. They seem to elicit symptoms in their researchers by virtue of their own constant production of symptoms that never seem to cede the floor to an interpretation that would definitively dissolve them. To be clear, my intention here is not to provide a history of these cultural formations,[14] but rather to see how critics have generally attempted to characterize what appears beyond characterization—the pachuco's/a's and zoot suiter's nonsensical and indefinable nature. In the second section, I provide narrative, if not strictly speaking filmic, readings of two curious and odd cinematic treatments by Anglo male directors of the zoot suiter and pachuco/a figures.[15] George Stevens's 1956 film *Giant* teases the viewer with the possibility of offering a pachuco/a or zoot-suit figure through the character of Angel Obregon but then eliminates the kind of static this figure might have introduced into Stevens's drama of ethnic and racial tolerance by killing him off at war and providing us instead with a safer version of Mexican American male subjectivity through the character of Jordy IV. If Stevens's film can be said to repress this figure, David Lynch's 2001 film *Mulholland Drive* constitutes the return of the repressed pachuca through the secret Chicana-qua-Latina amnesiac, "Rita," who I argue represents the *"sinthomestiza* subject." Lynch's film offers a strangely compelling theorization of Chicana-qua-Latina identity and the politics of Chicano space and place in Los Angeles at the beginning of the twenty-first century that appears to, unwittingly perhaps, capture the Spanglish ethos that marks the contemporary discourse of Latinidad discussed in chapter 4.

Escobar insists that "despite the outlandish clothes and the sometimes outlandish behavior, what the zoot suiters and even the more defiant pachuco/as wanted" was respect.[16] I disagree. Might we not also understand the form of protest crafted here as the very undermining of the notion of respect and dignity, of recognition, even, as a deeper inquiry into the meaning of respect, dignity, and recognition as adjudicated by the dominant culture, given how pachucos/as and zoot suiters seem committed, in a general way, to scrambling the very structures of narrativity and signification in the first place? I know I have crossed the line in my shamefaced—why not call it what it is?—nostalgia for an anti-identity Chicano and Latino politics through which I never lived. This already places me significantly at odds with Sanchez-Tranquilino's and Tagg's insistence that the zoot suiter and pachuco/a cannot be claimed back for some protonationalist Chicano politics, for example.

I both am and am not guilty of this, insofar as what I'm nostalgic for is a politics of Latino subjectivity without identity, a depsychologized politics of the Latino subject as a subject of the signifier. We need to revisit their species of anti-identity politics, their reinvention of ethnic-racialized subjectivity, their politicization of "nonsense,"[17] in the context of coercive mid-twentieth century assimilatory imperatives in order to reinvigorate contemporary Chicano and Latino identity politics, which increasingly seem to possess a bloodless and joyless feel, given how obsessed we've become again with the placid notions of respect and dignity.

There is no other way to say it: the zoot-suit outfit seems like the most spectacularly weird sartorial expression. Escobar provides some nice detail:

> The zoot-suit, or drapes, as the boys who wore it liked to call the outfit, can generally be described as an exercise in excess, a composition in conspicuous consumption. It consisted of very baggy pants that fit very high on the waist (in the most extreme cases, all the way to the armpits), deep "reat" pleats, and extremely narrow cuffs. The coat had wide lapels and shoulder pads that resembled epaulets and was sometimes so long it reached the knees. Accessories to the zoot suit included a wide-rimmed "pancake" hat, long watch chains, and thick-soled shoes. The female equivalent to the zoot suiters, the "cholitas," also wore distinctive, if not as outlandish, clothes. Their outfits consisted of either flared or tight short skirts, tight sweaters, and distinct styles of earrings and makeup.[18]

Noriega reminds us that the zoot suiter's outfit was in fact an oversized exaggeration of the American businessman's suit.[19] The use of excessive fabric, a wartime prohibition, flaunted these restrictions, and its exaggerated masculine display of the business suit actually made the Anglo male business suit code as feminine. The zoot suiter's over-the-top spectacular re-signification of the business suit could also be read as a symptom formation of capitalism's very own excesses.

Noriega explains that with Chicano fashion, "the ornamental is utilitarian because it advertises a social conflict, yet it also disguises an identity from the State."[20] To translate this into my own terms, I would say that the clothes do not disguise an identity from the state as much as they reveal identity as a disguise itself. I would further add that the strategy of disguising identity from the state, from the social science researchers, from everyone except each other, can be read as a symptomatic and politicized response to the pressure coming from Anglos and other Mexican Americans that they code as manageable, calculable evidence of Mexican American identity. I think Franz Fanon had zoot suiters and pachucos/as in mind when he wrote in one of the most stirring passages in the concluding chapter of *Black Skin, White Masks*, "I should constantly remind myself that the real leap consists in introducing invention into existence. In the world through which I travel, I am endlessly creating myself."[21] Noriega puts us on the track to understanding how Fanon's

145

notion of "endlessly creating myself," when read in concert with the "uses and not just the abuses of fashion for everyday life,"[22] reveal the zoot suiters as able to extract both pleasure from the goods and care for the self, capturing what Foucault in his later work might have called a "care of the self."[23] In our specific example, we are afforded the opportunity of attending to the politics of resistance embedded in these self-regarding practices of pleasure revealed when one deigns to care for one's own disprized body.

One of the most luxurious accounts of what we are calling, after Foucault, the zoot suiter's "care of the self" is depicted in African American poet Gwendolyn Brooks's 1945 poem "The Sundays of Satin-Legs Smith."[24] Its narrator cobbles together a zoot suiter who pays his skin the utmost respect by applying a lotion of "lavender and oil" since "life must be aromatic." The pajamas, carrying the trace of "shabby days," are shed before the transubstantiating bath can ready the "kneaded limbs" for "the kiss of silk" and the embrace of the "equivocal wool" of "wonder suits." These "wonder suits," also known as "zoot suits" or "drapes," crowd his lavish closet:

> Let us proceed. Let us inspect, together
> With his meticulous and serious love,
> The innards of this closet. Which is a vault
> Whose glory is not diamonds, not pearls,
> Not silver plate with just enough dull shine.
> But wonder-suits in yellow and wine,
> Sarcastic green and zebra-striped cobalt.
> All drapes. With shoulder padding that is wide
> And cocky and determined as his pride;
> Ballooning pants that taper off to ends
> Scheduled to choke precisely.
> Here are hats
> Like bright umbrellas; and hysterical ties
> Like narrow banners for some gathering war. (44)

In one of the most famous and rigorous studies of pachuco/a culture, published in 1950, George Barker seems less impressed with the sartorial splendor of pachucos/as at the same time that he appears to be positively bewitched by a young man named "Toro," "the individual who, of all those interviewed, most nearly fits what might be called the pachuco stereotype":

He is of medium height, about twenty-two years of age and of athletic build. His dark-complexioned face might be considered handsome were it not for numerous scars and pockmarks on his cheeks. He has a wide mouth, fringed by a thin moustache, and when he smiles, his nostrils dilate broadly, a feature which may be the source of his nickname of Toro (bull). His coarse black hair is combed straight back, and he wears an old army shirt open at the neck, army pants with narrow cuffs, and thick-soled shoes. When he talks Pachuco he constantly uses his hands, and his voice drawls out the endings of words in a sonorous manner.[25]

Barker's tone in this scholarly piece is quietly melancholic and forlorn. One sees him trying to balance a kind of beauty he doesn't quite know how to make sense of in the terms of his argument—that seemingly "gets him off"—along with what he interprets as the ugliness that yields from the young pachucos'/as' general sense of defeat, "Pachuco values may be said to have two basic premises, which may be stated briefly as follows: (1). We'll probably die young so we may as well get our thrills out of life now; and (2) the laws are against us but we can outsmart them."[26]

Both the dress and demeanor turn Beatrice Griffith on in 1948. In *American Me*, she dwells lovingly on the personage of "Chacho Martinez":

> Who is this Chacho Martinez who stands before the Judge in a Los Angeles Juvenile court charged with possession of a gun while involved in a gang fight? Dressed in drapes and finger-tip coat, hair cut long and swept back from the front and sides of his brown face into ducktail haircut, wearing shoes with triple soles, he stands unemotional and unprotesting before the judicial authority of the society that produced him.
>
> His impassive face hides his defiance against society and authority. He will take with little show of feeling the tongue-lashing of the judge and any punishment that is handed out to him.[27]

When the *Nation* reviewed *American Me* in 1949, Ward Moore remarked on the "fine, economical prose" and its affecting quality—"an experience immediately satisfying yet sequentially agitating."[28] Moore has really hit on two of the favorite poles of affective charge inspired by pachucos/as and zoot suiters in the research of the 1940s and 1950s: "satisfying" yet "sequentially agitating."

Griffith suggests that society has produced the pachuco as a symptom of sorts. The Chicano intellectual George Sánchez might be read as agreeing with her when he wrote in the journal *Common Ground* in 1943 that "the pachuco is a symbol not of the guilt of an oppressed 'Mexican' minority but of a cancerous growth within the majority group which is gnawing at the vitals of democracy and the American way of life. The pachuco and his feminine counterpart, the cholista, are spawn of a neglectful society—not the products of an humble minority people who are defenseless before their enforced humiliation."[29] Sanchez-Tranquilino and Tagg have a different way of reading pachucos/as and zoot suiters; their symptoms are forms of knowledge production: "It was a cultural affirmation not by nostalgic return to an imaginary original wholeness and past, but by appropriation, transgression, reassemblage, breaking and restructuring the laws of language: in the speech of Calo and pochismos, but also in the languages of space, the city, the barrio, the street."[30]

Reading Griffith, Sánchez, and Sanchez-Tranquilino and Tagg together on the question of the symptom, we witness the general interpretative tension that elects itself when researchers attempt to explain the pachuco's/a's raison d'être: either pachucos/as are seen as produced by the social and cultural forces of racism and discrimination or pachucos/as make themselves, not entirely free of social and cultural contingencies, but in such a way that the reason given for their *being* can't comfortably rest on an explication that simply interprets them as an X-ray of the power relations in a particular social order. Symptoms won't yield up their meaning, and even when an interpretation is offered, the pachuco/a and zoot suiter, like Lacan's hysteric, produces another symptom to take its place, more knowledge and thus more need for interpretation.

Although the young pachucos/as and zoot suiters seemed to require some engagement with Mexican American youth as complicated psychological subjects, an engagement with them that could not simply understand their personality and behavior as reflective of so-called deficiencies in the Mexican American community, the nonsensical, troubling, and incalculable nature of these figures seemed to make them generally recalcitrant to being captured by standard ego- and social psychological approaches to human psychology. Again, ego and social psychology, as I have explained earlier, focuses on, among other things, questions of adaptation and the autonomous, masterful ego's role in being able to adjust to whatever environment, revealing an abiding faith in the ultimate harmony that might eventually be struck between the ego and its environment; there is a commonsensical notion for what passes as both "reality" and "mental health" internal to these ideas of adjustment and adaptation. One of the widely circulating assumptions in social science research at this time was that any group who did not or could not assimilate must be flawed, a defect that would be extended as a defining characteristic to the entire ethnic-racialized group in question. The perception that Mexicans were not assimilating meant that the defect had to be located in them.

The pachuco/a and zoot-suit figure seem mostly uninterested in these ideals, revealing an implicit critique of the values of assimilation, not to mention laying bare how regardless of the utility of the concept of assimilation it was clear that Mexican Americans in the 1940s and 1950s were not going to be accepted in the same way white ethnic minorities were accepted at the beginning of the twentieth century. Importantly, young pachucos/as and zoot suiters were not failing to assimilate; they were unconcerned with assimilating —big difference. Given the guiding notions of mental health, as determined by a dominant cultural perspective, as well as what would pass as the agreed-upon notion of reality, as determined, again, by a dominant cultural perspective, and the religious faith in the subject's ability to adjust to any hostile environment, pachucos/as and zoot suiters could only have seemed somewhat pathological and even a little self-destructive. A Lacanian approach would not have pathologized these figures but would have understood these countercultural youth formations instead as expressions of protest along the lines of the hysteric's protest, a protest against the psychologization of the Mexican American subject, whereby the ego is collapsed with the subject and where all manner of explication is drawn from whatever can be gleaned from an analysis of the social and cultural context in which the subject is immersed.

Really?

149

As it turns out, zoot suit and pachuco/a culture is at its height precisely during the time of the consolidation of ego psychology's hegemony in the United States. In fact, one can establish quite solid historical links between ego psychology and the pathologization of zoot suit and pachuco/a culture. In a fascinating section in *American Encounters*, José E. Limón provides us with the necessary historical background to understand how the pathologization of pachucos/as and zoot suiters came directly from a tradition of ego psychology. The Mexican philosopher and psychoanalytic enthusiast Samuel Ramos published what would become an enduring and widely used psycho-cultural study of Mexicans in 1934, *El perfil del hombre y la cultura en México* (*Profile of Man and Culture in Mexico*). Limón writes, "For Ramos, the central Mexican psycho-cultural condition can best be understood as stemming from an inferiority complex generated by history. Like the child who feels inferior in his confrontation with the adult world, pre-Conquest indigenous civilization in

Mexico 'at first found itself in the same relationship to the civilized world as that of the child to his parents. It entered Western history at a time when a mature civilization already prevailed, something which an infantile spirit can only half understand.' "[31]

Limón implicitly links Ramos to the ego psychological school of thought by noting that Ramos was an enthusiastic supporter of Alfred Adler's work. Adler had broken with Freud in 1911, and although he is not generally known as a psychoanalyst who popularized ego psychology like, for example, Hartmann, Kris, and Loewenstein, his work is regarded by many as a precursor to the psychoanalytic work that would later be collected under the rubric of ego psychology. In the prologue to the third edition of *Profile of Man and Culture in Mexico*, Ramos writes, "Here, in brief resume, I have presented the psychological doctrine of Alfred Adler, who at first was a disciple of Freud but later followed his own course in creating a new interpretation of nervous character. Some years ago, while observing psychological traits common to a large group of Mexicans, it occurred to me that these traits could be explained from the point of view indicated by Adler."[32] Octavio Paz's infamous *Labyrinth of Solitude*, another psycho-cultural study of Mexicans, which I will discuss in more detail below, essentially recycles Ramos's ego-psychological views in his own pathologizing case study of the working-class pachuco/a figure in the United States. Limón reminds the reader that Paz never rejects the "inherited universe"[33] provided by Ramos's seminal ego psychological study of Mexicans.

Translated into the terms of my own project, what Paz inherits from Ramos, as do countless other psychological studies of so-called Mexican and Mexican American "character," are the problematic and reductive assumptions that inform ego psychology's understanding of the human psyche and the related issues of how to theorize trauma, loss, adaptation, and assimilation. Unfortunately, in the critiques of this kind of work virtually no mention is made of the fact that what is passing as psychoanalytic theory in these studies is ego psychology and its particular version of Freudian theory—its "Americanization of psychoanalysis," as Limón puts it. In other words, the critiques of the use of psychoanalysis in studies of the psychology of Mexicans and Mexican Americans that claim it is a white, Eurocentric colonialist paradigm would do better to understand more precisely how these studies reflect a certain North American distortion of Freudian theory and how, as I explain in chapter 2, this distortion of Freudian theory can be read as part and parcel to the increasing hegemony of the United States over the rest of the world in the post–World War II years. This will provide us with new critical terrain and material by which to explore the politics of U.S. imperialism with respect to Mexico—a "geopolitics of the psyche,"[34] as it were. From this angle, we are provided with a different view for understanding how and why ego psychology would come to figure in popular cultural and academic narratives about Mexican and Mexican American psychology and why, given its central tenets and theories, the figure of the zoot suiter and pachuco/a could only register as pathological when not simply beyond its grasp entirely.

The pachuco's/a's and zoot suiter's endless production of meaning, not pathology, shows them to be as enthralled with knowledge as is the hysteric; they get off on knowledge too. In this regard, I will argue that they are not only an enigmatic symptom of a racist culture that tries to wrestle ethnic-racialized subjects down into recognizable, manageable identities but are also what Lacan calls the "sinthome."

The sinthome, in the later work of Lacan, is introduced as a new way of thinking the symptom. In "The Function and Field of Speech and Language in Psychoanalysis," Lacan writes that "the symptom can be entirely resolved in an analysis of language because a symptom is itself structured like a language: a symptom is language from which speech must be delivered."[35] As Lacanian commentators have noted, by the time Lacan delivers *Seminar XXIII: The Sinthome* in 1975–76, his thinking has changed regarding the symptom.[36] He now understands that there is something in language immune to interpretation, something that cannot be dissolved—something that one would, in fact, want to steer clear from dissolving.

Lacanian theorists Dominiek Hoens and Ed Pluth explain the paradox of the sinthome as Lacan develops it in his later work:

> This is the paradox: the sinthome is meaningless, but at the same time it is enjoyment-in-meaning. . . . The sinthome is meaningless, in the sense that it does not have any particular signification. It is a pure signifier, and in that respect, it is meaningless. For Lacan, meaning is always produced through the connection of signifiers, in what he called a signifying chain. The sinthome is an enjoyment-in-meaning, however, in the following sense: as a production of meaning, the sinthome is not concerned with the meanings produced, but with the activity of production itself.[37]

This describes quite nicely the zoot suiter's and pachuco's/a's investment in the production of meaning not so much for meaning's sake, but for produc-

151

Def (?)

Sinthome

tion's sake. We should understand the "enjoyment-in-meaning" in the passage above as calling up the pleasure of the pachuco's/a's and zoot suiter's uses of fashion in the service of caring for the self by lending that self the pleasure of indeterminacy.

In this respect, the sinthome represents a form of signification that is beyond interpretation. The politics I'm trying to shamefacedly extrude from this notion for a contemporary Chicano and Latino anti-identity politics—a politics initially taught to us by pachucos/as and zoot suiters—values this beyond to interpretation as precisely what must, again, destroy the illusion that ethnic-racialized subjects are transparent to the signifier, to themselves and to others. The freedom squeezed out from this attempt to fully exhaust them as the perfect sum of the calculation of the relations of power, knowledge, and domination has to do with an insistence on the incalculable nature of the subject in language, an insistence that should count as an antiracist practice in our work as Latino and Chicano studies scholars.

Octavio Paz would certainly find my attempt to cobble together a contemporary politics of Latino identity from the lessons we learn from pachucos/as and zoot suiters preposterous, given the very little respect and dignity he attributes to pachucos/as in his somewhat ferocious account of them in the first chapter of his infamous *Labyrinth of Solitude*. In the process, he reveals himself to be no less turned on by them than Griffith and Barker.

But to be clear, I am not after dignity and respect. I'm engaging Paz's well-worn account here because, regardless of what we may think of its mean-spiritedness and the wall-to-wall pathologization of the pachucos/as he offers, Paz appears to understand that what the pachucos/as reveal is a refusal of identity on *anyone's* terms. It's this refusal, and particularly the fear, dread, and confusion that this refusal unleashes in a multicultural society, that contemporary Latino and Chicano identity politics needs to reconsider. By the way, I don't see why any of the descriptions included in the passages that follow from Paz can't serve us as good, *but really bad*, scripts for Latinos and Chicanos to follow, things being as they are. Paz writes,

> When you talk with them, you observe that their sensibilities are like a pendulum, but a pendulum that has lost its reason and swings violently and erratically back and forth. . . . the pachucos do not attempt to vindicate their race or the nationality of their forebears. Their attitude reveals an obstinate, almost fanatical will-to-be, but this will affirms nothing specific except their determination—it is

152

an ambiguous one, as we will see—not to be like those around them. . . . His whole being is sheer negative impulse, a tangle of contradictions, an enigma.[38]

It may be that the pachucos/as figured out a way as to how *not* to be their own Mexican descendants or their later Chicano progenitors, as the passage from Richard T. Ford explains: "It may be that the price of providing our descendants with a world free of social stigma and oppression of identities such as race, a world we could be proud to call more just, is that they would not share our identities, that they would be our heirs but *not* our descendants."[39] Having never left a record, as we noted earlier, and having never read from the identity manuals, they have had difficulty transmitting to us what they appeared to be busy ridding themselves of.

Readers familiar with Paz's text will recall that he seems never to be more at a loss for final words than when he's describing this figure. He writes, "This duality is also expressed in another, perhaps profounder way: the pachuco is an impassive and sinister clown whose purpose is to cause terror instead of laughter. His sadistic attitude is allied with a desire for self-abasement which in my opinion constitutes the very foundation of his character: he knows that it is dangerous to stand out and that his behavior irritates society, but nevertheless he seeks and attracts persecution and scandal."[40] What is fascinating in Paz's "case study" of the pachuco/a—and this is precisely what irks Paz—is that the pachuco/a is a symptom that refuses to yield to an interpretation that would dissolve it, and moreover a kind of symptom that can't be entirely captured according to analyses attuned to social and cultural contexts, say, in the manner in which Beatrice Griffith and George Sanchez account for the whys and wherefores of the pachuco's/a's existence in passages quoted earlier. The pachuco/a appears to be identifying with his or her symptom, leaving the reader, cultural critic, and analyst in the dust.

The freedom the zoot suiter and pachuco/a squeeze out has to do with the space left open between the attempt to wrestle them down into types, as per Palumbo-Liu, of ethnic-racialized subjects and what they give back as the impossible text to be read and interpreted. Their text makes no sense and cannot be understood, ultimately, by Mexican Americans or by Anglos, and in this way they win back the pleasure that comes from luxuriating not in a particular meaning but rather in the constant *production* of meaning, as related to Lacan's *sinthome*. I may be overstating the value of this troubling of meaning, but I risk it in order to suggest again that this kind of troubling of

153

understanding and meaning is precisely what contemporary Latino and Chicano identity politics may fruitfully mine in the context of the falsely amplifying multiculturalist discourses of recognition and visibility in, especially, university contexts today that appear inoculated against creating any real changes in the ongoing unequal distribution of social and material resources impacting Latino and Chicano lives.

In the epigraphs to this chapter, I coupled together passages by Octavio Paz and Lee Edelman suggesting in a rather forced way—but one impossible to resist—the homology between Paz's description of the pachuco/a and Edelman's description of "sinthomosexuality"—a neologism that Edelman claims grafts "at an awkward join the sounds of French and English"[41] the words *homosexuality* and Lacan's late notion of the *sinthome*. Edelman appropriates Lacan's notion of the sinthome, and by suturing it with the word *homosexuality* proffers a species of queer critique that operates a nasty cut in the social that makes again and again a "scandal of civilized meaning," to borrow the resonant term used by Sanchez-Tranquilino and Tagg to describe the wreckage of signification represented by the pachuco/a. Edelman writes, "Sinthomosexuality, then, only means by figuring a threat to meaning, which depends on the promise of coming, in a future continuously deferred, into the presence that reconciles meaning with being in a fantasy of completion—a fantasy on which every subject's cathexis of the signifying system depends."[42]

I interpret the antisignifying labor of the "sinthomosexual" as precisely the "scandal of civilized meaning" operated by the pachuco/a in the social. Brooks wrote in 1945 of "wonder-suits in yellow and wine, Sarcastic green and zebra-striped cobalt," and Edelman deepens, according to my reading, the description of these "wonder-suits" by telescoping in on "the fraying knots that hold each sequin in place"[43]—the fraying, we might add, of the seams that try to keep meaning fixed and contained, sewn in, as it were. Paz appears to give us less sartorial texture, since the point for him is to describe not the suit but the "wound that laughs at itself"—it's not a man who dons the suit, but a wound that "decks itself out for the hunt."[44] The wound makes the man. Let's think of this as Lacanian zoot suiter and pachuco/a shorthand to say that the constitutive loss, the primordial wound suffered by the human speaking organism, creates the generative conditions for subjectivity and desire.

Some readers might find my assertion that George Stevens's 1956 film *Giant* hallucinates for its viewers a pachuco/a or zoot-suit figure through the character of Angel Obregon, the soldier who is summarily dismissed from the filmic text when he dies at war, a bit farfetched, perhaps even a hallucination on my part. After all, there are no actual pachucos/as or zoot suiters in the film. To be clear, I base my assertion on what *could have been.*

Over the years Stevens's film has come to occupy a more and more exalted place within the canon of Chicano cinema. Assessments such as the following one, made by Charles Ramirez Berg, capture some of the reasons for the heightened interest in this film over the last twenty years: "It's also time for a full-blown appreciation of *Giant*, one of the most enlightened of all of Hollywood's wide-screen epics. Its female protagonist allows it to question some of the key principles of the dominant ideology: patriarchy, the imperialistic bent of America's westward expansion, . . . racism, the class system, and the social construction of manhood."[45] A cursory description of the plot of the film might read as follows: Rock Hudson and Elizabeth Taylor play Jordan and Leslie Benedict, the heads of a wealthy cattle-ranching family in Texas. They have three children, Jordy III, Judy, and Luz. Although the entire support system for the family and its business is provided by the labor of Mexican people, Jordan has only contempt for them. Leslie's white liberal progressive agenda makes her the Mexican community's visiting-missionary activist. Leslie outlines the film's position on ethnic-racialized tolerance from within a feminist analysis of patriarchy. Her critique of Hudson's character's idea of Texas history and Anglo-Mexican relations will eventually convince him to accept the Mexican people. Their son, Jordy III, played by a plucky, wide-eyed Dennis Hopper, forces the issue on both parents when he marries the Mexican woman Juana, played by actress Elsa Cardenas, and brings the ethnic-racialized other into the intimate space of the Benedict family.

The film offers two visions of young Mexican American male subjectivity in the 1940s and 1950s that actually constitute two different versions. In addition to Angel, the film provides us with Jordy IV, the half-Mexican, half-Anglo baby born to Jordy III and Juana, whose brown face fills and overflows the screen at the very end of the film, signifying the fulfillment of Stevens's professed goal of making a film about ethnic and racial tolerance. Presumably,

155

Jordy IV will stand at some point to inherit the wealth of the Benedict family as one of its future patriarchs.

In order to understand the version of Mexican American male subjectivity that Angel might have stood for, we need to remind ourselves what Chicano historians have taught us, that when Mexican American soldiers—upward of 500,000 enlisted or were drafted for World War II—came back from the war, they found themselves still having to play the role of second-class citizens, to put it mildly.[46] Mexican American soldiers returning to Los Angeles, for example, would have found themselves contending with the virulent and systemic anti-Mexican racism and police abuses that, as Escobar has argued, helped galvanize the Mexican American community and helped ignite the rebellious Mexican American youth culture that we have been referring to as pachucos/as and zoot suiters.

That Stevens's film manages to overlook this particular history is interesting, given that Edna Ferber's 1952 novel *Giant*, on which the film is based, makes explicit the links between the returning Mexican American soldiers and the zoot suiters. Late in the novel, one character opines, "I heard some of the younger Mexican fellas since the war's over they've come home and haven't settled down right, they've been rabble-rousing, shooting their mouths off, getting together saying they're American citizens without rights and that kind of stuff. They want to be called Latin Americans, not Mexicans any more. I hear they're getting up organizations, the boys who fought in the war, and so on. Spreading all over, they say. *Got some fancy names for their outfits*."[47] The critical Mexican American soldier who would begin shooting off at the mouth while decked out, one presumes, in a fancy-named outfit never materializes in the film. Angel is, after all, killed off at war, and the potential zoot suit he might have donned is traded for the military outfit in which he's buried. The film safeguards itself against the precipitation of a critique potentially embodied in Angel that would have certainly created some thematic interference for Stevens's film's project of ethnic and racial tolerance.

Although the film can be said to bury the Mexican American body from which this critique might have issued, the vague outlines of this critique appear to surface anyway in the soundless performance of a yawn. In a complex passage in the film, Angel's shabby funeral begins with a curious image absent from the several versions of the screenplay that I've read. A Mexican American boy's head is shown in profile, close-up; he's watching the funeral from a distance. As the camera rests on his profile, the boy lets out a jaw-unhinging yawn. I read the yawn as a fatigued expression of defiance that registers as disbelief, critical boredom, and wisdom, knowing that all of the national iconographic drag marched into the mise-en-scène of Angel's funeral doesn't really address or interest him, recalling for me an affective variation on the impassiveness and indifference that Beatrice Griffith and Octavio Paz attribute to the zoot suiter and pachuco/a. I also read the yawn as a symptom formation for what Stevens's film tries to repress and effectively bury: the rebellious Mexican American returning soldier. Stevens's film tinkers with the past and comes up with a Mexican American male subject who might be more amenable to accepting the Benedicts' wealth, and possibly even their name. In the aforementioned funeral scene, Stevens establishes an associative link between Angel's death and the births of two significant babies. The images of Angel's funeral are intercut with images of the birth of the Benedicts' daughter Judy's baby, named Judy II, and the birth of Jordy and Juana's Anglo-Mexican baby, Jordy IV, the film's new, preferred, and manageable version of the Mexican American male citizen subject.

Stevens's film's so-called fulfillment of the theme of ethnic-racialized tolerance proceeds apace with several filmic and extrafilmic-spectacles of what I can only think to call "gender trouble." In fact, the film's ability to achieve a kind of consistency with respect to the theme of ethnic and racial tolerance appears oddly reliant on the troubling of normative gender and sexuality categories. What has always intrigued me about this film, "one of the most enlightened of all Hollywood's wide-screen epics," as Ramirez Berg puts it, and its treatment of Anglo and Mexican relations in Texas concerns its generous citation of queer Hollywood stars from the 1950s: Rock Hudson, James Dean, and Sal Mineo all have central roles. I'm granting Dennis Hopper partial inclusion in this list as well, given his on-again, off-again queer posturings in the 1960s and 1970s. In addition, there is Elizabeth Taylor, the film's matriarch, who has contributed in complicated ways to the accumulation of knowledge about gay male actors in Hollywood and gay male sexuality, more generally, in her real and fictive screen roles as gay male confidante and AIDS activist. Also, Hudson's character's sister, played by actress Mercedes McCambridge—who, as Judith Halberstam explains, seemed over the years to definitively make the "category of predatory butch her very own"[48]—in her role as the Benedict ranch's horse wrangler, delivers a subtle, dreamy, and furrowed performance of female masculinity.

With respect to the filmic text, critics have remarked on how Jordy III is presented as troubled with a kind of "effeminacy."[49] There are many scenes where Jordy III appears to disappoint his father over the years by simply not behaving and desiring like a "normal" boy. For example, he pitches a hysterical fit when he's forced to ride a pony at his birthday party, and worse, he takes absolutely no interest in the family's cattle-ranching business. In the scene where he meets Juana for the first time, on the eve of Angel's departure to war, he tries on a ten-gallon hat at a Christmas party. The hat literally smothers his head, covering the better part of his face, underscoring the ill fit between the demanding cowboy-ranch life and Jordy's sensitivity; he wants to be a doctor.

It is certainly worth noting here that the film's story seems destined to eventually include the Mexican presence in the private familial Benedict space—as something other than laborers—as a result of Jordy III's dubious heteromasculinity, since his love for Juana is elaborated—from the perspective of the racist patriarch played by Hudson—as a kind of embattled masculine weakness itself, a weakness for something other than women. In fact, Jordy III and Juana never register as the proper heterosexual couple.[50] A final curiosity worth mentioning has to do with the sex-gender of the actor playing the role of Jordy III and Juana's son, Jordy IV, at the very end of the film: I have come across information suggesting that Jordy IV is actually played by a female child.

"Gender trouble" seems to stick to and wreak havoc with whatever comes into contact with the film *Giant*. In the 1982 film *Come Back to the Five and Dime, Jimmy Dean, Jimmy Dean*, based on Ed Graczyk's play and directed by Robert Altman, the viewer revisits the making of Stevens's film, witnessing not only a sublimely weird holy trinity of queer popular culture icons—Karen Black, Cher, and Sandy Dennis—but also seeing the coiling together of portraits of adolescent gay male sexuality and the vicissitudes of sex-reassignment surgery. The film *Giant* is at the center of all of this, since its filming in a neighboring town sets in motion certain delusional fantasies on the part of Mona, played by Sandy Dennis.

Altman's entire film takes place in a five-and-dime in a small, mostly forgotten town of McCarthy, Texas, where a twenty-five-year reunion is being held in 1975 by the "Disciples of James Dean" to commemorate Dean's untimely death. The Disciples consist of a group of old high school girlfriends. In flashbacks we see Sandy Dennis's character, Mona, develop a very close relationship with the only male member of the group, Joe Qualley. Joe is shown in one of these flashbacks as the victim of a severe gay bashing suffered after a school dance that he attended in drag. The viewer learns that when

Stevens and his crew were filming *Giant* in a neighboring Texas town, Mona and Joe traveled to the set to spy the likes of the great James Dean and to see if they might land roles as extras. According to Mona's story, one evening after shooting for the day had wrapped up, James Dean approached their car and asked for a light. She recalls spending a night of "love making" with Dean and claims to have become pregnant as a result. Mona's son, whom we never see in the film and who Mona insists is "retarded," over the years becomes a small-town celebrity; folks from all over visit the five-and-dime, where Mona continues to work in order to see "the son of James Dean."

As guests begin to gather for the reunion, a mysterious, sharply dressed, urban-looking woman named Joanne, played by Karen Black, drives up in a Porsche and enters the store. The others can't place her until finally, in a very dramatic scene, Joanne tells them that she's Joe, that she had a "sex change," and that she has every right to attend the reunion. A second shock wave is sent through the five-and-dime when Joanne eventually reveals Mona's secret—that Mona's son is not the son of James Dean, but is rather her son, Joe's son, Joanne's son, and that she and Mona were intimate that night, all of which Mona refuses to acknowledge. The historical and narrative bits and shreds of gender trouble that constellate around the film *Giant* in concert with the disappearance of the pachuco/a and zoot-suit figure constitute a kind of queer interpretive lens through which the theme of ethnic and racial tolerance asks to be read.

One reviewer, H. Wayne Schuth describes the final scene of *Giant* as follows: "Back home, Leslie and Bick sit and watch their two grandchildren, who are in a playpen. A white sheep and a black calf are behind the playpen. One grandchild has light skin and one has dark skin in this visual image of the importance of acceptance."[51] The final scene's use of the dissolve with a superimposition has been variously described as uncanny, nonsensical, powerful, and breathtaking. Chicano film and culture theorist, Chon Noriega remarks that the final image "stops the narrative cold."[52] Why and how does this image manage to signify the theme of ethnic and racial tolerance? The burden of proof—that is, to prove ethnic and racial tolerance as well as providing the proof of ethnic-racialized difference—is on the very final image we see: the brown body and giant brown face of the Anglo-Mexican child, Jordy IV.

I agree with the Chicano literary scholar Rafael Pérez-Torres who, like me, doesn't quite buy the film's utopic rejoinder. He suggests that ultimately the emergence of the mestizo voice is contained, quite literally, in the fold of the

159

Benedict family, and that the film never quite abandons the center-periphery model as it tries to articulate relations across ethnic-racialized differences: "Though difference in *Giant* becomes part of a discourse of liberal humanism and pluralistic democracy, difference still marks alterity and inferiority. That is, there is still an 'us' at the center of discourse, agent and subject of history, and a second constituency comprising 'them,' the Others who are not yet (and may never be) 'us.'"[53] In a critique of Pérez-Torres's reading of the film, José Limón writes, "Pérez-Torres has offered a stimulating counter-reading of the film. What is missing in it for me, however, is any historically specific appreciation of how radical the film was in including such a Mexican presence as it did in the 1950s, and how precisely sophisticated, as opposed to naïve, it was in ensuring that the audience knew that Mexican-Americans had a real active presence in American life but did not yet have a full and continuous appearance in the American narrative."[54] Limón has a point, although when read in the context of twenty-first-century discourses of soft multiculturalism and vacuous diversity rationales, the film's inclusion of the Mexican presence seems predicated on strategies of containment and management, as Pérez-Torres sharply maintains. Missing in all of the readings of this film that I've come across is any note of how the inclusion of the Mexican presence or the mestizo body, as Pérez-Torres puts it, is secured through the elimination of another version of Mexican American politicized subjectivity—the pachuco/a and zoot suiter who might have been, could have been, if Angel had not been killed off.

160

I close this chapter with a brief narrative reading of David Lynch's film *Mulholland Drive* (2001), adding to the link already forged between Edelman's "sinthomosexual" and the pachuco/a and zoot suiter on the basis of their shared labors of scandalizing civilized meaning. This link couples Lacan with Anzaldúa, grafting Lacan's *sinthome* to Anzaldúa's *mestiza* to create the term *sinthomestiza*, an antipsychologist reading of Chicano and Latino identity that stays alive to the effects of language as structure on the speaking organism as well as staying sharply attuned to the cultural and historical particularities of Chicano and Latino experience in the twenty-first century.

Lynch's film narrativizes the return of the pachuca that Stevens's film tried to repress from the narrative of Texas history through the secret Chicana-qua-Latina amnesiac, sinthomestiza subject, Rita. The narrative that pools around Rita embeds a certain interpretive incoherency that has historically attended the take-up with the pachuco/a and zoot-suit figure in Anglo social science research and in Chicano critical and artistic responses to that research.

When we first meet the character Rita, played by Laura Elena Harring, she has just survived a nasty car accident along Mulholland Drive, suffering only a strangely fetching gash on her forehead and the loss of one pearl earring. I liken the gash to the slash through the S in Lacan's symbol for the barred subject, the symbol that also represents, for our purposes, Latino studies' border subject. This gash, as the price to be paid for survival, announces Rita as the *sin-thomestiza border subject*. Dressed in a smart black cocktail dress, she wanders down the Hollywood Hills, already anticipating the film's later engagement with the consummate wandering Mexican woman, La Llorona. In black sling-backs, Rita click-clacks her way across a neighborhood street and tucks herself in behind a tangle of palm fronds for a night's sleep.[55]

In the morning, she sneaks into an apartment. When the apartment owner's niece, Betty, played by Naomi Watts, arrives later the same day from Ontario, Canada, she finds the wandering woman taking a shower. When the wandering woman is asked her name, she goes silent; she cannot remember her name, or anything else for that matter. After spying a poster in the bathroom (of the 1946 film *Gilda*, directed by Charles Vidor) bearing Rita Hayworth's name and image, she assumes this name as her own. Some might recall that Rita Hayworth was made to function as a secret Latina in Hollywood.[56] Hayworth was born Margarita Cansino. She starred in twelve films using the Cansino name and was made to play, without exception, Mexican señoritas. Considered too ethnic, she was encouraged to lose weight and dye her hair. It was also recommended that she have her low hairline moved up and broadened because it was also considered too ethnic. More brow, less brown was the order of the day. The film might itself be read as engaging the ethnic-racialized politics of Rita Hayworth's hair when Rita decides to don a blond wig midway through the film in order to elude the men she imagines are in pursuit of her.[57] She fears these men as much as she fears the LAPD and refuses to allow Betty to contact the police. Although we cannot claim that Rita is a pachuca, she certainly evokes the particular history of crime, the LAPD, and the general mistrust among Mexican Americans for the increasingly corrupt police force that Escobar details.[58]

After some mostly unsuccessful detective work performed by Rita and Betty in an effort to help Rita regain her memory, Rita eventually appears to win some of it back. What returns to her traffics in *lo Chicano y lo Latino*. In the scene where Rita begins to regain her memory, she lets on that what she forgot was that she spoke Spanish. After a night of vigorous sex with Betty, Rita begins to talk in her sleep in Spanish. She mutters, "No hay banda" [there's no band]. The Spanish words wake Betty up, at which point Rita asks her to go with her somewhere. They hail a cab and head for Club Silencio. The filmic sequence of their taxicab ride to the club looks unlike anything else up to that point in the film. The images speed up and then cloud over. The viewer finds himself skidding through murky streets at tremendous speed, traveling in spaces that had been cordoned off from the other city spaces of Los Angeles that the viewer has seen to this point. A new Los Angeles has awoken along with Rita's newfound Spanish tongue. The two women enter the club, a slender upright structure, through a magic slit of a facade that immediately goes jittery. The image of the club vibrates nervously among a cluster of other ghostly facades. Inside the club, they witness the performance of a singer introduced as La Llorona de Los Angeles, played by Latina popular singer Rebekah Del Rio, who lip-synchs to her own stirring Spanish-language version of Roy Orbison's "Crying." Once inside the club, the film suddenly becomes bilingual. For example, the master of ceremonies who introduces "La Llorona de Los Angeles" speaks all of his lines first in Spanish and then repeats them in English.[59] The choice of the *Medea*-like folklore story of La Llorona seems to indirectly repeat the theme of amnesia as suffered by Rita. It locates us in the cognitive force field of remembering and forgetting—remembering and forgetting, in the case of La Llorona's story, where a mother has buried the three children she has just killed.

Lynch's film's attempt to traffic in first, the Spanish language (and bilingualism) that is refound by Rita, and then the Mexican folklore story of La Llorona, in conjunction with the significantly different looking images the viewer gets of the spaces of Los Angeles at this point in the film, reads like a quasi-Chicano historiographic study of Los Angeles, that Los Angeles is Chicano history's history. The sinthomestiza pseudohistorian Rita, who helps facilitate the unearthing of this knowledge, does so through a critical methodology guided by what we might call, while continuing to mine the critical overlap between Lacan and Anzaldúa, "sinthomestiza consciousness." Anzaldúa has famously written, "*En unas pocas centurias*, the future will belong to the mestiza. Because the future depends on the breaking down of paradigms, it depends on the straddling of two or more cultures. . . . The work of *mestiza* consciousness is to break down the subject-object duality that keeps her a prisoner and to show in the flesh and through the images in her work how duality is transcended."[60]

These points, read together, are what the film struggles to remember, and this struggle proceeds apace with Rita's attempt to dispel her amnesia in order to help the viewer locate these ghostly remnants of the Chicano past in a Janus-faced, sinthomestiza view of history whose temporality, we can say, is defined by the future anterior tense of a Lacanian analysis. Dispelling her amnesia also means recalling that as a Chicana-qua-Latina subject, she is a subject in language whose right it is to deliriously slide in the chain of the signifier, in thrall with the metonymy of desire. The passage from Lacan's "The Function and Field of Speech and Language in Psychoanalysis" quoted in chapter 4 denotes here the temporality and tense in which *Mulholland Drive* appears to locate the rediscovery of Chicano history. We can imagine that Lacan here is to be seen as impersonating not only Latinidad but also Anzaldúa's mestiza consciousness: "I identify myself in language, but only by losing myself in it as an object. What is realized in my history is neither the past definite as what was, since it is no more, nor even the perfect as what has been in what I am, but the future anterior as what I will have been, given what I am in a process of becoming."[61]

163

Note the clear resonances between Lacan's "future anterior," "what I am in a process of becoming," and Anzaldúa's "the future will belong to the mestiza," as well as the pachuco's/a's and zoot suiter's—to use Fanon's words—"invention into existence," deeply ensconced as they were in the practice of "endlessly creating myself." Rita and Los Angeles, a veritable character by the end of the film, like two hysterics, never cease getting off on knowledge, never stop producing symptoms and thus generating more and more meaning. Although we might argue that a certain identifiable Chicano history emerges in the film in some ghostly fashion, it is never wrestled down into a final signification since it is constantly in the process of becoming, portraying as it does the transformation of the United States that we are currently calling the Latinization of the United States. In Lynch's film, Latinidad and, more specifically, a Chicano history of Los Angeles, although initially forgotten, refuses not to be remembered. In Stevens's film, Angel dies. In Lynch's film, Rita survives to tattletale on the Chicano past that Anglo history tried to forget.

The latter half of this chapter has been built around cognitive spectacles of remembering and forgetting. Stevens's film, *Giant*, selectively forgets what

Ferber's novel warns against: the emergence of the pachuco/a and, related to that, the emergence of a Chicano politicized discourse and critique that can also be read as a species of Lacanian anti-identity politics before its time. In Lynch's film, Latinidad, and more specifically a Chicano history of Los Angeles, although initially forgotten, refuses not to be remembered. The film seems unable to repel the delirious pull that we are calling the Latinization of the United States. Latinidad and a Spanglish ethos emerge in ghostly fashion in the film through the secret Chicana-qua-Latina amnesiac, Rita.

In chapter 4, I established a homology between Latino studies critique and the "hysteric's discourse" with respect to how both attempt to undermine the master's pretension to absolute knowledge, to being the subject who is not divided so as to divide the spoils in the master's favor. In this chapter, I fixed on the figure of the pachuco/a and zoot suiter for roughly similar reasons, because of how this figure undermined the master's discourse embedded in social science research's attempts to make a kind of perfect, moribund sense about these cultural formations, to wrestle these figures down into manageable ethnic-racialized subjects and how its politics of refusal, not resentment, may serve us as a model by which to reinvigorate contemporary Chicano and Latino identity politics today.

It seems to me a wonderful coincidence that Brooks glosses the sartorial splendor of zoot suiters with the following gorgeous line from "The Sundays of Satin-Legs Smith": "*hysterical* ties like some narrow banner for some gathering war." The pachuco's/a's and zoot suiter's incomprehensible, generative nonresponse to the hailing "Hey you, Mexican American" strikes me, from the vantage point of the twenty-first-century United States, forty years after the gathering wars of the civil rights movement, as, oddly enough, a supremely reasonable, politicized response.

164

Emma Pérez Dreams the Breach: Rubbing Chicano History and Historicism 'til It Bleeds

His words were big, his message mindless.

EMMA PÉREZ, *Gulf Dreams*

I'm brooding in a meeting. Confessing. Healing. Forgiveness was once impossible. In the meeting people gather to release transgressions. We speak words and as they mingle in mid-air, grief dissolves. Infused with air, injuries evaporate. Tears streaming down my face.

EMMA PÉREZ, *Gulf Dreams*

When a typical cultural theorist deals with a philosophical or psychoanalytic edifice, the analysis focuses exclusively on unearthing its hidden patriarchal, Eurocentrist, or identitarian bias, without even asking the naïve, but nonetheless necessary question: okay, but what is the structure of the universe? How is the human psyche really working? Such questions are not even taken seriously in cultural studies; they simply get reduced to historicist reflection upon conditions in which certain notions emerged as the result of historically specific power relations.

SLAVOJ ŽIŽEK, "A Symptom—of What?"

Whatever momentum of re-identification and re-territorialization nationalisms make possible, they always turn on their own strategy of terror: their own interiorization of a center, their own essentializing of a dominant frame of differentiation, their own pograms and expulsions. Whatever the tactical value of their reactive inversions, nationalist discourses remain prisoner to the very terms and structures they seek to reverse, mirroring their fixities and exclusions. But the attachment is also deeper and its effects more pervasive and unconscious, as nationalisms are fractured by the drive of a desire for the very Other they constitute, denigrate, and expel, yet to which they continue to attribute enormous powers.

MARCOS SANCHEZ-TRANQUILINO and JOHN TAGG,
"The Pachuco's Flayed Hide: Mobility, Identity and Buenas Garras"

Few theorists working in Chicano and Latino studies over the years have attempted to articulate psychoanalysis with politics as has the Chicana historian, writer, and queer theorist Emma Pérez. In her bold, unflinching work, Pérez unpacks the limits in historicist thinking. She reveals its inability to attend to what may get remaindered in critical, fictional, and historical narratives of Chicano subjectivity and experience that deploy an approach primarily, if not solely, attuned to (returning to Copjec's definition of "historicist") "the indwelling network of relations of power and knowledge."[1] For a historian like Pérez, who appears committed to exploring the full range of losses (and the full range of meanings that explain the effects of those losses) a human subject stands to suffer in the world, a solely historicist explication of Chicano experience runs the risk of exiling questions that open onto the psychical and, more generally, the unconscious.

Pérez opens an interpretative space between historicist and psychoanalytic approaches by fathoming a Chicano subject who is not just a social and political subject but also a psychoanalytic subject in language. For her, the Chicano subject's freedom and liberation is secured through the ethical psychoanalytic insistence that the Chicano subject in language is incalculable, indeterminate, and can therefore never, as a rule, be fully transcribed in historicist analyses. Moreover, for Pérez, this species of Lacanian psychoanalytic understanding of the subject in language does not prevent us from attending to the texture of individual and collective Chicano historical losses and traumas. It merely crowds the field for what can be contemplated as evidence of Chicano historical loss and trauma by considering the additional narrative of loss that attends every human subject's inscription in language.

I read the challenges that Pérez poses in her history monograph *The Decolonial Imaginary: Writing Chicanas into History* and her novella *Gulf Dreams* to be roughly similar to those I pose to critical race and ethnicity studies scholars who continue to theorize ethnic-racialized subjectivity as though it were not partly determined by the effects of language as structure on the speaking organism. These scholars inadvertently give new life to precisely the ego- and social psychological notion of the ethnic-racialized subject as full, calculable, and potentially whole that is the hallmark of the racist discourses we imagine ourselves as fighting. Pérez's recognition of the seemingly messier, more unwieldy, and less tangible questions that elect themselves in the historicist's attention to the psychical, generally speaking, means engaging with the difficult forms of knowledge production that Copjec describes: "We know now, more concretely than ever before, what goods men and women of various classes were supposed to find pleasurable, which of these were denied them, which allowed, and how the inequalities in the distribution of goods affected the actions of these men and women. *We learn nothing, however, of the historical effects of the fact that men and women often act to avoid pleasure, to shun these goods.*"[2]

The news Pérez brings is not always good, a fact that may explain scholars' reticence to engage her work over the years. Her activism is of the species Michel Foucault identified as his own and on which my book has shrilly insisted throughout—a "pessimistic activism," one that does not insist that everything is bad, but that everything is dangerous.[3] Pérez's attribution of danger to the forces that impact and envelop the subject compels constant action on the part of the Chicano activist, not paralysis. To be clear, I do not think that Pérez should be read as critiquing historicism in simple deference to a psychoanalytic approach. I do not think Pérez's engagement with history and psychoanalysis and the critique of traditional historiographic approaches that she launches more directly in *The Decolonial Imaginary* can be reduced to a debate, strictly speaking, between psychoanalytic versus historicist approaches.

I use the terms of this debate—psychoanalytic versus historicist—cautiously, since Pérez's psychoanalytic critique of historicist thinking emerges where the borders of her history monograph overlap with the borders of her novella, *Gulf Dreams*—where the two, in effect, work to finish each other's sentences, as it were. Thus these two texts should be read together in order to understand the full and complex nature of Pérez's intervention into both historicist and psychoanalytic approaches to Chicano subjectivity, history, and experience.

Pérez's mining of psychoanalysis is never straightforward or necessarily obedient to its perceived codes, protocols, and shibboleth. Like Hortense Spillers, Pérez storms the house of psychoanalysis and demands that, as Chicano and Latino studies scholars, we take up with psychoanalysis if for no other reason than for the fact that we have denied it for so many years. In her theoretical and conceptual universe as historian and artist, this denial registers as a cowardly ceding on one's desire, however impossible and unseemly that desire might seem. Pérez, like Spillers, is not interested in the fixity and rigidity that mark knowledge projects guided by the ego's will to mastery. She is interested in precipitating the historical and psychoanalytic Chicano subject of desire.

Her elaboration of this debate in both the monograph and the novella is organized around two major points of related concern: ethnic-racialized mimicry and coercive ethnic-racialized politicized identity formations. One of the difficult questions the unnamed narrator of the novella appears to ask is whether appeals to the state for protection and recognition from the site of politicized ethnic-racialized identity formations, that seem already to be determined by scripts—psychologistic scripts, we might add—do not risk codifying ethnic-racialized subjectivities as always already lost, copied, transparent, and disprized in legal and extralegal contexts. The question that drives the monograph similarly mines the dynamics of mimicry and coerced performance insofar as it asks after the effects on understandings and inhabitations of Chicano subjectivity in the present and future, if we are condemned to continue historicizing the Chicano past according to what Pérez refers to as U.S. "colonial imaginar(ies)." Both the monograph and novella elaborate on Rey Chow's theory of "coercive mimeticism" but effect a noticeable shift in the original focus of the concept: here the question of laboring to resemble what is recognizably ethnic is rotated slightly to show how this labor is assigned from within Chicano activist and intellectual communities. As the well-worn line spoken by those sage authorities who finally manage to locate the threatening menace in that species of horror film we all recall seeing or living through at some point or another in our lives goes, "The caller is inside the house."

I want to begin with a brief explanation for how the psychoanalytic versus the historicist debate has been articulated before I turn to Pérez's critique of traditional Chicano historiographic approaches. We shall see that Pérez's critique sits somewhere between a psychoanalytic and historicist approach to understanding the meanings we give to Chicano subjectivity and experience. Pérez's engagement with this debate is interested less in proving the benefits of a psychoanalytic critique over a historicist one or vice versa and rather more in the service of insisting on the crucial balancing act critical race and ethnicity studies scholars must strike between these two analytics.

In *Read My Desire*, Copjec critiques historicist thinking by arguing against Foucault—by setting Lacan up against Foucault, essentially, whom she considers, in the end, to be a historicist. She begins with Foucault's critique of linguistically informed analyses:

A corollary of Foucault's denigration of the supposed idealism of language-based analyses is his complaint that they "flatten out" the phenomena they purport to study, that they place all phenomena on the same plane. This is certainly true in one sense; a linguistically informed analysis is obliged to forgo the possibility of a metalanguage; the field of phenomena to be analyzed, therefore, cannot be stratified. No phenomenon appearing there my [*sic*] be taken to account for, to interpret, all the others; none stands above the others as the final interpretant, itself beyond interpretation.[4]

In her explanation of how "reduction" might be said to figure in Foucault's explanation of phenomena, Copjec addresses negation in language:

> His belief that every form of negation or resistance may eventually feed or be absorbed by the system of power it contests depends on his taking this point to mean that every negation must be stated. Thus the prohibition "you shall not do X" must spell out what X is, must incite us to think about X, to scrutinize ourselves and our neighbors to determine whether or not we are guilty of X. . . . *What Foucault seems to overlook is that form of negation which, while written in language, is nonetheless without content. This type of negation cannot, by definition, be absorbed by the system it contests.*[5]

Copjec insists on the need for some notion of "transcendence" if one "is to avoid the reduction of social space to the relations that fill it."[6]

Copjec's point here regarding the "negation which, while written in language, is nonetheless without content" and her insistence on some notion of transcendence can be clarified in the context of our discussion if we link the idea of negation to the loss we've been discussing throughout the book that is attributed to the effects of language as structure on the speaking organism. We can interpret the negation that cannot be absorbed by attempts to symbolize it as roughly similar to Lacan's notion of the irremediable loss suffered by the speaking organism who must at some point choose the distorting medium of language to represent her or his needs in the form of an articulated demand. Recalling the explication of Lacan's elementary cell of the graph of desire that I offer in my introduction, the Real is the name Lacan gives to the order pertaining to a hypothesized fullness of being prior to the moment when the vector representing the movement of life as experienced by the mythic organism of needs is intersected by the vector of language, $S \rightarrow S'$. What is lost by the human organism when it is inscribed in language persists as a remainder, as a remnant of the Real, but it persists as something that cannot be rendered as such in language and that, at the same time, compels all ongoing future attempts at symbolization. Returning to Copjec's language, we can now think of this remainder, roughly speaking, as the outcome of a type of negation—loss—that although written in language is without specific content.

EMMA PÉREZ DREAMS THE BREACH

Regarding how this negation in language figures in Lacan's notion of historicity, Slavoj Žižek explains, "Lacan grounds historicity in a different way: not in the simple empirical excess of 'society' over symbolic schemas but in the resisting kernel within the symbolic process itself."[7] That historicist analyses do not seem to consider this "resisting kernel" is what leads Copjec to ultimately define historicism as "the reduction of society to its indwelling network of relations of power and knowledge."[8] Historicism as Copjec and Žižek understand it has no theory of the Real; it sees every cause as necessarily immanent in the field of its effects.

In his discussion of some of the more problematic effects yielding from historicist analyses, Marc Bracher notes, "The major one is narcissistic closure, which entails repression of both internal and external difference. Historicism promotes narcissistic closure in several ways. It does so first of all by constructing a system of knowledge in which one can situate one's own identity securely and in which an identity group to which one belongs, or values and ideals that one has identified with, are the protagonists."[9] I want to explore this notion of narcissism with the ethnic-racialized subject in mind. In *The Protestant Ethnic and the Spirit of Capitalism*, Chow writes, "At this juncture, representation such as writing becomes an intricate matter. How is the experience of an inaccessible narcissism to be represented? How can something that has not, as it were, been allowed to develop, and is therefore not empirically available, be written about?"[10] Although Chow and I might differ regarding the value that should attach to narcissism and whether we need even consider being pulled in the direction of its elaboration as part of a reparative strategy, I think we agree that ethnic-racialized subjects, given the terms and conditions that instantiate us as socially and culturally intelligible, are coerced and seduced into writing under the sign of narcissism because it seems to represent a form of social and material loss that threatens never to be subject to any remedy.

I think this point is one that Bracher's passage above does not sufficiently consider. Historicism, in the general way Bracher discusses it here, may indeed provide a compensatory narcissism, but his critique of historicism does not take issue with the duping effect for ethnic-racialized subjects of narcissism's promised luminosity—the way that a racist, white supremacist regime always threatens to sink certain marked subjects into the Imaginary quicksanded swamp of the ego. We must make important distinctions between different kinds of historicist projects in an effort to understand what is at stake in the politics of knowledge production in the university. To use a somewhat limited example drawn from my experiences in the humanities, this battle is reflected in the resources that support and underwrite research on Shakespearean drama and the English Renaissance in comparison to, say, Chicano movement politics and Chicano poetry.

Pérez's intervention is an attempt to shed light on the "resisting kernel," the negation in language that historicist work must attend to as well as shedding light on how historicizing a minoritized experience like that of Chicanos immerses its researcher in debates about the politics of knowledge production wherein one must come to grips with the risk of "narcissistic closure" that historicism sometimes necessarily entails.

In *The Decolonial Imaginary*, Pérez already seems to put us on the track of tracing the distinction between historicist and psychoanalytic approaches insofar as she repeats Copjec's gesture of identifying Foucault and Lacan as representative of these approaches. However, whereas Copjec is not interested in reconciling one with the other, Pérez attempts to strike a kind of tense balance between Foucauldian and Lacanian theory as necessarily central to her alternative approach to Chicano historiography. To begin with, Foucault's approach to history defines Pérez's own, as she explains: "My argument is that Chicana/o history, like any other subaltern history, will tend to follow history's impulse to cover 'with a thick layer of events,' as Foucault writes, 'the great silent, motionless bases' that constitute the interstitial gaps, the *unheard*, the *unthought*, the *unspoken*."[11] We should already hear in Pérez's appropriation of Foucault's passage the echoes of Lacan's description of the function of the ego as constituted by virtue of the sedimentation of a "thick layer(s)" of identifications (or identificatory events). We might even add to the terms *unheard*, *unthought*, and *unspoken* yet one more: *the unconscious*.

Lacan's Imaginary, one of the three orders he develops along with the Symbolic and the Real, figures in the central conception in Pérez's book and serves as part of its title, *The Decolonial Imaginary*. She explains, "In the Lacanian sense, the imaginary is linked to the mirror stage, at which a child identifies the 'I' of the self in a mirror, an image is reflected back, and the subject becomes object. For my purpose, the imaginary is the mirrored identity where coloniality overshadows the image in the mirror."[12] Pérez's version of Lacan's Imaginary is in keeping with Lacan's steady reworking of it throughout the 1950s and 1960s, in which the mirror, as a reflecting object in some real ontological event, is gradually replaced by the concept of the Other—that is, the Symbolic, as we saw in chapter 3. Pérez's notion of how "coloniality overshadows the image in the mirror" reflects Lacan's own understanding of how the symbolic operates in the imaginary. Pérez's resonant notion of "the decolonial Imaginary" can also be translated into the terms of my project's insistence on the need to theorize ethnic-racialized subjectivity as not only restricted to the Imaginary. If, as I explained in my introduction, the Imaginary is primarily linked to the ego and its rivalrous identifications and dreams of mastery and where ethnic-racialized subjectivity has been—and continues to be—theorized as all ego, then the idea of "decolonizing the Imaginary" can be read as effectively decolonizing ethnic-racialized subjects from this hegemonic mode of Imaginary engagement and confinement.

Although Foucauldian and Lacanian theory are both being mined to different degrees, Pérez embraces Foucauldian theory without questioning any aspect of it, whereas Lacanian theory is deployed, but with an announced difference, as she declares that she is making a particular use of the Imaginary, "for my purpose," even though her use and Lacan's, as the later version of his mirror-stage article bears out, are not that dissimilar.

What is Pérez's critique of what she terms "traditional" Chicano historiography? She begins with a simple and startling claim: that Chicano historians have come to rely by way of assumption at the very initial point of research on certain historical events and markers as providing the general coordinates around which the Chicano past will be recalled, recollected, and transcribed. Important, although not made explicit by Pérez, is how an agreed-upon version of the Chicano past bears on how the Chicano subject in the present is understood and how certain codified versions of the past participate in the processes and practices that we have named, after Chow and Ford, "coercive mimeticism" and "compelled performance." Pérez links this reliance to a more general problematic that persists, according to her, in all historiography:

> To learn history, we categorize time linearly and map regions geographically. Historians assign names to epochs and regions that reflect spatio-temporal characteristics: The Trans-Mississippi West, the frontier, the Renaissance, the Progressive Era, the Great Depression, the sixties. Within these categoric spaces, we continue to conceptualize history without challenging how such discursive sites have been assigned and by whom. One fundamental result of such traditional approaches to history is that these spatio-temporal models enforce a type of

colonialist historiography. . . . Restricted to the boundaries of arguments that came before, Chicano historians have tended to build a discipline that *mimics* the making of the frontier, or "American West," while at the same time opposing the ideological making of the "West."[13]

Pérez's critique of linear conceptions of time seems to recommend that interpretations of history begin to take seriously the psychoanalytic view of temporality and causality. This view employs the term *deferred action*, in which a subject's history is never simply conceived according to how the past acts on the present but rather understands how fresh impressions sometimes compel revisions of past events or how new impressions may actually compel something ostensibly from the past to suddenly *count* as an event. This view of psychoanalytic-historicist temporality will provide a much more variegated understanding of "how," to return to Pérez's words, "such discursive sites have been assigned and by whom."

After identifying the various assumed historical signposts that guide Chicano historiography, Pérez notes that missing from these versions is any serious engagement with sex and gender as categories that might impact the recalling and codifying of Chicano historical events as *the* events. She understands her intervention as answering precisely to these lacunae: "I want to provide another paradigm, an alternative model for conceptualizing a subaltern and self-consciously oppositional Chicano historiography that can account for issues of the modern, the postmodern, immigrations and diasporas, and genders and sexuality. I call it a theory of Chicano historical consciousness."[14] I want to recall here a point Lacan makes in *Seminar I* on the question of history, because I think Pérez's "Chicano historical consciousness" is very similar to how psychoanalysis theorizes the subject's history, and not only on the question of "deferred action." Pérez, like Lacan in the following passage, theorizes her intervention as a species of historical reconstruction and rewriting: "The precise reliving—that the subject remembers something as truly belonging to him, as having truly been lived through, with which he communicates, and which he adopts—we have the most explicit indication in Freud's writings that that is not what is essential. What is essential is reconstruction, the term he employs right up until the end. . . . I would say—when all is said and done, it is less a matter of remembering than of *rewriting* history."[15] Lacan's use of the phrase "rewriting history" recalls, in more ways than one, the latter part of the title of Pérez's monograph: *Writing Chicanas into History*.

EMMA PÉREZ DREAMS THE BREACH

Early in the first chapter, Pérez argues that Chicano historians have been trained "under the rubric of a U.S. history in which the Southwest does not exist before 1848," thereby becoming "historians under spatio-temporal bounds dependent upon a colonial moment. In this temporal scheme, the Mexican period from 1821 to 1836 is conflated with the coming of the U.S.-Mexican War of 1846–48 and the annexation of northern Mexico to the United States as a colony. Hence, post-1848 Chicana/o history is readily confirmed as 'real' Chicano history, the rupture where Chicanas/os become U.S. citizens."[16] Pérez's bracing critique regarding how Chicano history has been recalled and narrativized as "dependent upon a colonial moment" finds a remedy in her strategy of reading and writing Chicanas back into the various historical scripts, that is, her strategy of refinding Chicanas: "Women's voices and actions intervene to do what I call sexing the colonial imaginary, historically tracking women's agency on the colonial landscape."[17] To render this move, she enlists Chela Sandoval's concept of "differential consciousness": "Like differential consciousness, the decolonial imaginary in Chicana/o history is a theoretical tool for uncovering the hidden voices of Chicanas that have been relegated to silences, to passivity, to that third space where agency is enacted through third space feminism."[18] Recall Bracher's critique of "historicist" analyses as ruled by what he calls "narcissistic closure," "It does so first of all by constructing a system of knowledge in which one can situate one's own identity securely and in which an identity group to which one belongs, or values and ideals that one has identified with, are the protagonists."[19] On the one hand, one could certainly read Pérez's critique of the recollection of the same old past as a critique of a kind of male narcissistic closure. On the other hand, might one not also say of Pérez's project—her role and desires as Chicana subject and Chicana historian and the nature of the alternative model she puts forth—that it risks engaging in its own species of narcissistic closure insofar as the Chicanas who are refound in a historical approach that looks to the past differently provide the missing link that makes the story of the Chicano past whole? I do not think the thrust of her intervention can be characterized as a species of narcissistic closure because her attempt to read and write Chicanas back into history accomplishes the task not of repressing internal and external difference, to use Bracher's terms, but rather of making the repression of those differences visible, palpable, and audible. Moreover, Pérez's intervention, following the general example of Foucault's brand of historicism, never imagines that the story could be told in such a way that it would offer up a narrative that is whole and complete.

There is, however, an aspect to Pérez's intervention that in counterposing so starkly Chicana female invisibility to Chicano male visibility potentially opens her up to a queer and perhaps also Lacanian critique that might note how her intervention risks conjuring, behind her own back, as it were, the dream of complementarity between the sexes. To question the fact that certain Chicano historical signposts seem to elect themselves due to a pervasive and general mortification in approaches to the Chicano past, one needs also to question the framing of the intervention in terms of men and women, since that frame is a party to the petrification in question. Having said this, I want to give readers unfamiliar with debates that have figured in Chicano studies over the years some context explaining the capitulation in Pérez's argument to the assumption of a complementarity between the sexes in the guise of a lack of complementarity between the sexes.

There is a richly tense and conflictive history in Chicano studies scholarship regarding Chicana lesbian theorists' questioning of Chicano history, and historiographic practices more generally, over the last thirty years, not to mention how to situate the contributions of Chicana lesbian feminists—whose work has been broached and guardedly valued in other fields—in the larger context of the field of Chicano studies. Some may be familiar with the many interpretative contortions staged around the historical figure La Malinche, the Amerindian female slave who supposedly became Hernan Cortes's lover and translator during the conquest of Mexico—was she a sell-out, or was she sold out? She has been recuperated in differing degrees as a Chicana feminist figure, and a queer archetype. The controversies over Gloria Anzaldúa's so-called idiosyncratic (they use this word when they're feeling generous) version of history in *Borderlands/La Frontera* often seemed to break down into a Chicano men–versus–Chicana women battle onto death.

Some of the checkered past of the attacks against Chicana lesbian feminists is captured in the incendiary and invaluable collection *Living Chicana Theory*.[20] Chicana historians, queer or not, have always been construed as significantly dangerous—and we should read Pérez's project as dangerous, brilliantly so, because she wants to remap some of the past, to keep whatever may qualify as evidence of a past up for contention from within Chicano studies. For the benefit of the reader unfamiliar with these debates, I want to point to one characterization from an unflinching essay by the Chicana theorist Deena J. González of the internal tensions among Chicano scholars and the reparative, ethical work that still needs to be done. She writes, "Hostile interactions are common among academic Chicanas and Chicanos. . . . The historical record is silent on the subject of our internal dissension, but I raise it because I believe that undergraduates and graduates, a new generation for the academy, must practice new ways of living, of apologizing, and of confronting."[21] González's essay, which cites the work of Chicana lesbian feminists like Pérez—work that is woefully undercredited for the avenues of critique it has opened in a number of fields—provides some context for understanding why Pérez's monograph and her novella, as we shall see, risks conjuring the ghost of the complementarity of the sexes in her very attempt to undermine the assumption of that complementarity.

At stake for Pérez, among other things, is the status of the term *resistance* as it has been assigned to the work of Chicano historians and scholars, not to mention as it has become interlaced with the question of contemporary Chicano (and Latino) subjectivity itself. Although Pérez questions what kind of resistance could possibly yield from Chicano history scholarship that traces the same old events, she does not question the larger disciplinary issues that Chow explores regarding the assumption of resistance that attaches to ethnic-racialized subjects in the imperative "protest or remain invisible." Chow writes, "In this context, to be ethnic is to protest—but perhaps less for actual emancipation of any kind than for the benefits of worldwide visibility, currency, and circulation. Ethnic struggles have become, in this manner, an indisputable symptom of the thoroughly and irrevocably mediatized relations of capitalism and its biopolitics."[22] We may, however, read Chow's diagnosis here as internal to the diagnosis Pérez makes of the taming impact of familiar colonial imaginaries on new Chicano scholarship when she writes, "This means that even the most radical Chicano/a historiographies are influenced by the very colonial imaginary against which they rebel. The colonial imaginary still determines many of our efforts to write history in the United States."[23] The consequences of this are devastating on many levels, according to Pérez:

> But Chicano history is caught in a time lag between the colonial and the postcolonial, the modern and the postmodern, the national and the postnational. What remains is the ontological wish to become that which would allow a liberatory

future promised by the postcolonial, postmodern, and postnational. The historical inheritance, discursive and non-discursive, of the colonial imaginary in the United States has not permitted that ontological wish to come true. It is almost as if we are doomed to repeat the past, to move, not ahead, and certainly not dialectically, but in circles, over and over, as our communities "become" another kind of colonized / colonizer with the colonial imaginary overshadowing movements.[24]

I want to raise a few questions regarding this passage, which turns considerably bleak toward the end as Pérez invokes the doom of repetition compulsion and the death drive. Here, Lee Edelman's recent argument in *No Future* might be appropriate to take up with given the basic homology between both theorists' queer critique of the overlapping concepts of historicity and futurity and how these concepts seem tied in an elemental way to the ideology of hetero reproduction. Is the promise, to use Pérez's words, of a "liberatory future" carved from "historical inheritance[s]," "discursive and non-discursive," that are already spiked with the metaphors of hetero reproduction always doomed to failure when the potential for promise demands, and this seems integral to the alternative nature of her project, that the circuits of historical transmission be queered?

Edelman writes,

> Queers must respond to the violent force of such provocations not only by insisting on our equal right to the social order's prerogatives, not only by avowing our capacity to promote that order's coherence and integrity, but also by saying explicitly what Law and the Pope and the whole of the Symbolic order for which they stand hear anyway in each and every expression or manifestation of queer sexuality: Fuck the social order and the Child in whose name we're collectively terrorized . . . fuck the whole network of Symbolic relations and the future that serves as its prop.[25]

Perhaps Pérez isn't critical enough of the concept of "futurity." Or do the added dimensions in her inquiry that are absent in Edelman's—gender-sex, in the specific context of certain institutional and intellectual power-knowledge issues in Chicano studies to which I referred above, and ethnicity and race— qualify the extent to which her idea of a Chicano future extruded from a reassembled Chicano past can dismiss "futurity" outright when the blighted past struck from the historical record always already seems to place a Chicano future in jeopardy?

Although her critique of traditional, increasingly moribund approaches in Chicano historiography is not a straightforward psychoanalytic critique of historicism, it does still unambiguously betray a certain psychoanalytic frustration and fatigue with a conceptualization of Chicano subjectivity as wholly reducible to an analysis of the relations of power and knowledge in a particular historical formation that is, in her project's terms, determined by coloniality. She challenges a historicist conceptualization of Chicano subjectivity and experience that does not consider what may remain unremarked upon in such an approach, that something about Chicano subjectivity and experience persists as a remainder that cannot be taken up in the order of language. Her critique of traditional Chicano historiographic approaches locates her alternative model somewhere between a psychoanalytic critique of historicism and a historicist critique of a psychoanalytic approach, when the psychoanalytic approach does not—as I gestured to in my reading of Bracher's critique of historicist analyses above—draw any significant distinctions between historicist projects that are in the service of recalling previously invisible, minoritized experiences and those experiences that already reflect dominant white European traditions and cultures.

178

I read Pérez's *Gulf Dreams* as a "thesis novella." In the manner in which Jean Paul Sartre wrote "thesis plays" that theorized the philosophical arguments he made in his essays and nonfiction books, Pérez writes a thesis novella that articulates her theoretical position in *The Decolonial Imaginary* and where interestingly the questions that she doesn't bring up there regarding the viability of a Foucauldian analysis and the qualification of a Lacanian approach for her historiographic concerns ends up being turned around. By this I mean that in her thesis novella the psychoanalytic corrects or amends for what the historicist approach can't shed light on, for what gets remaindered.

In *Gulf Dreams* Pérez's novella's unnamed Chicana lesbian narrator's refusal to be successfully hailed by Chicano movement discourse begs a number of questions regarding ethnic-racialized minoritarian discourse and its ability to address, in this case, its queer Chicano contingencies. Lacanian analyst and theorist Colette Soler reminds us that the master/hysteric couple is found throughout history.[26] Pérez narrativizes this couple within the very field of Chicano history and locates historicism in the position of the master, the master discourse for producing knowledge about Chicano subjectivity and experience.[27] The hysteric's discourse in the monograph is embodied in the critique of traditional Chicano historiographic approaches whereas in the novella the unnamed, queer Chicana narrator is made to inhabit the role of hysteric as she challenges and puts to the test Chicano movement discourse itself. She pressures it to prove its mettle, to prove that it indeed has what it takes.

The text seems to pose the project of becoming politicized as a Chicana subject through the dictates of Chicano movement discourse as, oddly enough, intolerable. The novella although clearly historicist and historical also collects and gathers knowledge about the Chicano subject through a species of psychoanalytic inquiry. Let me explain. It certainly does not, in any explicit way, apply psychoanalysis to read social and cultural issues. The novella engages the psychoanalytical insofar as it points to precisely the kind of remainder that historicist work, however copious and rigorous, cannot account for, which is to say that the novella points to and encircles the Lacanian Real.

What gets remaindered, according to this grim text, is something traumatic that cannot be explained according to its historical effects, something that resists being taken up entirely in the order of language. Try as a reader might, the experiences of the narrator in this text cannot be explained by relying solely on an analysis of her specific sociocultural, economic, and political formation. I know some critics might use the text's refusal to provide an exhaustive explication of the narrator according to this explanatory framework as an argument for why the text is a failure. However, given Pérez's larger critical project of dwelling ferociously in the interpretative space between historicist and psychoanalytic approaches in order to offer the fullest, most complex theory of Chicano subjectivity, I read her strategy of gesturing to what gets remaindered about Chicano subjectivity and experience in any historical narrative as precisely that which secures a bit of freedom and liberation for the Chicano subject. Pérez crafts a historically textured and nuanced narrative of Chicano subjectivity that is informed by a Lacanian ethics of the Real through her insistence in this novella that the Chicano subject is not just a social and political subject but a subject of the signifier, who has the right to experience the fullest range of losses that a human subject stands to endure in the world. In line with the more infelicitous effects that issue from being bullied by a dominant racialized social order into prescriptive ways for understanding one's losses in the social as an ethnic-racialized subject, trauma in *Gulf Dreams*, through what amounts to a complicated boomerang narrative effect, is partly attributed to the politicized Chicano movement discourse, which one might have imagined as contributing to the lessening of the pain and not a deepening of the grief.

The events in the compact, terse, very dense novella *Gulf Dreams*—notoriously difficult to teach—take place primarily in El Pueblo, Texas, a somewhat mythically rendered town, with some events also recorded in Los Angeles. Threaded through the novella is the story of the relationship between the narrator and a "young woman from El Pueblo," a story most often understood by readers and critics as one of obsessive love. Neither woman is ever marked with a proper name. The novella is divided into four sections, "Confession," "The Trial," "Desire," and "Epilogue." The first section tracks the events leading up to and including the first meeting between the narrator and the young woman when the narrator is fifteen years old. In "Confession," the narrator describes the world she inhabited before meeting the woman, a world already seemingly organized to her disadvantage, to which she responds with deep sadness and concentrated practices of self-violence and mutilation. "Since an early age, I learned to exhibit indifference with sadness," she writes (18); "I remember we were poor" (31); "Before I met her I led a childhood filled with grim illusions and stomach-aches" (43); "Self-inflicted wounds marked me at an early age" (71).

While her father's upholstery shop provides some semblance of financial security, the family continues to rely on the labor performed by the narrator and her mother and brother in the cotton fields. By the age of fifteen, the narrator has become profoundly versed in the experiences of poverty, sexual abuse, and ethnic-racialized denigration: "As a young woman of fifteen in a rural Texas coastal town, I didn't recognize love. In a town where humidity bred hostility, I memorized hate" (15).

The two women have a tempestuous relationship, to put it mildly, until the narrator decides to leave El Pueblo after graduating from junior college during the time of the Chicano movement and the Vietnam War. The relationship becomes unbearable for the narrator once the young woman begins a love affair with a Chicano movement activist, César Díaz, referred to as "Pelón" throughout the text. After a ten-year absence, the narrator returns to El Pueblo, Texas, upon reading of the rape of a young Chicana, Ermila. She discovers that Pelón is defending the rapists and decides to attend the trial. The reader, midway through the text, also discovers that one of the five men accused of raping Ermila, Chencho, the ringleader, is also the man who sexually molested the narrator when she was a child. Chencho becomes a fascinating and yielding figure for the narrator; he's gay, but closeted, a rapist, and himself a rape victim at the hands of his uncle when he was a child.

Of the five men accused of raping Ermila, only Chencho is convicted. After a short one-year stint in prison, he's viciously murdered in Los Angeles. Ermila is also murdered around the same time, her bones found on a cove off the beach. By the close of the text, the relationship between the narrator and the young woman has dissolved into real and hallucinatory violence, Chencho and Ermila have been murdered, and the narrator has, curiously, left the reader with the impression that she murdered Chencho and that this murder serves some psychically compensatory and exorcizing function to rid herself of the young woman, Pélon, and the rapist.

Let's begin by tracking in Pérez's novella the work performed by the signifiers "that dare not speak [their] name": *Chicano movement* and the politicized ethnic-racialized identity term *Chicano*. I am intentionally tying the "unspeakability" of homosexuality to the similar unspeakability that accrues to the terms *Chicano* and *Chicano movement* in the novella, since it appears to me that queerness and this specific politicized identity formation and movement play a kind of zero-sum game of intelligibility with each other. One can be spoken only at the cost of the other's elision. The terms actually never once appear in the text. Chicano politicization and the Chicano movement become traumatic kernels around which the more grief-stricken bundles of narrative threads coil and unravel, given how they are floated into the text through the nefarious character named Pélon, "president of the Mexican American Youth Organization," who wears "the typical Pancho Villa, Emiliano Zapata mustache" (54). Pélon figures as the narrative's condensation of Chicano politicization practices and the attending Chicano movement, as well as the obstacle standing between the two women. Is the narrator's rejection of Pélon based on his affiliation with the Mexican American Youth Organization (MAYO)?

MAYO was founded in 1967 in San Antonio, Texas, by five young men: Jose Angel Gutierrez, Mario Compean, Nacho Pérez, Willie Velasquez, and Juan Patlan.[28] These men nurtured their emerging radical Chicano politics on the works of black nationalists like Eldridge Cleaver, Stokely Carmichael, and Malcolm X. MAYO's brand of confrontational politics did not sit well with older, more accommodationist styles of Mexican American politicking. Various so-called leaders of the Mexican American community, such as San Antonio congressman Henry B. Gonzalez, despised the militancy of MAYO. Gonzales argued on the floor of Congress in 1969 that the Ford Foundation should be ashamed for funding "militant groups like MAYO [who] regularly distribute literature that I can only describe as hate sheets designed to inflate passions. . . . The practice is defended as one that will build race pride, but I have never heard of pride being built on spleen."[29] Given the narrator's own adversarial and confrontational posturing throughout the text—"Don't misunderstand me, even when I'm told to hide from public, to meet only in unlit rooms where you can't see us, I'm defiant" (73)—one cannot reasonably assume that MAYO's radical brand of politicking would serve to alienate her along these lines.

We should of course keep in mind that the Chicano movement did not speak in one singular, dominant political voice. There were two primary modes of address: one strategy was largely rural and included César Chávez's attempt to end rampant discrimination against Mexican immigrants working in agricultural labor as well as including the attempts of Reies López Tijerina and his Alianza de las Mercedes movement, which sought to regain the lands stolen from Mexicans after the Mexican-American War. The second mode of address regarded "the urban reality of socioeconomic deprivation and persistent racism" and took the form of political mobilization organized largely by Chicano students: Rudy "Corky" Gonzalez's Chicano Power Movement and Jose A. Gutierrez's La Raza Unida party.[30] Pélon's and the narrator's brand of Chicano politics, resistance, and defiance at first glance would appear to overlap most with this second mode of address to Chicano social injustices.

The narrator in *Gulf Dreams* holds herself responsible to no one except, one might argue, the "young woman from El Pueblo"—"Her hold on me will not cease . . . she controls me in yet another way, in unexplainable ways unknown to me." She mocks the heteromasculinist posturings of Pélon and tries to draw attention to the empty rhetoric he's seen as bringing to her college campus: "Pélon was ordinary, the kind of ordinary who remakes himself with boasting words to exaggerate mediocre talent. . . . He preached to men, parading himself almost charismatically, unaware that he looked and sounded like an adolescent stumbling through clichés" (47, 54–55).

What is Pérez up to in her tirelessly dismissive and negative characterization of Pélon and his brand of emergent Chicano politics, a politics that on some level might certainly have been perceived as helping lessen the deep grief and alienation that appears to be choking and suffocating the town, El Pueblo? In a particularly macabre passage toward the end of the novella, the

182

narrator concludes, "We're lost, you see. Not just you and me, but all of us. We live a violent, psychic horror daily" (139). Some readers have remarked that the disparaging portrait she offers has to do with the narrator's positioning as a queer Chicana who feels utterly erased by a Chicano heteromasculinist nationalist political discourse. Her only defense is to reject anything linked to that discourse. In other words, the critique registered here is the familiar one of most politicized movements of the 1960s organized around race and ethnicity, in which queer minorities were marginalized, when not excluded entirely from membership in these embattled communities.

Although this is clearly an aspect to the critique animating the text, I do not think this reading is sufficient to the task at hand, since Pérez appears also to be commenting on the function of politicized ethnic-racialized nominatory terms, which have a coercive, prescriptive, and compelling nature. This critique stands mostly alone in the annals of Chicano literature. It is, for example, very unlike the moment in Richard Rodriguez's *Hunger of Memory* where "Richard" mocks early expressions of Chicano resistance at Berkeley: "Walking on campus one day with my mother and father, I relished the surprised look on their faces when they saw some Hispanic students wearing serapes pass by. I needed to laugh at the clownish display. I needed to tell myself that the new minority students were foolish to think themselves unchanged by their schooling."[31] Richard is consumed with guilt and is embarrassingly forthcoming about his pathetic, self-amplifying need to mock them.

Pérez's narrator, on the other hand, feels neither guilt nor embarrassment as she identifies Pélon's clownish display as having to do with the mandatory performance of Chicano masculinity that she interprets as the plaster cast of what passed as ethnic-racialized resistant politics during her junior college days as a young Chicana: "The day he recruited students for the university, his words were big, his message mindless, mimicking phrases of genius he'd read, but none came from the core of him. He threw up other's words, not his own" (64). There are no apologies on the narrator's part, but rather a delirious celebration of her unreachable place with respect to the heady discourse of Chicano resistance spun by Pélon: "He told friends and strangers I was a sellout, 'una vendida,' he'd call me and anyone who didn't bow to him, rumoring I wasted time with queers. I enjoyed how I threatened him" (65).

The narrator's description of Pélon during his early MAYO days, when he lectured at the community college, and of how the "young woman from El Pueblo" began to come under his spell effectively empties his lectures of their specific political content. The attention he compels in his listeners seems cobbled and sutured together from prior moments of Imaginary fascination and narcissism—love—between "men" and "women":

> Always within sight of him, she mirrored him back to him. He was her purpose. When they were together in a crowd, he demanded the crowd's attention. To impress. He sought attention, especially from men. And while he did, he dismissed others' successes, his own superior. He worked harder than anyone, he would boast. No matter what job or skill, Pélon reminded others he had excelled in high school and in college. Claiming he was the expert, more competent than anyone, he would speak into air. He didn't converse. He lectured. (46–47)

The narrator describes how the desire to be the subject-supposed-to-know is what centrally informs the transmission of Chicano movement discourse as discourse-supposed-to-know and does not necessarily say anything about the content of the movement's discourse itself.

Pélon tries to pass as having never been subjected to symbolic castration, as never having had to suffer the effects of language as structure, as not having lost any semblance of Real being. He is master, will be master, and might certainly compel the belief in the fantasy that there is at least one who avoids symbolic castration, but he won't fool the narrator. That his primary mode of inhabiting the fantasy of the undivided subject is when he speaks as Chicano activist disseminating Chicano movement discourse is compelling and troubling.

In an earlier, short-story version of the novella that appeared in the now classic Chicana lesbian feminist collection, *Chicana Lesbians: Girls Our Mothers Warned Us About*, Pérez provides a passage expunged from the novella:

> I was born in 1954, the year civil rights was initiated once again through "Brown vs. the Board of Education" in Topeka, Kansas. In the 1950s, pretension superseded reality. McCarthy must have frightened some Mexicans into patriotic idiocies. How many turned their back on mojados? The wetbacks of ancestry forgotten. How many got caught in the American dilemma of scapegoats, communists, and be-bop? In that Texas town there were no civil rights marches, no activists. Only rice paddies and cotton fields where Mexicans and Blacks couldn't even earn a livelihood. El Pueblo was far from Washington and closer to Kansas. Distance, however, was inconsequential, El Pueblo only slept.[32]

Given that most of the text that appears in the short story also appears in the novella, in most cases unchanged in word, syntax, and grammar for pages

184

on end, I was struck by the fact that this particular passage was stricken from the novella. The *Brown v. Board of Education* decision and its impact appears to go missing in the El Pueblo of the novella version in more ways than one.

The novella offers a fascinating microhistory of the Chicano movement as it may have been experienced by a queer Chicana subject in the Southwest in the late 1960s. Again, although MAYO might be understood as ready to address at least some of the concerns raised by the narrator in the novella regarding the various injustices fracturing and circumscribing Mexican American lives and the need to have some politicized group formation willing to address those issues, there is some profound disconnect between what Pélon and MAYO can offer and the narrator's vision of social justice, a vision that is never spelled out for the reader. Where the narrator in the passage from the short story bemoaned the lack of precisely this type of politicized activism in her town, the narrator in the novella, getting what the narrator in the short story wanted, simply eclipses it, ignoring its potential to intervene in the social's profoundly wounded state. This seems to be the case because MAYO's politics, as floated into the text through Pélon, is already presented as irredeemably wounded, even though the reasons for this woundedness are never precisely spelled out.

185

Later the narrator will take up a second time with an extended characterization of Pélon where she links the first narrative sequence with the later context of the courtroom:

> César Díaz, el Péloncito, was a man with devout opinions, true to himself and to men, unaware of how much he loathed women, yet he revealed himself daily when he described how women's words were never truths, only lies and fantasies. Slogans he had once sworn by, he repeated in the courtroom. Pélon defended the rapists, accusing a white media of framing innocent young men, making them a gang of barrio punks. He was so sure of himself that when he spoke about gringo enemies, he forgot who Ermila was and where she came from.[33]

Here Pérez links Pélon's prior take-up with the movement's discourse with his mastery of courtroom Chicano victimization discourse. The text's way of pitting the Chicano sexes against each other is captured perfectly here. The text belabors a certain point of irreconcilability between the sexes at the same time that it constantly hallucinates them in relation to each other in the first place. Pérez's alternative historiographic model in *The Decolonial Imaginary*, as we saw, similarly hallucinates this nonrelation between the sexes in a way that risks reinscribing complementarity in the very act of dissolving the assumed link of correspondence between male and female.

Regarding how the text functions to impart lessons in Chicano and Mexican history in the twentieth century, the novella illustrates through Ermila's story one very specific goal that Pérez set out to fulfill in the history monograph: her attempt to write Chicanas back into history. "Women's voices and actions intervene to do what I call sexing the colonial imaginary, historically tracking women's agency on the colonial landscape," she writes.[34] "The decolonial imaginary in Chicana/o history is a theoretical tool for uncovering the hidden voices of Chicanas that have been relegated to silences, to passivity, to that third space where agency is enacted through third space feminism."[35] The novella labors to uncover these voices by detailing Ermila's difficult, painful family life and the powerful role played by the women in the family, reading the women back into the history of the Mexican Revolution and into the history of Chicano resistance, more generally, "The sturdy, spirited child crossed the *rio Bravo* when she was ten. She would outlive war, fights, and battles; she would witness lynchings during *la Revolucíon*."[36]

186   The narrative also flashcards the naturalized historical links in the U.S. social imaginary between Chicanos and crime as it plays out in the legal system, discussed in chapter 5, through the trial of the five Chicanos accused of raping Ermila. However, Pérez's ferocious characterization of Pélon, the Chicano activist attorney defending the accused Chicano rapists, seems to turn the historical discourse regarding the unjust criminalization of Chicanos by Anglo media and the judicial system and the vigorous Chicano contestations over the years of these characterizations on its head. In Pérez's example, an equals sign suggesting shared ideological beliefs is set up between very different historical agents in this drama of justice and injustice: the Chicano activist defending the young Chicanos, the racist Anglo media, the Chicano defendants who appear guilty beyond question, and, finally, the Mexican-hating attorney in charge of defending Ermila.

No one is let off the hook in this text. Everyone appears to participate in diminishing the life chances of Mexican Americans and Chicanos, those inside the Mexican American and Chicano community and those outside the community. *Gulf Dreams'* coverage of the trial calls up a historic event like the 1943 Sleepy Lagoon Murder trial in which seventeen young Chicano male defendants were unjustly convicted of the murder of José Díaz, although Perez's text's Chicano defendants are far from not guilty, and asks whether there has ever been any room to conceptualize Chicanas in this history of Chicanos, law, and order. Pérez also gives the reader the impression that the narrator murdered Chencho, the leader of the group of rapists, which seems to be an attempt to illuminate the role of Chicanas in Chicano historical scripts of criminality, however problematic on some level it may seem to some. It would be more problematic to continue participating in the ongoing relegation of these Chicana voices, criminal or not, to silence and passivity.

Can the meaning of the narrator's life be reduced down to the power relations that might be seen to partly determine it? Does the narrator employ this interpretative practice when she narrativizes the lives of others? This is a question that returns us to the distinction between psychoanalytic and historicist critical analyses. Let's look at the end of the text. The dynamic of transference where someone—or in this case, with my somewhat idiosyncratic use of the concept, some discourse—is positioned as the subject/discourse-supposed-to-know offers us an additional way of exploring the narrator's relation to Pélon and Chicano movement discourse. The narrator's relationship to the Chicano movement, its discourse of politicization, its heteromasculinist bias, creates a situation we might refer to as negative transference, insofar as the narrator hates in a profoundly unforgiving way the figure or object who represents all of the above. This hatred for Pélon finds itself obsessively "signifierized" through her attempt to write out the unnamed woman's story, whose story is also linked in complicated ways to the rape the narrator suffered as a child at the hands of Chencho, one of the five men accused of raping Ermila. These four passages from different moments in the text give the reader a sense of how these characters and events are knotted together and how the potential vaporization of one might in effect help dissolve the other:

187

Her story suffocates me, anxious for resolution. (91)

In the courtroom, his trial becomes her. (71)

Throughout the trial, I hated her. She, with her husband and his rapists, so proud, refusing to reclaim Ermila. (88)

The time had come. I mustered courage to help me execute the loud rapist, the *costurera's* [seamstress's] son, to purge him from my nightmares, the ones that kept me tied to the woman from El Pueblo. (133)

The narrator's obsessive relationship to writing and the ongoing pressure she feels to narrativize her own history, the history of the "young woman from El Pueblo," and the history of the town throughout the text—"I was addicted to words and she had spawned the addiction" (52)—reveals her to be in thrall with nothing less than the signifier, than with the act of metaphorizing, specifically, metaphorizing the "enigma of the feminine object," to borrow Lacan's characterization of what's at stake in the tradition of courtly love.

In Lacan's discussion of courtly love, which he dates from the eleventh to the beginning of the thirteenth century in Germany, he explains that a form of poetry codified a certain erotics in which woman was conceptualized as a "terrifying," "inhuman partner": "The poetry of courtly love, in effect, tends to locate in the place of the Thing certain discontents of the culture. And it does so at a time when the historical circumstances bear witness to a disparity between the especially harsh conditions of reality and certain fundamental demands. By means of a form of sublimation specific to art, poetic creation consists in positing an object I can only describe as terrifying, an inhuman partner."[37] The unnamed woman-qua-object of the unnamed narrator's affec-

188 tion—we'll use this last term rather loosely—is, if anything, the narrator's "terrifying," "inhuman partner." Lacan's discussion of "courtly love" is apropos in our discussion of Pérez's mining of historicist and psychoanalytic approaches. Lacan's analysis helps show how a historicist study of this tradition comes up short in explaining why it first appeared and why it persisted for so long:

> I am not forcing things in saying that once one has examined all the historical, social, political, and economic evidence, and applied all the available modes of interpretation of the superstructure, our contemporary historians are unanimous in giving up on the question. Nothing offers a completely satisfying explanation of the success of this extraordinary fashion at a period which was not, believe me, so mild or civilized—on the contrary. Society was just emerging from the first feudal period, which in practice can be summed up as being dominated across a large area of geographical space by the manners of bandits; and then one suddenly finds codes that regulate the relations between man and woman that have all the characteristics of a stupefying paradox.
>
> . . . It will have to do with the ambiguous and enigmatic problem of the feminine object.[38]

This notion of the "enigmatic problem of the feminine object" frames the project of Chicano historicization in Pérez's work. The narrator of *Gulf*

Dreams and the Chicana historian in the monograph both appear compelled by the question of the enigma of the feminine object in Chicano history.

The *other* subject in this text is always the *other* woman, who is also the terrifying, inhuman partner, the enigmatic feminine object:

> How can I explain she was the core of me? I repeat this over and over, to you, to myself. We merged before birth, entwined in each other's souls, wrapped together like a bubble of mist, floating freely, reflecting rainbows. This was before flesh, before bones crushed each other foolishly trying to join mortal bodies before the outline of skin shielded us from one another. We both knew this, that we came from the same place, that we were joined in a place so uncommon that this world, which bound and confined us, could not understand the bond that flesh frustrated. (27)

Described here, I maintain, is not so much the fact of fusion with another human organism but rather the dream of having never been subjected to language as structure. Pérez has created a narrator who writes out her refusal to accept symbolic castration in the guise of her love for another woman; this is what sexuality means in this text. On this level, she is like Pélon, who she appears to lambaste for his attempts to come across as the one not subjected to symbolic castration.

Is the narrator dreaming of an opportunity to metaphorize *woman* from a site outside of language? What bond could flesh be said to frustrate? Are we approaching something like a distinction between being and appearance? Being in the Real versus the subject's inscription in language? Pérez appears to want to locate the bond between the women in the Real. In order to insist on the women's Real bond, Pérez must, on some level, deny that she is a subject in language in the very act of operating language in her attempt to symbolize the bond's Real status. In these moments, Pérez's novella interprets sexuality not from the point of view of men and women but rather, following Tim Dean's characterization of his own queer Lacanian theoretical project in *Beyond Sexuality*, "from the perspective of language and its effects": "We misconstrue sexuality's functioning when we begin our analysis of it from the point of view of men and women, rather than from the perspective of language and its effects."[39]

In recalling various aspects of "the young woman from El Pueblo," the narrator cannot make sense of the built-in logical aporias in language, especially when the project at hand is to narrativize woman: "For an instant, I

189

forgot her name. I couldn't place her. She was foreign, a stranger."[40] This is significant if we keep in mind that no final sense can be made of the woman and the relationship between the narrator and the woman. It is this relationship and what happens between them that I argue cannot be explained by an analysis of the narrator's or the woman's sociocultural, economic, and political formation. What cannot be inscribed in language has to do with something else, something that cannot be taken up in the order of language. In this text, what cannot be taken up completely in the order of language is the meaning of "Chicana woman."

The text asks after the enigma of woman as Chicana. What is a Chicana, as materialized in writing by another Chicana? Pérez's narrator is not only hystericizing Chicano movement discourse by incessantly asking after its masterful claims to defining Chicano identity and politics, she is doing so through the very question that Lacan attributes to the clinical structure of "hysteria" itself: "What is a woman?"[41] Pérez hystericizes Chicano movement discourse through the question of the hysteric, with a slight difference: "What is a *Chicana* woman?" Pérez writes,

190

> With phrases I create you. I create you here in text. You don't exist. I never wanted you to exist. I only wanted to invent you like this, in fragments through text where the memory of you inhabits those who read this. You have no name. To name you would limit you, fetter you from all you embody. I give you your identities. I switch them when it's convenient. I make you who I want you to be. And in all my invention, no matter how much I try, you don't have the skill to love, to love me as I am.[42]

A riptide in the narrative has to do with whether or not the narrator will be able to rid herself of the young woman. In the opening lines of the third section (fortuitously for our concerns here, titled "Desire"), she writes, "Her hold on me will not cease. After the trial, in Los Angeles, she controls me in yet another way, in unexplainable ways unknown to me, unfathomable to my conscious habits" (129).

We have already discussed in some detail in chapter 5 how Lacan's notion of the symptom changes from his early teaching to his late teaching, how by *Seminar 23* in 1975–76 he understands that there is something in language immune to interpretation, prompting him to develop the neologism *sinthome*, which is "meaningless, but at the same time it is enjoyment-in-meaning. . . . The sinthome is meaningless, in the sense that it does not have any particular signification. It is a pure signifier, and in that respect, it is meaningless. . . . The sinthome is an enjoyment-in-meaning, however, in the following sense: as a production of meaning, the sinthome is not concerned with the meanings produced, but with the activity of production itself."[43] Pérez's novella and her grappling with the symptom through writing is a species of enjoyment in meaning, in the production of meaning about why she is the way she is, why the town hurts, all the time luring readers into accepting possible reasons that always come up lacking. To consider the labors of the narrator as more closely resembling those of the hysteric, I could say that she is enthralled with the constant production of new symptoms, more knowledge, that she gets off on knowledge.

Have we stumbled upon the good interpretative sense it made to remove from the novella version of *Gulf Dreams* the passage from the short-story version that made reference to the *Brown v. Board of Education* decision? The passage is too clean, too clear-cut about the endless whys and wherefores. A passage like that one threatens to, on some level, dissolve the town's symptom. There's no fun in that, Pérez's unforgiving, symptom-producing narrator might be overhead as saying. However, there's also another way of reading the deletion of that passage: it provides a reason for the town's inhabitants' misery that is entirely reducible to a discursive analysis of the relations of power and knowledge. Pérez puts us, instead, on the track of the split subject in language, the Chicano subject as subject of the signifier. The novella, minus that passage, tells us that the town's misery cannot be explained through even the most copious analysis of the social, economic, and political forces of racism and discrimination. There are the effects of language on the speaking subject: "I thought writing this years later would release me from her. But I feel no reprieve. Not yet. Maybe the only resolution is in the act of loving. Maybe I had to love her enough to let her go. I had to begin to love her more than I loved my selfishness. I disavowed what I had to do. I wasn't ready: I cried" (27–28). Is Pérez's narrator here illustrating the move from symptom to sinthome, from dissolving the symptom through interpretation—meaning, in a basic way, that one has to *believe* in the symptom—to identifying with the symptom—thus the resolution in loving?

In the last section, "Epilogue," the narrator concludes, "You were a symptom, a symptom of my irrevocable illness. I warned you how I fell in love with women easily. I was careful to warn you about my dishonesty, my carelessness. There is no cure for my illness, the insanity I rehearse. Nothing will change me, not even you, my beautiful symptom, the one who will not judge me harshly."[44] What the narrator cannot acknowledge, it would appear, in this passage is that the lack is structural. The illness is language, so to speak—language makes the human subject sick with meaning. On the one hand, the narrator appears to be transitioning from an obsessive interpretation of the symptom to an *identification* with it, and this would appear to embed a prior acknowledgment that the Other is lacking. On the other hand, the narrator's claim that "there is no cure for my illness" gives the impression not so much that there is no cure for the generative sickness that language introduces, but rather that *her* particular illness is enigmatic and that no cure for it has been found. The hope for a cure continues, however. What accounts for this static?

Lacan's later work on the sinthome was heavily informed by his readings of James Joyce's work, in particular *Finnegans Wake*. He spoke of how Joyce's text appears to get off on itself. Pérez's narrator, like Lacan's Joyce, is getting off on language, addicted to words as she claims to be, but Pérez's narrator, unlike Joyce, seems to harbor some guilt about this. The narrator dreams partly of being cured of symbolic castration. The "gulf dreams" in the title might be read as the dream of being beyond the gulf, beyond the breach introduced in the human organism by language, the dream of a moment prior to the subversion of the biological by language and the system of signifiers. No cures assuage the pain of the loss constitutive of subjectivity. In "The Signification of the Phallus," Lacan writes, "This passion of the signifier thus becomes a new dimension of the human condition in that it is not only man who speaks, but in man and through man that it speaks; in that his nature becomes woven by effects in which the structure of language of which he becomes the material can be refound; and in that the relation of speech thus resonates in him, beyond anything that could have been conceived of by the psychology of ideas."[45] On one level, the text seems to know this—"There are no cures. People like us can't be cured. Remedies don't exist, they haven't been invented"[46]—and then it also forgets that it knows.

What does the impasse here tell us? How does it pick up on broader concerns in my project? I think the text illustrates the difficulty for some subjects of maintaining a certain kind of knowledge about the truth, the lack in the Other, because of issues related to Chow's notion of "coercive mimeticism." When the coordinates for one's subjectivity appear to be entirely afforded one from the big Other, how does one keep the kind of distance one needs to maintain and not dissolve in the very moment when one encounters the lack in the Other, that the Other cannot answer the question about one's existence?

If "coercive mimeticism" partly indicates to us that ethnic-racialized subjec-

192

tivity is scaffolded in the manner of a symptom, then what I am proposing, and what I read Pérez and Spillers as proposing on some level, is the dissolving of the symptom and thus the ego. That is, I imagine, an intolerable and ultimately unsustainable project, but it is available as a politics of resistance.

Returning to the discussion regarding how the Chicano movement is posited as the discourse-supposed-to-know, the big Other who grants the coordinates according to which the narrator is to situate herself, we will need to consider whether the novella shows that in the master's discourse a certain remainder persists. I want to focus my attention on the movement discourse's role in attempting to veil the constitutive division of the subject. Since I am arguing that, generally, ethnic-racialized subjectivity is theorized as not subject to the effects of language, the way the movement discourse operates here should make us pause. We need to consider whether the narrator in *Gulf Dreams* is able to articulate the basic question of the hysteric in Lacan's four social discourses: the hysteric's, the analyst's, the university's and the master's. Žižek explains, "The hysterical question articulates the experience of a fissure, of an irreducible gap between the signifier that represents me (the symbolic mandate that determines my place in the social network) and the nonsymbolized surplus of my being-there. . . . The hysteric embodies this 'question of being': his/her basic problem is how to justify, how to account for his/her existence (in the eyes of the big Other)."[47]

Chicano movement discourse in the novella works in such a way that it wants to draw this species of question and answer to a definitive close. I think it's quite clear that Pérez's narrator in effect attempts to hystericize the movement discourse by showing it up for what she thinks it doesn't have, revealing that it cannot, in the end, prove its mettle. However, she does not break free from its power to continue providing the symbolic coordinates of her existence. She is still responding to a demand that she imagines the movement discourse to be issuing to her because of her hatred and contempt for the figure made to embody the movement in the text, Pélon, in relation to whom she continues to see herself in conversation. To be clear and to be fair, given the text's very complicated manner of condensing and aligning the figures and events that come to represent, in no particular order, Chicano movement activism, the Mexican American Youth Organization, the objectionable figure Pélon, the narrator's obsessive desire to signifierize the enigma of *Chicana woman*, and her attempt to make sense of her rape as a child, by lending them all virtually equivalent weight with respect to what motivates the basic production of signification in the text, it feels like sleight of hand on my part to single out the Chicano movement as that which the narrator imagines as continuing to issue seemingly superegoic demands to her, to which she cannot help but keep responding. I cannot resolve these issues here because—and here I'm affording myself an alibi of sorts—I do not think the text allows for their resolution. It won't allow the reader to make complete sense of these rich difficulties because of how the text inscribes a reading of the symptom as the late Lacan of *Seminar 23* understood it, as that which cannot be dissolved through language and interpretation.

In closing, I want to return to the final passage included in the epigraphs to this chapter, a passage that I will deploy as a kind of rationale for the negatively charged affect that suffuses Pérez's narrative. Marcos Sanchez-Tranquilino and John Tagg write,

> Whatever momentum of re-identification and re-territorialization nationalisms make possible, they always turn on their own strategy of terror: their own interiorization of a center, their own essentializing of a dominant frame of differentiation, their own pograms and expulsions. Whatever the tactical value of their reactive inversions, nationalist discourses remain prisoner to the very terms and structures they seek to reverse, mirroring their fixities and exclusions. *But the attachment is also deeper and its effects more pervasive and unconscious, as nationalisms are fractured by the drive of a desire for the very Other they constitute, denigrate, and expel, yet to which they continue to attribute enormous powers.*[48]

The closing sentence has an obvious Lacanian psychoanalytic resonance. The Other in this passage could be read as the symbolic Other, and the enormous powers attributed to it can be interpreted as illustrating, in the context of Pérez's novella, the narrator's dependence on the demand seen to issue from this Other-qua-Chicano nationalist discourse. This captures precisely the power of Chicano movement discourse's function for the narrator in Pérez's text, as I described above.

It is perhaps irritatingly clear to the reader that I have not read Perez's novella for the empowering angles of vision it lends to ethnic-racialized, queer minoritarian politics as currently conceived. I have instead attempted to isolate those moments where the text theorizes Chicano subjectivity not only according to historicist analyses but also in accordance with a Lacanian psychoanalytic literacy that stays alive to the effects of language on speaking Chicano subjects, inscribing, in the process, an understanding of Chicano subjects as not only social and political subjects but as, additionally, subjects of the signifier.

The text is bleak, and this grimness, I argue, is indirectly tied to the bullying effects of the Chicano movement discourse that tries to strong-arm the unnamed narrator. To use the characterization offered by Sanchez-Tranquilino and Tagg above, the Chicano movement discourse in *Gulf Dreams* makes trouble for Pérez's narrator because these types of nationalisms "turn on their own strategy of terror." I do not mean to suggest that the existence of this species of Chicano nationalism embedded in movement discourse does more harm than if it simply did not exist at all as a point of identification or disidentification. I am trying to shed light on how "coercive mimeticism" and "compelled performance" appear to work as internal mandates to the politicization projects detailed in this novella as well as in how traditional Chicano historiographic practices, as Pérez explains in *The Decolonial Imaginary*, routinely recall and narrativize a useable Chicano past. So then what is the problem? Am I suggesting that given the force of "coercive mimeticism" and "compelled performance" that there is no way for any ethnic-racialized group — whether in seeming capitulation or resistance—to not slavishly respond to and fulfill the mandates of mimicry and resemblance that grant them a modicum of social and cultural intelligibility in post–civil rights U.S. culture? I am suggesting that the best way to intervene here would be to take more seriously and pursue more rigorously the Lacanian resonances in the passage above by Sanchez-Tranquilino and Tagg. In the failure of compelling an interpretative strategy that is both psychoanalytically attuned to the losses that are constitutive of subjectivity—the effects of language on the speaking subject—and attentive to the deep historical texture of those losses attributable to social and material inequities, we develop an Imaginary politics of the ego.

I think this is how we might read Pérez's novella's negatively charged affective universe. In it, the available Chicano politicization practices are not only heterosexist and masculinist, they also appear to smuggle all viable expressions of resistance and defiance into the arena of the ego, precipitating, to return to some choice words from the fourth epigraph to this chapter, "terror," "denigration," and "expulsion." In the end, ego politics terrorize, denigrate, and expel.

For Lynda Hart, still

The Clinical, the Speculative, and What Must Be Made Up in the Space between Them

> Who, for example, decides what constitutes a problem for the patient? And by what criteria?
>
> ADAM PHILLIPS, "Keeping It Moving"

The phrase "clinical and speculative" in this chapter's title is borrowed from a conversation between Adam Phillips and Judith Butler. In it, they attempt to craft a psychoanalytic dialogue between a clinical and a speculative perspective "on questions of gender, melancholia, and performativity."[1] In this chapter I attempt to forge both a psychoanalytic and a psychological dialogue between clinical and speculative perspectives not on questions of gender, strictly speaking, but on questions of ethnic-racialized subjectivity. Although I have not intentionally focused on the additional questions of melancholia and performativity as do Phillips and Butler, they seem to draw attention to themselves anyway insofar as melancholia and performativity appear embedded in the larger topic around which I've organized these psychoanalytic and psychological dialogues—the coerced and compelled performances of ethnicity that must be staged by ethnic-racialized subjects in order for them to qualify as socially and culturally intelligible subjects in contemporary U.S. culture. These labors of resemblance operate, as David Eng and Shinhee Hann remind us, as a "melancholic process"[2] that is, in turn, responsible for engendering what Rey Chow describes as the "profound sense of self-hatred and impotence among ethnics," because no matter how obediently we follow these scripts of *nativeness*, no matter how well we read for the part, we will always come across as "copies that are permanently out of focus."[3]

Much of this book has insisted on the need to engage a more Lacanian psychoanalytic reading of the ethnic-racialized subject as a subject in language, as a subject of the signifier in our work as critical race and ethnicity studies scholars, so that we might theorize in the richest, most complex manner possible the full spectrum of psychical, material, and social losses that a human subject stands to endure in the world. This recommendation has, no doubt, at times appeared restricted to the realm of theory. That is to say, the movement in thinking it tries to inspire appears restricted to the limited range of motion allotted an intervention at the theoretical level in predominantly academic contexts where so often one walks heavily, and where movement of any sort is generally slow and plodding.

In this chapter, the deployment of a more Lacanian psychoanalytic account of ethnic-racialized subjectivity will take on the more definitive and recognizable shape of an actual critical and interpretative practice, a practice inspired by the psychoanalytic hermeneutic practice developed by Hortense Spillers, "interior intersubjectivity." Spillers's psychoanalytic hermeneutic serves as a practice that we can engage in at all levels of society, and it interrupts, if not stalls, the hailing practices, both within and outside of ethnic-racialized communities, that call out to us with names that promise legibility on the condition that through the searing, branding process that accepting the name entails we then tacitly, quietly agree to authenticate for ourselves and others the full, transparent, and mortified account of who and what it is we are imagined and hallucinated to be.

In the first section of this chapter, I pair Spillers with Franz Fanon in the service of exploring clinical and speculative perspectives in psychoanalysis on the question of ethnic-racialized subjectivity and the cultivation of politicization practices among ethnic-racialized subjects and analysands inside and outside the clinical setting. Spillers, an African American cultural and literary theorist, is positioned here as representing the speculative perspective, whereas Fanon, the psychiatrist, is seen as representing the more properly speaking clinical perspective. However, we shall see that this distinction is ultimately rendered quite porous as both theorists break down this opposition and reconfigure it in the course of their own arguments.

In the second section, Spillers's theory of "interior intersubjectivity" still finds ample room to circulate as a possible interpretative strategy and practice of resistance. It finds itself, however, in a slightly altered terrain, as my ongoing exploration of the dialogue between clinical and speculative perspectives shifts from psychoanalysis to material from the fields of ethnic psychology, Hispanic psychology, and Latino psychiatry in order to see how clinicians and therapists imagine one is to treat an ethnic-racialized patient and, related to that, how they theorize the therapeutic value that attaches to the assumption of a strong ethnic-racialized identity. Chow's meditations on the psychological impact of "coercive mimeticism" on ethnic-racialized subjects serves in this section to represent the speculative perspective on psychology in the dialogue between it and culture criticism on the political, economic, and psychical questions related to the inhabitation of ethnic-racialized identities in twenty-first century U.S. multicultural society. I also look briefly to material in the emergent field of political psychology to understand how ethnic-racialized children in the United States are described as developing either strong or weak ethnic-racialized identities and how the positive value ascribed to acquiring strong ethnic-racialized identities is to be understood when compared to Lacanian theory's critique of the clinical strategy of strengthening the ego.

SPILLERS, LACAN, AND FANON:
LET'S GET DECENTRALIZED, DISPERSED, AND DISARRAYED

Discussing interior intersubjectivity, Spillers insists that "race"—that is, the meanings and significations that accrue to and yield from the idea of race—is around making signifying trouble prior to language and the subject's inscription in language. I had interpreted this reading as introducing some potential static with a Lacanian position. If we understand the signifierness of race as being of the Symbolic order and acknowledge that the Symbolic preexists the infant's entry into the world, Spillers does have a point, one that could be defended through Lacanian theory. Here I will read Spillers's claim regarding race's prelinguistic signifierness in relation to sexual difference.

Spillers's idea may be read as keying the debate between Lacanian psychoanalytic theorists and feminist theorists on the inaugural and anterior status lent to "sexual difference" by Lacanians in a theory of subjectivity constitution. Characterizing the Lacanian psychoanalytic position as it's been elaborated by Joan Copjec and Kaja Silverman, Jean Walton writes, "The matter of 'racial, class, or ethnic identity' is invoked only to function as a foil to sexual identity; it is presumed that we already know what it means to say that racial identity, for instance, is 'inscribed in the symbolic.' Is it that the intractability of sex is being contrasted to a presumed mobility of race?"[4] One might regard a claim that states the existence of something prior to language as lending that existence a Real status in Lacanian theory. Think back to my explication of the elementary cell of the graph of desire in the introduction, where we noted that the mythic organism of needs prior to being intersected by and thus

198

inscribed through the vector of language is to be located in the register of the Real. Returning to Spillers's point, might we say that she is claiming a Real status for race, that race is in the Real in the way many Lacanians claim sexual difference is of the Real?

The Lacanian argument as to why sexual difference is a different kind of difference from racial or class difference is very complicated. Although I have not given myself the time and space here to unpack this argument in its entirety, I would like to give the reader a sense for how some Lacanians explain this difference. In a careful engagement with Butler's *Gender Trouble*, Copjec writes, "While sex is, for psychoanalysis, never simply a natural fact, it is also never reducible to any discursive construction, to sense, finally. For what such a reduction would remain oblivious to is the radical antagonism between sex and sense."[5] We have spoken previously of the distorting medium of language that the organism of needs must eventually choose in order to express her or his needs in the form of a demand. Language is a differentially constituted system of signifiers, in which signifiers mean something only in relation to each other, in their difference from each other. There are no positive terms in language.

As many Lacanians understand it, language does not somehow fail to fully grasp sex; sex does not elude language, but rather sex coincides with the very failure in language to provide determinate meaning. Again, Copjec explains, "Sex is, then, the impossibility of completing meaning, not . . . a meaning that is incomplete, unstable. Or, the point is that sex is the structural incompleteness of language, not that sex is itself incomplete."[6] Sexual difference, therefore, cannot be inscribed in language—which is to say, inscribed in the Symbolic, except as the failure of its inscription, as a mark of its failure. Some Lacanians believe that this is not the case with other kinds of difference like racial or class difference. These latter differences can be inscribed in the Symbolic. These inscriptions are still, of course, subject to the distorting medium of language in which they appear, but they do not constitute, like sexual difference, the very built-in failure in language's attempt to provide determinate meaning. According to Copjec, this fact "should not disparage the importance of race, class, or ethnicity, it simply contests the current doxa that sexual difference offers the same kind of description of the subject as these others do. . . . It is always a sexed subject who assumes each racial, class, or ethnic identity."[7]

THE CLINICAL, THE SPECULATIVE

The Lacanian theorist Kalpana Seshadri-Crooks provides a somewhat different reading of the relation between racial and sexual difference and the question of their Real status. She writes:

> I suggest that race should be understood in its particularity as something that is neither totally like sexual difference, which is indeterminate and exceeds language, nor purely symbolic or cultural like class or ethnicity. Race resembles class in that it is of purely cultural and historical origin, but it is also like sex in that it produces extra-discursive effects. From a certain perspective, it seems marked on the body, something inherited like sex; from a Lacanian perspective, one might even suggest (erroneously) that it seems to exceed language.[8]

Seshadri-Crooks maintains the privileged status of sexual difference in relation to racial difference at the same time that she does not simply align racial with class and ethnic difference, as do some other Lacanians. For her, race is unlike sexual difference, and it is also unlike ethnic and class difference. They are related, according to Seshadri-Crooks, but they cannot be analogized: "The order of racial difference attempts to compensate for sex's failure in language."[9]

In the following lyrical passage in Spillers's essay, she engages this debate by suggesting that race, although previously theorized by her as existing prior to language, now appears to come second, after something else. Is it sexual difference? In section 5 of her essay, Spillers begins by remarking on her childhood and her minister's odd pronouncement of "send go." Later in the same section, she returns to the scene of the church to entertain another conundrum: racial and sexual difference:

> But if we move back in the direction of a "prior" moment, the seven year old in the front pew, for instance, we can then go forward with another set of competencies that originate, we might say, in the bone ignorance of curiosity, the child's gift for strange dreams of flying and bizarre, yet correct, notions about the adult bodies around her—how, for example, her father and brothers bent forward in a grimace when mischievously struck in a certain place above the knees by a little girl, propelling herself off a rollaway bed into their arms. *The foreignness had already begun in the instant grasp of sexual and embodied division.* But from that moment on, the imposition of homogeneity and sameness would also be understood as the great text of the "tradition" of "race." The Fanonian abyss requires this urtext as the "answer" that fosters a two-way immobility. *But before "race," something else has happened, both within the context of "race" and alongside it.*[10]

In the context of our discussion, we are compelled to read the two italicized passages together: "The foreignness had already begun in the instant grasp of sexual and embodied division" & "But before 'race,' something else has happened, both within the context of 'race' and alongside it." Are we to understand the "sexual and embodied division" in the first passage as that which happens before "race" in the second? That understanding would resemble the Lacanian position. However, the passage's syntax also appears to suggest that race is already present in the moment carved out as preliminary to it. What kind of temporality is this? That is, before race, *something else* has happened, but this something else already appears determined in some way by the context of race, and so what happens before race also appears to happen alongside race.

If Spillers can be read, as I'm suggesting, as remarking on the question of the status we are to afford racial and sexual difference in Lacanian psychoanalytic theory, she looks to scramble the question from the get-go. The temporality in which Spillers operates the question makes the argument for one or the other's prior status seem ultimately undecidable. Spillers appears to subject Copjec's claim that "it is always a sexed subject who assumes each racial, class, or ethnic identity"[11] to Lacan's notion of "reversible time," discussed in chapter 4. This temporality is split between anticipation and retroaction, which adds a certain tone of bemusement to the debate and effectively transforms Copjec's claim into a question: "Is it always a sexed subject who assumes each racial, class, or ethnic identity? Really?" We might also characterize the temporality introduced by Spillers as the psychical temporality and causality of "deferred action" in which, for example, a fresh impression of the significance of the function of racialized difference as experienced by ethnic-racialized subjects in a Symbolic order suffused with racialized meanings may compel a revision of the event previously experienced in some way as "sexual and embodied division," or vice versa.

I have tried to attend carefully to the riotously complex meanings that Spillers attaches to race. The signifying labor she needs it to perform in relation to both language as structure and to sexual difference allows her to craft a theory of the subject who precipitates through the practice of "interior intersubjectivity." This is homologous to Lacan's theory of the subject who emerges at the end of analysis, which makes explicit Spillers's attempt at articulating Lacanian psychoanalysis with a politics of race.

Briefly, for Lacan, the subject at the end of analysis is no longer a slave to

201

the demand seen to issue from the Other; the subject learns to assume responsibility for herself by becoming her own cause, as it were. For Spillers, the subject who vigorously practices an "interior intersubjectivity" achieves a similar release from the Other insofar as he is no longer a slave to the demand that issues from race as a structure of narrativity and signification that attempts to exhaust the meaning of human subjectivity. She writes:

> The question, then, for this project is not so much why and how "race" makes the difference—the police will see to it—but how it carries over its message onto an interior, how "race," as a poisonous idea, insinuates itself not only across and between ethnicities but within. What I am positing here is the blankness of "race" where something else ought to be, that emptying out of which I spoke earlier, the evacuation to be restituted and recalled as the discipline of a self-critical inquiry. In calling this process an interior intersubjectivity, I would position it as a sort of power that countervails another by an ethical decision.[12]

The practice of interior intersubjectivity helps the speaking subject locate the space in which race falsely dwells as a structure of narrativity and significa-
202   tion that attempts to explain the nature of the human subject. At the same time, it helps evacuate and restitute that space for other knowledge projects of "self-critical inquiry" that risk precipitating a nontransparent subject who can no longer be wrestled down through the calculus of race. Simply and forcefully, interior intersubjectivity concerns rescuing the blank space that race somehow came to fill in the constitutive work of subjectivity formation in order to reclaim it as a surface of inscription for other interpretative efforts.

The homologous critical operations performed in Spillers and Lacan precipitate a kind of subject who is necessarily dispersed, decentralized, and in disarray. In the last paragraph in her essay, Spillers writes, "My interest in this ethical self-knowing wants to unhook the psychoanalytic hermeneutic from its rigorous curative framework and try to recover it in a free-floating realm of self-didactic possibility that might *decentralize* and *disperse* the knowing one."[13] Toward the end of *Seminar VII*, Lacan notes, "At the end of a training analysis the subject should reach and should know the domain and the level of the experience of absolute *disarray*. It is a level at which anguish is already a protection, not Abwarten as Erwartung. Anguish develops by letting a danger appear, whereas there is no danger at the level of the final experience of Hilflosigkeit [helplessness]."[14] Lacan's notion of disarray is internal to what Spillers calls "decentralization" and "dispersal." It is this disarray—Spillers's attempt to decentralize the ego and thus undermine its pretension to mastery as the center of consciousness as well as her attempt to promote the subject's dispersal into spaces of possibility outside its incarceration in solitary Imaginary confinement—that the ethnic-racialized subject must experience in order to understand that she is a subject of the signifier who is incalculable, indeterminate, and always in the process of becoming.

Lacan's and Spillers's homologous critical approaches to theorizing the dispersed, decentralized subject in disarray are also revealed in the nature of the kind of interpretative labor each thinks must be performed, one that is not curative in nature nor in the service of amplifying the ego. She writes,

> I have chosen to call this strategy the interior intersubjectivity, which I would, in turn, designate as the locus at which self-interrogation takes place. It is *not an arrival but a departure, not a goal but a process,* and it conduces toward neither an answer nor a "cure," because it is not engendered in formulae and prescriptions. More precisely, its operations are torque-like to the extent that they throw certainty and dogma (the static, passive, monumental aim) into doubt. *This process situates a content to work on as a discipline, as an askesis, and I would specify it on the interior because it is found in economy but is not exhausted by it.* Persistently motivated in inwardness, in-flux, it is the "mine" of social production that arises, in part, from interacting with others, yet it bears the imprint of a particularity.[15]

What Spillers has in mind is not the working on the subject that would resemble the reconsolidation of the ego's masterful powers or the restoration of the ego as whole, "It is not an arrival but a departure, not a goal but a process."[16] This strategy has to do with frontally challenging the fixity and rigidity that characterizes the ego's resistance to subjective growth and change: "its operations are torque-like to the extent that they throw certainty and dogma (the static, passive, monumental aim) into doubt."[17] Her specification of an interior as that which is "in economy" but not exhausted by it indirectly critiques the more routine approach to ethnic-racialized subjectivity and experience through explications attuned solely to social, cultural, and historical but not psychical analyses. Her use of the term, *askesis* reminds one of how Lacan characterized psychoanalysis's species of interpretative labor. In "The Function and Field of Speech and Language in Psychoanalysis," Lacan writes, "Of all the undertakings that have been proposed in this century, the psychoanalyst's is perhaps the loftiest, because it mediates in our time between the care-ridden man and the subject of absolute knowledge. This is also why it requires a long

203

subjective ascesis, indeed one that never ends, since the end of training analysis is not separable from the subject's engagement in his practice."[18]

Although throughout her essay Spillers speaks generally of psychoanalysis, sometimes referring to "classical psychoanalytic theory" and mentioning the names of both Freud and Lacan, I see her model as primarily Lacanian. Spillers wants to pursue the ethnic-racialized subject's signifying dependence. Understanding the nature of that dependence and the signifying elements that constitute the subject's symbolic universe are precisely the nature of the interpretative labor that Spillers has in mind: "The one that I am after, then, must be built up from the ground, so to speak, inasmuch as classical psychoanalytic theory and its aftermath contradictorily point toward it—a subject in its 'signifying dependence,' which means that the subject's profound engagement with, and involvement in, symbolicity is everywhere social."[19]

Now that we have unpacked some of the essential elements that make up Spillers's psychoanalytic hermeneutic practice of interior intersubjectivity, I want to explore the specific relation between what Spillers refers to in the passage above as "a subject in its 'signifying dependence'" and the larger goal announced in the practice of interior intersubjectivity: the "evacuation," "that emptying out" of race "where something else ought to be" in an effort to compel new modes of "self-critical inquiry" not determined by the calculus of race. There is an exceedingly seductive, utopic charge to the project of emptying the space filled by race. It implies that the subject's signifying dependence on race would no longer exist, insofar as race in the position of the Other—to continue mining the similarity between Spillers's subject and the subject at the end of the Lacanian analysis—whose demand we think we are still called upon to respond to has been evaporated.

Seshadri-Crooks sharply describes the stubborn ways in which we continue to hold on to the idea of race:

> As a system of organizing difference, race is very distinctive in relation to other forms of organization such as caste, ethnicity and nation. It is distinctive as a belief structure and evokes powerful and very particular investments in subjects. Consider the peculiar intensification of racial identification and racial discourse even as the scientific untenability of race is ever more insisted upon by scientists and anthropologists. Even though it has now become commonplace to utter rote phrases such as "race is a construct" or "race does not exist," etc., race itself shows no evidence of disappearing or evaporating in relevance. It is common sense to

believe in the existence of race. Why do we hold on to race? What is it about race that is difficult to give up?[20]

Seshadri-Crooks's questions appear not to bode well for Spillers's ultimate goal. The positing of "the blankness of 'race' where something else ought to be" might be an impossible task that when actively engaged may in fact serve only to perpetuate the ongoing hallucination of race in new and no less damaging disguises.

I want to return to one sentence from Spillers's essay and read it in a way that would suggest less tension between Seshadri-Crooks's insight and Spillers's goal. Again, Spillers writes, "What I am positing here is the blankness of 'race' where something else ought to be, that emptying out of which I spoke earlier, the evacuation to be restituted and recalled as the discipline of a self-critical inquiry."[21] If we agree that race may register in any number of ways but "blankness" won't be one of them, then we could still understand the "discipline of a self-critical inquiry" as an interpretative practice that understands that race won't disappear any time soon. A scrutinous analysis of its stubborn hold on us and its ongoing role in the constitution of human subjectivity are the "something else" that Spillers is after. She names this discipline "interior intersubjectivity," a hermeneutic strategy that, although it may not render race blank, will lay bare the processes—psychical, social, economic, and political— that explain to us why race won't budge, why, to return to Seshadri-Crooks's words, it "shows no evidence of disappearing or evaporating in relevance."[22] Spillers imagines her hermeneutic as a species of psychoanalytics, since race cannot be addressed simply through historicist genealogies that describe its discursive construction. I think Spillers believes, like Seshadri-Crooks, that race makes certain constitutive psychical claims on our existence that don't simply go away because we describe, ad nauseam, its scientific untenability, its social constructedness, its variability over time and cultures, and so on.

The discussion so far, in focusing on Spillers, was supposed to have broached only the speculative perspective on ethnic-racialized subjectivity in the context of psychoanalysis, as I positioned Spillers as representing the speculative and not the clinical. Yet the reader will surely have noticed how Spillers's approach has effectively broken down that opposition and even reconfigured it.

The discussion here and throughout this book has attempted to grapple with the form if not the actual content of Phillips's characterization of the question he sees Butler asking the psychoanalytic community: "What would have to happen in the so-called psychoanalytic community for an ethos to be created in which patients were encouraged to mourn the loss of all their repressed gender identities?"[23]

In a partial response to Butler, Phillips asks the vexing question: "Who, for example, decides what constitutes a problem for the patient? And by what criteria?"[24] Moving on to Fanon's text and the more clinical perspective on psychoanalysis, I want to begin with the power-knowledge-questions Phillips raises regarding who decides what constitutes a problem for the analysand when the analysand, in our example, must assume an ethnic-racialized identity through coercive and compelled mandates.

Fanon describes his encounter with a friend/patient's dream. Fanon, in good form, brings up the hardest questions: how to intervene, inside and outside the clinical setting; what is to be done to bring the dreaming man into an understanding of what ails him; and how the dreamer might be compelled to think differently, to think for his advantage and survival in a white supremacist society in a manner that is not ambiguously politicized. How does Fanon decide there may be a problem, and how does he imagine treating it?

First, the dream: "A Negro tells me his dream: 'I had been walking for a long time, I was extremely exhausted, I had the impression that something was waiting for me, I climbed barricades and walls, I came into an empty hall, and from behind a door I heard noise. I hesitated before I went in, but finally I made up my mind and opened the door. In this second room there where white men, and I found that I too was white.'"[25]

Fanon's initial response is, "When I try to understand this dream, to analyze it, knowing that my friend has had problems in his career, I conclude that this dream fulfills an unconscious wish."[26] But then something changes for Fanon and the shift in interpretation, which is really a deepening of the interpretation, is precipitated by the change in locale, from inside the clinician's office to outside in the world:

But when, *outside my psychoanalytic office*, I have to incorporate my conclusions into the context of the world, I will assert: 1. My patient is suffering from an inferiority complex. His psychic structure is in danger of disintegration. What has to be done is to save him from this and, little by little, to rid him of this unconscious desire.

2. If he is overwhelmed to such a degree by the wish to be white, it is because he lives in a society that makes his inferiority complex possible, in a society that

derives its stability from the perpetuation of this complex, in a society that proclaims the superiority of one race; to the identical degree to which that society creates difficulties for him, he will find himself thrust into a neurotic situation.[27]

What he begins to introduce next as a way of intervening as analyst must by necessity involve another form of intervention, a politicized one if you will: "As a psychoanalyst, I should help my patient to become *conscious* of his unconscious and abandon his attempts at a hallucinatory whitening, *but also to act in the direction of a change in the social structure*. In other words, the black man should no longer be confronted by the dilemma, *turn white or disappear*; but he should be able to take cognizance of a possibility for existence."[28] Although Fanon is not explicit about this, I read his intervention as Lacanian. He introduces into the analysis—or would want to introduce (recall that he remarks on what he *may* have done, not on what he actually did)—the register of the Symbolic. Still, though, "Who, for example, decides what constitutes a problem for the patient? And by what criteria?"[29]

Upon hearing in Fanon's passage the direct mention of "racism," the "social structures," and the language, generally, of politicization that he would want to imbue his patient with, some readers might imagine that his intervention is anything but Lacanian. Even Spillers writes, "to that extent, Lacanian psychoanalytic theory is simply heavenly, insofar as it has no eyes for the grammar and politics of power."[30] This captures a widely accepted misunderstanding about Lacanian theory. The register of the Symbolic in Lacan must be read as precisely that which offers if not the grammar, then the syntax of the politics of power. The Symbolic is the locus in which is situated the chain of the signifier. Some clinical therapists who are not Lacanians agree that Lacanian theory's concept of the Symbolic generates a "politically attentive analysis" in a way other psychoanalytic theories do not. Patrick Colm Hogan has argued in a sharp analysis of one of D. W. Winnicott's case studies that "object-relations theorists quite generally lack the sorts of theoretical concepts which might encourage the type of politically attentive analysis I am advocating. In the work of Jacques Lacan, however, such concepts are indeed available—the most obvious cases being the Symbolic Order and the Other."[31]

Where some have read these passages in *Black Skin, White Masks* as offering a corrective to Lacanian and Freudian psychoanalytic theory for its inability to address the significance of ethnic-racialized difference in the overall context of racism and white supremacy, I see Fanon's analytical intervention as ultimately

Lacanian. Fanon engages the significance of race by considering the Symbolic order that envelops his patient. Returning to Fanon's passage, we will note a couple of things going on. First, let's reengage Phillips's question: "Who, for example, decides what constitutes a problem for the patient? And by what criteria?" Fanon feels like he needs to intervene in the immediate clinical setting to make the analysand conscious of his unconscious wish to be white. But there's an additional intervention—and it's not clear how Fanon as analyst might go about compelling this change—"to act in the direction of a change in the social structure."

Fanon is attempting to compel a species of politicization in his analysand, and this must begin to take shape in the clinical setting as *additional* to the interpretative labor that would make the analysand conscious of his unconscious wish to be white. Let's return to Spillers: "What I am positing here is the blankness of 'race' where something else ought to be, that emptying out of which I spoke earlier, the evacuation to be restituted and recalled as the discipline of a self-critical inquiry."[32] The double analytical labor Fanon is describing is revealed in the moves Spillers outlines. Acting for change in the social structure must be cultivated in the patient: "If society makes difficulties for him because of his color, if in his dreams I establish the expression of an unconscious desire to change color, my objective will not be that of dissuading him from it by advising him to 'keep his place'; on the contrary, my objective, once his motivations have been brought into consciousness, will be to put him in a position to *choose* action (or passivity) with respect to the real source of the conflict—that is, toward the social structures."[33]

Let's think about the nature of Fanon's intervention, keeping in mind the discussion in chapter 2 of Lacan's critique of what he considered the touchstone of ego psychology and, to some extent, object relations theory: the technique of "suggestion" as the reflection of power, as the analyst's domination of the analysand. Is Fanon's intervention a form of "suggestion"? In "The Direction of the Treatment and the Principles of Its Power," Lacan reminds the reader that the analyst directs the treatment, not the analysand; the analyst is not in the business of ordering the patient's conscience around, however much the patient may beg for it:

I intend to show how the inability to authentically sustain a praxis results, as is common in the history of mankind, in the exercise of power.

2. Assuredly, a psychoanalyst directs the treatment. *The first principle of this*

208

treatment, the one that is spelled out to him before all else, and which he finds throughout his
training, so much so that he becomes utterly imbued with it, is that he must not direct the
patient. The direction of conscience, in the sense of the moral guidance a faithful
Catholic might find in it, is radically excluded here.[34]

Lacan's vigorous critique of forms of psychoanalysis in which the analyst takes
on the role of directing the patient is closely related to his critique of how the
notion of "reality" is arrived at in ego psychology and object relations theory,
where the agreed upon "reality" is determined, of course, by the analyst's idea
of "reality." Bruce Fink explains,

> How, then, could the analyst possibly "know reality," "know what is real and what it
> [*sic*] not," better than the analysand? Lacanian psychoanalysis is certainly not a dis-
> course of mastery wherein the analyst is considered some sort of master of reality. In
> the course of his or her own "training analysis," the analyst does not learn what is
> real and what is not, but learns something about his or her own fantasy (even as it is
> reconfigured) and how to prevent it from impinging on work with patients.[35]

Fanon is very careful. At no point in the passage is it suggested that the
analysand is to take Fanon's ego as the healthy ego or Fanon's "reality" as the
accepted "reality." But can we be so sure? Is Fanon's fundamental fantasy as a
tireless anticolonialist, antiracist activist not finding some room to impinge on
his work with this patient? In *Identification Papers*, Diana Fuss reminds us that
Fanon, as perhaps one of the most active and famous members of the National Liberation Front, repeatedly warned of how psychoanalysis might be
appropriated in the colonies and used to adjust colonized subjects to the
conditions of their subordination.[36] Fanon's response to his black friend's
dream appears to straddle a Lacanian psychoanalytical position that strives
against directing the analysand's conscience while taking a revolutionary position that wants to mine in psychoanalysis material that might compel a real
intervention in changing racist structures. Some critics have argued that after
the publication of *Black Skin, White Masks*, Fanon effectively abandoned psychiatry and psychoanalysis for politics.[37] I agree, instead, with Fuss's interpretation of Fanon's very complicated relationship to psychoanalysis, psychiatry, and anticolonialist activism, "The critical debate over the relation between
Fanon's psychiatric training and his political education—posed in the oppositional terms of dramatic break or seamless continuity—obscures the critical
faultlines upon which Fanon's own work is based, for Fanon himself was

interested precisely in the linkages and fissures . . . the translations and transformations of the theory-politics relation."[38]

We might also understand these critical fault lines as reflected in the ways Fanon, like Spillers, breaks down the opposition between clinical and speculative perspectives in psychoanalysis at the moment when the question of racism and the cultivation of politicization practices to contest racism emerge inside the clinic. Fanon illustrates how the political may precipitate in the clinical setting as a prompting, a compelling of the analyst to interpret and to act and where this dimension is to be addressed at the Symbolic register. Fanon challenges us to understand that his work, given the specific context of racism and a black man's dream of being white, must think about the possibility of affecting the social structures that serve as the discursive framework lending the residual daily elements to this man's dream.

In a parting shot in the second-to-last chapter of *Black Skin, White Masks*, Fanon suddenly and unexpectedly returns to his friend's dream. He makes it clear that a clinical intervention on his watch would ultimately need to compel nothing less than bringing a racist world to its knees:

> If I were an Adlerian, then, having established the fact that my friend had fulfilled in a dream his wish to become white—that is, to be a man—I would show him that his neurosis, his psychic instability, the rupture of his ego arose out of this governing fiction, and I would say to him: "M. Mannoni has very ably described this phenomenon in the Malagasy. Look here: I think you simply have to resign yourself to remaining in the place that has been assigned to you." Certainly not! I will not say that at all! I will tell him, "The environment, society are responsible for your delusion." Once that has been said, the rest will follow of itself, and what that is we know. *The end of the world.*[39]

Is Fanon ultimately practicing a species of politicized suggestion? Perhaps. The question persists: "Who, for example, decides what constitutes a problem for the patient? And by what criteria?"

STRENGTHENING ETHNIC-RACIALIZED CHILDREN'S EGOS, DEAD ON ARRIVAL

Since I don't think we can study contemporary ethnic-racialized subjectivity and experience in the United States without attending to the codification of understandings for ethnic-racialized subjectivity and experience as produced and circulated within the field of psychology in both legal and extralegal contexts, my reason for engaging analyses below of ethnic psychology, Hispanic psychology, and political psychology is somewhat obvious. Although the discussion that follows is in no way exhaustive of all approaches in psychology to questions of ethnicity and race, it does, I think, capture an accurate overall view of the situation. The clinical and speculative exchange I craft here collects together the work in these subfields of psychology along with the culture criticism and ideology critique of Chow in order to understand on what points the dialogue goes silent. We must also ask whether in fact there can even be a dialogue if what we witness consistently in the psychological investigations is the proffered strategy of strengthening the ethnic-racialized ego, with no questioning of the coercion internal to the demand that one identify as ethnic-racialized in order to be considered a socially and culturally legible subject.

This second section of the chapter is, in the end, concerned with young ethnic-racialized subjects and how the increasingly rigid mandates demanding that one come to resemble what is recognizably ethnic-racialized are fooling younger generations out of crafting more effective politicized responses to racism. Does this material's handling of ethnicity and race and the larger question of the rewards and hazards that come with assuming an ethnic-racialized identity allow Spillers's suggestion "that an aspect of the emancipatory hinges on what would appear to be simple self-attention," or "to the extent that the psychoanalytic provides, at least in theory, a protocol for the 'care of the self' on several plans of intersecting concern, it seems vital to the political interests of the black community"?[40] I think that the emancipatory may still be located in the psychoanalytical, insofar as it has freed itself from all psychologistic thinking.

In "Ethnicity and Culture in Psychological Research and Practice," an essay collected in *Psychological Perspectives on Human Diversity in America*, a lecture series published by the American Psychological Association in 1991, Stanley Sue considers various things "therapists" should keep in mind when dealing with Hispanics, Asian Americans, and African Americans. In the literature on race, psychoanalysis, and psychotherapy focused on the specific context of the clinical setting, there seems to be a consensus that there are significant resistances in patients as well as countertransferences in therapists that are associated with race.[41] What I found remarkable about the research is the number of times the analysis of the function of race concerns itself almost exclusively with a theory of the transference, how race emerges as a problem with respect to the transference. I have chosen Sue's essay because the collection that includes it imagines itself intervening in an important debate that wasn't being staged in psychology regarding race and ethnicity. In addition, Sue's essay attempts to speak directly to the question of what should take place in the therapeutic setting with ethnic-racialized clients. He writes,

> In response to the need for more concrete suggestions on how to conduct therapy, some clinicians attempted to devise what was considered culturally consistent forms of intervention. For example, Asian Americans tend to prefer psychotherapists who provide structure, guidance, and direction rather than nondirectness in interactions (Kim, 1985). Clinicians were advised to be directive with Asian Americans. Similar suggestions were made for other minority group clients. For Latinos, some clinicians felt that therapists should focus on reframing problems as medical ones in order to reduce client resistance; for Blacks, action-oriented and externally focused rather than intrapsychic approaches were recommended (see Sue and Zane, 1987).[42]

212   With respect to these clinicians' attempts to devise "culturally consistent forms of intervention," the ethnic-racialized clients in question are being theorized as what David Palumbo-Liu refers to as "types," "groups," and not as "individuals." The therapeutic strategies listed in Sue's passage are obviously based on a woefully problematic under-reading of the human subject, who is not here a human subject but rather an ego who follows a script. Sue realizes that this approach is problematic and offers an alternative.

> However, these recommendations also raised questions. Is it possible for therapists to change their therapeutic orientations in working with ethnic clients? For instance, a psychoanalytic therapist might find it very difficult to become more action-oriented when working with a Black client. By using a specific approach—one presumably based on the culture of the client—how does one deal with intragroup variability, as ethnic minority clients may show a great deal of individual differences? Is there a single, culturally consistent form of treatment for each group? Given the inability to address these questions fully, I believe we should investigate therapeutic processes rather than simply argue for cultural knowledge or culturally specific forms of treatment. The two processes that appear to be critical, at least in the initial treatment sessions, are credibility and gift giving (i.e. seeing that the client receives a benefit early in the treatment process).[43]

Sue's dismissal of attempts to come up with a treatment that can be codified for any particular ethnic-racialized group would appear to place him generally in agreement with our position. However, through the particular way that credibility and gift giving are conceptualized here, we will see how the notion of ethnic-racialized subjects as types, as memorizable-qua-codifiable experiences, creeps back into the therapeutic setting, despite Sue's initial criticisms of just this type of approach. Sue abandons the ridiculous search to discover the perfect language of exhaustive cross-cultural translation for an approach that ends up introducing a whole new set of problems, since it turns the therapeutic environment into a space where the analysand must see the analyst as a gift giver. This dynamic cannot help but complicate the transference and may indeed make it impossible for the analysand to work through her transference onto the analyst in productive ways. Sue explains the first of the two important processes in the treatment, "credibility": "Credibility can also be achieved. Achieved credibility refers more directly to the skills and actions of the therapist in treatment. The therapist does something that is perceived by the client as being competent or helpful. Ascribed and achieved credibility undoubtedly are related, *but they tend to have distinct and different implications for ethnic clients in terms of psychotherapeutic process.*"[44]

As the italicized portion of Sue's passage makes clear, "ethnic clients" are still being separated from other types of clients, insofar as "ascribed and achieved credibility" have "different implications" for "them." Why? Allow me to return to a passage quoted in chapter 1. There, Joel Kovel writes, "Within our culture, introspection signifies participation in a particular class and social relation. . . . I am not saying that working-class people do not develop insight, but for them to do so in analysis means pursuing an activity foreign to their experience of the world."[45] Sue is still conceptualizing ethnic-racialized clients as types, and presuming that developing, to use Kovel's words, "insight" in analysis "means pursuing an activity foreign to their experience of the world." Accepting this claim about ethnic-racialized clients as a kind of truism only deepens the problems Sue is trying to resolve. It in fact participates in naturalizing the idea, not too far removed from early-twentieth-century North American psychoanalyst Dr. Lind's conclusions in chapter 1 that African American subjects can't metaphorize, that ethnic clients don't do insight.

Sue goes on to explain that the most critical aspect that will push the therapy with an ethnic-racialized patient toward success will have to do with offering immediate satisfaction. The immediacy attending the illusion of credibility and the speed of the offering of the gift speak as much to the therapist's anxiety over her skills as to the ethnic-racialized patient's anxiety over the same. Although Sue imagines these two processes have stripped away the endless considerations and qualifications that come with trying to isolate particular cultural beliefs and traditions, he only calls up new problems, immersing us more squarely in the magnetic fields of capitalism by making the success or failure of a therapy contingent on the "goods" that it produces and the speed by which they are delivered.

What Sue seems to be telling us about ethnic-racialized patients in particular is that they're not going to stand for going to session after session, paying for session after session, unless being shown the goods in one form or another. "This better work," they appear to think, "and it better work fast." We're more effectively served if we direct our attention to how these new and improved strategies on the part of the therapist will only end up complicating the transference beyond repair, given how the exchange between therapist and client is now structured around the strategies of credibility and gift-giving. These strategies give no breathing room to the therapy outside the dominating technique of "suggestion" and the attending insistence on the power of the analyst-therapist as the one who's able to provide the goods. Sue's good intentions notwithstanding, the unambiguous contradictions in his approach reflect the vexed, impossible place seemingly occupied by ethnic-racialized subjects in the treatment setting precisely because the view of them as types, as groups and not individuals, never quite evaporates.

Although psychoanalytic theory has been historically underengaged in Latino and Chicano studies, to the same extent that Spillers claims is the case with respect to African American studies, the field of psychology has not. In an early collection on Chicano psychology, Alfredo Castañeda links Chicano psychology to the social justice agenda of the Chicano movement: "One word has come to symbolize the basic, underlying motivation of the Chicano movement in the United States—justice. Appropriately, one of the major concerns permeating Chicano psychology was the need for social justice, long denied to Mexican-Americans as the direct result of policies and practices developed in American institutions on the basis of ethnocentric interpretations of data related to psychological tests of intelligence and achievement."[46] In a paper delivered in 1972, Cervando Martinez explicitly links the social justice concerns of the Chicano movement with those of the community mental health movement: "Community psychiatry emphasizes the early detection, treatment, and prevention of mental disorders by a mental health system serving a distinct population or catchment area. The Chicano movement calls upon Mexican-Americans to strengthen their sense of community (or barrio) and to make care-giving institutions responsive and responsible."[47] Hispanic psychology, according to one of the pioneers in the field, Amado P. Padilla, "has its roots in ethnic psychology and in cross cultural psychology." He explains that "the basic premise [of Hispanic psychology] is that it is a valuable enterprise both theoretically and empirically to study the behavior of Hispanics."[48] This sentence might be said to say it all, as it were. It's a behavioral approach through and through. The question of what precisely is the value in studying and codifying the behavior of an ethnic-racialized group, not to mention asking after whose needs this codification serves, is not broached. It appears somehow structurally outside the scope of how this field defines its critical inquiry.

I'll quote the rest of the abstract here, because I think it lays out nicely several topics we have been addressing thus far regarding psychology's failure to question the coercive and disciplinary imperatives undergirding the assumption of an ethnic-racialized identity in U.S. culture today: "Over the past 25 years, research in Hispanic psychology has given way to a new scholarship or paradigm that calls for the recognition of intragroup variation which values within-group comparisons rather than relying exclusively on between-group effects. Acculturation and biculturalism have taken on special significance in Hispanic psychology. Further, Hispanic psychology must also consider the effects of racism and oppression on people and how these affect ethnic identity, attitudes toward the dominant group, and intergroup relations."[49] In the field of Latino psychiatry, the theoretical and clinical goals and aspirations reveal themselves as roughly quite similar to those outlined by Padilla above. In a recent collection, *The Latino Psychiatric Patient*, Ernestina Carrillo writes,

> A comprehensive and accurate evaluation of the Latino psychiatric patient requires that clinicians take into account information beyond what is usually considered necessary in a conventional psychiatric intake. It is insufficient to concentrate solely on recent symptoms and circumstances when reaching diagnostic and treatment conclusions. Latinos in the United States are a diverse population, who are often influenced by cultural, social and political systems quite different from those of the mainstream American population. Inquiry must be made about how these different factors affect the patient's behavior and psychiatric presentation.[50]

In this collection the authors break down their analyses of the Latino experience by addressing in separate chapters the experiences and histories of Columbians, Cubans, Dominicans, Salvadorans, Mexicans, Nicaraguans, Peruvians, and Puerto Ricans. Although they provide useful historical background on each of these groups and explain how their specific historical experiences may bear on their lives as immigrants in the United States, there is no questioning of the coercive force and psychological impact of the term *Latino*. In other words, the "Latino psychiatric patient" described in this collection presents with psychological disturbances that have nothing to do with the labors of ethnic resemblance—with the forced labor, that is, of having to resemble what is recognizably ethnic. The manner in which the term *ethnic identity* is used in this collection, and in Hispanic and Chicano psychology more generally, shows that the fact that one must inhabit an ethnic-racialized identity is never thought of as a problem potentially contributing to the patient's claims of psychological distress.

Padilla specifies other investigative interests, mostly behavioral in nature and design. What does "influence" mean in the following passage? What is the nature of those things contending for influence?

216

> How oppression and racism *influence* the perceptions, feelings, and behavioral expressions of Latinos is not easily dismissed in Hispanic psychology. . . . The reason that themes of oppression and racism are important in Hispanic research is that these topics emerge frequently in the accounts of Hispanics as they relate their experiences with majority institutions and individuals.[51]

How might we explore the relevance of the quasi-psychological diagnostic question asked in the following passage by Chow while keeping in mind how Padilla has defined the investigative work in Hispanic psychology? She writes, "If the colonized subject that is being theorized at the second level of mimeticism is a neurotic being permanently shuttling back and forth between black and white but basically still identified with whiteness as the ultimate superior value, what is the condition of the ethnic subject who feels she must try to resemble, to appear as herself—to be ethnic?"[52]

To begin with, we would have to complicate our understanding of the effects of racism to include "coercive mimeticism" as a species of racist practice that Hispanics contend with daily. Chicano and Hispanic psychology have battled admirably over the years to make the American Psychological Association (APA) address its ethnocentrism. Eligio R. Padilla describes how the first challenges to the APA by Chicano psychologists came on the heels of the Black Student Psychological Association's (BSPA) challenges to the APA at the annual APA convention in 1969. Although the BSPA was successful in forcing the APA to develop a committee that would work to increase black graduate student enrollment in psychology programs, Chicanos with similar concerns were initially less successful. Padilla writes, "As a result of the 1969 confrontation between BSPA and APA a guarded, yet undeniable feeling of optimism has precipitated among certain black individuals and members of the APA that psychology may be entering a stage in its development where psychologists may be willing, as well as able, to have some kind of professional impact on the lives of black Americans in significant numbers. Unfortunately, for Chicanos to have similar hopes at this time is far removed from the realm of reasonable consideration."[53] Chicano psychologists should no doubt continue to keep their attention trained on the APA's ethnocentric assumptions but must also, crucially, now direct their attention to the problematic, coercive function of ethnic-racialized identity categories. Chow's argument challenges us to understand how these ethnic-racialized nominatory terms also name contemporary divisions of labor, and how they are internal to a particular style of controlling and dominating life, which Michel Foucault terms "biopower," the management and reproduction of biological life marked out as ethnic-racialized.

217

In the opening essay to the recent *Oxford Handbook of Political Psychology*, the editors describe the field of political psychology as "an application of what is known about human psychology to the study of politics. From psychology it draws on theory and research on personality, cognitive psychology, and intergroup relations. It addresses political phenomena such as individual biography and leadership, mass political behavior, mass communication effects, political socialization and civic education, international conflict, foreign policy decision-making, conflict resolution, intergroup conflicts involving race, gender, nationality, and other groupings, political movements, and political mobilization."[54] The editors note that the field is interdisciplinary, drawing scholars from history, sociology, anthropology, psychiatry, communications, education, and the law, in addition to psychology and political science—but not psychoanalysis.

An essay in the collection authored by David O. Sears and Sheri Levy, "Childhood and Adult Political Development," illustrates how Chow's notion of "coercive mimeticism" might be seen to function in young ethnic-racialized children. However, Sears and Levy do not address the power-knowledge relation that compels this mimicry internal to biopower. The authors' work is interesting in the context of this discussion because of how they link the acquisition of ethnic-racialized identity to "political development." Political development on these grounds, although perhaps necessary at a particular stage in the development of a young ethnic-racialized subject's politicization, must ultimately, given the contemporary politics of multiculturalism in U.S. universities today, be subjected to serious criticism. The notion of politicization around ethnic-racialized identity that is being compelled in young people is a form of coercion, taking the shape of a compelled unpaid labor of ethnic-racialized resemblance and representation on college and university campuses in the service of following through on the post-Bakke 1978 decision's "diversity rationale."[55] Richard T. Ford explains, "The diversity rationale is benign when understood as one of many possible reasons a university might care about the racial demographics of its student body. But it is dangerous when codified as the only reason race is significant. . . . A more subtle and much more pernicious implication hovered over post-Bakke university life: only by highlighting their own distinctiveness could minority students justify their presence in the universities that admitted them."[56]

In attempting to understand children's ethnic identity development, Sears and Levy turn to Jean S. Phinney's and William E. Cross's three-stage model of ethnic identity.

> In the first stage, "unexamined ethnic identity" (Phinney) or "preencounter" (Cross), children have not explored their ethnic identity. . . . *Children who have not examined their ethnic identity might have negative feelings toward their own group* (Cross 1978, see Phinney 1989). In the second stage, "ethnic identity search" or "encounter and immersion," young persons seek out information about their group (e.g., reading books on ethnicity, visiting ethnic museums). This stage is considered a turning point akin to an identity crisis (Erikson 1968). Active identity exploration often begins in high school or college but may begin in middle school or even younger as children express identity through joining ethnicity-based peer groups (Rotheram-Borus 1993).[57]

Regarding the negative feelings arising in the children discussed in the italicized sentence, perhaps it has less to do with the children having not examined their ethnic-racialized identity and more to do with their having come to understand in some way that their identity—insofar as they will be seen to actually possess one by others—will be predicated on the labors of ethnic-racialized resemblance. At the very least, we need to entertain this possibility. In a culture like that of the United States, where virtually all aspects of daily life are profoundly suffused with racialized meanings, to deny that children's negativity regarding their respective cultural groups might not also be a protesting response to the imperative that they accept being marked out as culturally different material to begin with is to deny the complicated cognitive and intellectual work carried out by children. The authors continue, "In stage 3, 'achieved ethnic identity' or 'internalization,' adolescents have developed positive self-concepts as members of their group."[58]

This three-step process describes how children learn to assume an identity as ethnic-racialized in U.S. culture. They internalize the various disciplinary codes and rules of proper ethnic-racialized comportment in order to be able to resemble the acceptable American ethnic-racialized subject. The process also describes how this internalization works to preempt the interpretative labor—to engage, we might say, in Spillers's practice of interior intersubjectivity—that might allow the children to ask why these extra categories attach to them and not others and why fully assuming these ethnic-racialized identity categories provides the primary means upon which they will be thought to have reached the status of intelligible human subject.

Children are in fact manifesting these questions. We are not listening closely enough to this embattled speech, because we are not sufficiently imbued, like the lame psychoanalyst who can't intervene at the Symbolic because she prefers to play cat and mouse in the Imaginary, with the new terms and conditions lending social and cultural intelligibility to ethnic-racialized subjects on the basis of self-mimicry. In the passage that ends chapter 3, Ford writes, "It may be that the price of providing our descendants with a world free of social stigma and oppression of identities such as race, a world we could be proud to call more just, is that they would not share our identities, that they would be our heirs but *not* our descendants."[59] Our deafness to this embattled, learned speech among young ethnic-racialized subjects, who are choking on these coercive edicts, amounts to our irresponsible and shameful refusal to not allow them to choose *not* to be our descendants, to *not* be plagued by our symptoms.

We need to take seriously that these young people may draw their inspiration from the difficult and, for some, impossible declaration that Fanon startles his readers with in the concluding pages to *Black Skin, White Masks*: "In no way should I derive my basic purpose from the past of the peoples of color. . . . I will not make myself the man of any past. I do not want to exalt the past at the expense of my present and my future."[60] Why should these children have to suffer the persistent ghosts and symptoms of their ancestors? The three steps outlined in the experiment above describe the implantation of ethnicity and race as, to use Spillers's language, "a poisonous idea . . . insinuates itself not only across and between ethnicities but within."[61] The researchers never ask: Why do the children do this? Why do they think they have to do this? What compels an understanding of identity, ethnic-racialized or otherwise, in this way? Again, the question arises: "Who, for example, decides what constitutes a problem for the patient? And by what criteria?"[62]

One of the researchers they rely on, Cross, understands a "strong ethnic identity as serving the protective function of filtering one's social worldview so as to . . . make it less dehumanizing."[63] A strong ethnic-racialized identity, as I have been arguing, is predicated on a strengthened ego. This is held out to some as the instantiating condition defining their humanness and, from a Lacanian position, could result only in a more thorough alienation of the human subject. What if the very idea of a "strong ethnic-racialized identity" is what in fact dramatizes a racialization practice that, to return to Cross's words, reveals to the child the "social worldview" as more "dehumanizing"? What would constitute a weak ethnic-racialized identity? More important, what is the purported effect of a weak ethnic-racialized identity on a child? Sears and Levy claim, "The protection comes from accepting that racism exists and affects all blacks, that negative outcomes are because of a racist system and not the self, and that one can use various strategies to deal with racism (withdrawal, assertion, avoidance, passivity). Other functions that a strong identity may serve include providing purpose, meaning, and affiliation, often expressed in celebration of accomplishments of the black community."[64] The commonsense nature of this claim is very seductive, and I certainly don't want to be construed as suggesting that celebrating the cultural productions, histories, or traditions of a group to which you understand your self linked to or belonging to is bad. I am saying that this characterization of the best defense against racism is hardly that. It works as an Imaginary explanation, however, as long as one remains intoxicated by the idea of a strong ethnic-racialized ego. These approaches seem to accept that race won't budge, as we argued earlier, without understanding the need for an interpretative practice like Spillers's interior intersubjectivity that tries to explain to oneself and to others why race won't budge, why, as Seshadri-Crooks writes, "it shows no evidence of disappearing or evaporating in relevance."[65]

These clinical and speculative exchanges on ethnic psychology, Hispanic psychology, and political psychology reveal a tremendous disparity. A culture criticism and ideology critique like Chow's or a legally inflected critique like Ford's understands the consequences of accepting the terms of being an ethnic-racialized subject in a way very different from what is imagined by the "clinical" material as the major stumbling block: weak ethnic-racialized identities–qua–egos. Let me restate the central problem as this book has seen it: we have developed no language to talk about ethnic-racialized identity that is not entirely ego- and social psychological and that does not imagine a strong ego as the desired outcome in a racist, white supremacist world.

Continuing with the general spirit of this chapter regarding the possibility of a dialogue between the clinical and the speculative, I would like to end this discussion with a look at David Eng's and Shinhee Hann's essay "A Dialogue on Racial Melancholia."[66] Eng and Hann meditate on the devastating psychical effects the model minority stereotype has had on Asian American college students. They develop a theory of racial melancholia that not only resignifies the routine negative assessments of the mechanism of melancholia in psychoanalysis but lays bare the psychical consequences on young ethnic-racialized subjects of the disciplinary protocols of "coercive mimeticism."

Eng and Hann write about the popular cultural construction of Asian Americans as the model minority and the bullying effects that this stereotype construction has had on young Asian Americans who may come up short of fulfilling the ridiculous demands of the stereotype: "Asian Americans are forced to mimic the model minority stereotype in order to be recognized by mainstream society—in order to be at all. To the extent, however, that this mimicry of the model minority stereotype functions only to estrange Asian Americans from mainstream norms and ideals (as well as from themselves), mimicry can operate only as a melancholic process."[67] They name this process "racial melancholia" and link it to Freud's notion of splitting, introduced in his late essay, "The Splitting of the Ego in the Process of Defense." Eng and Hann write, "In this regard, racial melancholia might be described as splitting the Asian American psyche. This cleaving of the psyche might be productively thought about in terms of an altered, racialized model of classic Freudian

221

fetishism. This assimilation into the national fabric demands a psychic split-ting on the part of the Asian American subject, who knows and does not know, at once, that she or he is part of the larger group."[68]

I would prefer here to shift from Freud's notion of splitting to Lacan's idea of splitting as revealed in his notion of the barred subject. We should recall that Lacan amplifies Freud's notion of splitting in his effort to understand splitting as constitutive of subjectivity itself and as having to do with the impact of language on the speaking subject. In Lacan, the subject is split by the very fact that she is a speaking organism; the split or division is structural and not the consequence of social and material forces. I think Lacan's notion of splitting works more to our advantage here, since Freud's understanding can be used to suggest that the splitting in the ego is equivalent to the subject's division in language and that we may therefore be able to cover over this breach, stitch it up. The authors reach a grim conclusion: "This material failure leads to a psychic ambivalence that works to characterize the colonized subject's identification with dominant ideals of whiteness as a pathological identification. It is an ambivalence that opens upon the landscape of melan-cholia and depression for many of the Asian American students with whom we come into contact on a regular basis. Those Asian Americans who do not fit into the model minority stereotype (and this is probably a majority of Asian American students) are altogether erased from—not seen in—main-stream society."[69] For young ethnic-racialized subjects to acknowledge that the division is structural may provide a more empowering angle of vision from which to understand "racial melancholia," because they will have reclaimed their right to take up a position in the chain of the signifier as subjects in language. This will, in effect, multiply the objects that can be considered as lost as well as the narratives that can be crafted to explain the meanings of those losses.

Spillers's theory of interior intersubjectivity serves to lay bare the processes whereby these young ethnic-racialized subjects experience a psychic ambiva-lence due to the function of ethnicity and race in the larger narrative of subjectivity constitution. Reading Chow's, Eng's and Hann's, and Spillers's powerful pieces together, we might say that Chow provides a general outline for the contemporary instantiation of ethnic-racialized subjectivity in the United States as predicated on mimicking what is recognizably ethnic-racial-ized, that Eng and Hann painfully illustrate the devastating psychical consequences of this self-mimicry, and that Spillers offers a hermeneutic that might interrupt the process from its inception by adding what has always been missing: a Lacanian, psychoanalytically-inflected theory of the ethnic-racialized subject in language. Still, "who, for example, decides what constitutes a problem for the patient? And by what criteria?"[70]

223

Ruining the Ethnic-Racialized Self and Precipitating the Subject

I don't think one can find any normalization in, for instance, the Stoic ethics. The reason is, I think, that the principal aim, the principal target of this kind of ethics, was an aesthetic one. First, this kind of ethics was only a problem of personal choice. Second, it was reserved for a few people in the population; it was not a question of giving a pattern of behavior for everybody. It was a personal choice for a small elite. The reason for making this choice was the will to live a beautiful life, and to leave to others memories of a beautiful existence. I don't think we can say that this kind of ethics was an attempt to normalize the population.

MICHEL FOUCAULT, "On the Genealogy of Ethics"

At the very least, I am suggesting that an aspect of the emancipatory hinges on what would appear to be simple self-attention, except that reaching the articulation requires a process, that of making one's subjectness the object of a disciplined and potentially displaceable attentiveness. To the extent that the psychoanalytic provides, at least in theory, a protocol for the "care of the self" on several planes of intersecting concern, it seems vital to the political interests of the black community, even as we argue (endlessly) about its generative schools of thought. I should think that the process of self-reflection, of the pressing urgency to make articulate what is left in the shadows of the unreflected, participates in a sociopolitical engagement of the utmost importance.

HORTENSE SPILLERS, "'All the Things You Could Be by Now'"

What kinds of social, material, and psychical losses can a human subject stand to endure in the world? What if answering this question, or even simply entertaining a response, required one to understand that a more fundamental question of loss persists for ethnic-racialized subjects? Before contemplating such a huge and ridiculous question, we are challenged to understand that, as ethnic-racialized subjects, we have already lost, have been made to lose, that is, by a kind of generous racist exemption, an interpretation of human subjectivity that takes into account the primordial loss endured by all human speaking organisms who must at some point choose language in order to express needs. Abandoning the loss that attends every human's inscription in language as a part of the clinical, extraclinical, legal, and extralegal narrative histories we reconstruct and rewrite about ourselves is part of those social and material resources more likely to be unequally distributed to ethnic-racialized subjects. It is probably only in this context that ethnic-racialized subjects get *less* loss and not more.

Throughout this project, I have been attempting to craft meaningful, hopefully transformative clinical and speculative exchanges on psychoanalysis and psychoanalytic treatment when the question of ethnic-racialized difference elects itself into these discussions. My argument in chapter 1 makes the case that the history of psychoanalysis and psychology in the United States appears reliant, by definition, on the spectacle and meaning of ethnic-racialized difference in order to tell a story about itself as a discipline, a field of study, a potential science, a therapeutics of adjustment, and a practice of care. The clinical and speculative exchanges in this book have been tracked through dialogues between critical race and ethnicity theorists and legal scholars like Hortense Spillers, Rey Chow, Emma Pérez, and Richard T. Ford, as well as clinicians, analysts, therapists, and theoreticians working in Lacanian psychoanalysis and various forms of psychology. I have also explored this species of clinical and speculative exchange by placing Latino studies and Lacanian theory into conversation as predicated on the critical space of overlap that I think can be discerned and productively mined between Lacan's barred subject and Latino studies' border subject.

My version of the question Adam Phillips imagines Judith Butler to be posing to the psychoanalytic community does not ask after the ethos that would have to be created in the psychoanalytic community to encourage patients to "mourn the loss of all their repressed gender identities."[1] Rather, it wonders, What would have to happen in the fields, for example, of ethnic and Hispanic psychology and Latino psychiatry for an ethos to be created in which ethnic-racialized patients were encouraged to mourn their false constitution as ethnic-racialized subjects, coerced as they are into resembling what is recognizably ethnic-racialized in order to figure as socially and culturally intelligible subjects?

I don't hazard a clear response in chapter 7 about what kind of ethos we might go about cultivating. Here, I do. As I have insisted throughout, this ethos would have to understand the ethnic-racialized subject's experience of

225

loss as attributable to the social structures in place in a racialized social hierarchy as well as understand the experience of loss as attributable to the effects of language as structure on the ethnic-racialized subject. This ethos would understand that the ethnic-racialized subject is also a subject of the signifier, a social, political, and psychoanalytic subject in language.

Ethnic-racialized subjects would certainly not be encouraged to mourn their failure to coincide with an ethnic-racialized identity or their failure to inhabit their ethnic-racialized identity in a strong as opposed to weak manner, as we saw in the political psychology experiment. This was the species of mourning that plagued and paralyzed Piri Thomas in the novel *Down These Mean Streets*. The mourning I have in mind would not, returning to the terms in Butler's question, have to do with mourning the loss of other possible ethnic-racialized identity positions—although this could be an interesting and generative line of thinking. Rather, it would have to do with mourning the loss of a theory of subjectivity constitution in clinical and extraclinical contexts that understands that ethnic-racialized subjects are, first and foremost, subjects in language who lose Being in the Real like all other human speaking subjects. The mourning we have in mind is the mourning of the loss of *loss*.

The hegemony of ego and social psychology and the virtual eradication of psychoanalysis in the United States has, as I have maintained, significant effects on how ethnic-racialized subjectivity is theorized and inhabited at so many levels—at individual and collective levels distributed across economic, cultural, legal, and political realms. Where the psychoanalytic ego psychology specifically associated with Heinz Hartmann and his group in the post–World War II years may, in the words of Martin Bergmann,[2] have passed, we should keep in mind that it has not passed away but rather has passed *into* most forms of psychology as influenced by the meeting up early on of social, culturalist, and behavioral psychology with ego psychology in the 1940s and 1950s. It has also passed into the legal apparatus's definition of the ethnic-racialized subject as a juridical, rights-bearing subject and into the various civil rights movement's discourses' precipitation of the protesting ethnic-racialized subject under siege and more generally into the culture's extralegal, extraclinical values and norms on the question of what it means to be an ethnic-racialized subject in all manner of speaking.

Those of us teaching in the fields of ethnicity and race studies who work closely with ethnic-racialized students in various contexts—for example, in attempting to create programs like Latino studies or in participating in students' protests to the university as they battle against myriad manifestations of racist and discriminatory behavior—see the consequences of this ongoing and widely accepted strategy of strengthening the ethnic-racialized ego that is being assailed. In the context of contemporary forms of fiscally driven multiculturalism discourses and diversity rationales, a woefully undertheorized position on ethnic-racialized subjectivity is being cultivated in ethnic-racialized and non-ethnic-racialized subjects alike. The codification of this limited explanation of the full range of losses a human subject endures in the world then nurtures an a-dialectical ego politics of the Imaginary.

Again, this is the problem as the book has seen it: we have developed no language to talk about ethnic-racialized subjectivity and experience that is not entirely ego- and social psychological and that does not imagine a strong, whole, complete, and transparent ethnic-racialized subject and ego as the desired therapeutic, philosophical, and political outcome in a racist, white supremacist world. In the process, we fail to see how the repeated themes of wholeness, completeness, and transparency with respect to ethnic-racialized subjectivity are what provide racist discourse with precisely the notion of subjectivity that it needs in order to function most effectively.

227

In the fields of psychology, psychiatry, and psychoanalysis, we have over the course of more than a century managed to find different ways of articulating more or less the same reductive position with respect to ethnic-racialized, nonwhite, non-European subjects. They are either not psychically complicated enough to warrant a sustained engagement at the same time that they are riotously bestowed with, as Juliet Flower MacCannell puts it, an "animal-like" jouissance,[3] a lurid and obscene fullness of being. Or, when analyzed, their experience is entirely reducible to and fully and exhaustively captured by an analysis of, as Joan Copjec writes, "the indwelling network of relations of power and knowledge."[4] In this context, ethnic-racialized subjects' experiences of loss are entirely attributable to whatever social, cultural, and historical obstacles have stood in their way. This interpretation, in effect, renders them nonhuman, if we understand the specifically human dimension—the dimension that distinguishes human difference from animal ethology—as having to do with language, the effects of the signifier on the human organism. Looking back on the research now, it seems to me as though the history of this engagement in the United States is still trying to make sense of the very first questions that emerged after the Civil War with respect to African American subjects: can recently freed African American subjects really make claims to madness and insanity? Are they psychologically different or the same as white subjects? What can they be said to stand to lose psychically? Do they metaphorize? Do they practice insight?

I want to use the opportunity afforded by Butler's mention of "grief" and "mourning" in the psychoanalytic setting in her conversation with Phillips to open a general discussion and description of the analysand at the end of a Lacanian analysis. Grief and mourning may, from this angle, lose their significance entirely. Additionally, I would like to complete my attempt to read Spillers with Lacan by reading both of them in concert with Foucault and his notion of "care of the self." On Spillers's cue, we can insist on the homology between Foucault's care of the self and a Lacanian ethics of psychoanalysis. The psychoanalytic hermeneutic practice Spillers names interior intersubjectivity, which ethnic-racialized subjects can deploy as an antiracist interpretative practice, must care for the ethnic-racialized subject by ruining the ethnic-racialized self (read: ego).

LOSING EVERYTHING WE CAN STAND TO LOSE

In the exchange between Phillips and Butler, Phillips, although not a Lacanian analyst, gestures to precisely the sort of critique Lacan lodges at ego psychological (and object-relations theory as well) treatment strategies regarding the role of the analyst and the topic of suggestion. As I discussed earlier with regards to Fanon's intervention as well as Stanley Sue's suggested treatment strategies for ethnic-racialized patients, suggestion, according to Lacan, is an exercise of power on the analyst's part. He reminds the reader that the analyst directs the treatment, not the patient's conscience. Phillips characterizes the speculative question he imagines Butler putting forth: "What would have to happen in the so-called psychoanalytic community for an ethos to be created in which patients were encouraged to mourn the loss of all their repressed gender identities?"[5]

Although Phillips doesn't quite spell it out in the way I will, he does seem to be asking what Butler imagines the labor of psychoanalysts to entail, not to mention the role psychoanalysis is to play in a society. He writes, "If the convinced heterosexual man, in Butler's words, 'becomes subject to a double disavowal, a never-having-loved and a never-having-lost,' the homosexual attachment, is it therefore to become integral to the psychoanalytic project to analyze, or engineer the undoing of this disavowal if the heterosexual man claims to be relatively untroubled by it? To me, the absolute plausibility of Butler's argument poses some telling clinical quandaries. *Who, for example, decides what constitutes a problem for the patient?* And by what criteria?"[6] He is right to consider that Butler's position, on a swift, somewhat careless reading, could be construed as suggesting that psychoanalysts in this regard should play the role of social engineers.

Butler's question is characteristic of a sustained meditation that has been present throughout all of her work over the last twenty years, the relationship generally between politics and psychoanalysis, and more specifically the potential emancipatory angle of vision opened up by some psychoanalytic theories, precisely the question that Spillers pursues in her essay. In response to Butler, if the social and cultural milieus do not reflect even the faintest outlines of Butler's alternative, can one really push psychoanalysis into the role of compelling new, alternative understandings to what passes as currently accepted cultural norms and values? In another essay, Phillips appears to come closer to detailing the kind of social, cultural, and political interventions that Butler imagines could be effected in psychoanalytic theory and treatment. He writes,

> There is clearly a question here about how we go about legitimating our psychoanalytic aims, bound up as they are with fantasies about the kind of world we would prefer to live in. . . . If psychoanalysis saw itself as rhetoric rather than metaphysics (as persuading people to prefer certain ways of living to others, rather than revealing the truths about, and causes of themselves) we might have better descriptions not only of the aims of analysis, but of why we should value such aims.[7]

I have banked on this possibility throughout this book. In following Spillers's model, which is psychoanalytic without the burdensome consideration of the psychoanalytic community's training protocols, institutional histories riotously conflicted since even before Freud died, name calling, and very nasty politics,[8] I have imagined a psychoanalytic hermeneutic the ethnic-racialized subject may practice in relation to herself. Spillers's model of a scrutinous self-regarding practice for ethnic-racialized subjects provides a kind of critical balance to Fanon's cautious but decisive embrace of a form of politicized persuasion that he's willing to enact in the clinical setting when analyzing his black analysand's dream of being white. Recall that Fanon writes, "As a psychoanalyst, I should help my patient to become *conscious* of his unconscious and abandon his attempts at a hallucinatory whitening, but also to act in the direction of a change in the social structure. In other words, the black man should no longer be confronted by the dilemma, *turn white or disappear*; but he should be able to take cognizance of a possibility for existence."[9] Comparing the language Fanon uses to that of Phillips, it appears that Fanon's intervention actualizes the move Phillips claims could be productive for psychoanalysis: to see itself as rhetoric rather than metaphysics, "as persuading people to prefer certain ways of living to others." The intervention that begins to take shape, as Fanon tells us, outside the clinician's office, must, by a kind of politicized necessity, consider the function of racism in the social structure in order for Fanon to provide the fullest and most textured analysis of the black analysand's dream of being white and to, in the process, perhaps persuade his friend to prefer a certain politicized way of living his life as a black man in a white supremacist society.

Phillips gently critiques what looks like Butler's focus on mourning and the privileged place it may be read as being promoted as occupying in the analysis: "These seem to be questions of considerable interest, provided they do not entail the idealization of mourning—its use as a spurious redemptive practice, as a kind of ersatz cure for repression or the anguishes of uncertainty."[10] Butler writes in response, "Phillips is right to warn psychoanalysis against an idealization of mourning itself, the sacralization of mourning as the consummate psychoanalytic ritual. It is as if psychoanalysis as a practice risks becoming afflicted with the very suffering it seeks to know. The resolution of grief becomes unthinkable in a situation in which our various losses become the condition for psychoanalysis as a practice of interminable mourning."[11]

I want to concentrate on how grief and mourning might resonate in Lacanian theory and in the theory of the Lacanian end-of-analysis in order to discuss the kind of *knowing-grief* that attends Spillers's Lacanian antiracist hermeneutic, one that cannot be simply reduced to the mandate "know thyself" because of how it is primarily organized around a form of difficult care. In order to flesh this out, I'd like to comment briefly on what we can call the ethics of psychoanalysis, Lacanian-style, by looking to some passages from *Seminar VII: The Ethics of Psychoanalysis*.

The following passage from *Seminar VII* bears on Phillips's and Butler's discussion on the question of the role of mourning in an analysis. There may be very different notions of what an analysis is and should be and what an analyst can reasonably assume as her responsibilities without capitulating to the demands of the analysand-qua-consumer. Lacan asks, "Are we analysts simply something that welcomes the suppliant then, something that gives him a place of refuge? Are we simply, but it is already a lot, something that must respond to a demand, to the demand not to suffer, at least without understanding why?—in the hope that through understanding the subject will be freed not only from his ignorance, but also from suffering itself."[12] In a later passage, Lacan meditates on the role of the analyst as the analyst must contend with the world of goods and the lure of placing herself in the position of one who is capable of granting them to the analysand:

> At every moment we need to know what our effective relationship is to the desire to do good, to the desire to cure. . . . I will even add that one might be paradoxical or trenchant and designate our desire as a non-desire to cure. . . .
>
> Here the question of different goods is raised in their relation to desire. All kinds of tempting goods offer themselves to the subject; and you know how imprudent it would be for us to put ourselves in a position of promising the subject access to them all.[13]

The ethics of psychoanalysis that Lacan develops in this seminar is intimately related to desire, to not cede on one's desire and to first understand the coordinates of one's desire: "And it is because we know better than those who went before how to recognize that nature of desire, which is at the heart of this experience, that a reconsideration of ethics is possible, that a form of ethical judgment is possible, of a kind that gives this question the force of a Last Judgment: Have you acted in conformity with the desire that is in you?"[14] This ethic rejects ideals of happiness and health: "I wanted to make you feel the extent to which we approach these things differently, how far we are from any formulation of a discipline of happiness."[15]

What does suffering mean in the Lacanian clinical setting? How might the suffering in the Lacanian clinical setting in the context of the end-of-an-analysis relate to the suffering that must be risked by ethnic-racialized subjects, a risk for which Spillers's interior intersubjectivity provides the general outlines? If a practice of suffering and mourning are seen to mark a certain full address to gender identity, if we trust Phillips's characterization of Butler's question, can we theorize something similar for ethnicity and race? Instead of Butler's and Phillips's focus on the melancholia of gender, my engagement looks to understand the melancholia of the ego, more generally, and the place of ethnicity and race in that melancholia.[16] With respect to ethnicity and race, we need to attend to a kind of mourning that addresses the constitutive subjective losses that refuse to be acknowledged as losses that undergird an Imaginary theory of the ego as center of consciousness and that effectively codifies an understanding of the ethnic-racialized subject as immune to the effects of language as structure.

My address and theirs is not parallel, because Butler—at least in the essay I refer to here and in *Gender Trouble* (1990)—is discussing the acquisition of gender identity as part of the formation of the ego. Butler focuses on the discoveries Freud makes after 1914 regarding the importance of identification as constitutive of the ego and how melancholia becomes crucial as a process in the formation of the ego, since the ego is now seen to be formed by its identifications with lost objects. In 1923, Freud writes,

> We succeeded in explaining the painful disorder of melancholia by supposing that [in those suffering from it] an object which was lost has been set up again inside the ego—that is, that an object-cathexis has been replaced by an identification. At that time, however, we did not appreciate the full significance of this process and did not know how common and how typical it is. Since then we have come to understand that this kind of substitution has a great share in determining the form taken by the ego and that it makes an essential contribution towards building up what is called its "character."[17]

Lacan, to begin with, doesn't discuss melancholia in this way, and he certainly doesn't read it in tandem with a theory of ego formation. As the reader will have gathered from my discussion of the mirror stage in chapter 3, Lacan's theory of ego formation doesn't talk about a *history* of losses as constituting the ego, nor does he talk about gender acquisition as part of this process.[18]

In Freud, the ego is like Dr. Frankenstein's monster, put together from bits, pieces, and shreds of losses, whereas in Lacan there is something strangely immaculate about the ego. The ego in Lacan is certainly worked over, constituted by what is outside it—the specular image that secures the foundational alienation and misrecognition of the ego—but it is pristine, too, bearing few lines or marks, and although we wouldn't use the ego psychologist's language of ego autonomy to describe Lacan's ego, it does seem strangely self-possessed in the very process of its own production as other. As Shuli Barzilai explains, "The self is also the agent of its own production as radically other."[19] Where fragmentation as a concept might figure in Freud's theory of the ego insofar as the ego is built up of fragments and shreds, in the early Lacan, fragmentation is what the fledgling organism experiences as its first disarray because of what Lacan theorized at that time as a Real biological lack concerning the human's general prematurity, its motor uncoordination when compared to other species. The organism narcotizes itself against the feeling of fragmentation by identifying with and assuming the specular image.

Grief doesn't really seem to come up that much in Lacanian analytical theory. Lacan was just shy of loquacious regarding his *own* grief suffered at the hands of the International Psychoanalytic Association and of ego psychology.[20] In an admittedly somewhat speculative move on my part, I would like to identify three dominant modes in which loss and grief figure in Lacanian theory.

The first is part of Lacanian theory itself, complete with its theory of technique and analysis presented by Lacan as a return to Freud. One returns to Freud because in the various psychoanalytic theoretical "aftermaths," to use Spillers's term, the true discovery of Freudian psychoanalysis has been lost, especially by those who claim to be its true heirs, the troika, Heinz Hartmann, Ernst Kris, and Rudolph Loewenstein. Lacan's trenchant critique of ego psychology would appear to transform ego psychology into a theory predicated on the loss of basic Freudian theoretical insights and discoveries. Freudian theory goes missing in ego psychology, and Lacanian theory overall can be read as a thorough, rigorous mourning of that loss, metaphorizing that loss over the course of twenty-seven seminars and twenty-seven-odd years and counting, if we include the ongoing metaphorization of that loss in the work of Lacanian theorists and commentators writing since Lacan's death in 1980. This has resulted in a characterization of ego psychology as a thoroughly bereaved enterprise and Lacanian theory as its ethical, garrulous Greek chorus.

In a second mode, loss marks that which is introduced by the dimension of language in the organism's life. A Real "existence" prior to the effects induced by the signifier is lost and this "existence" prior to language can be written only as a hypothesis, since the articulation of its having been lost must take place in the medium and in the material which made it go missing in the first place: language. The subject in Lacan, we might say, is afflicted by language and is constituted by that affliction, just as Pérez's unnamed narrator in *Gulf Dreams*, *sick* as she is with words. Language is surely afflicted by the certainty that it will compel the precipitation of a subject. A signifier, to tweak a famous Lacanian aphorism, gets saddled with the responsibility of having to represent a subject for another signifier.

CONCLUSION

In the third mode, closely related to the second, grief and loss emerge in the analysis, not in the manner both Phillips and Butler warn against, as an ongoing psychoanalytic ritual, but at the end of analysis, when the analysand has been lifted to the strange dignity of a kind of destitution and disarray.

I'd like to briefly characterize the end of the Lacanian analysis to give the reader a sense of how the arrival at disarray and subjective destitution suggest a kind of beyond to grief and loss, insofar as grief has lost its objects and thus its footing. After all, where is one to locate the suffering that attends the symptom when the end of the Lacanian psychoanalytic process is conceptualized as the moment when the analysand *identifies* with her or his symptom by becoming her or his own cause?

To what state or condition is the analysand brought at the end of an analysis? Lacan's answer in 1960 is: "At the end of a training analysis the subject should reach and should know the domain and the level of the experience of absolute disarray."[21] I wonder if Butler's question to the psychoanalytic community regarding an ethos where analysands would be encouraged to mourn the loss of all of their repressed gender identities can be read as part of a process of subjective destitution whereby the analysand would come to feel the experience of "absolute disarray." Is what transpires at the end of analysis—this subject in disarray—at all subject to being characterized in Butler's language of mourning and melancholia? What is lost in the Lacanian clinical setting along the way to the end of analysis?

Although I do not have the time and space to give a detailed account of what is entailed in a Lacanian analysis, I do want to point to two very specific things: what the analysand must come to identify with at the end of analysis and what prior to that should be seen as the goal of an analysis. To return to some of the points of chapter 2, Lacan was adamantly opposed to the idea that seemed to organize the analysis in ego psychology and object relations theory, where the end of analysis is seen to conclude with an identification with the analyst, since this would simply repeat another form of alienation for the analysand. In the Lacanian setting, what is required instead is the most radically opposite notion of identification with the analyst, since by the end of the analysis the analyst should come to represent a profoundly unassimilable difference. The Lacanian psychoanalyst Anne Dunand explains:

> We can see how the end of analysis, in order to fit in with the distinction between the real and reality, must needs be an end without identification: the unconscious

234

can be interminably interpreted, for it is words, words, words. . . . One cannot identify with the object; one can only space it out with signifiers around the gap. And this has to be worked through, several times, for according to Lacan, it is not a mirage or mere illusion, it is the cause of desire. That is the only way of crossing the plane of identification. That analyst cannot be absorbed in the identification.[22]

What is the goal of analysis? The Lacanian psychoanalyst Paul Verhaeghe answers,

> At first sight, the answer is strange: a successful analysis brings the subject to the point where s/he can identify him or herself with the symptom. This identification is a special one, because it concerns an identification with the real of the symptom, and thus concerns an identification on the level of being. This is exactly the counterpart to what the analysand experienced before, namely the identification/alienation with the Other and the accompanying belief in this Other, and thus in its existence. The analytic experience make clear that this Other does not exist, and hence that the subject does not exist either. This paves the way to the real being of the subject.[23]

Lacan illustrates this vanishing analysand and Other when, in a slightly different context, he teaches, "How can man, that is to say a living being, have access to knowledge of the death instinct, to his own relationship to death? The answer is, by virtue of the signifier in its most radical form. It is in the signifier and insofar as the subject articulates a signifying chain that he comes up against the fact that he may disappear from the chain of what he is."[24]

I am stringing these passages together to force a feeling for the sense of loss, and then to ask what there's left to suffer for. How might one characterize the acceptance of the lack of the Other in Lacanian theory? Is this acceptance a sign of something successfully mourned? Is the refusal to acknowledge lack and loss a melancholic operation? Related to this but cast in a much broader way is the refusal to accept or consider that language as structure has certain privative and generative effects on the speaking human organism a melancholic refusal? Does the Lacanian end-of-analysis with the analysand's acknowledgment that the Other doesn't exist and that, likewise, the analysand-qua-subject doesn't exist either, mark the consummate act of successful grieving, where one has been given the strangest and most deliciously morbid opportunity to mourn one's death while still alive?

The idea of accepting the lack in the Other recalls for me the queer ethic

235

Michael Warner elaborates in *The Trouble with Normal*, in which he posits a community of queer folk organized around a kind of indignity and shame. Warner writes,

> I call its way of life an ethic not only because it is understood as a better kind of self-relation, but because it is the premise of the special kind of sociability that holds queer culture together. A relation to others, in these contexts, begins in an acknowledgment of all that is most abject and least reputable in oneself. Shame is bedrock. Queers can be abusive, insulting, and vile toward one another, but because abjection is understood as the shared condition, they also know how to communicate through such camaraderie a moving and unexpected form of generosity. No one is beneath its reach, not because it prides itself on generosity, but because it prides itself on nothing. The rule is: Get over yourself.[25]

I think one could imagine a similar kind of charge attaching to the general acknowledgment that the Other is lacking. We might understand the "special kind of sociality that holds" humans together on the basis of everyone's subjection to language as structure.

Regarding the subject's experience of primordial loss due to the privative and generative effects of language as structure on the speaking organism and the subject's subsequent division in language, we might say to each other, with the warmest regards, "Get over yourself!" Lacan might be read as telling us as much when he writes, "This passion of the signifier thus becomes a new dimension of the human condition in that it is not only man who speaks, but in man and through man that it speaks; in that his nature becomes woven by effects in which the structure of language of which he becomes the material can be refound."[26] There's enough of this to go around because there's all of it to go around. Warner writes, "Spread around the room, leaving no one out, and in fact binding people together, . . . it begins to resemble the dignity of the human."[27]

CARING FOR THE LOSS

I would like to return to the epigraphs to my concluding chapter. In his characterization of Stoic ethics, Foucault writes, "The reason for making this choice was the will to live a beautiful life, and to leave to others memories of a beautiful existence."[28] I would add one word to this sentence: "And to leave to others memories of a beautiful [analyzed] existence." The notion of something left to others—or rather, something that is *not* being left to others because it has yet to emerge in any sustained way—compels this addition. That notion comes from my reading of Spillers's essay, an essay I have been working with for years and which I read before coming across Foucault's interview. The others and what might be left to them in Spillers's essay are boldly announced in a quandary she brings up early on, regarding how an engagement with psychoanalytic theory "now constitute[s] the missing layer of the hermeneutic/interpretive projects of an entire generation of black intellectuals now at work."[29]

Working with Spillers's assessment and translating it into my terms, then, what will not be left, what hasn't been *being* left, to a generation of African American intellectuals will have been a tradition of psychoanalytic theory and certain interpretative and emancipatory possibilities yielding from it. Spillers's practice of interior intersubjectivity, as I have argued, could constitute something along the lines of an analyzed existence left behind to others. I have argued in this book that psychoanalytic theory also constitutes a missing hermeneutic, and this continues to be the case, among generations of Latino and Chicano studies scholars and their research. More importantly, it has been an analytical literacy missing among ethnic-racialized subjects in the United States more generally. This has had serious consequences for how we imagine a politics of emancipation. Currently, we're bullied into crafting an ego politics of the Imaginary that goes mostly unquestioned by us and this is having a withering effect on young Latinos and other young ethnic-racialized subjects, whether inside or outside the university apparatus, who are having to perform the labors of ethnic-racialized resemblance in order to code as legible subjects. They are bereft of a psychoanalytic hermeneutic that might allow them to at least stall the delivery of the hailing practice that tries to name and fossilize them as culturally "different" material in U.S. culture. Reading Spillers's epigraph with Foucault's, I hope to show that despite all that has been written regarding Foucault's general hostility, even dismissal, of certain aspects of psychoanalytic theory, a synthesis of Spillers's interior intersubjectivity and Lacan's theory of the subject who emerges at the end of analysis could constitute something along the lines of Foucault's notion of care of the self.

Before I describe the nature of this care as it emerges from a reading of Spillers, Foucault, and Lacan together, I would like first to establish a link between Foucault and Lacan predicated on their shared critique of psychology and psychiatry, two fields in which each received his initial training.

Didier Eribon understands Foucault's early interest in psychology as a reflection of a particularly vexed time in Foucault's life: "It was during this psychologically troubled period, when he was face-to-face with psychiatric medicine embodied in one of its most eminent practitioners, that Foucault chose to direct his education toward psychology and psychiatry. In 1949 he received a diploma from the Institut de psychologie de Paris. In 1952 he received a diploma in psychopathology." Eribon goes on to explain how "psychology would be Foucault's professional specialization for many years. He was hired to teach psychology in Lille in 1952, and he was hired as a psychology professor in Clermont-Ferrand in 1960."[30]

It is certainly worth mentioning that just as Foucault is embarking on a professorial career in psychology, Lacan is just beginning to deliver his first private seminars from 1951 to 1953 in the apartment of Sylvia Bataille. Lacan comes to psychoanalysis from psychiatry in the 1930s, turning to it because he thought it would help him with his psychiatric research. He begins training as an analyst in the 1930s, and although initially convinced that psychoanalysis could assist psychology in becoming a real science, he eventually dissociates the two quite radically. He will argue from the 1950s on that psychology cannot really address what is uniquely human about the subject, that is, the effects of language on the subject, and finds himself wondering as late as 1972 and 1973 why psychologists refuse to understand that the structure of thought is based on language. At some point in their intellectual careers, we know that both Lacan and Foucault came to vigorously and tirelessly oppose psychology.

Foucault, as much as Lacan, understood the Freudian discovery of the unconscious as presenting a serious challenge to the philosophical foundations of the phenomenological and existentialist discourses in his day. Arnold Davidson writes, "It was the psychoanalytic discovery of the unconscious that, as Foucault emphasizes in 'The Death of Lacan,' allowed one to question the old theory of the subject; whether described in Cartesian or phenomenological terms this theory of the subject was incompatible with the concept of the unconscious, an incompatibility that Jean-Paul Sartre embraced and carried to its ultimate conclusion in *Being and Nothingness*."[31] Foucault also shared Lacan's interest and focus on language as structure and the effects of language on the speaking subject: "Since Foucault, in consonance with Lacan, understood the unconscious as a system of logico-lingusitic structures, he could oppose the primacy of the subject, of psychological forms, to the search for logical structures, structures that could not be understood or explained in

238

psychological terms and whose existence could not be reconciled with the Sartrean sovereignty of the subject."[32]

Although it is downplayed in queer theoretical and in ethnicity- and race-theoretical appropriations of Foucault for critical minoritarian discourses, both Foucault and Lacan had an interest in linguistics and in the role linguistic structures played in the definition of the subject and the intentionality of consciousness. Both Lacan and Foucault, unlike most structuralists, understood that the human subject is not simply mortified by these structures but rather that something in the way of a remainder persists. However, they theorize this remainder very differently. Understanding the overlaps between them in this way should make us refrain from posing their projects as irreconcilable, even if we want to insist on the differences between historicist and psychoanalytic methodological approaches.

It shouldn't strike us as too odd or curious that the late Lacanian theory of the sinthome that I discuss in chapters 5 and 6 and Lacan's later analytical goal of identifying with one's symptom can be read as homologous to what Foucault in his later work would name "care of the self." At the risk of twisting the arm of this analogy to the point of breaking it, might we not understand the notion of identifying with one's symptom as the ultimate form of care of the self?

This is a form of care, as I've said before, that works by way of a kind of ruination of self so that the subject might be precipitated, if we can understand *self* as I'm using it here to mean "ego." In "The Ethics of the Concern for Self as a Practice of Freedom," Foucault writes, "It is what one could call an ascetic practice, taking asceticism in a very general sense—in other words, not in the sense of a morality of renunciation but as an exercise of the self on the self by which one attempts to develop and transform oneself, and to attain to a certain mode of being."[33] Compare this passage to one by Spillers:

> I have chosen to call this strategy the interior intersubjectivity, which I would, in turn, designate as the locus at which self-interrogation takes place. It is not an arrival but a departure, not a goal but a process, and it conduces toward neither an answer nor a "cure," because it is not engendered in formulae and prescriptions. . . . This process situates a content to work on as a discipline, as an askesis, and I would specify it on the interior because it is found in economy but is not exhausted by it.[34]

Spillers's strategy of interior intersubjectivity works as an illustration of the ascetic practice Foucault has in mind but is importantly, as I've been remark-

ing throughout these final chapters, a strategy mined from Lacanian psychoanalytic theory given her interest in understanding the subject's "signifying
dependence."

Psychoanalytic theory, in Spillers's model, serves the function of care, first
because of how she seems to care enough to ask after its disappearance in
African American intellectual work. Second, care announces itself in the
scrutinous analytical regard for the subject that psychoanalytic theory compels, which may then lend itself to the emancipatory. Her strategy is no more
pinned to a morality of renunciation than Lacan's theory of the analysis. Paul
Rabinow explains Foucault's critique of a kind of renunciation that gets linked
to certain practices of self-knowledge: "For Foucault the equation of philosophical askesis with renunciation of feeling, solidarity, and care for one's self
and for others—as the price of knowledge—was one of our biggest wrong
turnings." He continues, "One of the main themes Foucault explored in the
early eighties was 'the care of the self.' The nearly complete uncoupling of this
imperative from its twin, 'know yourself,' is an essential element of his diagnosis of modernity, in which the latter was gradually to eclipse the former as a
philosophical object."[35]

The adage "know thyself" does not quite define the object of psychoanalysis. On this point, Lacan writes:

> Kern unseres Wesen, "the core of our being"—it is not so much that Freud
> commands us to target this, as so many others before him have done with the futile
> adage "Know thyself," as that he asks us to reconsider the pathways that lead to it.
> Or, rather the "this" which he proposes we attain is not a this which can be the
> object of knowledge, but a this—doesn't he say as much?—which constitutes my
> being and to which, as he teaches us, I bear witness as much and more in my whims,
> aberrations, phobias, and fetishes, than in my more or less civilized personage.[36]

Lacan's theory of the subject and the work, quite specifically, the analysand
should perform in the clinical setting is still entirely within the project Foucault names "care of the self." Many might find this counterintuitive or just
plain wrong-headed on my part. After all, where do we locate care? Consider,
for example, this passage characterizing the end of analysis: "At the end of a
training analysis the subject should reach and should know the domain and
the level of the experience of absolute disarray. It is a level at which anguish is
already a protection."[37] At the very least we might agree that there's no
renunciation of feeling or solidarity in the Lacanian setting.

I have tried, perhaps unconvincingly, to argue that the solidarity we might understand in the Lacanian context is organized around the collective understanding that the Other is lacking, that the Other is not complete. This is both a queer ethic and an antiracist Lacanian ethic. I want to end with a point I have been making throughout: this practice on the self that risks ruination in order to precipitate the subject is in the service of an emancipatory politics for the ethnic-racialized subject who must take up her rightful place in the chain of the signifier in order to luxuriate in and suffer the full range of losses that a human subject stands to endure in the world. From here, one can then engage in the full range of meanings that can be made of those losses as well as engage in the full range of strategies that can be crafted in response to those losses. Given the history of how ethnic-racialized subjectivity and experience has been theorized as one subject to being fully exhausted in language because ethnic-racialized subjects have been made into the perfect captives of representation and because those who outfit themselves for the hunt have figured themselves as the masterful, undivided operators of language, then the turn to a Lacanian psychoanalytic model that understands all of us as necessarily divided seems crucial for the simple fact of effecting something new and *keeping it moving.*

The phrase "keeping it moving" comes from the title of Phillips's essay response to Butler. Phillips chooses this resonant term to characterize the movement in thinking that Butler's language of performance keeps inciting, as opposed to how mourning puts the veritable brakes on thinking: "Butler's language of performance keeps definition on the move, which is where it is anyway. Mourning slows things down."[38] Transposing this attribution of movement to Lacanian theory's particular grappling with the function of mourning in the Lacanian analysis, we must today theorize the ethnic-racialized subject as a subject in language, as the incalculable and indeterminate subject of the signifier, as "what slides in a chain of signifiers, whether he knows which signifier he is the effect of or not."[39] Spillers uses "disperse" to name this sliding movement in which the subject is engaged. She reminds us that this generative drift is crucial to the new forms of knowledge we might risk producing regarding ethnic-racialized subjectivity if we dare to mine the intersections between race, psychoanalysis, and politics: "But my interest in this ethical self-knowing wants to unhook the psychoanalytic hermeneutic from its rigorous curative framework and try to recover it in a free-floating realm of self-didactic possibility that might *decentralize* and *disperse* the knowing one."[40]

The precipitation of the subject in Lacanian analysis is in the service of keeping it moving, a goal that is in direct opposition to the ego's desire for mastery, fixity, rigidity, wholeness, and transparency, themes that we still find operative in forms of ego- and social psychologically inspired conceptualizations of ethnic-racialized subjectivity and experience in clinical, extraclinical, legal, and extralegal contexts. This affectively moving species of mourning that the ethnic-racialized subject must commit to is outlined in Spillers's theory of interior intersubjectivity and in Pérez's psychoanalytic-historiographic alternative model for Chicano knowledge production. It keeps it moving because this mourning is incited by the endless possibility of action and intervention that Foucault has named "pessimistic activism": "My point is not that everything is bad, but that everything is dangerous, which is not exactly the same as bad. If everything is dangerous, then we always have something to do. So my position leads not to apathy but to a hyper- and pessimistic activism."[41]

242

Notes

INTRODUCTION: ALL THE THINGS YOU *CAN'T* BE BY NOW

The title of my introduction plays on the title of Hortense Spillers's landmark essay on race and psychoanalysis, first published in *boundary 2* in 1996, "'All the Things You Could Be by Now If Sigmund Freud's Wife Was Your Mother': Psychoanalysis and Race." Her title, in turn, comes from a Charles Mingus composition of the same name. I replace the possibilities and the general hope that Spillers might be said to gesture to with her use of "can" with "can't" not to be unnecessarily gloomy—although a certain gloom does figure here nonetheless—but rather more to suggest the interpretative possibilities for a critique of ideology that have been left unconsidered as a result of critical race and ethnicity studies' reluctance to engage psychoanalytic theory over the years. I would like to take this moment to refer readers to some of the bold, transformative, trailblazing, inspirational work that, in addition to the work of Spillers, has directly attempted to mine psychoanalytic theory while remaining attuned to questions of race and ethnic-racialized subjectivity. For me, a selective contemporary list would at the very least include Mauricio Mazón's *The Zoot-Suit Riots: The Psychology of Symbolic Annihilation*; Claudia Tate's *Psychoanalysis and Black Novels: Desire and the Protocols of Race*; Ann Pellegrini's *Performance Anxieties*; Emma Pérez's *The Decolonial Imaginary: Writing Chicanas into History*; José Estéban Muñoz's *Disidentifications: Queers of Color and the Performance of Politics*; Diana Fuss's *Identification Papers*; Anne Anlin Cheng's *The Melancholy of Race: Psychoanalysis, Assimilation, and Hidden Grief*; David L. Eng's *Racial Castration: Managing Masculinity in Asian America*; Jean Walton's *Fair Sex, Savage Dreams*; Ranjana Khanna's *Dark Continents: Psychoanalysis and Colonialism*; Patricia Gherovici's *The Puerto Rican Syndrome*; Neil Altman's *The Analyst in the Inner City: Race, Class, and Culture through a Psychoanalytic Lens*; Christopher Lane's edited volume *The Psychoanalysis of Race*; and David Eng and David Kazanjian's edited volume *Loss: The Politics of Mourning*.

1 Lacan, *The Seminar of Jacques Lacan, Book XX*, 110.

2 Thomas, *Down These Mean Streets*, 299.

3 I borrow the characterization of the effects of language on the speaking human organism as both privative and generative from Tim Dean's exemplary analysis of Lacanian theory in *Beyond Sexuality*. Dean's study has served as a constant source of inspiration for my thinking on the potential relevance of Lacanian theory to a politics of ethnic-racialized minoritarian discourse. His chapter, "How to Read

Lacan" (22–60), in which he periodizes Lacan's thinking from the 1940s to the 1970s, is an indispensable and sophisticated overview of Lacan's work.

4 Yale Kramer, "Freud and the Culture Wars," 44.

5 Grosfoguel and Georas, "Coloniality of Power and Racial Dynamics," 104.

6 Thomas, *Down These Mean Streets*, 299.

7 Lacan, "The Function and Field of Speech and Language," *Écrits*, 39.

8 Clark, "The Social Scientists, the Brown Decision, and Contemporary Confusion," xlvi.

9 Herman, *The Romance of American Psychology*, 179.

10 Dean, *Beyond Sexuality*; Edelman, *No Future*. The exceptions here, to my mind, are Joan Copjec's "Sex and the Euthanasia of Reason," in *Read My Desire*, Kalpana Seshadri-Crooks's razor-sharp *Desiring Whiteness*, and Juliet Flower MacCannell's *The Hysteric's Guide to the Future Female Subject*, especially the indispensable chapter 3, "The Postcolonial Unconscious; or, The White Man's Thing," and chapter 4, "Race/War." Copjec's powerful and persuasive argument in "Sex and the Euthanasia of Reason" regarding how the Lacanian definition of the incalculable subject in language lends itself to an antiracist theory of human subjectivity has served as an invaluable source of inspiration for my project over the years.

11 Copjec, "Sex and the Euthanasia of Reason," 209.

12 See Teresa Brennan's important *History after Lacan* for a detailed analysis of what she refers to as Lacan's under-remarked-upon theory of history and the "ego's era," in which we currently live, that thrives on rivalry and competition among human subjects and the steady and seemingly inevitable destruction of the environment that appears to be the natural outcome to this rivalry and competition.

13 Fraser, *Justice Interruptus*. See chapter 1, "From Redistribution to Recognition? Dilemmas of Justice in a 'Postsocialist' Age."

14 See, for example, the work of other psychoanalysts in this group, such as Rene Spitz, Edith Jacobson, Margaret Mahler, Anna Freud, and Kurt Eissler.

15 Hartmann, *Ego Psychology and the Problem of Adaptation*.

16 Hartmann, introduction to Loewenstein and Newman, *Psychoanalysis*, ix.

17 Hartmann, *Essays on Ego Psychology*, x.

18 Bergmann, *The Hartmann Era*.

19 Ibid., 11.

20 Yale Kramer, "Freud and the Culture Wars," 46.

21 David Beres, "Ego Autonomy and Ego Pathology," 23.

22 Lacan, *The Seminar of Jacques Lacan, Book II*, 41.

23 Lacan, "The Function and Field of Speech and Language," 42–43.

24 Verhaeghe, "Lacan's Answer to the Classical Mind/Body Deadlock," 128.

25 Bhabha, "The Other Question," 66.

26 The debates on identity politics have failed to comment on the fact that there is, first and foremost, a strong assumption of the ego-psychological subject both in the work condemned as essentialist as well as in the work that condemns certain other work as essentialist. What we might more properly understand as "essen-

tialist thinking" regards the assumption that the ego is the center of consciousness and, moreover, that in this grounding assumption the ego can be confused and conflated with what we might more properly speaking refer to as the subject, the speaking subject in language. As we know, the ego and the subject are not identical. The condemnations of essentialist identity politics have in many ways always struck me as expressions of bad faith insofar as the condemnation more often than not is guided by the very same assumptions regarding the ego as center of consciousness and the related conflation of the ego with the subject. In my reading, what defines an essentialist approach to questions of human subjectivity and experience is precisely this confusion regarding the ego and the subject and the refusal to consider the effects of language as structure on the speaking human organism.

27 Gurewich, "Who's Afraid of Jacques Lacan?" 21.

28 Bergmann, *The Hartmann Era*, 15.

29 Ibid., 3.

30 Kohon, "The Greening of Psychoanalysis," 50.

31 Ibid., 33–34, emphasis added.

32 Lacan, "The Function and Field of Speech and Language in Psychoanalysis," 36.

33 Edelman, 11.

34 Miller, "Microscopia," xxxi.

35 Y. Kramer cited in Bergmann, *The Hartmann Era*, 58–59.

36 Miller, "An Introduction to Seminars I and II," 25.

37 Foucault, "On the Genealogy of Ethics," 256.

38 Van Haute, *Against Adaptation*, 25. In my discussion of Lacan's understanding of language as structure, I have drawn much inspiration from Van Haute's incredibly cogent and wonderful text. For readers in search of an introduction to Lacan's early work in the 1950s, I highly recommend this very readable and learned text.

39 Lacan, "The Instance of the Letter in the Unconscious," *Écrits*, 139.

40 Ibid., 142.

41 Maire Jaanus, " 'A Civilization of Hatred,' " 325.

42 Fink, *The Lacanian Subject*, 50. Fink's text is a clear-headed exposition of the most compelling aspects of Lacan's theory of the subject that I think is infinitely useful for readers interested in the serious promise of Lacanian psychoanalytic theory for critical race and ethnicity studies knowledge projects attempting to theorize the ethnic-racialized subject outside of the moribund confines of ego and social psychology. All of his work over the years has served me as an indispensable touchstone, and like the texts by Dean and Van Haute, Fink's *The Lacanian Subject* serves as an excellent introduction to Lacan's work.

43 Lacan, *The Seminar of Jacques Lacan, Book I*, 157.

44 Dean, *Beyond Sexuality*, 59.

45 Ibid., 205.

46 I attribute this question to the astute anonymous reader of my book at Duke University Press.

47 Fink, *A Clinical Introduction to Lacanian Psychoanalysis*, 250 n.45.

48 Lacan, "The Subversion of the Subject and the Dialectic of Desire in the Freudian Unconscious," *Écrits*, 291.

49 Van Haute, *Against Adaptation*, 21.

50 Spillers, " 'All the Things You Could Be by Now,' " 78.

51 Soler, "Time and Interpretation," 64, emphasis added.

52 I understand that *queer* has been theorized as a term that disturbs all binarial categories, not just those that appear to have something to do with sexual difference, gender, and sexuality. In other words, there is no reason to think that *queer* does not in theory also disrupt binarial thinking around race and ethnicity. For my purposes here, in my attempt to liken "queer" to "Latino" and "Latino" to "queer" as critical operations, I am assigning the disruption of binarial thinking on race and ethnicity to "Latino" and not "queer" in this specific example.

53 This anecdote is reported by Nathan G. Hale Jr. in his *Freud and the Americans*, 73.

54 Although Freud was certainly concerned with "wild analysis" conducted by folks who had little exposure to Freudian theory, one should keep in mind that Freud was very opposed to—and felt positively betrayed by—his North American colleagues' insistence that any practicing psychoanalyst must have a medical degree. I extrapolate on this point more in chapter 2.

55 Copjec, *Read My Desire*, 6.

56 Lacan, *The Four Fundamental Concepts of Psycho-Analysis*, 263.

57 Whether in English or in the original French, working with Lacan's seminars already appears to be a vexed exercise if one keeps in mind how the seminars have been compiled and transcribed. In the preface to the English edition of *The Seminar of Jacques Lacan, Book XX: On Feminine Sexuality—The Limits of Love and Knowledge*, Bruce Fink reminds the reader that this seminar from 1972–73 "was not a text at all originally, but rather a series of largely improvised talks given from notes. The French editor, Jacques-Alain Miller, had to work from a stenographer's faulty transcription of those talks, and was obliged to invent spellings for certain of Lacan's neologisms and condensations and new ways of punctuating for Lacan's idiosyncratic speech" (viii–ix). It was only in the early 1990s that I began to hear of the so-called egregious translations of Lacan's work that I had been reading for years as well as the so-called problematic and sometimes equally egregious North American commentaries on Lacan's work, commentaries that often worked with just the very little of Lacan's seminars and writings that had been published up to that time. Still, as of this writing in 2006, of the twenty-seven seminars Lacan delivered from 1953 to 1980, only six have been collected, translated into English, and made available to the general English-language reader. Earlier this year, Bruce Fink released his long-awaited English translation of the mammoth French version of the *Écrits*. These English translations do not include all of the unofficial English translations of Lacan's seminars by Cormac Gallagher from unedited French manuscripts, which are available for purchase at Karnac Books in London (karnacbooks.com). In this book, I work with all of the latest English official transla-

tions. I have tried to imbue myself with all of the critical commentary on Lacan, including that of actual practicing analysts, literary critics, and philosophers.

58 Zupančič, *Ethics of the Real*, 241.

59 Miller, "Commentary on Lacan's Text," 425.

60 MacCannell, *The Hysteric's Guide to the Future Female Subject*, 109.

61 Fink, *A Clinical Introduction to Lacanian Psychoanalysis*, 213.

62 The use of interpreters in clinical settings with Latino and Hispanic patients is not as unusual as one would think. This is not to say that it represents anything like an ideal situation for the clinician and the patient. In Lopez and Carrillo, *The Latino Psychiatric Patient*, Ernestina Carrillo writes, "Interpreters are recommended in situations where clinicians and patients do not share a common language. The efficacy of interpreted sessions depends on whether interpreters have been trained to work in psychiatric settings and on whether clinicians have been trained in how to work with an interpreter. Interpreters who do not understand the psychiatric interview process normalize patients' responses and omit details they do not understand or that embarrass them" (39).

63 Gallop, *Reading Lacan*, 112.

64 Lacan, *The Seminar of Jacques Lacan, Book II*, 44.

65 Oboler, "Anecdotes of Citizens' Dishonor in the Age of Cultural Racism," 27.

66 Chow, *The Protestant Ethnic*, 107.

67 Kirsner, *Unfree Associations*, 3.

68 Malone and Friedlander, *The Subject of Lacan*, 4.

69 Fink, "Science and Psychoanalysis," 62.

70 "Science and Truth" is now available to the English-language reader as part of Bruce Fink's complete translation of all of the thirty-five texts that originally appeared in the French version of *Écrits* in 1966.

71 Fink, "Science and Psychoanalysis," 62–63.

72 Lacan, *The Seminar of Jacques Lacan, Book II*, 147–48.

73 Spillers, "'All the Things You Could Be by Now.'" The term comes up several times in her study. In its first appearance in the essay, she defines it in the following manner: "A psychoanalytic culture criticism not only would attempt to name such contradictions but would establish the name of inquiry itself as the goal of an *interior intersubjectivity*" (83).

74 Foucault, "Afterword: The Subject and Power," 216.

CHAPTER ONE: HOLLOWED BE THY NAME

1 Witmer, "Insanity in the Colored Race in the United States." The census figures come from Witmer's article. They are identical to the figures provided by Du Bois in *Black Reconstruction in America*, 3.

2 Witmer, "Insanity in the Colored Race in the United States," 20.

3 McGuire, "The Sexual Crimes among Southern Negroes," 106.

4 "The Nature and Definition of Insanity," 521, emphasis added.

5   Rubio, *A History of Affirmative Action*, 2.

6   See Gherovici's *The Puerto Rican Syndrome* for a searing account of how mental health service facilities, like the one I worked in many years ago, in urban centers have, due to the pressures exerted by insurance companies, virtually jettisoned sustained analytical treatment in preference for drug treatment.

7   Kohon, "The Greening of Psychoanalysis," 42.

8   Nathan Hale Jr. provides a cogent overview of some of the debates in the nineteenth-century North American professional neurological community in his introduction to *James Jackson Putnam and Psychoanalysis*. Regarding the use of electrical stimulation to localize brain functions, see his discussion on page 6.

9   Davidson, "Closing Up the Corpses," 3.

10 Ibid., 2, emphasis added.

11 Mama, *Beyond the Masks*, 23.

12 Heinze, "Schizophrenia Americana," 233.

13 Hall cited in Guthrie, *Even the Rat Was White*, 65.

14 Guthrie, *Even the Rat Was White*, 35.

15 Ferguson, "The Psychology of the Negro," 3–4, emphasis added.

16 Ibid., 124.

17 Ibid.

18 Lacan, "The Freudian Thing," 109.

19 Lacan, *The Four Fundamental Concepts of Psycho-Analysis*, viii.

20 Gallop, *Reading Lacan*, 58.

21 Given that this project looks to, whenever appropriate, the specificity of Latino experience in the United States and later to the field of Hispanic psychology and its relationship to North American psychology and psychoanalysis more generally, the reader might expect me to talk a little bit about the emergence of psychoanalysis in Spanish-speaking countries. Although I cannot do justice to a detailed account of psychoanalysis's emergence in Spanish-speaking countries regarding issues relative to technique and theory, I do want to point briefly to some information that may interest the reader. According to Maria Luisa Muñoz and Rebecca Grinberg in their entry for "Spain" in *Psychoanalysis International: A Guide to Psychoanalysis throughout the World, Volume 1: Europe*, the first appearance of Freud's work in Spanish scientific journals was in 1893, when Freud's article "On the Psychic Mechanism of Hysterical Phenomena" was published in both the *Gaceta Medica* of Granada and the *Revista de Ciencias Medicas* of Barcelona. In 1911, José Ortega y Gasset wrote an essay, "Psychoanalysis, the Problematic Science," where he took Freud's theories to task for being unscientific. In 1917, Ruiz Castillo, a Spaniard, acquired the rights to the publication in Spanish of all of Freud's completed and subsequent work. The first volume of Freud's work translated into Spanish appeared in 1932, including a preface by Ortega y Gasset (252). Angel Garma is generally thought to be the figure who introduced psychoanalysis in Spain. Fascinated by Freud's work, he studied at the Institute of Psychoanalysis in Berlin and returned to Madrid in November 1931 to start his work as an analyst

and to begin organizing Spain's first psychoanalytic group (253). In Mexico, Freud's name first appears in print in 1922 when a "provincial doctor," José Torres Orozco, published the article "Freudian Theory in Relation to Mental Illness" in the journal *Mexico Moderno* (149). In the entry for "Peru," Hilke Engelbrecht and Alvaro Rey de Castro write that Peru in 1915 was the first country in the Spanish-speaking world into which psychoanalysis was introduced. Evidence shows that a young psychiatrist, Honorio Delgado, was in correspondence with Freud during this time. In fact, Freud mentions him by name in his 1914 essay "The History of the Psycho-Analytic Movement."

22 Hale, *James Jackson Putnam and Psychoanalysis*, 10. Unfortunately, my attempts to access records of any sort from the Massachusetts General Hospital that might give me some idea of how "immigrants" in the 1870s were able to access "magnetic and electric" mental health care, especially at the hands of Putnam himself, and, more generally, what the intake process looked like, not to mention what the majority of complaints might have been, and so on, have been entirely unsuccessful.

23 Ibid., 7.

24 Ibid.

25 Putnam, "Personal Impressions of Sigmund Freud and His Work."

26 Ibid., 294–95.

27 Ibid., 294.

28 Ibid., 301, emphasis added.

29 Hale, *James Jackson Putnam and Psychoanalysis*, 92.

30 Ibid., 92.

31 Ibid., 43.

32 Lacan, *The Four Fundamental Concepts of Psycho-Analysis*, 77.

33 Hale, *James Jackson Putnam and Psychoanalysis*, 95, emphasis added. Putnam never provides the closing bracket for the passage beginning with "as."

34 Lacan, *The Seminar of Jacques Lacan, Book VII*, 8.

35 Librett, "Medicalized Psychoanalysis and Lay Analysts," 56.

36 Ibid., 56.

37 Ibid., 64–65.

38 Lacan, "The Freudian Thing," 108–9.

39 Lind, "The Dream as Simple Wish-Fulfillment in the Negro," 296–97.

40 Lind, "The Color Complex in the Negro."

41 Foucault, "Psychiatric Power," 48, emphasis added.

42 Gilroy, *Against Race*, 45.

43 A. L. Stoler, *Race and the Education of Desire*, 23.

44 Chow, *The Protestant Ethnic*, 3.

45 Foucault, *Society Must Be Defended*, 81.

46 I borrow this term from Joan Copjec, who uses it to offer, as I explained in the introduction, a tentative definition of "historicism" in *Read My Desire*, 6.

47 Žižek, "Love Thy Neighbor: No Thanks!" 164.

48 Mama, *Beyond the Masks*, 18–19.

49 I mean for "hollow" to refer to the lack of any remarkable psychical interiority or complexity. I am aware that up to this point in the chapter, the use of the word "interiority" seems problematic insofar as I am assuming a profound bipartition in the subject—the inside versus the outside—that goes against the kind of non-Euclidian psychical topology that Lacan demonstrated with the example of the Möbius band; as a result I may appear to be lending a kind of substantialization to the word *unconscious*, which might then lead us down the wrong path in how we understand the term as a thing into which repressed thoughts are deposited like some magical container. This tension notwithstanding, I defend myself to the reader by claiming that I do follow Lacan's reading of the unconscious, one that offers a significantly desubstantialized interpretation even if I depart from Lacan's basic understanding for the purposes of this specific demonstration. I'm aware that this alibi just may not work and may, in fact, itself ring hollow to some readers. In "The Instance of the Letter in the Unconscious," Lacan writes, "The unconscious is neither the primordial nor the instinctual, and what it knows of the elemental is no more than the elements of the signifier" (161).

50 Foucault, *History of Sexuality, Volume 1*, 127.

51 Ibid., 126.

52 Pfister and Schnog, *Inventing the Psychological*.

53 Kovel, *The Radical Spirit*, 152–53.

CHAPTER TWO: SUBJECTS-DESIRE, NOT EGOS-PLEASURES

1 Copjec, *Read My Desire*, 209.

2 Lacan, *The Seminar of Jacques Lacan, Book XX*, 50.

3 Khanna, *Dark Continents*, 221, emphasis added.

4 Spillers, "'All the Things You Could Be by Now,'" 78.

5 MacCannell, *The Hysteric's Guide to the Future Female Subject*, 109. MacCannell's text has been instrumental in my thinking through how the logic of racism depends on a refusal to read those who come to be marked as ethnic-racialized subjects as subjects in language, subjects subjected to the effects of language as structure. The interested reader might consult two especially important chapters that articulate in rich and complicated ways the intersection between race, politics, and psychoanalysis: chapter 3, "The Postcolonial Unconscious; or, The White Man's Thing," and chapter 4, "Race/War."

6 Lacan, *Encore*, 110.

7 Lacan, "Instance of the Letter in the Unconscious," 161.

8 Lacan, "The Function and Field of Speech and Language," 52.

9 Van Haute, *Against Adaptation*, xvii.

10 Zeitlin, "The Ego Psychologists in Lacan's Theory," 212.

11 Leupin, *Lacan Today*, 15.

12 Roudinesco, *Jacques Lacan and Co.*, 123.

13 Kirsner, *Unfree Associations*, 21.

14 Ibid., 33.

15 Fink, *Lacan to the Letter*, 41.

16 Lacan, *The Seminar of Jacques Lacan, Book II*, 10.

17 Ibid., 11.

18 See Fink, *Lacan to the Letter*, 45.

19 Miller, "Contexts and Concepts," 13.

20 Lacan, *The Seminar of Jacques Lacan, Book I*, 171, emphasis added.

21 Lacan, "The Function and Field of Speech and Language," 88.

22 Laplanche and Pontalis, *The Language of Psycho-Analysis*, 136.

23 Lacan, *The Seminar of Jacques Lacan, Book II*, 41.

24 Lacan, "The Function and Field of Speech and Language in Psychoanalysis," 42–43. Keep in mind that *jouissance* as a term, like many other terms in the Lacanian corpus, does not maintain a stable definition over time. This essay, also referred to as the "Rome Discourse," was delivered in 1953. At this point in Lacan's theory, *jouissance* is meant to refer to pleasure. After *Seminar VII, The Ethics of Psychoanalysis*, in 1959–60, the term takes on a different resonance, as it indicates a kind of suffering, or as Dylan Evans puts it, pain and pleasure in a single packet ("From Kantian Ethics to Mystical Experience").

25 Bergmann, *The Hartmann Era*, 14.

26 Lacan, *The Four Fundamental Concepts of Psycho-Analysis*, 203.

27 Van Haute, *Against Adaptation*, xxix.

28 Lacan, "The Freudian Thing," 124.

29 Lacan, *The Seminar of Jacques Lacan, Book I*, 138.

30 Ibid., 139.

31 Lacan, *The Seminar of Jacques Lacan, Book VII*, 293, 298.

32 Lacan, "The Direction of the Treatment and the Principles of Its Power," 234.

33 Lacan, *The Four Fundamental Concepts of Psycho-Analysis*, 177.

34 Safouan, *Four Lessons of Psychoanalysis*, 3.

35 Hale, *James Jackson Putnam and Psychoanalysis*, 43.

36 Lacan, *The Seminar of Jacques Lacan, Book I*, 193. Given my claim that Lacan's critique of ego psychology's theory of the ego interprets their focus on adaptation and harmony as trying to make good—by covering over—on the basic lack of complementarity between the sexes, we may want to consider the relevance, with regard to Balint's theory (see his *Primary Love and Psycho-Analytic Technique* [1956]), of Balint's leadership (along with his future wife, Enid Flora Eichholz) at the Tavistock Institute of Human Relations in 1949 of a group expressly and intensely devoted to the investigation of "marital problems." Balint became the leader of this group on marital woes.

37 Fink, preface to *Reading Seminar XI*, xi.

38 Lacan, *The Seminar of Jacques Lacan, Book I*, 12.

39 Lacan, *The Seminar of Jacques Lacan, Book VII*, 303.

40 Lacan, *The Four Fundamental Concepts of Psycho-Analysis*, 11.

41 Lacan, *The Seminar of Jacques Lacan, Book I*, 3.

42 Brousse, "Language, Speech, and Discourse," 128.

43 Lacan, "The Freudian Thing," 127.

44 For a sharp explanation of the variable-length session and the practice of "punctuation" and "scanding" in Lacanian analysis, see Fink, *The Lacanian Subject*, 66–68.

45 Ibid., 129.

46 Lacan, *The Seminar of Jacques Lacan, Book I*, 3.

47 Lacan, *The Four Fundamental Concepts of Psycho-Analysis*, 77.

48 Chow, *The Protestant Ethnic*, 107.

49 Chow, *Ethics after Idealism*, xxi.

50 Lipsitz, *American Studies in a Moment of Danger*, xvii.

51 Dean, *Beyond Sexuality*, 205.

52 Chow, *The Protestant Ethnic*, 30–33.

53 Rowe, *The New American Studies*, 32.

54 Miller, "Microscopia," 26.

55 Lacan, *The Seminar of Jacques Lacan, Book I*, 73.

56 MacCannell, *The Hysteric's Guide to the Future Female Subject*, 109.

57 Lacan, "The Freudian Field," 108–9, emphasis added.

58 Champagne, *The Ethics of Marginality*, 31.

59 Lacan, *Television*, 32.

60 Evans, "From Kantian Ethics to Mystical Experience," 20.

61 Foucault, *The History of Sexuality, Volume 1*, 157.

62 Ibid., 98.

63 Ibid., 147.

64 Ibid., 129.

65 Davidson, "Foucault, Psychoanalysis, and Pleasure," 212.

66 Lacan, *The Four Fundamental Concepts of Psycho-Analysis*, 45.

67 Ibid., 142.

68 Ibid., 149.

69 Gherovici, *The Puerto Rican Syndrome*, 192.

CHAPTER THREE: BROWNED, SKINNED, EDUCATED, AND PROTECTED

1 K. Clark and M. Clark, "Racial Identification and Preference in Negro Children," 308.

2 Ibid., 308–9.

3 Kenneth Clark quoted in Kluger, *Simple Justice*, 318. Much of the information on the *Brown v. Board of Education* case that I draw upon in this chapter is pulled from this important study written by Klueger.

4 Lacan, *Television*, 3.

5 Lacan, *The Seminar of Jacques Lacan, Book I*, 193–94.

6 Spillers, " 'All the Things You Could Be by Now,' " 76.

7 K. Clark, "The Social Scientists, the Brown Decision and Contemporary Confusion," xlvi.

8 Foucault, "About the Concept of the 'Dangerous Individual' in Nineteenth-Century Legal Psychiatry," 6.

9 Clark, "The Social Scientists, the Brown Decision and Contemporary Confusion," xlvi.

10 Spillers, "'All the Things You Could Be by Now,'" 108.

11 Ibid., 78.

12 Gilman, *Freud, Race, and Gender*, 3.

13 Ibid., 6.

14 Khanna, *Dark Continents*, 16.

15 Spillers, "'All the Things You Could Be by Now,'" 89.

16 Rand and Torok, *Questions for Freud*, 141.

17 Regarding precisely how Jews were racialized as other-than-white in race science literature of the nineteenth century, Gilman writes, "The general consensus in the ethnological literature of the late nineteenth century was that Jews had 'black' skin, or were at least 'swarthy.' . . . The Jews' disease is written on the skin. The appearance, the skin color, the external manifestations of Jews mark them as different" (*Freud, Race, and Gender*, 20).

18 Freud, "Lines of Advance in Psycho-Analytic Therapy," 167, emphasis added.

19 Regarding the aforementioned clinics for the masses, they never came to be when the primary funder for this effort, Anton Von Freund, lost most of his money to the high inflation set off by the Hungarian revolution. No money, no free treatment.

20 Gherovici, *The Puerto Rican Syndrome*, 25.

21 Bergmann, *The Hartmann Era*, 66.

22 Lacan, *The Seminar of Jacques Lacan, Book II*, 147–48.

23 Jay, *The Dialectical Imagination*, 92.

24 N. Altman, *The Analyst in the Inner City*, xv.

25 Chryssochoou, *Cultural Diversity*, xvii.

26 Fink, *Lacan to the Letter*, 97.

27 Gherovici, *The Puerto Rican Syndrome*, 18.

28 Darder and Torres, "Mapping Latino Studies," 320.

29 Ibid.

30 Herman, *The Romance of American Psychology*, 179.

31 Ibid., 185.

32 Another equally crucial case is the *Hernandez v. Texas* case of 1954, the first Supreme Court case to grant constitutional protection to Mexicans, issued just two weeks before the *Brown v. Board of Education* decision.

33 Escobar, *Race, Police, and the Making of a Political Identity*, 169.

34 Section 1 of the Fourteenth Amendment to the U.S. Constitution reads, "All persons born or naturalized in the United States, and subject to the jurisdiction thereof, are citizens of the United States and of the State wherein they reside. No State shall make or enforce any law which shall abridge the privileges or immunities of citizens of the United States; nor shall any State deprive any person of

life, liberty, or property, without due process of law; nor deny to any person within its jurisdiction the equal protection of the laws."

35 Kluger, *Simple Justice*, 399.

36 See Oboler, *Ethnic Labels, Latino Lives*, 59–64.

37 K. Clark and M. Clark, "The Development of Consciousness of Self and the Emergence of Racial Identification in Negro Preschool Children," 593.

38 Cross, *Shades of Black*, 15. I highly recommend Cross's careful and cogent analysis of Horowitz's and the Clarks' work in chapter 1, "Landmark Studies of Negro Identity." He provides the kind of detail that I can only hint at here.

39 K. Clark and M. Clark, "The Development of Consciousness of Self and the Emergence of Racial Identification in Negro Preschool Children," 593.

40 Spillers, "'All the Things You Could Be by Now,'" 76.

41 K. Clark and M. Clark, "Racial Identification and Preference in Negro Children," 308.

42 Ibid.

43 Ibid., 308–39.

44 Ibid., 309.

45 Ibid., 314.

46 I focus more centrally on this issue in my manuscript *Latino Histories of Sorrow and Anxiety: Everything You Wanted to Know about the Latinization of the U.S. but Were Afraid to Feel*, where I trace the scaffolding of the Latino subject as a psychological subject in psychology, psychoanalysis, and psychiatry in the twentieth century.

47 Garretson, "A Study of Causes of Retardation among Mexican Children in a Small Public School System in Arizona," 31–40.

48 Kluger, *Simple Justice*, 319.

49 Robinson quoted in ibid., 336.

50 K. Clark quoted in ibid., 353.

51 Mama, *Beyond the Masks*, 56, 52.

52 Spillers, "'All the Things You Could Be by Now,'" 89.

53 Lacan, "The Mirror Stage as Formative of the I Function," 4.

54 Ibid., 6.

55 Spillers, "'All the Things You Could Be by Now,'" 76.

56 The reader should keep in mind that Lacan does not work out the three orders Imaginary, Symbolic, and Real until 1953, the year of the first seminar, and so the use of these terms is absent in the articles written between 1936 and 1949.

57 Hoens and Pluth, "The Sinthome," 4, emphasis added.

58 Lacan, *The Seminar of Jacques Lacan, Book I*, 140.

59 Nobus, "Life and Death in the Glass," 120, emphasis added.

60 Fink, "Science and Psychoanalysis," 62.

61 Lacan, "The Direction of the Treatment and the Principles of Its Power," 223.

62 Butler, Laclau, and Žižek, *Contingency, Hegemony, Universality*, 174–75.

63 Crenshaw, Gotanda, Peller, and Thomas, *Critical Race Theory*, xxiv.

64 K. Clark, "The Social Scientists, the Brown Decision, and Contemporary Confusion," xvli.

65 See David S. Caudill's *Lacan and the Subject of Law: Toward a Psychoanalytic Critical Legal Theory* for a more sustained attempt to do just this. In his introduction, Caudill writes, "Lacan is not yet a fixture in the theory and criticism of legal processes and institutions. My primary intention in this book is to explore the promise of Lacanian theory as a critical supplement to the discipline of law" (xi).

66 Cited in ibid., 23.

67 Michel Foucault, "Afterword: The Subject and Power," 216.

68 Crenshaw et al., *Critical Race Theory*, xxxiii–xiv.

69 Williams, *The Alchemy of Race and Rights*, 153.

70 Ibid., 152.

71 Brown, *States of Injury*, 121.

72 Lacan, *The Seminar of Jacques Lacan, Book VII*, 209.

73 Dean, *Beyond Sexuality*, 198.

74 Lacan, "The Direction of the Treatment and the Principles of Its Power," 253.

75 Crenshaw et al., *Critical Race Theory*, xxv.

76 Ford, "Beyond 'Difference,'" 75.

77 Ibid., 53.

78 Ibid., 61.

79 Brennan, *History after Lacan*, 28. The relevant passage where Lacan discusses "rewriting history" is found in *The Seminar of Jacques Lacan, Book I*. See the end of the class session for January 13, 1954: "I would say—when all is said and done, it is less a matter of remembering than of rewriting history" (14).

80 Bergmann, *The Hartmann Era*, 66.

81 Ford, "Beyond 'Difference,'" 76.

255

CHAPTER FOUR: LATINO STUDIES' BARRED SUBJECT AND LACAN'S BORDER SUBJECT

1 See *Boletín Demográfico*, July 1998.

2 Ford, "Beyond 'Difference,'" 76.

3 The symbol of the rhomboid, lozenge, or diamond, ◊ is defined by Lacan in n. 17 to "The Direction of the Treatment and the Principles of Its Power": "The sign registers the relations envelopment-development-conjunction-disjunction" (270). Generally it is read as signifying "in relation to." For example, the formula for fantasy, can be read as "the barred subject *in relation to* object a."

4 Lacan, *The Seminar of Jacques Lacan, Book I*, 171, emphasis added.

5 Lacan, "The Subversion of the Subject and the Dialectic of Desire," 301.

6 For Lacan's incredibly dense, hallucinatory, and fascinating discussion on "string theory" and the Borromean knot, see chapter 10, "Rings of String," in *The Seminar of Jacques Lacan, Book XX*.

7 Lacan, *The Seminar of Jacques Lacan, Book XX*, 50.

8 Ibid., 33.

9 Lacan, "The Subversion of the Subject and the Dialectic of Desire," 301.

10 Dean, *Beyond Sexuality*.

11 Fink, *The Lacanian Subject*.

12 I am fully aware of how odd it may strike some readers that I am attributing the theory of the border subject to Latino studies and not Chicano studies. I will discuss this problematic attribution and the pressures that attend and motivate it in the argument that follows. For now, I want readers to understand that my attribution of the border subject to Latino studies follows on the heels of Frances R. Aparicio's remarks in a recent interview: "I think that the theorization and development of the concept of a border subject and hybrid identity has been one of the most significant contributions of Latino studies to cultural studies" (Aparicio, "Latino Cultural Studies," 20). The slippage between Latino studies and Chicano studies reflects very complicated and unwieldy institutional and political issues within and outside the university, and I will address these issues head on in this chapter.

13 Darder and Torres, "Mapping Latino Studies," 307, emphasis added.

14 Davis, *Magical Urbanism*, 14.

15 Huntington, "The Hispanic Challenge," 1. These issues are also tracked in his book, *Who Are We*. In particular, consult chapter 9, "Mexican Immigration and Hispanization."

16 Huntington, "The Hispanic Challenge," 1.

17 I borrow the term *Spanglish ethos* from Ed Morales's *Living in Spanglish*.

18 Gutiérrez and Padilla, *Recovering the U.S. Hispanic Literary Heritage*, vol. 1, 18.

19 Ibid., 21.

20 Herrera-Sobek and Sánchez Korrol, *Recovering the U.S. Hispanic Literary Heritage*, vol. 3, 1–2.

21 Ibid., 5.

22 See the excellent essay in Herrera-Sobek and Sánchez Korrol, *Recovering the U.S. Hispanic Literary Heritage*, by Kenya C. Dworkin y Mendez, "From Factory to Footlights: Original Spanish-Language Cigar Workers' Theatre in Ybor City and West Tampa, Florida," addressing this period and the development of this genre.

23 *Arrepentida* means "ashamed" in Spanish and is most often used as a term of derision from one Latino to another Latino who's trying to get over as an Anglo.

24 Cruz, *Anna in the Tropics*, 50.

25 Rivera, *Marisol and Other Plays*, 68.

26 Davis, *Magical Urbanism*, 51–57.

27 If we insist on the difference between the terms *Latino* and *Hispanic*, might we say there is a shift of tense struck between *Hispanic* and *Latino*, with the latter the future perfect tense of the first?

28 Long, *The Sentence and Its Parts*, 47.

29 Soler, "Time and Interpretation," 64, emphasis added.

30 Chow, *The Protestant Ethnic and the Spirit of Capitalism*, 107.

31 Morales, *Living in Spanglish*, 17.

32 Valle and Torres, *Latino Metropolis*, 194.

33 I deal with this specific topic in much more detail in the introduction to my new manuscript, *Latino Histories of Sorrow and Anxiety*.

34 Lacan, "The Function and Field of Speech and Language," 84.

35 For a detailed analysis of how Lacan strategically adopts the analysand's discourse in one of his most difficult pieces of writing, "The Instance of the Letter in the Unconscious," that Lacan explicitly situates in the first pages as somewhere between writing and speech, see Bruce Fink's very informative chapter, "Reading 'The Instance of the Letter in the Unconscious'" in his text *Lacan to the Letter*. See especially the discussion on pages 68–72.

36 *Luchando* means "to toil" or "to struggle" in Spanish.

37 The term is from Chela Sandoval's *Methodology of the Oppressed*.

38 Aparicio, "Latino Cultural Studies," 13.

39 See, for example, Yvonne Yarbro-Bejarano's critique of Marjorie Garber's use of Anzaldua's work in "Gloria Anzaldua's *Borderlands/La frontera*," and Marcus Embry's more general critique of misappropriations of Anzaldua's work, "Cholo Angels in Guadalajara."

40 Saldívar, *Chicano Narrative*, 7.

41 Chow, *The Protestant Ethnic and the Spirit of Capitalism*, 32.

42 Copjec, *Read My Desire*, 209.

43 Mignolo, *Local Histories/Global Designs*, 12.

44 Ybarra-Frausto, "Rasquachismo," 157.

45 Ibid., 156.

46 Sandoval, "U.S. Third World Feminism," 3.

47 Muñoz, *Disidentifications*, 11–12.

48 Aparicio, "Latino Cultural Studies," 20–21.

49 Lacan, *The Seminar of Jacques Lacan, Book XX*, 50.

50 Anzaldúa, *Borderlands/La Frontera*, 26.

51 Ibid., 79–80.

52 Ibid., 53–57.

53 Mignolo, "Capitalism and Geopolitics of Knowledge," 46.

54 Poblete, *Critical Latin American and Latino Studies*, xv.

55 For a similar reading of the hysteric's discourse in relation to Latin Americanist discourse, and not Latino studies, see Moreiras, *The Exhaustion of Difference*, 81–82.

56 See Lacan, *The Seminar of Jacques Lacan, Book XVII*.

57 For stimulating essays on *Seminar XVII*, see *Jacques Lacan and the Other Side of Psychoanalysis*, edited by Justin Clemens and Russell Griggs.

58 Copjec, "Dossier on the Institutional Debate," 51.

59 Lacan, "Impromptu at Vincennes," 121.

60 In the *Introductory Dictionary of Lacanian Psychoanalysis*, Dylan Evans explains that Lacan identifies "four possible articulations of the symbolic network which regulates intersubjective relations. These 'four discourses' are the discourse of the master, the discourse of the university, the discourse of the hysteric, and the discourse of the analyst" (44). My readings of Lacan's four discourses draw

generously on Bruce Fink's cogent explanation of them in his introduction to Lacanian theory, *The Lacanian Subject*. See chapter 9, "The Four Discourses." The diagram that I use to represent the "four positions" to be filled by the "four mathemes" appears on page 131.

61 Fink, *The Lacanian Subject*, 130.

62 However, to be honest, all ethnic-racialized students and laborers in the university, insofar as they too serve as pedagogical texts of difference in most university settings, are also cleverly put to work as spectacles of differences. They perform the labor of representation. One could use this formula to describe how they slave away for the university too. Whereas the university as master can come clean more or less about the fact that it knows that it's putting the professor to work and lets the professor know that it has to produce work, it can't let the students know about the representational labor they're producing by their simply being there, by their appearances in classrooms, meetings, university brochures, and so on, because their labor goes for the most part unpaid.

63 Fink, *The Lacanian Subject*, 133.

64 Darder and Torres, "Mapping Latino Studies," 305.

65 Fink, *The Lacanian Subject*, 133.

66 Ford, "Beyond 'Difference,' " 76.

67 Oboler, "Anecdotes of Citizens' Dishonor in the Age of Cultural Racism," 29.

258

68 Ibid.

CHAPTER FIVE: HYSTERICAL TIES, LATINO AMNESIA, AND THE *SINTHOMESTIZA* SUBJECT

1 See Lombroso, *Criminal Man*.

2 Palumbo-Liu, "Assumed Identities," 766–67.

3 L. Trujillo, "La Evolución del 'Bandido' al 'Pachuco,' " 54.

4 Gutiérrez-Jones, *Rethinking the Borderlands*, 1.

5 If we want to pursue a comparative analysis under the umbrella of "Latino," we might comment on the fact that mostly contemporaneous to the construction of the criminalized Chicano male is the construction of the hysterical Puerto Rican soldier beginning after the Korean war that culminated in the creation of the diagnosis of "Puerto Rican Syndrome" in 1953 by U.S. army psychiatrists, who stood bemused and confused at the sight of Puerto Rican men who couldn't fight, exhibiting as they did all manner of incomprehensible behavior.

6 Lacan, *The Seminar of Jacques Lacan, Book XX*, 110.

7 Thomas, *Down These Mean Streets*, 299.

8 Noriega, "Fashion Crimes," 2.

9 Mazón, *The Zoot-Suit Riots*, 9.

10 Escobar, *Race, Police, and the Making of a Political Identity*, 178.

11 Sanchez-Tranquilino and Tagg, "The Pachuco's Flayed Hide," 559.

12 Escobar, *Race, Police, and the Making of a Political Identity*, 17.

13 Sanchez-Tranquilino and Tagg, "The Pachuco's Flayed Hide," 559.

14 Many fine texts have done the work of historicizing pachuco/a and zoot suit cultures. I have found four to be absolutely indispensable: McWilliams, *North from Mexico*; Jones, *The Government Riots of Los Angeles, June, 1943*; Mazón, *The Zoot-Suit Riots*; and Escobar, *Race, Police, and the Making of a Political Identity*. I arrived at Escobar's text late in my research and would highly recommend it to a reader who wants an excellent overview of the issues involved here, because it builds generously upon the research and studies that I reference in the first three texts.

15 I have chosen not to look at films that address the zoot suiter and pachuco/a in more obvious and direct ways, like Luis Valdez's *Zoot Suit* and Edward James Olmos's *American Me*, because I'm interested in how these figures emerge somewhat symptomatically in the text, behind the backs, as it were, of the manifest content of the filmic text. My motivation here is to remain alive to the oblique nature of the figures themselves, the way they challenge the obvious. I do consider both Stevens's and Lynch's films to qualify as species of Chicano cinema. What exactly constitutes Chicano film has always been the subject of some debate. Traditionally, critics have considered "Chicano" film to mean that the writer, producer, or director is Chicano. However, there are significant films that belong to the Chicano cinema canon that do not respond to this criterion, films such as Herbert Biberman's 1954 *Salt of the Earth* or Robert M. Young's *Alambrista! The Illegal*. In these cases, the filmic texts are thought to be Chicano-like in their cultural sensibilities and in their politics of Chicano identity. By and large, Chicano cinema emerges as a component of the Chicano movement of 1965–75. For an excellent and still invaluable overview of these debates, see Chon A. Noriega's introduction to *Chicanos and Film*.

16 Escobar, *Race, Police, and the Making of a Political Identity*, 185.

17 The East L.A. multimedia art group Asco (1972–87) mined, among other things, nonsense and nonmeaning for a similar kind of quasi-Lacanian identity politics for Chicanos/as in the 1970s and 1980s.

18 Escobar, *Race, Police, and the Making of a Political Identity*, 178.

19 Noriega, "Fashion Crimes," 7.

20 Ibid.

21 Fanon, *Black Skin, White Masks*, 229.

22 Noriega, "Fashion Crimes," 7.

23 Foucault, *The Care of the Self*. See especially parts 2–4.

24 Brooks, "The Sundays of Satin-Legs Smith," 43–48.

25 Barker, "Pachuco," 18.

26 Ibid., 24.

27 Griffith, *American Me*, 42.

28 *Nation*, January 1, 1949, 1.

29 Sánchez, "Pachucos in the Making," 213.

30 Sanchez-Tranquilino and Tagg, "The Pachuco's Flayed Hide," 559.

31 Limón, *American Encounters*, 76. To my knowledge, the links between Samuel Ramos and Alfred Adler were first made in Mauricio Mazón's 1984 text *The Zoot-Suit Riots*, although Limon's presentation is more explicit regarding how Adler's views were considered by some to be a distortion of Freudian thought or to typify the "Americanization of psychoanalysis," as he calls it, something Mazón does not mention. See 114–16 for this discussion in Mazón.

32 Ramos, *Profile of Man and Culture in Mexico*, 8–9.

33 Limón, *American Encounters*, 86.

34 I borrow the term "geopolitics of the psyche" from Patricia Gherovici. It serves as the title of chapter 6 in *The Puerto Rican Syndrome*.

35 Lacan, "The Function and Field of Speech and Language," 58.

36 For a detailed reading of Seminar XXIII, see Roberto Harari's *How James Joyce Made his Name*.

37 Hoens and Pluth, "The Sinthome," 11.

38 Paz, *The Labyrinth of Solitude and Other Writings*, 13–14.

39 Ford, "Beyond 'Difference,'" 76.

40 Paz, *The Labyrinth of Solitude*, 16.

41 Edelman, *No Future*, 33.

42 Ibid., 114.

43 Ibid., 35.

44 Paz, *The Labyrinth of Solitude*, 17.

45 Ramirez Berg, "Bordertown," 43.

46 See David G. Gutiérrez's invaluable *Between Two Worlds* for a richly textured account of this period in American history.

47 Ferber, *Giant*, 424–25, emphasis added.

48 See Judith Halberstam's *Female Masculinity* for a sharp discussion of McCambridge's "predatory butch" role in Orson Welles's 1958 film *Touch of Evil* (195).

49 Noriega, "Citizen Chicano," 97.

50 Jordy III and Juana, in this regard, recall in more ways than one the odd heterosexual couple Pilar and Sam in John Sayles's *Lone Star* (1996). At the end of Sayles's film Pilar and Sam, who were once star-crossed lovers in their youth, are revealed to be half-brother and -sister, sharing the same Anglo father. Even after discovering this, they appear to agree to forge ahead in their relationship.

51 Schuth, *International Dictionary of Films and Filmmakers*, 388.

52 Noriega, "Citizen Chicano," 91.

53 Pérez-Torres, "Chicano Ethnicity, Cultural Hybridity, and the Mestizo Voice," 161.

54 Limón, *American Encounters*, 123.

55 Throughout the film, Rita is made to represent in her clothing and makeup what is today recognized popularly as a Latina fashion aesthetic in the U.S.—the "Latina beauty" construction. She is consistently outfitted in either black or red colors, her lips are always painted red, and even in her worst moments she appears "well put together," as they say.

56 Rodríguez, "Visual Retrospective," 81.

57 Rita Hayworth, far from being dismissed as a sell-out by new generations of Latinos, has been recuperated as an important Latina icon. In the June 2005 issue of *Urban Latino*, which boasts on the masthead, "The Culture, the Movement, the Magazine," Rita Hayworth is featured and celebrated in the monthly "Urban Legends" section (64). Hayworth could hardly be demonized as a sellout during the heyday of her popularity. Along with Orson Welles, with whom she had a child, she was openly supportive of the young Mexican American men unjustly convicted for the murder of José Díaz in the 1943 case that came to be referred to as the Sleepy Lagoon Murder trial, on which Luis Valdez's 1981 film *Zoot Suit* is based. Hayworth died in the grips of Alzheimer's disease in 1987 and is considered the first person in Hollywood to raise awareness for Alzheimer's. We could certainly push at my reading of Rita and Chicana-qua-Latina amnesia to suggest as well that the link to Rita Hayworth for Rita is also colored by the memory loss that characterizes this disease.

58 Escobar, *Race, Police, and the Making of a Political Identity*.

59 We might add here that the very last utterance in the film—"silencio"—is spoken in Spanish.

60 Anzaldúa, *Borderlands/La Frontera*, 80.

61 Lacan, "The Function and Field of Speech and Language in Psychoanalysis," 84.

CHAPTER SIX: EMMA PÉREZ DREAMS THE BREACH

1 Copjec, *Read My Desire*, 6.

2 Ibid., 68, emphasis added.

3 See Foucault, "On the Genealogy of Ethics," 256.

4 Copjec, *Read My Desire*, 8.

5 Ibid., 10, emphasis added.

6 Ibid., 6.

7 Žižek, "The Real of Sexual Difference," 72.

8 Copjec, *Read My Desire*, 6.

9 Bracher, "'Always Psychoanalyze!'" 3.

10 Chow, *The Protestant Ethnic*, 142.

11 Pérez, *The Decolonial Imaginary*, 5, emphasis added.

12 Ibid., 6.

13 Ibid., 3–4, emphasis added.

14 Ibid., 4.

15 Lacan, *The Seminar of Jacques Lacan, Book I*, 14, emphasis added.

16 Pérez, *The Decolonial Imaginary*, 8–9.

17 Ibid., 7.

18 Ibid., xvi.

19 Bracher, "'Always Psychoanalyze!'" 3.

20 Trujillo, *Living Chicana Theory*.

21 González, "Speaking Secrets," *Living Chicana Theory*, 66–67.

22 Chow, *The Protestant Ethnic*, 48.

23 Pérez, *The Decolonial Imaginary*, 5.

24 Ibid., 20.

25 Edelman, *No Future*, 29.

26 Soler, "Hysteria in Scientific Discourse," 47.

27 The reader may want to return to my explication of the hysteric's discourse in chapter 4 to remind herself how the hysteric undermines the master's discourse in the hysteric's pursuit for the ongoing production of new and more knowledge.

28 García, *United We Win*, 15.

29 Cited in Rosales, *Chicano!*, 219.

30 Oboler, *Ethnic Labels, Latino Lives*, 59.

31 Rodriguez, *Hunger of Memory*, 159.

32 Pérez, "Gulf Dreams," 102–3.

33 Pérez, *Gulf Dreams*, 89.

34 Ibid., 7.

35 Pérez, *The Decolonial Imaginary*, xvi.

36 Pérez, *Gulf Dreams*, 91.

37 Lacan, *The Seminar of Jacques Lacan, Book VII*, 150.

38 Ibid., 125.

39 Dean, *Beyond Sexuality*, 18.

40 Pérez, *Gulf Dreams*, 14.

41 Lacan, *The Seminar of Jacques Lacan, Book III*. See the chapter, "The Hysteric's Question (II): What Is a Woman?"

42 Pérez, *Gulf Dreams*, 139.

43 Hoens and Pluth, "The Sinthome," 11.

44 Ibid., 149.

45 Lacan, "The Signification of the Phallus," 274.

46 Pérez, *Gulf Dreams*, 150.

47 Žižek, *Looking Awry*, 131.

48 Sanchez-Tranquilino and Tagg, "The Pachuco's Flayed Hide," 561, emphasis added.

CHAPTER SEVEN: THE CLINICAL, THE SPECULATIVE, AND WHAT MUST BE MADE UP IN THE SPACE BETWEEN THEM

1 The term first comes up in the context of Butler's reply to Phillips's commentary in "Melancholy Gender/Refused Identification," chapter 5 of *The Psychic Life of Power*. Butler writes, "Adam Phillips's welcome commentary confirms that there might be a dialogue, even perhaps a psychoanalytic one, between a clinical and speculative perspective on questions of gender, melancholia, and performativity. Clearly the positions here are not as 'staked out' as is often the case, for Phillips is himself both a clinician and a speculative thinker, and thus furthers the doubly dimensioned writing inaugurated by Freud. Indeed, what might at first seem a

strict opposition—the clinician, on the one hand, and the cultural theorist on gender, on the other—is broken down and reconfigured in the course of this exchange" (160).

2 Eng and Hann, "A Dialogue on Racial Melancholia," 350.

3 Chow, *The Protestant Ethnic*, 127.

4 Walton, *Fair Sex, Savage Dreams*, 7.

5 Copjec, *Read My Desire*, 204. For readers interested in this debate, I highly recommend Copjec's careful unpacking of this argument in chapter 8, "Sex and the Euthanasia of Reason." The reader may want to read Copjec's chapter in tandem with Lacan's *Seminar XX* in order to understand Copjec's engagement with Lacan's complex formulas of sexuation. Also see Verhaeghe's "Lacan's Answer to the Classical Mind/Body Deadlock."

6 Ibid., 206.

7 Ibid., 207–8.

8 Seshadri-Crooks, *Desiring Whiteness*, 4.

9 Ibid., 7.

10 Spillers, "'All the Things You Could Be by Now,'" 118–19, emphasis added.

11 Copjec, *Read My Desire*, 208.

12 Spillers, "'All the Things You Could Be by Now,'" 89.

13 Ibid., 141, emphasis added.

14 Lacan, *The Seminar of Jacques Lacan, Book VII*, 304.

15 Spillers, "'All the Things You Could Be by Now,'" 84–85, emphasis added.

16 Ibid., 84.

17 Ibid.

18 Lacan, "The Function and Field of Speech and Language," 102.

19 Spillers, "'All the Things You Could Be by Now,'" 103.

20 Seshadri-Crooks, *Desiring Whiteness*, 4.

21 Spillers, "'All the Things You Could Be by Now,'" 89.

22 Seshadri-Crooks, *Desiring Whiteness*, 4.

23 Phillips, "Keeping It Moving," 154–55.

24 Ibid., 155.

25 Fanon, *Black Skin, White Masks*, 99.

26 Ibid., 99–100.

27 Ibid., 100, emphasis added.

28 Ibid., emphasis added.

29 Phillips, "Keeping It Moving," 155.

30 Spillers, "'All the Things You Could Be by Now,'" 89.

31 Hogan, "The Politics of Otherness in Clinical Psychoanalysis," 37.

32 Spillers, "'All the Things You Could Be by Now,'" 89.

33 Fanon, *Black Skins, White Masks*, 100.

34 Lacan, "The Direction of the Treatment and the Principles of Its Power," 216, emphasis added.

35 Fink, *A Clinical Introduction to Lacanian Psychoanalysis*, 245 n.8.

36 Fuss, *Identification Papers*, 161.
37 See, for example, Gendzier's *Franz Fanon*, 64.
38 Fuss, *Identification Papers*, 164.
39 Fanon, *Black Skin, White Masks*, 216.
40 Spillers, "'All the Things You Could Be by Now,'" 108.
41 See Holmes, "Race and Transference in Psychoanalysis and Psychotherapy." In this essay, Evans, a black female analyst, offers five fascinating case studies of her own. Race emerges as an obstacle in the transference that is then interpreted and worked through, to the benefit of the analysis.
42 Sue, "Ethnicity and Culture in Psychological Research and Practice," 71.
43 Ibid.
44 Ibid., emphasis added.
45 Kovel, *The Radical Spirit*, 152–53.
46 Castañeda, foreword to Martinez, *Chicano Psychology*, xiii.
47 Martinez, "Community Mental Health and the Chicano Movement," 294.
48 A. Padilla, "Hispanic Psychology."
49 Ibid., 1.
50 Carrillo, "Assessment and Treatment of the Latino Patient," 37.
51 Ibid., 2, emphasis added.
52 Chow, *The Protestant Ethnic*, 108.
53 E. Padilla, "The Relationship between Psychology and Chicanos," 283.
54 Sears, Huddy, and Jervis, "The Psychologies Underlying Political Psychology," 3.
55 For readers not familiar with the *Regents of University of California v. Bakke* case, decided in 1978, I provide here a very brief summary. When Alan Bakke applied to the medical school at the University of California at Davis, he was denied admission. He subsequently came to discover that racialized minorities with lower test scores and grades than he had were accepted as part of an affirmative action program. He sued the university, claiming that his right to equal protection under the Fourteenth Amendment had been violated, and he ended up winning the case.
56 Ford, "Beyond 'Difference,'" 46.
57 Sears and Levy, "Childhood and Adult Political Development," 67–68, emphasis added.
58 Ibid., 68.
59 Ford, "Beyond 'Difference,'" 76.
60 Fanon, *Black Skin, White Masks*, 226.
61 Spillers, "'All the Things You Could Be by Now,'" 84.
62 Phillips, "Keeping It Moving," 155.
63 Sears and Levy, "Childhood and Adult Political Development," 69.
64 Ibid., 69.
65 Seshadri-Crooks, *Desiring Whiteness*, 4.
66 See also Cheng, *The Melancholy of Race*, for a sophisticated and rich meditation on "racial melancholia" and Asian American subjectivity.

67　Eng and Hann, "A Dialogue on Racial Melancholia," 350.

68　Ibid., 348.

69　Ibid., 351.

70　Phillips, "Keeping It Moving," 155.

CONCLUSION

1　Phillips, "Keeping It Moving," 154–55.

2　Bergmann, *The Hartmann Era*, 60.

3　MacCannell, *The Hysteric's Guide to the Future Female Subject*, 109.

4　Copjec, *Read My Desire*, 6.

5　Phillips, "Keeping It Moving," 154–55.

6　Ibid., emphasis added.

7　Phillips, "Taking Aims," 167.

8　See Kirsner, *Unfree Associations*, a detailed and learned study of the supremely inglorious history of psychoanalytic institutes in the United States.

9　Franz Fanon, *Black Skin, White Masks*, 100.

10　Phillips, "Keeping It Moving," 155.

11　Butler, "Reply to Adam Phillips's Commentary on 'Melancholy Gender / Refused Identification,'" in *The Psychic Life of Power*, 162–63.

12　Lacan, *The Seminar of Jacques Lacan, Book VII*, 8.

13　Ibid., 218.

14　Ibid., 314.

15　Ibid., 292.

16　Although I do not engage with her argument here because it is more Freudian than Lacanian, I highly recommend to readers that they consult with Anne Anlin Cheng's excellent book *The Melancholy of Race* for a detailed analysis of race and melancholia. I also highly recommend chapter 2, "Photographies of Mourning: Melancholia and Ambivalence in Van Der Zee, Mapplethorpe, and *Looking for Langston*," in José Estéban Muñoz's *Disidentifications*, for a cogent and lyrical meditation on racial melancholia.

17　Freud, *The Ego and the Id*, 28.

18　"Gender" and "sexual difference" are not really part of the Lacanian theoretical vocabulary, even though in *Seminar 20* Lacan will talk about how the human organism becomes a sexuated subject.

19　Barzilai, *Lacan and the Matter of Origins*, 88.

20　See especially the chapter "Excommunication," in *The Four Fundamental Concepts of Psycho-Analysis* and Lacan's "Letter to Rudolph Loewenstein," in *Television*.

21　Lacan, *The Seminar of Jacques Lacan, Book VII*, 304. Four years after this seminar, in *Four Fundamental Concepts of Psycho-Analysis*, Lacan does not make any distinction between a training analysis and a therapeutic analysis: "There is only one kind of psycho-analysis, the training analysis" (274).

22　Dunand, "The End of Analysis I," 247.

23 Verhaeghe, "Causation and Destitution of a Pre-ontological Non-entity," 182–83.

24 Lacan, *The Seminar of Jacques Lacan, Book VII*, 295.

25 Warner, *The Trouble with Normal*, 35.

26 Lacan, "The Signification of the Phallus," 274.

27 Warner, *The Trouble with Normal*, 36.

28 Foucault, "On the Genealogy of Ethics," 254.

29 Spillers, " 'All the Things You Could Be by Now,' " 76.

30 Eribon, *Insult and the Making of the Gay Self*, 252–53.

31 Davidson, "Appendix: Foucault, Psychoanalysis, and Pleasure," 209.

32 Ibid., 209–10.

33 Foucault, "The Ethics of the Concern for Self as a Practice of Freedom," 282.

34 Spillers, " 'All the Things You Could Be by Now,' " 84.

35 Rabinow, "Introduction: The History of Systems of Thought," xxiv–xxv.

36 Lacan, "The Instance of the Letter in the Unconscious," 164–65.

37 Lacan, *The Seminar of Jacques Lacan, Book VII*, 304.

38 Phillips, "Keeping It Moving," 159.

39 Lacan, *The Seminar of Jacques Lacan, Book XX*, 50.

40 Spillers, " 'All the Things You Could Be by Now,' " 141, emphasis added.

41 Foucault, "On the Genealogy of Ethics," 256.

Bibliography

Altman, Neil. *The Analyst in the Inner City: Race, Class, and Culture Through a Psychoanalytic Lens*. Hillsdale, N.J.: Analytic Press, 1995.

Altman, Robert, dir. *Come Back to the Five and Dime, Jimmy Dean, Jimmy Dean*. M.C.E.G./Virgin Visi Studios, 1982.

Anzaldúa, Gloria. *Borderlands/La Frontera: The New Mestiza*. San Francisco: Spinsters/Aunt Lute, 1987.

Aparicio, Frances R. "Latino Cultural Studies." Interview by Juan Zevallos Aguilar. Translated by Dascha Inciarte and Carolyn Sedway. In *Critical Latin American and Latino Studies*, edited by Juan Poblete, 3–31. Minneapolis: University of Minnesota Press, 2003.

Barker, George C. "Pachuco: An American-Spanish Argot and Its Social Functions in Tucson, Arizona." *Social Science Bulletin* 18 (1950): 4–37.

Barzilai, Shuli. *Lacan and the Matter of Origins*. Stanford, Calif.: Stanford University Press, 1999.

Beres, David. "Ego Autonomy and Ego Pathology." *Psychoanalytic Study of the Child* 26 (1971): 3–24.

Bergmann, Martin S. "Introduction." In *The Hartmann Era*, edited by Martin S. Bergmann, 1–78. New York: Other Press, 2000.

Bhabha, Homi. "The Other Question: Stereotype, Discrimination, and the Discourse of Colonialism." In *The Location of Culture*, 66–84. New York: Routledge, 1994.

Bracher, Marc. "'Always Psychoanalyze!' Historicism and the Psychoanalysis of Culture and Society." *Journal for the Psychoanalysis of Culture and Society* 2, no. 1 (1997): 1–16.

Brennan, Teresa. *History after Lacan*. New York: Routledge, 1993.

Brooks, Gwendolyn. "The Sundays of Satin-Legs Smith." In *Blacks*, 43–48. Chicago: Third World, 1991.

Brousse, Marie-Hélène. "Language, Speech, and Discourse." In *Reading Seminars I and II: Lacan's Return to Freud*, edited by Richard Feldstein, Bruce Fink, and Maire Jaanus, 123–29. Albany: State University of New York Press, 1996.

Brown, Wendy. *States of Injury*. Princeton, N.J.: Princeton University Press, 1995.

Butler, Judith. *The Psychic Life of Power: Theories in Subjection*. Stanford, Calif.: Stanford University Press, 1997.

Butler, Judith, Ernesto Laclau, and Slavoj Žižek. *Contingency, Hegemony, Universality*. London: Verso Books, 2000.

Carillo, Ernestina. "Assessment and Treatment of the Latino Patient." In *The Latino Psychiatric Patient: Assessment and Treatment*, edited by Alberto G. Lopez and Ernestina Carrillo, 37–53. Washington, D.C.: American Psychiatric Publishing, Inc., 2001.

Castañeda, Alfredo. Foreword to *Chicano Psychology*, edited by Joe L. Martinez Jr., xiii–xiv. New York: Academic Press, 1977.

Caudill, David S. *Lacan and the Subject of Law: Toward a Psychoanalytic Critical Legal Theory*. Atlantic Highlands, N.J.: Humanities Press, 1997.

Champagne, John. *The Ethics of Marginality: A New Approach to Gay Studies*. Minneapolis: University of Minnesota Press, 1995.

Cheng, Anne Anlin. *The Melancholy of Race: Psychoanalysis, Assimilation, and Hidden Grief*. New York: Oxford University Press, 2001.

Chow, Rey. *Ethics after Idealism: Theory-Culture-Ethnicity-Reading*. Bloomington: Indiana University Press, 1998.

———. *The Protestant Ethnic and the Spirit of Capitalism*. New York: Columbia University Press, 2002.

Chryssochoou, Xenia. *Cultural Diversity: Its Social Psychology*. Oxford: Black Publishers, 2004.

Clark, Kenneth B. "The Social Scientists, the Brown Decision and Contemporary Confusion." In *Argument: The Oral Argument before the Supreme Court in Brown v. Board of Education of Topeka, 1952–55*, edited by Leon Friedman, xxxi–l. New York: Chelsea House, 1969.

Clark, Kenneth B., and Mamie P. Clark. "The Development of Consciousness of Self and the Emergence of Racial Identification in Negro Preschool Children." *Journal of Social Psychology* 10 (1939): 591–99.

———. "Racial Identification and Preference in Negro Children." In *Basic Studies in Social Psychology*, edited by Harold Proshansky and Bernard Seidenberg, 308–17. New York: Holt, Rinehard and Winston, 1947.

Clemens, Justin, and Russell Grigg, eds. *Jacques Lacan and the Other Side of Psychoanalysis*. Durham, N.C.: Duke University Press, 2006.

Copjec, Joan. "Dossier on the Institutional Debate: An Introduction." In *Television: A Challenge to the Psychoanalytic Establishment*. Text established by Jacques-Alain Miller. Edited by Joan Copjec. Translated by Denis Hollier, Rosalind Krauss, Annette Michelson, and Jeffrey Mehlman, 49–52. New York: W. W. Norton, 1990.

———. *Read My Desire: Lacan against the Historicists*. Cambridge: MIT Press, 1995.

Coda-Cárdenas, Margarita. *Puppet*. Translated by Barbara D. Riess and Trino Sandoval with the author. Albuquerque: University of New Mexico Press, 2000.

Crenshaw, Kimberlé, Neil Gotanda, Gary Peller, and Kendall Thomas, eds. *Critical Race Theory: The Key Writings That Formed the Movement*. New York: New Press, 1995.

Cross, William E., Jr. *Shades of Black: Diversity in African American Identity*. Philadelphia: Temple University Press, 1991.

———. "The Thomas Cross Models of Psychological Nigrescence: A Literature Review." *Journal of Black Psychology* 4 (1978): 13–31.

Cruz, Nilo. *Anna in the Tropics*. New York: Theatre Communications Group, 2003.

Darder, Antonia, and Rodolfo D. Torres. "Mapping Latino Studies: Critical Reflections on Class and Social Theory." *Latino Studies* 1, no. 2 (2003): 303–24.

Davidson, Arnold. "Appendix: Foucault, Psychoanalysis, and Pleasure." In *The Emer-*

gence of Sexuality: Historical Epistemology and the Formation of Concepts, 209–15. Cambridge: Harvard University Press, 2001.

——. "Closing Up the Corpses." In *The Emergence of Sexuality: Historical Epistemology and the Formation of Concepts*, 1–29. Cambridge: Harvard University Press, 2001.

Davis, Mike. *Magical Urbanism: Latinos Reinvent the U.S. Big City*. London: Verso, 2000.

Dean, Tim. *Beyond Sexuality*. Chicago: University of Chicago Press, 2000.

Du Bois, W. E. B. *Black Reconstruction in America: 1860–1880*. Cleveland: Meridian Books, 1964.

Dunand, Anne. "The End of Analysis I." In *Reading Seminar XI: Lacan's Four Fundamental Concepts of Psychoanalysis*, edited by Richard Feldstein, Bruce Fink, and Maire Jaanus, 243–49. Albany: State University of New York Press, 1995.

Edelman, Lee. *No Future: Queer Theory and the Death Drive*. Durham, N.C.: Duke University Press, 2004.

Embry, Marcus. "Cholo Angels in Guadalajara: The Politics and Poetics of Anzaldua's Borderlands/La Frontera." *Women and Performance: A Journal of Feminist Theory* 8, no. 2 (1996): 87–109.

Eng, David L. *Racial Castration: Managing Masculinity in Asian America*. Durham, N.C.: Duke University Press, 2001.

Eng, David L., and Shinhee Hann. "A Dialogue on Racial Melancholia." *Loss: The Politics of Mourning*, edited by David L. Eng and David Kazanjian, 343–71. Berkeley: University of California Press, 2003.

Eng, David L., and David Kazanjian, eds. *Loss: The Politics of Mourning*. Berkeley: University of California Press, 2002.

Eribon, Didier. *Insult and the Making of the Gay Self*. Translated by Michael Lucey. Durham, N.C.: Duke University Press, 2004.

Erikson, Erik H. *Identity, Youth, and Crisis*. New York: Norton, 1968.

Escobar, Edward J. *Race, Police, and the Making of a Political Identity: Mexican Americans and the Los Angeles Police Department, 1900–1945*. Berkeley: University of California Press, 1999.

Evans, Dylan. *Introductory Dictionary of Lacanian Psychoanalysis*. New York: Routledge, 1996.

——. "From Kantian Ethics to Mystical Experience: An Exploration of Jouissance." In *Key Concepts of Lacanian Psychoanalysis*, edited by Dany Nobus, 1–28. New York: Other Press, 1999.

Fanon, Franz. *Black Skin, White Masks*. Translated by Charles Lam Markmann. New York: Grove Press, 1967.

Ferber, Edna. *Giant*. New York: Doubleday, 1952.

Ferguson, George Oscar, Jr. "The Psychology of the Negro: An Experimental Study." *Archives of Psychology* 36 (April 1916): 1–138.

Fink, Bruce. *A Clinical Introduction to Lacanian Psychoanalysis: Theory and Technique*. Cambridge: Harvard University Press, 1997.

——. *Lacan to the Letter: Reading Écrits Closely*. Minneapolis: University of Minnesota Press, 2004.

———. *The Lacanian Subject: Between Language and Jouissance.* Princeton, N.J.: Princeton University Press, 1995.

———. Preface to *Reading Seminar XI: Lacan's Four Fundamental Concepts of Psychoanalysis,* edited by Richard Feldstein, Bruce Fink, and Maire Jaanus, ix–xv. Albany: State University of New York Press, 1995.

———. "Science and Psychoanalysis." In *Reading Seminar XI: Lacan's Four Fundamental Concepts of Psychoanalysis,* edited by Richard Feldstein, Bruce Fink, Maire Jaanus, 55–64. Albany: State University of New York Press, 1995.

Ford, Richard T. "Beyond 'Difference': A Reluctant Critique of Legal Identity Politics." In *Left Legalism/Left Critique,* edited by Wendy Brown and Janet Halley, 38–79. Durham, N.C.: Duke University Press, 2002.

Foucault, Michel. "About the Concept of the 'Dangerous Individual' in Nineteenth-Century Legal Psychiatry." *International Journal of Law and Psychiatry* 1 (1978): 1–18.

———. "Afterword: The Subject and Power." In *Michel Foucault: Beyond Structuralism and Hermeneutics,* edited by Hubert L. Dreyfus and Paul Rabinow, 208–26. Second edition, Chicago: University of Chicago Press, 1983.

———. *The Care of the Self: The History of Sexuality, Volume 3.* Translated by Robert Hurley. New York: Vintage Books, 1988.

———. "The Ethics of the Concern for Self as a Practice of Freedom." In *Ethics, Subjectivity, and Truth,* edited by Paul Rabinow, translated by Robert Hurley, 281–302. New York: New Press, 1997.

———. *History of Sexuality, Volume 1: An Introduction.* Translated by Robert Hurley. New York: Vintage Books, 1978. Reprint, New York: Vintage Books, 1990.

———. "On the Genealogy of Ethics: An Overview of Work in Progress." In *Ethics, Subjectivity and Truth,* edited by Paul Rabinow, translated by Robert Hurley, 253–80. New York: New Press, 1997.

———. "Psychiatric Power." In *Ethics, Subjectivity and Truth,* edited by Paul Rabinow, translated by Robert Hurley, 39–50. New York: New Press, 1997.

———. *Society Must Be Defended: Lectures at the Collège de France, 1975–1976,* English series edited by Arnold I. Davidson, translated by David Macey. New York: Picador, 2003.

Fraser, Nancy. *Justice Interruptus: Critical Reflections on the "Postsocialist" Condition.* New York: Routledge, 1996.

Freud, Sigmund. *The Ego and the Id* (1923). In *The Standard Edition of the Complete Psychological Works of Sigmund Freud,* edited and translated by James Strachey, 19:3–66. London: Hogarth Press and the Institute of Psychoanalysis, 1953–74.

———. "Lines of Advance in Psycho-Analytic Therapy" (1918). In *The Standard Edition of the Complete Psychological Works of Sigmund Freud,* edited and translated by James Strachey, 17:157–68. London: Hogarth and the Institute of Psychoanalysis, 1953–74.

Fuss, Diana. *Identification Papers.* New York: Routledge Press, 1995.

Gallop, Jane. *Reading Lacan.* Ithaca, N.Y.: Cornell University Press, 1985.

García, Ignacio. *United We Win: The Rise and Fall of La Raza Unida Party.* Tucson: University of Arizona Mexican American Studies Research Center, 1989.

Garretson, D. K. "A Study of Causes of Retardation among Mexican Children in a Small Public School System in Arizona." *Journal of Educational Psychology* 19 (1943): 31–40.

Gherovici, Patricia. *The Puerto Rican Syndrome*. New York: Other Press, 2003.

Gilman, Sander L. *Freud, Race, and Gender*. Princeton, N.J.: Princeton University Press, 1993.

Gilroy, Paul. *Against Race: Imagining Political Culture Beyond the Color Line*. Cambridge: Harvard University Press, 2000.

González, Deena J. "Speaking Secrets: Living Chicana Theory." In *Living Chicana Theory*, edited by Carla Trujillo, 46–77. Berkeley: Third Woman, 1998.

Griffith, Beatrice. *American Me*. Cambridge: Riverside, 1948.

Grosfoguel, Ramón, and Chloe S. Georas. "Coloniality of Power and Racial Dynamics: Notes toward a Reinterpretation of Latino Caribbeans in New York City." *Identities* 7, no. 1 (2000): 85–125.

Gurewich, Judith Feher. "Who's Afraid of Jacques Lacan?" In *The Subject and the Self: Lacan and American Psychoanalysis*, edited by Judith Feher Gurewich, Michel Tort, and Susan Fairfield, 1–30. New York: Other Press, 1997.

Guthrie, Robert V. *Even the Rat Was White*, 2nd ed. Boston: Allyn and Bacon, 1998.

Gutiérrez, David G. *Between Two Worlds: Mexican Immigrants in the United States*. Wilmington, Del.: Scholarly Resources, 1996.

Gutiérrez, Rámon A., and Genero M. Padilla, eds. *Recovering the U.S. Hispanic Literary Heritage, Volume I*, edited by Rámon A. Gutiérrez and Genero M. Padilla, 17–25. Houston: Arte Público, 1993.

Gutiérrez-Jones, Carl. *Rethinking the Borderlands: Between Chicano Culture and Legal Discourse*. Berkeley: University of California Press, 1995.

Halberstam, Judith. *Female Masculinity*. Durham, N.C.: Duke University Press, 1998.

Hale, Jr., Nathan G. *Freud and the Americans: The Beginnings of Psychoanalysis in the United States, 1876–1917*. New York: Oxford University Press, 1971.

——, ed. *James Jackson Putnam and Psychoanalysis: Letters Between Putnam and Sigmund Freud, Ernest Jones, William James, Sandor Ferenczi, and Morton Prince, 1877–1917*. Cambridge: Harvard University Press, 1971.

Harari, Roberto. *How James Joyce Made His Name: A Reading of the Final Lacan*. Translated by Luke Thurston. New York: Other Press, 1995.

Hartmann, Heinz. *Ego Psychology and the Problem of Adaptation*. Translated by David Rapaport. New York: International Universities Press, Inc., 1958.

——. *Essays on Ego Psychology: Selected Problems in Psychoanalytic Theory*. New York: International Universities Press, 1964.

——. *Psychoanalysis: A General Psychology*, edited by Rudolph M. Loewenstein and Lottie M. Newman. New York: International Universities Press, 1966.

Heinze, Andrew. "Schizophrenia Americana: Aliens, Alienists and the 'Personality Shift' of Twentieth-Century Culture." *American Quarterly* 55 (2003): 220–42.

Herman, Ellen. *The Romance of American Psychology: Political Culture in the Age of Experts*. Berkeley: University of California Press, 1996.

271

Herrera-Sobek, María, and Virginia Sánchez Korrol. "Introduction." *Recovering the U.S. Hispanic Literary Heritage, Volume III*, edited by María Herrera-Sobek and Virginia Sánchez Korrol, 1–14. Houston: Arte Público, 2000.

Hoens, Dominiek, and Ed Pluth. "The Sinthome: A New Way of Writing an Old Problem." In *Re-Inventing the Symptom: Essays on the Final Lacan*, edited by Luke Thurston, 1–18. New York: Other Press, 2002.

Hogan, Patrick Colm. "The Politics of Otherness in Clinical Psychoanalysis: Racism as Pathogen in a Case of D. W. Winnicott." *Literature and Psychology* 38, no. 4 (1992): 36–43.

Holmes, Dorothy Evans. "Race and Transference in Psychoanalysis and Psychotherapy." *International Journal of Psychoanalysis* 73, no. 1 (1992): 1–11.

Huntington, Samuel P. "The Hispanic Challenge." *Foreign Policy*, March/April 2004, 1–12.

——. *Who Are We: The Challenges to America's National Identity*. New York: Simon and Schuster, 2004.

Jaanus, Maire. "'A Civilization of Hatred': The Other in the Imaginary." In *Reading Seminars I and II: Lacan's Return to Freud*, edited by Richard Feldstein, Bruce Fink, and Maire Jaanus, 323–55. Albany: State University of New York Press, 1996.

Jay, Martin. *The Dialectical Imagination: A History of the Frankfurt School and the Institute of Social Research, 1923–1950*. Berkeley: University of California Press, 1973.

Jones, Solomon James. *The Government Riots of Los Angeles, June, 1943*. San Francisco: R&E, 1973.

Khanna, Ranjana. *Dark Continents: Psychoanalysis and Colonialism*. Durham, N.C.: Duke University Press, 2003.

Kim, S. C. "Family Therapy for Asian Americans." *Psychotherapy* 22 (1985): 342–48.

Kirsner, Douglas. *Unfree Associations: Inside Psychoanalytic Institutes*. London: Process Press, 2000.

Kluger, Richard. *Simple Justice: The History of Brown v. Board of Education and Black America's Struggle for Equality*. New York: Knopf, 1976.

Kohon, Gregorio. "The Greening of Psychoanalysis: André Green in Dialogues with Gregorio Kohon." In *The Dead Mother: The Work of André Green*, edited by Gregorio Kohon, 10–58. London: Routledge, 1999.

Kovel, Joel. *The Radical Spirit: Essays on Psychoanalysis and Society*. London: Free Association Books, 1988.

Kramer, Yale. "Freud and the Culture Wars." *Public Interest* 124 (Summer 1996): 37–51.

Kutter, Peter, ed. *Psychoanalysis International: A Guide to Psychoanalysis throughout the World, Volume 1—Europe*. Stuttgart–Bad Cannstatt: Fromann-Holzboog, 1992.

Lacan, Jacques. "The Direction of the Treatment and the Principles of Its Power" (1958). In *Écrits*, 215–70.

——. *Écrits: A Selection*. Translated by Bruce Fink in collaboration with Héloïse Fink and Russell Grigg. New York: W. W. Norton, 2002.

——. *The Four Fundamental Concepts of Psycho-Analysis*. Edited by Jacques-Alain Miller. Translated by Alan Sheridan. New York: W. W. Norton, 1981.

272

——. "The Function and Field of Speech and Language" (1953). In *Écrits*, 31–106.

——. "The Freudian Thing" (1955). In *Écrits*, 107–37.

——. "Impromptu at Vincennes." In *Television: A Challenge to the Psychoanalytic Establishment*. Text established by Jacques-Alain Miller. Edited by Joan Copjec. Translated by Denis Hollier, Rosalind Krauss, Annette Michelson, and Jeffrey Mehlman, 117–28. New York: W. W. Norton, 1990.

——. "Instance of the Letter in the Unconscious, or Reason Since Freud" (1957). In *Écrits*, 138–68.

——. "The Mirror Stage as Formative of the *I* Function" (1949). In *Écrits*, 3–9.

——. "Science and Truth" (1966). In *Écrits: The First Complete Edition in English*, translated by Bruce Fink in collaboration with Héloïse Fink and Russell Grigg, 726–45. New York: W. W. Norton, 2006.

——. *The Seminar of Jacques Lacan, Book I: Freud's Papers on Technique, 1953–1954*. Edited by Jacques-Alain Miller. Translated by John Forrester. New York: W. W. Norton, 1991.

——. *The Seminar of Jacques Lacan, Book II: The Ego in Freud's Theory and in the Technique of Psychoanalysis, 1954–1955*. Edited by Jacques-Alain Miller. Translated by Sylvana Tomaselli. New York: W. W. Norton, 1991.

——. *The Seminar of Jacques Lacan, Book VII: The Ethics of Psychoanalysis, 1959–1960*. Edited by Jacques-Alain Miller. Translated by Dennis Porter. New York: W. W. Norton, 1992.

——. *The Seminar of Jacques Lacan, Book III: The Psychoses, 1955–1956*. Edited by Jacques-Alain Miller. Translated by Russell Grigg. New York: W. W. Norton, 1993.

——. *The Seminar of Jacques Lacan, Book XVII: The Other Side of Psychoanalysis*. Edited by Jacques-Alain Miller. Translated by Russell Grigg. New York: W. W. Norton, 2007.

——. *The Seminar of Jacques Lacan, Book XX: Encore, On Feminine Sexuality: The Limits of Love and Knowledge, 1972–1973*. Edited by Jacques-Alain Miller. Translated by Bruce Fink. New York: W. W. Norton, 1998.

——. "The Signification of the Phallus" (1958). In *Écrits*, 271–80.

——. "The Subversion of the Subject and the Dialectic of Desire in the Freudian Unconscious" (1960). In *Écrits*, 281–312.

——. *Television: A Challenge to the Psychoanalytic Establishment*. Text established by Jacques-Alain Miller. Edited by Joan Copjec. Translated by Denis Hollier, Rosalind Krauss, Annette Michelson, and Jeffrey Mehlman. New York: W. W. Norton, 1990.

Lane, Christopher, ed. *The Psychoanalysis of Race*. New York: Columbia University Press, 1998.

Laplanche, J., and J.-B. Pontalis. *The Language of Psycho-Analysis*. Translated by Donald Nicholson-Smith. New York: W. W. Norton, 1967.

"Latin America: Population Projections 1970–2050." *Boletín Demográfico* 62 (July 1998): 1–158.

Leupin, Alexandre. *Lacan Today: Psychoanalysis, Science, Religion*. New York: Other Press, 2004.

Librett, Jeffrey. "Medicalized Psychoanalysis and Lay Analysts." *(a)* 1, no. 2 (2001): 56–67.

Limón, José E. *American Encounters: Greater Mexico, the United States, and the Erotics of Culture.* Boston: Beacon Press, 1998.

Lind, J. E. "The Dream as Simple Wish-Fulfillment in the Negro." *Psychoanalytic Review* 1 (1913): 295–300.

——. "The Color Complex in the Negro." *Psychoanalytic Review* 1 (1913): 404–14.

Lipsitz, George. *American Studies in a Moment of Danger.* Minneapolis: University of Minnesota Press, 2001.

Loewenstein, Rudolph M., and Lottie M. Newman, eds. *Psychoanalysis: A General Psychology.* New York: International Universities Press, 1966.

Lombroso, Gina. *Criminal Man, According to the Classification of Cesare Lombroso.* Montclair, N.J.: Patterson Smith, 1972.

Long, Ralph. *The Sentence and Its Parts: A Grammar of Contemporary English.* Chicago: University of Chicago Press, 1961.

Lopez, Alberto G., and Ernestina Carrillo, eds. *The Latino Psychiatric Patient: Assessment and Treatment.* Washington, D.C.: American Psychiatric Publishing, 2001.

Lynch, David, dir. *Mulholland Drive.* Canal 2001.

MacCannell, Juliet Flower. *The Hysteric's Guide to the Future Female Subject.* Minneapolis: University of Minnesota Press, 2000.

Malone, Karen Ro, and Stephen R. Friedlander, eds. *The Subject of Lacan: A Lacanian Reader for Psychologists.* Albany: State University of New York Press, 2000.

Mama, Amina. *Beyond the Masks: Race, Gender and Subjectivity.* London: Routledge, 1995.

Martinez, Cervando. "Community Mental Health and the Chicano Movement." In *Chicanos: Social and Psychological Perspectives,* edited by Carroll A. Hernandéz, Marsha J. Haug, and Nathaniel N. Wagner, 291–96. Saint Louis: C. V. Mosby, 1976.

Mazón, Mauricio. *The Zoot-Suit Riots: The Psychology of Symbolic Annihilation.* Austin: University of Texas Press, 1984.

McGuire, Hunter. "The Sexual Crimes among Southern Negroes." *Virginia Medical Monthly* 20, no. 2 (1893): 105–25.

McWilliams, Carey. *North from Mexico: The Spanish Speaking People of the United States.* New York: Greenwood, 1968.

Mignolo, Walter. *Local Histories/Global Designs: Coloniality, Subaltern Knowledges and Border Thinking.* Princeton, N.J.: Princeton University Press, 2000.

——. "Capitalism and Geopolitics of Knowledge: Latin American Social Thought and Latino/a American Studies." In *Critical Latin American and Latino Studies,* edited by Juan Poblete, 32–75. Minneapolis: University of Minnesota Press, 2003.

Miller, Jacques-Alain. "Microscopia: An Introduction to the Reading of Television." Translated by Bruce Fink. In *Television: A Challenge to the Psychoanalytic Establishment,* xi–xxxi. Text established by Jacques-Alain Miller. Edited by Joan Copjec. Translated by Denis Hollier, Rosalind Krauss, Annette Michelson, and Jeffrey Mehlman. New York: W. W. Norton, 1990.

——. "Contexts and Concepts." In *Reading Seminar XI: Lacan's Four Fundamental Con-*

cepts of Psychoanalysis, edited by Richard Feldstein, Bruce Fink, and Maire Jaanus, 3–15. Albany: State University of New York Press, 1995.

———. "An Introduction to Seminars I and II: Lacan's Orientation Prior to 1953 (II)." In *Reading Seminars I and II: Lacan's Return to Freud*, edited by Richard Feldstein, Bruce Fink, and Maire Jaanus, 15–25. Albany: State University of New York Press, 1996.

———. "Commentary on Lacan's Text." Translated by Bruce Fink. In *Reading Seminars I and II: Lacan's Return to Freud*, edited by Richard Feldstein, Bruce Fink, and Maire Jaanus, 422–27. Albany: State University of New York Press, 1996.

Moore, Ward. Review of *American Me*. *Nation*, January 1, 1949, 8.

Morales, Ed. *Living in Spanglish: The Search for Latino Identity in America*. New York: St. Martin's, 2002.

Moreiras, Alberto. *The Exhaustion of Difference: The Politics of Latin American Cultural Studies*. Durham, N.C.: Duke University Press, 2001.

Muñoz, José Estéban. *Disidentifications: Queers of Color and the Performance of Politics*. Minneapolis: University of Minnesota Press, 1999.

Nobus, Dany. "Life and Death in the Glass: A New Look at the Mirror Stage." In *Key Concepts of Lacanian Psychoanalysis*, edited by Dany Nobus, 101–38. New York: Other Press, 1999.

Noriega, Chon A. "Introduction." In *Chicanos and Film: Representation and Resistance*, edited by Chon Noriega, xi–xxvi. Minneapolis: University of Minnesota Press, 1992.

———. "Citizen Chicano: The Trials and Titillations of Ethnicity in the American Cinema, 1935–1962." In *Latin Looks: Images of Latinas and Latinos in the U.S. Media*, edited by Clara E. Rodríguez, 85–103. Boulder, Colo.: Westview, 1997.

———. "Fashion Crimes." *Aztlan: A Journal of Chicano Studies* 26, no. 1 (2001): 1–13.

Oboler, Suzanne. *Ethnic Labels, Latino Lives: Identity and the Politics of (Re)Presentation in the United States*. Minneapolis: University of Minnesota Press, 1995.

———. "Anecdotes of Citizens' Dishonor in the Age of Cultural Racism." *Discourse* 21, no. 3 (1999): 19–41.

Padilla, Amado P. "Hispanic Psychology: A Twenty-Five-Year Retrospective Look." *Online Readings in Psychology and Culture* (2002): 1–7. www.ac.wwu.edu/culture/padilla.htm (accessed June 6, 2004).

Padilla, Eligio R. "The Relationship between Psychology and Chicanos: Failures and Possibilities." In *Chicanos: Social and Psychological Perspectives*, edited by Carroll A. Hernandéz, Marsha J. Haug, and Nathaniel N. Wagner, 282–90. Saint Louis: C. V. Mosby, 1976.

Palumbo-Liu, David. "Assumed Identities." *New Literary History* 31 (2000): 765–86.

Paz, Octavio. *The Labyrinth of Solitude and Other Writings*. Translated by Lysander Kemp, Yara Milos, and Rachel Phillips Belash. New York: Grove, 1985.

Pellegrini, Ann. *Performance Anxieties*. New York: Routledge, 1996.

Pérez, Emma. *The Decolonial Imaginary: Writing Chicanas into History*. Bloomington: Indiana University Press, 1999.

———. "Gulf Dreams." In *Chicana Lesbians: The Girls Our Mothers Warned Us About*, edited by Carla Trujillo, 96–108. Berkeley: Third Woman, 1991.

———. *Gulf Dreams*. Berkeley: Third Woman, 1996.

Pérez-Torres, Rafael. "Chicano Ethnicity, Cultural Hybridity, and the Mestizo Voice." *American Literature* 70 (March 1998): 153–77.

Pfister, Joel, and Nancy Schnog, eds. *Inventing the Psychological: Toward a Cultural History of Emotional Life in America*. New Haven, Conn.: Yale University Press, 1997.

Phillips, Adam. "Keeping It Moving: Commentary on Judith Butler's 'Melancholy Gender/Refused Identification.'" In *The Psychic Life of Power: Theories in Subjection*, 151–59. Stanford, Calif.: Stanford University Press, 1997.

———. "Taking Aims: André Green and the Pragmatics of Passion." In *The Dead Mother: The Work of André Green*, edited by Gregorio Kohon, 163–72. London: Routledge, 1999.

Phinney, Jean S. "Stages of Ethnic Identity Development in Minority Group Adolescents." *Journal of Early Adolescence* 9 (1989): 34–49.

Poblete, Juan, ed. *Critical Latin American and Latino Studies*. Minneapolis: University of Minnesota Press, 2003.

Putnam, James Jackson. "Personal Impressions of Sigmund Freud and His Work, with Special Reference to his Recent Lectures at Clark University." *Journal of Abnormal Psychology* (December 1909–January 1910): 293–310, (February–March 1910): 372–79.

Rabinow, Paul. "Introduction: The History of Systems of Thought." In *Ethics, Subjectivity, and Truth*, edited by Paul Rabinow, translated by Robert Hurley, xi–xlii. New York: New Press, 1997.

Ramirez Berg, Charles. "Bordertown: The Assimilation Narrative and the Social Problem Film." In *Chicanos and Film: Representation and Resistance*, edited by Chon A. Noriega, 29–46. Minneapolis: University of Minnesota Press, 1992.

Ramos, Samuel. *Profile of Man and Culture in Mexico*. Translated by Peter G. Earle. Austin: University of Texas Press, 1962.

Rand, Nicolas, and Maria Torok. *Questions for Freud: The Secret History of Psychoanalysis*. Cambridge, Mass.: Harvard University Press, 1997.

Rivera, José. *Marisol and Other Plays*. New York: Theatre Communications Group, 1997.

Rodríguez, Clara E. "Visual Retrospective: Latino Film Stars." In *Latino Looks: Images of Latinas and Latinos in the U.S. Media*, edited by Clara E. Rodríguez, 80–84. Boulder, Colo.: Westview, 1997.

Rodriguez, Richard. *Hunger of Memory: The Education of Richard Rodriguez*. New York: Bantam Books, 1982.

Rosales, F. Arturo. *Chicano! The History of the Mexican American Civil Rights Movement*. Houston: Arte Público, 1997.

Rotheram-Borus, Mary Jane. "Biculturalism Among Adolescents." In *Ethnic Identity: Formation and Transmission Among Hispanics and Other Minorities*. Edited by M. E. Bernal and G. P. Knight, 81–102. Albany: State University of New York Press, 1993.

Roudinesco, Elisabeth. *Jacques Lacan and Co.: A History of Psychoanalysis in France, 1925–1985*. Translated by Jeffrey Mehlman. Chicago: University of Chicago Press, 1990.

Rowe, John Carlos. *The New American Studies*. Minneapolis: University of Minnesota Press, 2002.

Rubio, Philip. *A History of Affirmative Action: 1619–2000*. Jackson: University Press of Mississippi, 2001.

Safouan, Moustafa. *Four Lessons of Psychoanalysis*. Edited by Anna Shane. New York: Other Press, 2004.

Saldívar, Ramón. *Chicano Narrative: The Dialectics of Difference*. Madison: University of Wisconsin Press, 1990.

Sánchez, George I. "Pachucos in the Making." In *Chicano: The Evolution of a People*, edited by Renato Rosaldo, Robert A. Calvert, and Gustav L. Seligmann, 207–13. Minneapolis: Winston, 1973.

Sanchez-Tranquilino, Marcos, and John Tagg. "The Pachuco's Flayed Hide: Mobility, Identity, and *Buenas Garras*." In *Cultural Studies*, edited by Lawrence Grossberg, Cary Nelson, and Paula A. Treichler, 556–66. New York: Routledge, 1992.

Sandoval, Chela. "U.S. Third World Feminism: The Theory and Method of Oppositional Consciousness in the Postmodern World." *Genders* 10 (Spring 1991): 1–24.

——. *Methodology of the Oppressed*. Minneapolis: University of Minnesota Press, 2000.

Schreber, Daniel Paul. *Memoirs of My Nervous Illness*. Translated by Ida Macalpine and Richard A. Hunter. New York: New York Review Books, 2000.

Schuth, H. Wayne. Review of *Giant*. In *International Dictionary of Films and Filmmakers*, edited by Nicolet V. Elert and Aruna Vasudevan, 388. New York: St. James, 1993.

Sears, David O., Leonie Huddy, and Robert Jervis. "The Psychologies Underlying Political Psychology." In *The Oxford Handbook of Political Psychology*, edited by David O. Sears, Leonie Huddy, and Robert Jervis, 3–16. New York: Oxford University Press, 2003.

Sears, David O., and Sherry Levy. "Childhood and Adult Political Development." In *The Oxford Handbook of Political Psychology*, edited by David O. Sears, Leonie Huddy, and Robert Jervis, 60–109. New York: Oxford University Press, 2003.

Seshadri-Crooks, Kalpana. *Desiring Whiteness: A Lacanian Analysis of Race*. New York: Routledge, 2000.

Soler, Colette. "Hysteria in Scientific Discourse." In *Reading Seminar XX: Lacan's Major Work on Love, Knowledge, and Feminine Sexuality*, edited by Suzanne Barnard and Bruce Fink, 47–55. Albany: State University of New York Press, 2002.

——. "Time and Interpretation." In *Reading Seminars I and II: Lacan's Return to Freud*, edited by Richard Feldstein, Bruce Fink, and Maire Jaanus, 61–66. Albany: State University of New York Press, 1996.

Spillers, Hortense. "'All the Things You Could Be by Now If Sigmund Freud's Wife Was Your Mother': Psychoanalysis and Race." *boundary 2*, 23, no. 2 (1996): 75–141.

Stevens, George, dir. *Giant*. Warner Bros. Pictures, 1956.

Stoler, Ann Laura. *Race and the Education of Desire: Foucault's History of Sexuality and the Colonial Order of Things*. Durham, N.C.: Duke University Press, 1995.

Sue, Stanley. "Ethnicity and Culture in Psychological Research and Practice." In *Psychological Perspectives on Human Diversity in America*, edited by Jacqueline D. Goodchilds, 51–85. Washington, D.C.: American Psychological Association, 1991.

Sue, Stanley, and N. Zane. "The Role of Culture and Cultural Techniques in Psychotherapy: A Critique and Reformulation." *American Psychologist* 42 (1987): 37–45.

Tate, Claudia. *Psychoanalysis and Black Novels: Desire and the Protocols of Race.* New York: Oxford University Press, 1998.

"The Nature and Definition of Insanity." *Alienist and Neurologist* 9 (1888): 521.

Thomas, Piri. *Down These Mean Streets.* New York: Vintage Books, 1997.

Trujillo, Carla, ed. *Living Chicana Theory.* Berkeley: Third Woman, 1998.

Trujillo, Larry. "La Evolución del 'Bandido' al 'Pachuco': A Critical Examination of Criminological Literature on Chicanos." *Issues in Criminology* 9 (fall 1974): 43–67.

Valle, Victor M., and Rodolfo D. Torres. *Latino Metropolis.* Minneapolis: University of Minnesota Press, 2000.

Van Haute, Phillipe. *Against Adaptation: Lacan's "Subversion" of the Subject: A Close Reading.* New York: Other Press, 2002.

Vargas, Grace. "Urban Legends: Rita Hayworth, 1918–1987." *Urban Latino* 57 (June 2005): 64.

Verhaeghe, Paul. "Causation and Destitution of a Pre-ontological Non-entity: On the Lacanian Subject." In *Key Concepts of Lacanian Psychoanalysis,* edited by Dany Nobus, 164–89. New York: Other Press, 1999.

——. "Lacan's Answer to the Classical Mind/Body Deadlock." In *Reading Seminar XX: Lacan's Major Work on Love, Knowledge, and Feminine Sexuality,* edited by Suzanne Barnard and Bruce Fink, 109–39. Albany: State University of New York Press, 2002.

Walton, Jean. *Fair Sex, Savage Dreams.* Durham, N.C.: Duke University Press, 2001.

Warner, Michael. *The Trouble with Normal: Sex, Politics, and the Ethics of Queer Life.* New York: Free Press, 1999.

Williams, Patricia J. *The Alchemy of Race and Rights: Diary of a Law Professor.* Cambridge, Mass.: Harvard University Press, 1991.

Witmer, A. H. "Insanity in the Colored Race in the United States." *Alienist and Neurologist* 12 (1891): 19–30.

Yarbro-Bejarano, Yvonne. "Gloria Anzaldúa's *Borderlands/La frontera*: Cultural Studies, 'Difference,' and the Non-Unitary Subject." *Cultural Critique* 28 (1994): 5–28.

Ybarra-Frausto, Tomás. "Rasquachismo: A Chicano Sensibility." In *Chicano Art: Resistance and Affirmation, 1965–1985,* edited by Teresa McKenna, Yvonne Yarbro-Bejarano, and Richard Griswold del Castillo, 155–62. Los Angeles: Wright Art Gallery, 1991.

Zeitlin, Michael. "The Ego Psychologists in Lacan's Theory." *American Imago* 54 (1997): 209–32.

Žižek, Slavoj. "Critical Response: A Symptom—of What?" *Critical Inquiry* 29, no. 3 (2003): 486–503.

——. *Looking Awry: An Introduction to Jacques Lacan through Popular Culture.* Cambridge: MIT Press, 1992.

——. "Love Thy Neighbor: No Thanks!" In *The Psychoanalysis of Race,* edited by Christopher Lane, 154–75. New York: Columbia University Press, 1998.

——. "The Real of Sexual Difference." In *Reading Seminar XX: Lacan's Major Work on Love, Knowledge, and Feminine Sexuality,* edited by Suzanne Barnard and Bruce Fink, 57–75. Albany: State University of New York Press, 2002.

Zupančič, Alenka. *Ethics of the Real: Kant, Lacan.* London: Verso Books, 2000.

Index

280

282

285

287

Muñoz, José Estéban, 125, 127, 135, 265 n.16
Myrdal, Gunnar, 4, 86

Narcissism, 9, 57, 170–71, 174, 184
Narrator in *Gulf Dreams*: effects of language on, 191–92, 233; on emergent Chicano politics, 182–83, 185, 195; hysteric social discourse of, 178–79, 190, 191, 193; on performance of Chicano masculinity, 182–84; queer identity of, 178, 182–83, 185; symbolic castration and, 189, 192
Needs: concept of rights and, 101; language in articulation of, 8, 15, 19–20, 103, 168–70, 224–25
Nepantla, 128
Neurology, 32–33, 37–38
New York Psychoanalytic Association, 41, 55
Nobus, Dany, 96–97

Noriega, Chon, 141, 142, 145–46, 159

Object-relations theory, 60, 61, 207, 208
Oboler, Suzanne, 26, 136, 142
Olmos, Edward James, 259 n.15
Oppositional consciousness, 125, 126–27, 135, 174
Other, the: analysands' identification with, 235; Chicano movement discourse and, 194; cultural contexts and, 86; as difference, 159–60; end of analysis and, 235; interior intersubjectivity and release from, 202; jouissance of, 48, 58, 71; lacking in Lacanian theory, 235–36, 241; the mirror replaced by, 171–72; nationalisms and the drive of the desire for, 194; speech and, 86; subject emerges in language in relation to, 58; the Symbolic as, 14, 15, 27; the unconscious as, 27

Pachuco/a, 141, 142–43; in Anglo social science research, 161; anti-identity politics of, 143, 152–53; cinematic treat-

ments of, 143–44, 259 n.15; defiance of, 141–42, 146–47, 151–53, 164; descriptions of, 146–48; enjoyment-in-meaning of, 152; hysteric compared with, 148, 149, 151; knowledge production and, 148; Lacanian approach to, 148–49, 153; Angel Obregon as, 155, 160; production of meaning and, 151–52; psychological studies of, 148–50; racist culture and, 151; "a scandal of civilized meaning" and, 154; as *sinthome*, 151–52, 153
Padilla, Amado P., 215, 216
Padilla, Eligio R., 216–17
Padilla, Genaro M., 116
Palumbo-Liu, David, 139, 212
Paz, Octavio, 138, 150, 152–53, 157
Peller, Gary, 101
Pérez, Emma, 22–23, 165; on Chicano/Latino scholars' engagement with psychoanalysis, 167; on Chicanos and crime, 180–81, 185, 186; on colonial imaginary in Chicano historiography, 176–77; on Michel Foucault, 172; on futurity, 177; on the Imaginary, 171–72; on linear conceptions of time in historiography, 172–73; pessimistic activism of, 167; on politicized ethnic-racialized nominatory terms, 183; on psychoanalysis versus historicism, 166–67, 168, 171; on reinscription of Chicanas in history, 173–75, 186; on theory of Chicano historical consciousness, 173; on use of the term *resistance*, 176
Pérez-Torres, Rafael, 159–60
Pessimism, 12–13, 167, 242
Pfister, Joel, 47
Phillips, Adam, 206, 207, 220, 229; on aims of psychoanalysis, 229; on mourning the loss of repressed gender identity, 206, 225, 234; on treatment strategies, 228

Phinney, Jean S., 218
Piaget, Jean, 28
Pleasure, 8, 73, 145–46, 166–67
Pluth, Ed, 96, 151
Poblete, Juan, 130
Political psychology, 211, 217, 218
Pontalis, Jean-Bertrand, 57
Power, 41, 63–64, 104, 178
Prince, Morton, 38
Privileged marginal, 51
Protestant Ethnic and the Spirit of Capitalism, The, 170
Psychiatry, 33, 34–35, 44, 78. *See also* Fanon, Frantz
Psychoanalysis, 1; act of talking in, 61; African American subjects in, 36; biopower and, 11, 45, 51, 217, 218; capitalism, 82–83, 253 n.19; Chicano subject in, 166; death instinct and, 8; free treatments in, 82–83, 253 n.19; grief and mourning in, 66, 67, 206, 225, 230, 231–32, 233; happiness as goal of, 62; of heterosexual males, 228–29; imposters in, 22, 23; legacy of, 236–37; medical training and, 42, 246 n.54; neurology, 32–33; politicization of analysand, 208, 210; as protocol for the "care of the self," 79, 211, 224; as rhetoric, 229, 230; role of analysts in, 40–41; sex in, 199; social psychology and, 84–85; in Spanish-speaking countries, 248 n.21. *See also* Analyst/analysand relationship; Race and racism; Sex and sexuality
Psychoanalysis in the United States: Jewish psychoanalysts and, 3, 5, 68–69, 80, 82; Putnam on, 41; support for Freud and, 37, 38–40
Psychologization of the subject, 28
Psychology: African subjects in, 36; authority of, 3, 4; Chicano psychology, 214, 216, 217; ethnic, 62, 64, 211, 212, 213, 214, 215; ethnic identity and, 34; ethnology and, 36; Foucault on, 238; Hispanic, 64, 211, 215, 216, 221; Lacan's criticism of, 238; public policy and, 86; status of, in the United States, 3–4. *See also* Ego psychology; Social psychology

Puerto Ricans, 2, 73, 83, 86, 117, 258 n.5
Puppet, 138, 139, 140
Putnam, James Jackson, 37, 38–41, 249 n.22

Queer identity: abjection and, 236; binary categories and, 246 n.52; ethic of queer culture and, 235–36; of Hollywood actors, 157, 158; Latino, 21–22, 108, 109, 121, 127, 182–83, 185, 246 n.52; sinthomosexuality and, 138, 153, 154, 160–61, 162; unspeakability of, 181
Queer theory, 5, 11, 48, 59; Chicana lesbian feminists, 175–76

Race and racism: access to jouissance and, 68, 226; castration fantasies and, 48; cinematographic portrayals of, 157, 159, 160; Clarks' doll experiment and, 75–76, 89–93; critical race theory versus critical legal theory, 101–2; distinctiveness of, 200, 204–5; ego formation and, 94; eugenics movement and, 115, 139, 140; evacuation from the concept of, 205; Foucault on, 45; gender identity, 158; grief in response to, 67; insanity and, 30–31, 34, 44, 227–28; interior intersubjectivity and, 198, 204; Jewish identity and, 80, 81, 82, 253 n.17; language and, 5, 18–19, 45–46, 64, 66, 95–96, 198, 250 n.5; melancholia of, 221–22; public policy discourse and, 86–87; sexual difference and, 198, 199, 200, 201; as a structure of narrativity, 202; and the Symbolic, 79, 97–98, 198, 207, 208; transference and, 211–12; white supremacy and, 64, 104. *See also* African Americans; Coer-

289

Chicano historiography, 173, 175–65; cinematographic portrayals of, 157; complementarity between sexes, 175; deployment of, 45, 46, 48, 71–72; drive, 60–61, 109; ethnic identity and, 198, 199, 201; female masculinity, 157; Foucault on, 45–47, 71–72; gay male, 157, 158; genital love and, 59, 60; heterosexuality, 177, 182–83, 187, 228–29, 260 n.50; in Hollywood, 157; homosexuality, 154, 181; Lacanian psychoanalytic theory on, 71–72, 198, 199, 200, 210; language and, 189–90, 199; psychoanalysis and, 60; reciprocity between sexes, 59, 251 n.36; refusal to accept symbolic castration, 189; reproduction and, 46; sexual difference, 198, 199, 200, 201; sinthomosexuality, 138, 153, 154, 160–61, 162; social class and, 46–47; transsexuality, 159

"Signification of the Phallus, The" (Lacan), 192

Silverman, Kaja, 198, 199

Sinthome, 151–52, 153, 154, 190–91, 192, 194, 239

Sinthomestiza subject, 144, 160–63

Sinthomosexuality, 138, 153, 154, 160–61, 162

Sleepy Lagoon Murder trial, 186, 261 n.57

Social psychology: adaptation in, 148; border subjects and, 128; characterizations of, 84–85; culturalist school of, 28; doll experiments and, 75–76, 89–93; ego psychology and, 226; language in, 6; Latino studies and, 113; law and, 104–5; psychoanalysis and, 84–85; in the United States, 84

Soler, Colette, 21, 119, 178

Spanglish, 115–16, 120–21, 132, 137, 144, 164

Speech: of analysand, 61; human speaking subject and, 5–6, 13–14, 16, 58, 191–92, 195, 243 n.3, 244 n.10; irremediable loss and articulation of needs and, 15, 169, 224–25; Lacan on, 121, 132, 151, 203–4; the Other and, 86; symptom and, 151; temporality of, 21, 201

Spillers, Hortense, 50; on African American intellectuals' engagement with psychoanalysis, 237, 240; on the blankness of race, 205, 208; on causality of "deferred action," 201; on Chicano/Latino scholars' engagement with psychoanalysis, 167; on emancipatory potential of psychoanalytic theory for black cultural and political critique, 79; on end of analysis, 83; on the ethnic-racialized subject's signifying dependence, 204; on Freudian psychoanalysis, 233; on the juxtaposition of race and psychoanalysis, 79–80; on Lacanian psychoanalytic theory, 207; on Lacan's notion of disarray, 202–3; on psychoanalysis as protocol for the "care of self," 224; on race in psychoanalysis, 79–81, 88–89; on race preceding language, 18–19, 95–96, 98; on racialized difference, 95; on racialized difference and the formation of the ego, 97–98; on racial versus sexual difference, 200–201; on self-critical inquiry, 202; on speculative perspective on ethnic-racialized subjectivity, 205; temporality of, 201. *See also* Interior intersubjectivity

Split subject, 132

State, the, 99–100, 101, 103, 168

Stevens, George, 143–44, 155, 259 n.15. See also *Giant*

Stoler, Ann Laura, 45

Strong ego, 51, 53, 57–58, 61, 64, 136

Sue, Stanley, 211, 212–14

"Sundays of Satin-Legs Smith, The," 146, 154, 164

292

293

Antonio Viego is an associate professor in the Program in Literature and Romance Studies at Duke University.

LIBRARY OF CONGRESS CATALOGING-IN-PUBLICATION DATA

Viego, Antonio
Dead subjects : toward a politics of loss in Latino studies / Antonio Viego.
p. cm.
Includes bibliographical references and index.
ISBN-13: 978-0-8223-4099-7 (cloth : alk. paper)
ISBN-13: 978-0-8223-4120-8 (pbk. : alk. paper)
1. Hispanic Americans—Study and teaching (Higher)
2. Hispanic Americans—Psychology.
3. Loss (Psychology)—Social aspects—United States.
4. Racism—United States—Psychological aspects.
5. Psychoanalysis—Social aspects—United States.
6. Lacan, Jacques, 1901–1981.
7. United States—Ethnic relations—Psychological aspects. I. Title.
E184.S75V538 2007
371.829'68073—dc22
2007019197

Made in the USA
Monee, IL
24 September 2020